Only the Enemy in Front

ONLY THE ENEMY IN FRONT

(Every other beggar behind...)

The Recce Corps at War 1940-1946

Richard Doherty

LONDON   NEW YORK   SYDNEY   TORONTO

This edition published 1994 by BCA by arrangement with

Tom Donovan Publishing Ltd.
52 Willow Road
Hampstead
London NW3 1TP

CN 5174

Desk-top typeset by Tom Donovan Publishing Ltd.

Printed by The Bath Press, Bath

Contents

Maps

Illustrations

Twenty-two photographs will be found between pages 150-151. Numbers 1, 3-7, 9, 10, 12-17 are reproduced by kind permission of the Trustees of the Imperial War Museum, London. The remainder are reproduced by kind permission of the following: 2, Sir John Boynton; 8, 56 Recce OCA; 11, author's collection; 18, John Purdy; 19 & 20, Ken Baker; 21, Tank Museum, Brussels; 22, Royal Green Jackets Museum, Winchester (per John Newton).

DEDICATION

For all who served in The Reconnaissance Corps

Take these men for your example.
Like them, remember that posterity can only be for the free; that freedom
is the sure possession of those who have the courage to defend it.
(Pericles)

Introduction

When I was still at primary school my late father gave me a little booklet which is still in my possession. Published during the war, it illustrates the badges and headgear of regiments and corps of the British Army as well as some Commonwealth, Empire and Allied forces. In the pages of that booklet I first met The Reconnaissance Corps for, amid the lions, tigers, eagles, roses, harps and thistles, was an intriguing cap badge, the spear and lightning flashes of Recce. It was intriguing because it was so different from any other badge and, from that time, the very title Reconnaissance Corps, held a certain mystique for me.

Unfortunately, there was little else to be found about the Corps. Over the years I have even met men who saw active service in the same theatres as the Corps who were not aware of its existence. And yet this Corps was, in its time, an elite formation, with an ethos that set it apart and standards of the highest. Press publicity about Recce put it on a par with the commandos and the paratroopers but, since The Reconnaissance Corps did not survive in the post-war Army, its deeds have become overlooked. In the mid-50s, when battle honours were awarded for the Second World War, none were granted to The Reconnaissance Corps as it was no longer in existence. And yet so many honours could have gone the way of the Corps for it saw service in every theatre of war in which the British Army was to be found after 1941 and it served at all times with distinction.

In 1989 I began to research a history of The Irish Brigade of the Second World War and I soon came in contact with Recce, in the form of 56th Reconnaissance Regiment which served, as did The Irish Brigade, with 78th Division. One of my first interviewees on The Irish Brigade was Colonel Kendal Chavasse. It was talking with Colonel Kendal that sparked off the idea of writing a history of The Reconnaissance Corps. Two other 56th Reconnaissance Regiment members helped with my book on The Irish Brigade, Bill Croucher and John Newton and their contributions kindled the spark.

As a result I set about researching and writing a history of The Reconnaissance Corps. Along the way I had the invaluable assistance and guidance of a great many people from whom I learned so much more about the Corps that I began to understand the immense pride that there was in belonging to such a fine formation. This book is my tribute to all who served in The Reconnaissance Corps.

Acknowledgements

Compiling a history of a Corps that saw such varied service as The Reconnaissance Corps was a task that could not have been undertaken without the advice, support and co-operation of a considerable number of individuals and organisations and I therefore wish to place on record my appreciation of the help I received in writing this book.

My first thanks are due to Colonel Kendal Chavasse for all his help in the research for and writing of this history. Colonel Chavasse allowed me to borrow his collection of *The Reconnaissance Journal* and these volumes were invaluable as were other volumes which he loaned to me. Bill Croucher and John Newton provided copies of the 56th Reconnaissance Regiment OCA Newsletter as well as *This Band of Brothers,* Jeremy Taylor's original post-war history of the Corps. John Newton also introduced me to the secretaries of the various regimental associations which continue to flourish and which were a valuable source of information.

I was given access to private journals or detailed accounts of service in reconnaissance regiments by a number of individuals for which I am grateful to: Mr J.W. (Bud) Abbot, Major Ken Baker, Mr Arthur Barlow, Brigadier J.M.K.Bradford, DSO, Mr H.M.Brender, Colonel P.H.A. Brownrigg, DSO, Colonel K.G.F.Chavasse, DSO, Mr G.N.Glatley, Mr J.A.L.Hamilton, Mr R.Hand, Mr D.Henderson, Mr R.Minns, Mr R.Pite, Mr R.W.Robinson, Mr J.Rostron, Major D.Smith, MM, Mr E.C.Street, Mr J.Thompson, Mr E.C.West.

Many other individuals were generous with their assistance and I place on record my thanks to them. Former members of The Reconnaissance Corps include: Major G.Barrow, MBE, L.Bell, H.W.Bond, M.McE.Charlish, T.F.Clark, W.Croucher, MC, G.Dixon, E.Anderson, S.Firth, MM, R.J.Gibson, OBE, J.Goodman, R.Hall, P.Hedley, E.R.Howard, E.O.W.Hunt, DSO, G.Jackson, G.Kirkley, E.Lanning, S.R.Mansfield, E.Miller, D.K.MacFarlane, L.A.Meek, E.T.(John) Newton, Colonel A.R.Prince, J.Purdy, CMG, OBE, General Sir Antony Read, GCB, CBE, DSO, MC, M.R.Riesco, J.Rogers, J.C.Stokes, and Major D.Waugh.

Thanks are also due to Mrs A.Bastow and Mrs I.Bennett, both widows of reconnoitrers, my good friend Maurice Riley who helped me compile information on the Corps, Lieutenant Carol Liles, Royal Irish Regiment, who assisted in the search for books on the Corps, John Fairley, author of *Remember Arnhem* for his help with 1st Airborne Reconnaissance Squadron, Major K.H.Nash, who provided a number of contacts, Miss Josephine

M.A.Peel, for her help with 52nd (Lowland) Regiment, David Rooney, for contacts with the West African regiments and Tom Wylie for advice on a number of points.

. A number of institutions gave help that I could not have done without and I therefore gratefully acknowledge the help and co-operation of: The Public Record Office, Kew, Richmond, Surrey, especially the staff of the Reading, Search, Reprographic and Reference Rooms for all their help, patience and efficiency.

The Department of Printed Books and the Department of Photographs at the Imperial War Museum, London who were most helpful in identifying published references to the Corps and photographs of reconnaissance regiments. The National Army Museum, London, especially the staff of the Reading Room. The Tank Museum, Bovington, especially Colonel George Forty (Retd). The Tank Museum, Brussels. The Central Library, Foyle Street, Londonderry. The Prince Consort's Library, Aldershot.

Various quotations are used throughout the book and permission to use such is gratefully acknowledged from the various publishers as well as from the Controller of Her Majesty's Stationery Office for permission to use material from The Public Record Office, Kew. In a number of cases it has not been possible to trace copyright holders but the author and publisher are prepared to make the necessary arrangements to rectify this at the earliest opportunity.

Researching and writing this book has absorbed much of my time over the past three years. I am very grateful to my wife, Carol, and my children, Joanne, James and Catríona for their patience and support, without which the book would never have been possible.

Richard Doherty, May 1994

1
Formation

'Only the enemy in front; every other beggar behind' was the unofficial motto of The Reconnaissance Corps. Although not used by every reconnaissance regiment it nonetheless sums up the rôle, and the spirit, of the Corps which came into being in 1941 and was laid to rest in 1946. In its short existence it achieved elite status through the performance of its officers and men in action from the bloody battles of North Africa, through Sicily and Italy and from North-West Europe to the jungles of Burma.

Wars have always created expansion in the British Army. The Second World War was no exception; the Army which went to war in 1939 - already increased in size in recent years - expanded greatly as the war went on. That expansion was not simply in numbers: as in earlier wars names of new regiments and corps appeared on the Army List; one such was The Reconnaissance Corps.

Some of the new names came about at the suggestion of Winston Churchill who became Prime Minister in May 1940. He it was who inspired the formation of airborne forces, on the German model, and the commandos, both intended to develop high levels of morale and esprit de corps in units trained for special operations. Various other special forces and groups came into being as the war progressed. Some, such as the Chindits and the Special Air Service, were largely the work of individuals and reflected innovative thinking or, to some minds, flights of fancy.

No flight of fancy lay behind the creation of The Reconnaissance Corps. Its birth was the result of practical thinking and detailed analysis in the wake of the Dunkirk campaign. One immediate reaction to that campaign was to examine how it had been fought, the organisation of German forces, the organisation of the BEF and, from that examination, to identify lessons to be applied in the future with organisational structures to allow such lessons to be applied the better.

Within days of the end of Operation DYNAMO - the Dunkirk evacuation - and while another British force was being gathered to land in Brittany in a vain effort to bolster the French government, General Sir John Dill, newly-appointed Chief of the Imperial General Staff, established a committee under the chairmanship of General Sir William Bartholomew to carry out an enquiry into the recent campaign. This committee - the Bartholomew Committee - had, as its remit:

> 1 To consider lessons of the recent operations in Flanders which can be applied usefully to our present organisation and training.

2 To suggest modifications in our organisation, training and equipment which should be made to meet the problem with which the British Army will be faced in the event of an attempted enemy invasion of this country.[1]

The Bartholomew Committee was soon at work taking oral evidence from senior officers of the BEF from 12 to 18 June 1940; written reports were also received from a number of generals. Among those who presented evidence, either written or oral, were Alexander, Montgomery and Leese: Alexander was already a household name; Montgomery and Leese were to achieve similar status. By the end of July the Bartholomew Report had been submitted. The report was in three parts: a general review of the campaign; general lessons of the campaign; and suggestions arising from those lessons.

The second part, the lessons of the campaign, recommended a new organisation for infantry divisions that included a divisional reconnaissance unit. From that recommendation was born the Reconnaissance Corps.

This is not to say that the British Expeditionary Force had not possessed reconnaissance elements at divisional level. Such elements had been in the form of divisional cavalry regiments, the traditional 'eyes' of the infantry: the light cavalry regiments in France had been armoured to provide the speed necessary in modern warfare. (It is not generally recognised that the British Army was the only fully-mechanised army anywhere; the Germans, in spite of their highly mobile panzer and panzer grenadier formations, relied largely on horses in the early stages of the war and still had a very high proportion of horse transport in 1945.) Sorely deficient in tanks, the BEF's original small complement of such machines was used to carry out reconnaissance duties for infantry divisions. After the fall of France, new armoured divisions claimed all the cavalry regiments; those which had earlier provided the infantry with its reconnaissance 'eyes' came under the command of the Royal Armoured Corps to serve in the armoured rôle.

Thus the task of reconnaissance for infantry divisions had to be re-assigned. The final decision, of course, was to create a Corps specifically for that purpose. It could have been otherwise. Divisional troops already included machine-gun battalions - many of which were expanded into support battalions - which had been either regular or TA infantry battalions; yet during the First World War a Machine Gun Corps had been created and its rebirth was considered in 1940. It is possible, therefore, that the machine-gun/support battalion model could have been followed with infantry battalions re-rôled as reconnaissance battalions; nonetheless the Reconnaissance Corps was formed. As well as newly-created battalions, it also included re-rôled infantry battalions, one of which had had some mobile recce experience with motorcycles in France.

As 1940 faded away the Army continued training for a possible invasion and its infantry improvised to overcome the lack of a formal reconnaissance element at divisional level; many battalions formed recce platoons which proved hugely successful on exercises. (In fact the Bartholomew Report recommended that, as an interim measure, each "higher establishment" infantry division be allocated a motorcycle battalion as a reconnaissance unit. These were assigned on a brigade level within the divisions as brigade reconnaissance groups.) Improvisation was soon to be a thing of the past however.

> The Reconnaissance Corps came into the world while the snow of January, 1941, swirled outside on the window panes, to the sound of Ack-Ack, to the rehearsal of beach defences, to the tramp of the Home Guard, to the slow preliminary turning of the factories that had yet to produce the means by which the Corps was to live and work. The child was a puny one. Even Mother War Office, having laboured successfully, seemed at first not very proud of her off-spring and left it much to its own devices. But then, of course, she was very busy about that time.[2]

In late-July 1940 a meeting of General Staff Directors had considered the main recommendations of the Bartholomew Report in order to provide the CIGS "with a considered General Staff opinion on proposals concerning organisation and equipment."[3] Included in the discussion papers was a summary of the report's thinking on a divisional reconnaissance unit which was stated to be:

> ...clearly necessary. General Bartholomew recommends that, owing to the probability of its encountering armoured reconnaissance units, it should itself be armoured and preferably contain 2-pounder guns. ...the unit should be a tank unit and should belong to the RAC. The RAC is, however, fully occupied with the expansion of armoured formations which will also absorb, at any rate for the present, all tank production. Moreover, these reconnaissance units will usually operate under the general cover of armoured divisions. It is considered therefore that it should be an infantry unit suitably organised to carry out protective reconnaissance, the armoured element consisting of carriers and scout-cars and the un-armoured of motor-cyclists. The anti-tank gun element could be ...four 2-pounder guns on self-propelled and armoured mountings.[4]

The meeting recommended that divisional reconnaissance units should be infantry with an initial establishment of one unit per army corps - of which there were twelve - rather than one per division which would have placed too great a strain on existing manpower. There was still much shuffling of paper between departments before final acceptance that the units should be infantry. The Adjutant-General and Quartermaster-General both believed that reconnaissance units belonged in the RAC and not until 16 September was the decision made that the infantry arm should be the provider. In early October General Dill wrote to the Secretary of State for War to obtain agreement for the creation of twelve recce units; he also announced this and other changes in divisional structures to the Army.

When all administrative and political decisions had been made one act remained necessary to bring the new corps to life: on 14 January 1941 His Majesty King George VI signed a Royal Warrant "to authorize the formation of a corps to be entitled Reconnaissance Corps;" which was published by the War Office in a Special Army Order eight days later.

Now began the task of building the new Corps. It was not quite 'from scratch' as some of the new reconnaissance battalions already had a degree of experience in the rôle, having been formed from the brigade reconnaissance groups of their divisions. Others were converted from brigade anti-tank companies, many of which had seen action against German armour in France. Yet other recce battalions were converted en bloc from existing infantry battalions, including 3rd Tower Hamlets Rifles, formed in July 1940, which became 5th Battalion, The Reconnaissance Corps on 22 January 1941. Other battalions which followed in the transformation process included two of Royal Northumberland Fusiliers: 8th Northumberlands became 3rd Battalion, The Reconnaissance Corps and 4th Northumberlands became 50th Battalion, The Reconnaissance Corps in April 1941. The new 50th Recce had, as 4th Northumberlands, been a motorcycle battalion which had served in the reconnaissance rôle in France: its transfer to the new Corps was therefore logical.

The battalion numbers borne by these new formations indicated the divisions to which they were assigned; thus 3rd Recce Battalion was the reconnaissance unit of 3rd Division. However no-one with any knowledge of how the Army works would be surprised if this failed to work out in practice in all cases and exceptions were to be found as the war progressed.

Reconnaissance is as old as conflict itself and one of the basic tenets hammered home in training was that 'time spent on reconnaissance is seldom wasted;' one could very easily reword that to say 'never wasted.' The birth of the Reconnaissance Corps also brought the necessity for the establishment of training centres for its personnel. The Rifle Brigade depot at Winchester provided a temporary first home for a Reconnaissance Training Centre but as the Corps expanded three training centres were created. These were Nos 1 and 2 Reconnaissance Training Centres at Halleaths Camp, Lochmaben in Dumfriesshire and at Scarborough as well as a Tactical Training School at Annan, not far from No 1 Reconnaissance Training Centre. In August 1943 the two training centres were combined and located at Catterick, which became the spiritual home of the Corps.

While there were few doubts about the value of reconnaissance there were differences about the form it should take in this new era of warfare. Divisional commanders had been given no specific 'doctrine' on using their recce battalions and thus there was bound to be much trial and error. So much training was already taking place in mobile warfare for infantry divisions that it is hardly surprising that less attention than necessary was being paid to the reconnaissance battalions. With hindsight it is easy to argue that this proved that the Corps should have been part of the RAC from the very beginning since the whole ethos of a recce unit was essentially that of a divisional cavalry regiment. The result of this situation was argument that seemed unending at times, and intensive efforts to learn lessons from exercises; in this latter rôle the Tactical School was to play an important part in training officers and NCOs of the Corps.

Most members of the Corps were agreed that an offensive spirit was needed. Major General Montgomery, who had commanded 3rd Division in France had submitted his report on "Important Lessons from the operations of the BEF in France and Belgium - May 1940" to the Bartholomew Committee. Monty had described the German army "as quite first class" and, among other factors, had outlined their style of reconnaissance. The final report echoed his submission, describing German preparation for attack through "rapid reconnaissance, which taps along the front line until a weak spot or gap is effected" after which the obstacle is crossed, a small bridgehead established and then exploited to "allow the passage of more and more troops."[5] Such offensive spirit was to imbue the Corps and, from the composition of a battalion, this had clearly been foreseen by the planners, even if it was not communicated adequately to divisional commanders.

During the war the shape of a recce battalion changed little although the designation changed to 'regiment' in 1942. Normal strength was 40 officers and 733 other ranks divided, as shown in Table 1, into a headquarters element, a headquarters company and three recce companies; each company was further subdivided into a headquarters and four platoons, three recce platoons and an assault platoon. When battalions became regiments in June 1942 cavalry nomenclature was also applied in sub-units: thus companies became squadrons while platoons became troops. By early-1942, in fact, the divisional cavalry ethos had been adopted throughout the Corps.

TABLE 1
ORGANISATION OF A RECONNAISSANCE BATTALION

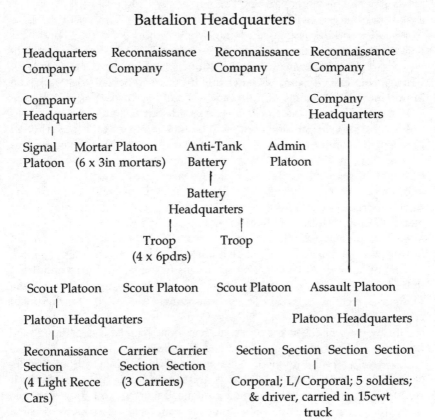

Battalion Headquarters

Headquarters   Reconnaissance   Reconnaissance   Reconnaissance
Company   Company   Company   Company

Company   Company
Headquarters   Headquarters

Signal   Mortar Platoon   Anti-Tank   Admin
Platoon   (6 x 3in mortars)   Battery   Platoon

Battery
Headquarters

Troop   Troop
(4 x 6pdrs)

Scout Platoon   Scout Platoon   Scout Platoon   Assault Platoon

Platoon Headquarters   Platoon Headquarters

Reconnaissance   Carrier   Carrier   Section Section Section Section
Section   Section   Section
(4 Light Recce   (3 Carriers)   Corporal; L/Corporal; 5 soldiers;
Cars)   & driver, carried in 15cwt
                                                      truck

Notes

1. After June 1942 battalions became regiments and cavalry designations were introduced: companies became squadrons and platoons became troops.

2. Towards the end of the Tunisian campaign armoured cars were issued to the reconnaissance troops which then deployed two armoured cars and three light reconnaissance cars each.

2
Finding a Rôle

Creating the Reconnaissance Corps had been a relatively easy paper exercise. With the Corps in being there were still many problems to be solved and difficulties to be overcome. Tactics and equipment featured among those problems and difficulties as did the identity or, more accurately, esprit de corps of the new battalions. The task of developing tactics and operational procedures would fall to the Reconnaissance Training Centre with great emphasis, in due course, on the operational experiences of fighting units. The first Corps units came into being in an Army still desperately short of equipment and reconnaissance battalions were well down the list for what was available. Not surprisingly, there was a 'make do and mend' emphasis within the Corps at first. That improvisation also helped to foster the unique esprit de corps of Recce, although to begin with there was not even a cap badge for its members.

The first Reconnaissance Corps Training Centre was established at the Rifle Depot in Winchester on 1 February 1941. Since the Corps had been charged with gathering "vital tactical information in battle for infantry divisions" the Training Centre's job was to teach them how to do just that. The standard reconnaissance battalion carried twice as much firepower as its infantry counterpart: it was designed to move quickly in armoured recce cars, universal carriers and trucks; and it was to send its information back by wireless. Sir Arthur Bryant summarised the rôle as "that of the cat's whiskers - armoured, mechanized transmitting whiskers. Those who served had to be intelligent, enterprizing, brave, enduring and highly skilled."[1] Bryant greatly admired the Corps and, in the final edition of *The Reconnaissance Journal* in 1950, he wrote:

> To take the place of the light divisional cavalry of the past, a succession of brilliant young soldiers of imagination evolved swift, adaptable and superlatively mobile fighting units with fast vehicles capable of taking heavy punishment, highly concentrated firing-power, and a complicated but efficient wireless network designed to convey, under the most trying conditions imaginable, accurate and balanced information to the general's battle map.[2]

The publicity fed to the general public in the Corps' early days seemed to indicate that a body of super soldiers was being created: the *Daily Mail* asserted that Reconnaissance Corps members "have to be tough with cold, scientific brains behind their brawn." The BBC went even further, claiming that Recce men would throw themselves across barbed-wire barriers so that the infantry could cross those barriers by running over their backs!

That idea seemed to have more to do with the battlefields of the Great War than with the mobile warfare of the current conflict.

For the men assembling at Winchester and, later, at the newer training centres, training was vastly different from the media's descriptions. As a mechanised force there was need of a large number of drivers and mechanics, and this at a time when driving was not so common as it is today, while men with the skills to operate radio sets, using morse, under battlefield conditions were another necessity. Having been taught basic skills, some elementary tactical work had to be done before men could be sent to a recce battalion or independent company where further training and practical exercises would polish their skills.

There was, however, some truth in what the media were saying about the Corps: its soldiers were of the very highest standard. Although an infantry battalion might transfer into the Corps it did not follow that all its men would be retained. All potential reconnoitrers were subject to an IQ test and those who failed were sent to other units. As Bob Pite of 4 Recce recalled: "Our egos were boosted greatly when [we were] told that only those who came out on top [in the IQ test] were being considered."[3]

As part of the learning process the battalions passed on recommendations from their experience in training and, later, from operations. In April 1941 the three-month old 4th Reconnaissance Battalion was suggesting changes in the War Establishment of a battalion based on lessons learnt in training. These included the use of No 11 radio sets instead of the higher-powered No 18 sets for communication between company and platoon; two additional carrier sections for the protection of battalion HQ; additional or alternative vehicles for a number of functions and some additional personnel.

The battalion's divisional commander, Major General Swayne, had also attended a model demonstration to outline the rôle of a reconnaissance battalion. Swayne described the battalion as having, "broadly speaking," two rôles, which were Reconnaissance and Protection:

> These two rôles are quite different and demand different methods and tactics.
>
> For reconnaissance you need dispersion.
>
> For protection you need concentration.
>
> Any one part of your unit cannot, therefore, at any one time carry out both rôles and must not be asked to do so.
>
> In this scheme your unit has been told to carry out both reconnaissance and protection but you will note that no one part of the unit has been told to do both at the same time. You can do either the one or the other but not both together. And when you change from one to the other you

must change your tactics and your dispositions.[4]

Expansion brought about the establishment of training centres at Lochmaben (No 1) and Scarborough (No 2, but later 63rd) with the Tactical Training School at Annan, close to No 1 Training Centre in Dumfriesshire. At the latter, operational training and analysis of lessons learnt in training or on operations was undertaken. By summer 1942, the Reconnaissance Corps was some twenty regiments strong and its equipment had improved considerably, but there was still uncertainty about how recce units would be employed in action.

> The argument in the Officers' Mess of the Tactical School was spiciest on the subject of how every reconnaissance regiment was invariably mis-handled all the time on every exercise. Not a great deal was said about the handling of squadrons and troops: there was a gentleman's agreement between the newly-arrived squadron and troop commanders that this was pretty good, and really it was a waste of time to come here to learn about it.[5]

At Annan the students were officers and NCOs of the Corps; they studied the tactical deployment of recce squadrons, troops and sections. Teaching methods included TEWTs (Tactical Exercises without Troops) during which students would be divided into syndicate groups to study a hypothetical situation with each syndicate having to present its solution to the school's directing staff who, inevitably, had heard it all before. The school solution would then be given and there would generally be further discussion on just who had got it right. TEWTs involved students going out into the neighbouring countryside and imagining that they were conducting a recce unit as it probed forward of its division towards an enemy. Situations that could confront a troop or squadron commander were discussed on the ground and solutions sought: thus students could find themselves arguing over the correct action to be taken by a troop commander who had just had his leading scout car knocked out as it rounded a bend into full view of a concealed enemy anti-tank gun some distance ahead (a not unlikely scenario in the eventual rôle of the Corps); should he attempt an outflanking movement with his carrier section? What should the commander of the scout section whose car had been hit do? Obviously his first duty was to report the presence of the anti-tank gun, but what then? Should he try to clear the opposition himself or wait for his troop commander who would be following behind? All of these scenarios led to lively debate and to the inevitable comparison between solutions offered by student syndicates and directing staff.

Sand-table exercises and discussions also featured highly in the programme. The sand table with its model vehicles, roads marked by tape, and bird's eye view was ideal for discussing tactics: how, for example, should a reconnaissance battalion take and hold a river? After deciding the approach to the river obstacle and the seizing of it, it became apparent that the object of the lesson, the directing staff solution, was that a river cannot be held simply by crossing it and sitting on the far bank: the reconnoitrers had to move forward of the river to deploy on the high ground beyond with vehicles concealed and soldiers positioned to fight off any counter-attack.

The points made by General Swayne when he spoke to 4 Recce in early 1941 about the protective rôle of a reconnaissance battalion in the defensive were also amplified. That rôle was taken further by examining how a battalion could cover the withdrawal of all or part of its division. For such a task a recce battalion was held to be ideal since it could move more quickly than an infantry battalion and had much more firepower. From that point, syndicates discussed the deployment of a battalion to cover a withdrawal; the location of troop positions to give supporting fire; the order of withdrawal of the battalion and the final withdrawal of the men who had provided the covering fire.

But the prime task of recce would be in the advance and much time was devoted to this rôle. Students learned of the three conditions under which a battalion might be advancing. Moving through country where it was unlikely that the enemy would be encountered was described as "moving in green" and the unit could travel speedily down its axis of advance without searching the surrounding countryside. Where contact with the enemy was possible, the unit was "moving in amber" and speed would be reduced so that scout cars could do some searching of the surrounding area by detouring along side roads off the axis of advance. Finally, where the enemy was known to be present, the unit was "moving in red" and close reconnaissance was called for with a much-reduced momentum.

At Annan students also learned about the School's notes on harbouring, something which most had already done many times but which the School considered needed emphasising through a demonstration by the resident Demonstration Troop which also helped at other times to give an air of reality to training by providing firepower and 'enemy' soldiers when needed. And, of course, students had to be familiar with the organisation of the enemy's army and so there were sessions devoted to unit markings, epaulette colourings - used by the Germans to denote operational functions - types of vehicles and methods of deployment for this, after all, was the prime task of a reconnoitrer - to send back detailed information about the enemy.

From Annan the student returned to his unit to put what he had learned into practice and pass on his new knowledge to his own squadron or troop. It was clear to see why the Corps demanded a very high standard from its officers: they were going to have to operate on their own initiative more than almost any others and field and junior officers were to have responsibilities with few equals in the wartime army. Many lessons from Annan would later be put to good use on battlefields from Tunisia to

Burma and to Germany itself.

In early 1941, when the Reconnaissance Corps was in its infancy, there were many demands from throughout the Army for equipment and vehicles. The newly-born Recce was hardly top of the priority scale for either; that was one of the factors that initially kept the Corps restricted to twelve battalions.

War Office letter 79/WE/2612 (SD3) of 28 November 1940 outlined the War Establishment of a divisional reconnaissance battalion: a battalion HQ company with Anti-Aircraft, Signals, Mortar, Anti-Tank and Administrative Platoons; three companies, each with three Scout Platoons - each Scout Platoon had one Armoured Reconnaissance Car Section with five armoured recce cars, also known as light recce cars or LRCs, and two Carrier Sections with three carriers apiece - and an Infantry or Assault Platoon of four sections. The battalion was therefore to have 45 recce cars and 67 carriers in its fighting transport plus the vehicles needed to move its headquarters, infantry sections and other elements: that amounted to a sizeable number of lorries, cars and motorcycles; 71 of the ubiquitous 15-cwt trucks were called for, four of which were to carry No 11 wireless sets, as well as six 3-tonners, 71 motorcycles and 6 utility cars. Firepower was to consist of 126 Bren light machine-guns, 4 twin Brens for anti-aircraft protection, 48 anti-tank rifles, 12 Thompson sub machine-guns, 18 2-inch mortars and two 3-inch mortars. Anti-tank rifles would later be replaced by 2-pounder anti-tank guns while the number of 3-inch mortars would be increased to six. For communication a battalion was to have twelve No 18 wireless sets, plus two spare, for intercommunication between companies and scout platoons and four No 11 sets, with another spare, for intercommunication between companies and battalion headquarters; in addition each battalion had a divisional signals' section attached to operate a No 9 set for communication between battalion and divisional headquarters.

By April 1941, the War Diary of 4 Recce was noting deficiencies in equipment that were afflicting all battalions of the Corps: 4 Recce had only 44 Bren guns; two 2-inch mortars and one 3-inch, while only nine anti-tank rifles had been received. Worse still was the issue of vehicles: the battalion had only nine carriers and no recce cars nor any information about the type of cars to be issued. Of other vehicles, only 30 motorcycles had been received against an establishment of 71 and one car against an establishment of five. "Lack of fighting vehicles was a serious impediment to tactical training and the training of drivers."[6]

The first armoured reconnaissance car supplied to the Corps was an improvised vehicle based on a Humber car fitted with armour plating and equipped with a machine-gun. Such vehicles were called Beaverettes and it was with these unwieldy cars that the Corps started its training.

Fortunately, by the time the Corps went into action the Beaverette was but a memory; it had served its purpose in providing a vehicle for training in the early months of 1941 although 4 Recce considered it "of little practical value" in that rôle although it might have been "of possible use against parachutists." Other stop-gap vehicles issued to the fledgling Corps included Standard 8s "with tin sides" and Ironsides, rudimentary armoured vehicles based on a Bedford 3-ton lorry chassis with an armoured box constructed from boiler-plating mounted on it. The Humber company also produced the replacement for the Beaverette and other interim vehicles in the shape of the Humber Light Reconnaissance Car (LRC) which had a crew of three and was fitted with a light machine-gun, a smoke discharger, two rifles and a No 19 radio set. Earlier versions were two-wheel drive but a four-wheel drive version was later developed. Weighing 3.6 tons, the Humber LRC had a maximum road speed of 61mph from a six-cylinder Humber petrol engine of 26.88 HP and a range of 175 miles from its 18-gallon fuel tank. As the war progressed the Humber LRC was to be supplemented with, or replaced by, a number of other vehicles, British and American, while heavy armoured cars were also to be introduced to the inventories of recce regiments. On 6 January 1942 six Humber Mark III LRCs with four-wheel drive were issued to 4 Recce, the first unit to receive any of these vehicles; they were described as a "considerable fillip to morale."

The carrier remained in service throughout the war. Although only lightly-armoured, it was versatile and reliable with good cross-country performance and served the Corps, and the Army, well. Best-known as the Bren-gun carrier, it was capable of carrying a range of weaponry, including mortars, and its armour was proof against most small-arms fire, although it was possible for a bullet to 'splash' through a joint in the armour-plating. There was no overhead armour so that the crew were vulnerable to airbursting shells. The carrier had no errant when faced by anti-tank guns or tanks: in such a situation the best option was to lay down smoke and move away quickly. Although very stable it could overturn when being driven fast across country. The first soldier of 4 Recce to die was Trooper 'Blondie' Richards who was decapitated when his carrier overturned on Exercise BUMPER, a major anti-invasion training scheme, in 1941.[7] Generally, however, the carrier was liked by its crews.

***

One of the distinctive marks of any regiment or corps is its cap badge. When the Reconnaissance Corps came into being there was no distinguishing badge for it and it was to be several months before the Corps received its badge. Meanwhile, soldiers joining a recce battalion from an existing regiment continued to wear their own regimental badges and buttons. Officers also wore the badges of the regiment into which they had been commissioned, but those newly commissioned into the Reconnaissance Corps itself wore General List badges.

The Corps was not totally without distinctions however: an arm-of-service strip of green and yellow, the colours of the Corps, was approved and several battalions used this as a basis for cloth badges. (Later, in July 1942, a shoulder title bearing the words Reconnaissance Corps in yellow letters on a green background was introduced: two months later this distinction was removed but in 1943 the shoulder title was restored with the single word Reconnaissance. According to the author of *Welsh Spearhead* this restoration of the shoulder title was due to the intervention of the prime minister himself).[8] Corps vehicles were to carry the number 41: this was the tactical number that identified recce vehicles throughout the Army.

The Corps cap badge had a long gestation and its design could almost be described as a campaign in itself for the first papers generated on the subject even showed doubt about the nature of the Corps. One staff officer wrote:

> It will be necessary to be quite clear that this will be a completely new Corps, having no connection with any other, i.e. not personnel of existing regiments performing a certain operational role.[9]

Badge designs were sought by the War Office and a number were submitted by the artist Rex Whistler who was serving in 24 Independent Company of the Corps.* These included compass-based designs with suggestions about the use of coloured enamel within a brass badge, which seemed rather extravagant for wartime days; the artist went so far as to submit suggestions for uniform details (Whistler's uniform designs were not adopted but in March 1942 the Corps was issued with green and yellow field-service caps which continued to be worn on occasion in some regiments after the introduction of the Corps' khaki beret at the end of the year). The compass designs also incorporated two suggestions for mottoes: Ab Uno Disce Omnes - From One Learn All - and Via Trita, Via Tuta - Beaten Paths are Safest. The rationale of the compass design was that it demonstrated the activities of a recce unit probing ahead of the main force. A similar idea was embodied in designs from an unknown artist in 18th Recce Battalion who used a design of a central boss with the title 'Recce' from which projected spearheads in the four principal directions. The intention was to signify the reconnoitring rôle forward and to the flanks, and the sending back of information; curves in the arms of the spearheads

---

*   Whistler was killed in action at the Bourguébus ridge in Normandy in 1944 when his battalion, 2nd Welsh Guards, was serving as the divisional reconnaissance unit of the Guards Armoured Division.[10]

were intended to show speed of movement.

The subtleties of such designs were too great for any of them to be accepted. In fact, one general principle for the required badge had been set down as being "conventional in design... It should not have subtle symbolism." Other qualities required were that the badge should be "easy to clean and easy to recognise, and strong enough to stand up to abuse."[11]

Among other suggestions was a badge incorporating twin bugle horns as the designer considered the Corps to be the lineal descendants of the light companies of the Peninsular War; this line of descent was rejected in Whitehall - the light companies had been skirmishers, wrote one officer, rather than reconnaissance troops - and with it the twin bugle horn badge.

Various designs were rejected for a series of reasons. A badge incorporating a hawk taking off was turned down as it might imply an aviation connection (the design produced by J.R.Gaunt bore a close resemblance to what later became the Army Air Corps badge). A design using a pointer was rejected on the grounds that it might lead to the nickname 'dogsbodies' and similarly the use of an Indian hunting leopard found no favour since that animal is commonly known as a cheetah which could lead to the nickname 'cheaters;' in addition the design submitted looked "more like a monkey, particularly in the rear portion." An American Indian's head badge was considered by one writer not to be British although it was pointed out to him that Canadian Indians were British and that many existing regimental badges had "un-British" designs. Six versions of this idea were designed and dies were struck for one version. Staff at No 1 Reconnaissance Training Centre at Winchester favoured the Indian's head and Lieutenant Colonel E.H.U.Bailey expressed their views in a letter dated 7 March 1941:

> Ref. your letter S/17 of 3rd March 41 the Hunting Leopard design is not at all popular. None of us like it.
>
> Of the Indian designs, I would like 05242 for the cap and 05243 for collar and buttons.
>
> If, however it is only intended that we are to have a cap badge for wear in battle dress, then I consider that 05243 would be most suitable.[12]

The design favoured by the Training Centre (05243) was that for which a die was struck.

Among the first designs considered was the old army scout's badge, the fleur-de-lys. It was felt that the Colonel of The Manchester Regiment might have to be consulted since his regiment used a similar badge. Again the idea was not proceeded with. The letters IRC, standing for Infantry Reconnaissance Corps, incorporated in a design also met with rejection; the stylised lettering looked too much like IRE although it was pointed out that the design could be sharpened to clarify the letters. A ferret badge was rejected almost out of hand since it "would lead to a lot of noisome discussion" and a series of centaur-based designs were also ruled out.

Not until 23 April 1941 was a final decision reached when the Adjutant-General wrote to the Deputy Adjutant-General to say that "QMG and I decided that the best badge is the Spear Head as submitted by the 56th Battalion Reconnaissance Corps..."[13]

The design which finally became the Corps badge was the work of Trooper George Jones of 56 Recce, a commercial artist in civilian life, and incorporated a spearhead flanked by two bolts of lightning. The designer was on the RHQ staff of 56 Recce at High Halden near Tenterden in Kent at the time he created the badge, a simple but strikingly effective design which embodied very clearly the rôle of the Reconnaissance Corps. As well as symbolising that rôle so well, the new badge also met the criteria of being robust, easy to clean and easily recognisable. It was also unlikely to attract any undesirable descriptions: apparently the only thing to which the badge was ever compared was a Christmas tree. The addition of a scroll reading 'Reconnaissance Corps' was the only significant change in George Jones's design which was submitted for the approval of the King at the end of June.

That approval was forthcoming and an ACI dated 29 July 1941 made the badge official but it was not until 1 September that units were invited to indent for supplies. One reason for the delay in supply had been bomb damage to the factory of J.R.Gaunt, who were manufacturing the badges. But at last a common identity could be clearly established with an end to the plethora of badges worn by Corps personnel until then.

Those delays undoubtedly caused a certain amount of frustration and some battalions tried to overcome the lack of a badge by producing their own cloth badges to be worn on the sleeve. Perhaps the most distinctive was a black panther on a diagonally split green and yellow background, the colours of the Reconnaissance Corps, designed by Second-Lieutenant E.M.Lyne of 4th Battalion for that unit and first issued on 18 July 1941. The distinctive black panther badge was not restricted to uniform sleeves: "our LRCs, HACs and carriers all carried the Black Panther painted on by [Sergeant] Bob Seal," an old soldier who had been just about to leave the Army at the end of his twenty-two years when war broke out.[14] The War Diary of 4 Recce noted that the official Corps' badge was "now in use" on 14 November 1941 but that "to render officers more distinctive it had been previously decided to alter finish of officers' badges."[14] This distinctive finish involved having the spear gilded while the lightning bolts and the title were nickel-plated; this was adopted by officers throughout the Corps.

By November 1941 the first battalion of the Corps to go overseas had arrived in the Middle East and was preparing for active service.

3
The Middle East

After the fall of France there was only one theatre in which the British Army was engaged with the enemy: North Africa. Initially the enemy was Italy but from February 1941 the Germans entered the desert war and the commander of the German expeditionary force, the Deutsches Afrika Korps, was to become one of the legends of the Second World War. He was Erwin Rommel, the Desert Fox.

Before Rommel's arrival in Tripoli the Italian Tenth Army had been destroyed in battle by the British Western Desert Force under Lieutenant General Sir Richard O'Connor. O'Connor had been forced to stop his advance at El Agheila when Wavell, the Commander-in-Chief, Middle East, had withdrawn men and equipment for the ill-fated campaign in Greece. Soon after arriving in Libya Rommel attacked the British and drove them back into Egypt. In November 1941 the newly-created Eighth Army launched Operation CRUSADER and Rommel was pushed back once again to El Agheila.

The Desert Fox had not been beaten; at the end of January 1942 his forces surged forward once more. Eighth Army was pushed back almost to its starting positions before CRUSADER. In the spring of 1942 the British defences were disposed between Gazala and Bir Hakeim. Included in those defences was a reconnaissance battalion, 50th Battalion The Reconnaissance Corps, of 50th Division, which had arrived in Egypt in late 1941.

Originally 4th Royal Northumberland Fusiliers, 50 Recce maintained many Northumberlands' traditions including using the designation Fusilier instead of Private. In France, in 1940, 4th Northumberlands had been used experimentally as a motorcycle battalion: on their machines, which included motorcycle combinations as well as other "odd transport," they had, in a sense, been the precursors of the Corps although in the retreat to Dunkirk there had been no real opportunity to develop their rôle. Still motorcycle-borne, the battalion transferred en bloc to the Reconnaissance Corps on 30 April 1941 and, in common with other battalions of the Corps, trained and practised for the recce rôle in the English countryside before moving to the Mediterranean.

After arriving in Palestine at the beginning of November 1941, 50th Division was alerted to a possible move to northern Iraq due to fears of a German breakthrough in the Caucacus which would bring Axis forces down from the north. That move did not materialise and 50 Recce was ordered to Alexandria in Egypt with 150 Infantry Brigade in late November.

Following training and exercises, the battalion re-formed in early 1942 as a motor battalion of 22 Armoured Brigade in 1st Armoured Division. They had hoped to reform as an armoured car regiment to replace 11th Hussars, who were due for a rest after service in the desert since the beginning of the campaign in North Africa. Any disappointment was shortlived as the battalion found 22 Armoured Brigade to be an extremely efficient and happy organisation and there was a high level of camaraderie with the armoured regiments, Royal Gloucestershire Hussars and 3rd and 4th County of London Yeomanry, which had sustained heavy losses during Operation CRUSADER. Artillery support for the brigade came from 107th Field Regiment, RA, The South Nottinghamshire Hussars, while fellow Northumbrians, The Northumberland Hussars, provided anti-tank protection as 102nd Anti-Tank Regiment.

In March 1942, 50 Recce joined 22 Armoured Brigade at Sidi Bishr camp on the outskirts of Alexandria. From Alex the brigade went to Mena for training and finally to Beni Yusif before setting out for the Gazala Line. Leaving Beni Yusif on St George's Day was a letdown for the Northumberlands as 1st Royal Northumberland Fusiliers were in the Citadel at Cairo and arrangements had been made for both battalions to celebrate St George's Day together.

'Front line' is a term that does not really apply to desert warfare. Although there was a loose line from Gazala to Bir Hakeim it was not defended along its entire length; instead there were defended localities and minefields stretching from Gazala southwards to Bir Hakeim. Around Gazala was 1st South African Division while, at the other end, Bir Hakeim was held by the Free French. In the central area was 50th Division, without its reconnaissance battalion, while the gaps were protected by the minefields. Behind the infantry, 1st and 7th Armoured Divisions held strongpoints, or 'boxes,' at Knightsbridge, Acroma and El Adem, Knightsbridge being 1st Armoured Division's responsibility.

The box concept was designed to provide a point around which the armour could manoeuvre and into which it could withdraw to refuel, replenish ammunition and carry out general maintenance. That point of manoeuvre was held by infantry, artillery and anti-tank guns.

Twenty-second Armoured Brigade formed three separate boxes, each of which included a battery of 107th Medium Regiment, two troops of 102nd Anti-Tank and a company of 50 Recce.

On the morning of 25 May Brigadier Carr, commanding 22 Armoured, decided to change his dispositions: all three boxes were moved and the troops took up their new positions that evening; the Gloucestershire Hussars box although somewhat isolated was still considered satisfactory. The CO of 50 Recce, Colonel des Graz, visited that box the following evening; he thought the box isolated and too far from its armour. That

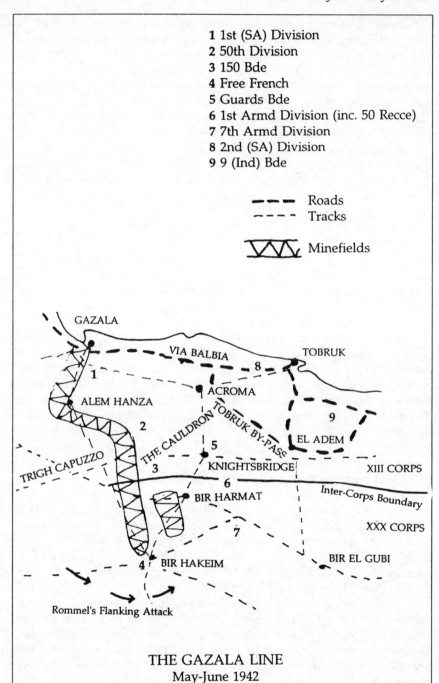

1 1st (SA) Division
2 50th Division
3 150 Bde
4 Free French
5 Guards Bde
6 1st Armd Division (inc. 50 Recce)
7 7th Armd Division
8 2nd (SA) Division
9 9 (Ind) Bde

--- Roads
- - - - Tracks

Minefields

GAZALA
VIA BALBIA
TOBRUK
8
1
ACROMA
ALEM HANZA
TOBRUK BY-PASS
2
9
THE CAULDRON
EL ADEM
5
TRIGH CAPUZZO
3
KNIGHTSBRIDGE
XIII CORPS
6
Inter-Corps Boundary
BIR HARMAT
7
XXX CORPS
4   BIR HAKEIM
BIR EL GUBI

Rommel's Flanking Attack

THE GAZALA LINE
May-June 1942

evening a report was received of enemy armour on the move about 30 miles west of the minefield; problems with communications - both land line and wireless - were also experienced.

On the morning of the 27th the sound of firing was heard to the south. Then, at 8.00am, the brigade was told to be ready to move north-westward at five minutes' notice to frustrate any enemy advance towards Tobruk from the southern end of the Gazala position. At the same time a large force of tanks was seen about 3,000 yards south of the Gloucestershire Hussars' box. Due to heat haze and mirage there was, at first, no certainty that the sighting was real, and the box commander reported as such to Brigade HQ. He was asked for confirmation and Lieutenant Neville Smith, commanding the box's motor platoon, established that the tanks were real - and German, about 60 in number. Brigade however thought Smith was mistaken and that the tanks were from 4 Armoured Brigade.

The Germans soon made matters clear. As the Brigade signal saying that the tanks were British was being decoded the first German shells were falling just north of the box. The anti-tank platoon of 50 Recce opened up with its 2-pounders but, although accurate, their fire was ineffective as the shells bounced off the enemy tanks. The panzers turned their attention to the Gloucestershires' Grant tanks, most of which were knocked out, after which the Germans returned to shelling the box. As a consequence of the change of position less than two days earlier the vehicles in the box had not been dug in and several were soon blazing while the guns of 107th Field were also targeted. As German armour advanced inside the box Major Herbert-Stepney of 50 Recce gave the order to withdraw. He himself was wounded and was one of only three Recce officers to escape. Box 1 had been destroyed; its survivors were absorbed into the remaining brigade boxes.

Brigadier Carr had, when he first learned that Box 1 was under attack, intended to move the remainder of his command to their aid. He soon realised that the box was unable to withstand the pressure being put on it and so ordered his brigade to withdraw northwards to a point east of Knightsbridge. The withdrawal was carried out successfully. There was already a strong defensive position at Knightsbridge, held by the Guards Brigade. Strengthened by the guns of 22 Armoured's Support Group it would provide a firm pivot for the armour. Boxes 2 and 3 of the Support Group, commanded by Colonel des Graz, were established close to Knightsbridge and linked by telephone: Box 2 faced west, Box 3 south; they were immediately to the east and north-east of the Knightsbridge Box.

For three days the defenders remained in those positions while the armour manoeuvred and fought around them. The boxes did their job effectively, their firepower breaking up enemy attacks while their own armour was able to fall behind the screen thus provided to refuel and replenish ammunition. Forced on to the defensive the Germans began to withdraw on 30 May due to shortage of ammunition; their supply columns were being harassed by the Free French at Bir Hakeim. German thrusts towards El Adem had also been pushed back thus permitting additional British formations to deploy against those Germans in the Knightsbridge area.

The enemy withdrawal allowed 50 Recce to be re-supplied with food and water and gave its soldiers a brief respite. On the last day of May there was a lull in the battle as the Germans withdrew into the 'Cauldron,' a bulge in the minefield, where mines, plus a line of 88mm guns deployed as an anti-tank screen, gave excellent protection. This gave the Germans the opportunity to re-organise for the next phase.

At dawn on 1 June the Germans attacked. Their first target was 150 Infantry Brigade, 50th Division's most southerly brigade, which was holding the eastern edge of the minefield north of the Cauldron; they had little support and were very low on ammunition. By that evening the brigade's ammunition stocks were so depleted that they could offer little further resistance and their positions were overrun. The Germans then cleared paths through the minefield and brought up supplies of badly-needed ammunition and fuel. Thus the British onslaught on the 'Cauldron,' which began at 2.50am on 5 June, was met by well-equipped and confident German troops.

By mid-day it was obvious that the attack had failed. Instead of executing the planned wide sweep the armoured regiments were holding the line of a ridge just ahead of the Support Group; both were being bombarded by enemy artillery. From the boxes the gunners were giving supporting fire to the armour. Expecting an order to withdraw when darkness fell, Colonel des Graz prepared his battalion but, although the armour was withdrawn at dusk, Support Group, with the survivors of the Indian infantry, was ordered to remain in position.

The next dawn brought a renewed enemy artillery bombardment. Realising that the British armour had been withdrawn, the Germans probed the British positions with tanks. There was sufficient weight of fire from the two boxes and the Indian troops to beat off any frontal attacks but the Germans were able to work round the flanks until the positions were completely encircled. This had been achieved by about 9 o'clock, just about an hour after Captain Maxwell, commander of HQ Company, had reached the boxes with some ammunition trucks.

Throughout the day the Germans made attempt after attempt to break in to the boxes. Each attack was beaten off but, every time this happened, guns or trucks were destroyed and ammunition levels reduced. Brigade Headquarters was told of the seriousness of the situation but the armour was now in action further north and no help could be given to the beleaguered Support Group. Sooner or later a German attack would succeed in breaking in. That happened at about 5.30 that evening. An assault from the north-west was met by the remaining guns but they had so little ammunition that they could not stop the German tanks. The enemy broke into the boxes where the final drama of the battle was played out.

Throughout the battle Colonel des Graz had driven around his battalion's positions, encouraging his fusiliers and giving orders as calmly as if he were on exercise. Showing a total disregard for danger, des Graz dominated the scene and imbued his men with his own spirit:

> He had one of the most bitter tasks that a commander can be called upon to face - that of holding, unsupported, an untenable position. He saw clearly what the end must be, but he never doubted where his duty lay, though in the execution of it he saw destroyed before his eyes the Battalion he had built up with so much labour and so much skill.[1]

One of the battalion's officers, Lieutenant G.F.Thistleton, witnessed his commanding officer's final moments:

> I was returning on foot from guns 5, 6, 7 and 8 to guns 1, 2, 3 and 4, and found that enemy tanks, after repeated attacks, had penetrated this position. One enemy tank was slowly approaching the gun positions and I tried to make my way past it to get a gun into action. I had reached my truck when Lt-Col des Graz appeared over the ridge, standing up in a carrier, and drove straight up to gun 2. He jumped out and brought the gun into action. No 1 of the gun fired two shots, which hit the tank but failed to penetrate. The tank stopped and opened fire, scoring two direct hits on the gun shield from a range of about one hundred yards, and silencing the gun.
>
> Colonel des Graz was standing immediately behind the two pounder and he and two of the gun crew were killed outright.[2]
>
> So he died, when his gallant and determined defence could no longer hold off the weight of superior armoured forces, himself directing at pointblank range the fire of a two pounder A/T gun.[3]

The outcome was inevitable: 50 Recce ceased to exist with most of its personnel being captured. Some suffered this fate for a second time, having been captured some days earlier then escaping to rejoin the battalion only to be present at its final struggle. Many gun-crews, on whom most of the fighting centred, died as did their commanding officer, while trying to stop the German tanks.

By the beginning of July the Axis army had forced Eighth Army back to the El Alamein line. There General Auchinleck fought a brilliant series of actions which stopped Rommel in his tracks and proved to be the turning-point of the desert war for it was on Auchinleck's achievements during July that Montgomery's victory at El Alamein that autumn was built. By then, of course, 50 Recce had ceased to exist although two other reconnaissance units had arrived in North Africa.

The new units were 44th and 51st Reconnaissance Regiments. The new nomenclature, with its echoes of the old divisional light cavalry and cavalry designations, had come into effect on 6 June, the day on which 50 Recce had virtually ceased to exist. As had been 50 Recce's lot, neither of the newcomers was destined to serve in a true 'recce' rôle.

Formed in January 1941, 44 Recce was created from 44th Division's anti-tank companies, each of which had in turn been built up from the respective brigades. These had all been Home Counties' brigades: 131 Brigade consisted of Queens and Buffs battalions; 132 of Royal West Kents and Queens and 133 of Royal Sussex. Initially A Squadron was made up of Queensmen and Buffs, B Squadron of Queensmen and Royal West Kents and C Squadron of Royal Sussex soldiers; RHQ and HQ Squadron had a cross-section of the battalions represented in the regiment.

After training in England, 44th Division sailed from Scotland in May 1942 with 44 Recce on board SS *Santa Elena* with divisional HQ. The voyage to Egypt via South Africa was memorable for a number of reasons: the ship carried twice as many men as it was designed to carry and therefore only two meals a day were served and, since it was American, no alcohol was permitted; not surprisingly its passengers quickly renamed it the *Altmark* after the German ship used to carry the *Graf Spee's* prisoners.

Arriving in Egypt in late July, the division concentrated between Cairo and Alexandria and 44 Recce spent two weeks in acclimatisation and training in desert conditions. A number of points were soon obvious: motorcycles would be useless in the desert; the Humber Light Recce Car was unsuited to driving in desert conditions where it would be an inviting target - the Humber LRC relied for survival in close country on its speed and the commander's eye for cover - but soft desert sand was passable if the skills and techniques of driving over it were mastered.

On 14 August 44th Division moved up to the Alamein line into a reserve position behind General Freyberg's NZ Division at the southern end. The recce regiment was placed under command of 7th Armoured Division, the Desert Rats, for a period of guidance. It had become clear that a reconnaissance regiment, as normally constituted, simply did not fit into the scheme of things for desert warfare. With its motorcycles written off and its LRCs of limited use, the regiment was left with its Bren-gun carriers and lorries and was far from being a balanced organisation. No-one had yet worked out a policy or a proper rôle for recce in the theatre.

During its time with the Desert Rats 44 Recce was split up to serve with the battalions and regiments of 4 Light Armoured Brigade. The assault troops and carriers were assigned to motor-battalions and the LRCs to cavalry regiments. When Rommel launched his attack on Montgomery's positions on 30 August elements of 44 Recce were engaged in action with their mentors of 4 Light Armoured Brigade during the Battle of Alam Halfa. On 4 September, the regiment concentrated once again under 44th Division but a week later it was placed under 22 Armoured Brigade which had become a permanent part of 7th Armoured Division on 7 September.

For two weeks the regiment had the task of guarding front-line positions at the British 'Nuts' and 'May' minefields, near Himeimat. Then came a withdrawal into reserve where it seemed as if someone had come up with a positive idea for the use of the regiment: the LRCs were sent to guard rear areas and the regiment was redesignated 44th Divisional Reconnaissance Carrier Regiment. This new organisation included one strong carrier squadron formed from all the regiment's carriers with two additional carrier squadrons made up from men and machines of 132 and 151 Brigades. Detachments of Royal Engineers were included in the order-of-battle and there was talk of Scorpions - tanks fitted with flails to explode mines - being allocated.

And so it became obvious that the regiment's job would be to clear paths through enemy minefields for Eighth Army's armour in the forthcoming offensive. Specifically, it was told that its rôle would be to clear four gaps for an armoured brigade and, in carrying out this task, to be prepared to seize and hold ground, 'to carry out reconnaissance in force and in so doing to be prepared to overcome minor resistance.'[4] There were shades of the original recce rôle in those orders but the task that lay ahead of 44 Recce was totally different to that for which it had trained for so long. Retraining was necessary and lasted into October.

A mineclearing drill was worked out, practised and then revised until a definitive drill was arrived at, which was then practised to perfection. Central to this drill were the Scorpions, six of which were issued to the regiment, one for each path with two tanks in reserve. As training continued a change in the shape of the regiment was thought necessary and so it re-formed into two carrier squadrons and an assault squadron; Matilda infantry tanks were to provide armoured support.

On 22 October the operation order was received: the regiment would go into action on the night of 23 October in Operation LIGHTFOOT. As the minefield task force of 7th Armd Division, 44 Recce had absorbed all the carriers of its division and also contained 4th Field Squadron, RE. The six Scorpions were in the van, supported by the Stuarts of A Squadron, Royal Scots Greys, rather than the intended Matildas, a battery of anti-tank guns and two companies of 1st KRRC. They had an approach march of almost ten miles over four parallel tracks through three British minefields before reaching their start line east of the German minefield codenamed 'January.' Clearing paths through 'January' and a second minefield, codenamed 'February,' was 44 Recce's task.

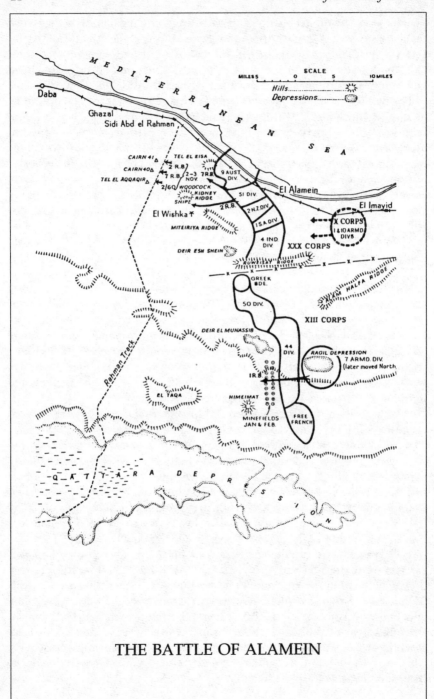

THE BATTLE OF ALAMEIN

B and C Squadrons led the regiment into 'January' ten minutes behind schedule. The gapping parties had arrived almost half an hour late at the start line, a delay caused by the fact that many of the lamps lighting the approach route had gone out. A number of further difficulties and mistakes beset the squadrons. Number 2 gap was cleared by C Squadron by 1.40am although the Scorpion had been damaged by a mine and then hit by anti-tank fire leaving the sappers to clear the gap by hand; number 1 gap was also cleared by C almost three hours later at 4.30am, but just west of the exit there was an enemy position. To the south gaps 3 and 4 presented even more difficulties for B Squadron: soon after leaving its start line the squadron had run into mines in a deep sandy wadi which claimed three carriers and, believing this to be the eastern edge of 'January,' the squadron leader ordered flailing to begin. It was not 'January,' but mines that had been laid in front of it. One Scorpion overheated several times and broke down; enemy fire was heavy with machine-guns, mortars and artillery and the squadron sustained heavy casualties before reaching the eastern edge of the enemy minefield where the Scorpions fortunately were all back in working order through the efforts of their crews. By 2.15am, number 3 gap was clear but was useless for wheeled vehicles due to soft sand; one Scorpion was now disabled at the western end of the gap. The final gap, number 4, was cleared by hand half an hour after midnight, the Scorpion assigned to it having been knocked out three-quarters of the way through.

The minefields had been bigger than anticipated and resistance very strong; B Squadron had been reduced to less than six carriers and casualties were severe. So bad were those casualties that 44 Recce's CO, Lieutenant Colonel Corbett-Winder, told Brigadier Roberts of 22 Armoured Brigade that his men could only clear two gaps instead of four in 'February;' the two squadrons could muster only one column each rather than two. The attack through 'February' was due to start at 5.30am. It had to be called off: one gapping party was unable to get to 'February;' the other reached it but came under heavy fire from the enemy. Dawn was breaking and, as any attempt to clear minefields in daylight would be suicidal, the operation was cancelled. One Scorpion, hit by anti-tank fire, had to be abandoned.

Daylight saw 22 Armoured Brigade deployed on either side of 'January.' Their situation worsened when the Free French were pushed off Himeimat and their commanding officer, the popular and inspiring Colonel Amilakvari, killed. Throughout that day there was heavy fighting all along the Alamein front and 7th Armoured Division had orders to extend their bridgehead westward through 'February' that night. The men of 44 Recce were to clear two gaps through which 22 Armoured would pass to be followed by 4 Light Armoured Brigade. Once again things did not go according to plan: although both gaps were complete by 2.30am, enemy fire was so heavy that the sappers were unable to mark the sides with dannert wire and lights; so much enemy anti-tank artillery was still operational that the British armour, after making one attempt to pass through, was forced to withdraw. For 7th Armoured Division the situation had been virtually stalemated; 44 Recce was pulled back to a reserve position at Deir el Ragil where it remained until 2 November. After forcing its way through 'February' the regiment had only four carriers surviving from 38; 13 officers and over 100 other ranks had been killed or wounded.

As the Axis forces began to withdraw from the El Alamein line 44 Recce, at the head of 44th Division, began a pursuit of the Germans and Italians from Himeimat. For 70 miles the division harried the retreating foe, taking hundreds of prisoners and large quantities of arms and equipment after a number of minor actions. Then came news of the division's withdrawal. Worse was to come: the CinC, Middle East Forces, General Sir Harold Alexander, judged that the need for reinforcements for Eighth Army, plus the supply problems of the advance, meant that two of his divisions could no longer be kept in being: the axe fell on 8th Armoured and 44th Infantry Divisions. Informed that it would be disbanded also, 44 Recce was sent to Qassasin, in the Nile delta, to await that fate.

However, a stay of execution was ordered and the regiment was re-organised with Marmon-Herrington armoured-cars replacing its Humber LRCs. Without an operational rôle it moved to the Citadel in Cairo in January 1943 to guard GHQ. That task ended in February and, by the end of that month, 44 Recce had moved to Gaza and 56th (London) Division which had left its own reconnaissance regiment in England on moving to the Middle East. By the beginning of April, 56th Division was moving westwards to join Eighth Army which had broken the Mareth Line and was operating in Tunisia.

Another reconnaissance regiment had fought its way through the El Alamein battle. This was 51st, the 'eyes' of the famous 51st (Highland) Division. Born in January 1941 in circumstances similar to those of 44 Recce, 51st had been formed from the brigade anti-tank companies of its division. (The division itself had been re-formed as the original 51st Division had been captured by the Germans at St Valery in 1940.) A Squadron had been 152 Anti-Tank Company made up of Camerons and Seaforths; B Squadron had been 153 Company with Black Watch and Gordons, while C Squadron had been 154 Company whose men had been Black Watch and Argylls. The CO was Lieutenant Colonel E.H.Grant, an Argyll, and the strong ethos of the division was reflected in his regiment. The Highland Division's recce regiment was one of those to adopt a distinctive appearance through its use of the highland infantry bonnet, the Tam O'Shanter, and the Hunting Stewart flash worn below the right shoulder; the divisional sign, the letters HD in white against blue, was worn below the left shoulder.

The division embarked for India in June 1942 but the North African situation meant a change in destination to Egypt. HMT *Stratheden* was home for divisional headquarters and 51 Recce until their arrival in Egypt almost two months later. The voyage was uncomfortable for most of the men: as a luxury liner in peacetime the ship normally carried about 800 passengers; in its wartime rôle it was carrying almost 5,000 although the highlanders found the shipboard catering standards more agreeable than the Home Counties men on board the *Santa Elena*.

Disembarking at Port Tewfik, 51 Recce entrained for Qassasin; the regiment's vehicles were later landed at Haifa. In the meantime training had begun with lectures on desert warfare and navigational exercises using sun compasses. On 22 August the Prime Minister and General Brooke, CIGS, inspected the Division and, two days later, Colonel Grant went to Cairo to discuss and reconnoitre positions to be occupied by the regiment in the event of an Axis attack on Cairo around the right flank of Eighth Army. It is interesting that such a plan existed, for Montgomery in his memoirs castigated General Auchinleck for having prepared plans for the defence of the Delta in the event of Axis forces breaking through the Alamein line. Nowhere in his writings did Monty mention that such plans continued after the Auk's removal and yet this was the case: the Highland Division was to form South Delta Force with 51 Recce responsible for the defence of Gezira Island and the four bridges connecting it with the mainland.

On 25 August squadron commanders were ordered to Cairo to reconnoitre positions for the defence of Gezira and the bridges across the Nile; Highland Division Headquarters and 239 Field Park Company, Royal Engineers, were placed under 51 Recce for this task. At the same time there was soul-searching about the rôle of a recce regiment in this theatre and, according to a note in Regimental Orders of late August:

> Until the role of a Recce Regt in the Middle East has been definitely decided, it is not possible to lay down anything but a provisional policy.[5]

While that uncertainty existed training continued with route marches, compass work, judging distances in the desert, patrols, moving into defence harbour on foot - vehicles had yet to arrive - and close order and battle drills.

For the first five days of September the regiment, less a mobile squadron under Major Hutchison, was given the task of defending the canal from Beni Yusif to the River Nile; the mobile squadron created a divisional reserve and patrolled until it ceased to exist on the 5th.

After participating in an exercise, 51st Division was ordered to join XIII Corps and moved to XXX Corps' area for training at which time the

Hunting Stewart and HD flashes were taken into use by 51 Recce. Soul-searching about the regiment's rôle continued: as the Humber LRCs were unsuitable for desert conditions Colonel Grant suggested to the divisional commander that the regiment should be equipped with heavy armoured-cars for recce work, or be converted into a divisional cavalry regiment with cruiser tanks and carriers - again in the recce rôle. Then, towards the end of the month, came another proposal: to create a carrier regiment with a HQ squadron and three carrier squadrons. This would have paralleled the experience of 44 Recce. But none of these proposals was put into effect and the first weeks of October found the regiment preparing for its part in the forthcoming offensive; this required re-organisation.

The regiment re-formed into two distinct elements, a composite squadron and an infantry squadron. The divisional plan of attack for Operation LIGHTFOOT was received on 19 October and, two days later, the composite squadron moved to Tel El Alamein. On the evening of 23 October, 11 and 17 Assault Troops were to cover sappers gapping enemy minefields but, whereas 44 Recce had been engaged on the southern flank of the line, 51 operated on the northern flank.

The composite squadron suffered its first casualties from enemy mortar fire almost as soon as it moved into action and one man was killed. By 11.30pm the squadron was moving into the gaps under heavy shellfire. There were many mines and Lieutenant Jocker, commanding the RE party, dismantled mines until he was wounded in the legs. A sapper sergeant then took over until he too was wounded. Captain R.R.Park of 51 Recce then went out to rescue both men. Park later returned to the minefield and re-appeared some time afterwards with 30 Italian prisoners:

> These casualties caused delay, with the result that the main RE party, escorted by A Scout Troop, caught up with the Assault Troops. The Germans had placed wire only on their own side of their minefields and the carriers entered it without knowing it was there. One was blown up. The RE main party then went on with the gapping while the Assault Troops protected them from the enemy side of the minefield. As soon as an eight-yard gap had been made, the Assault Troops went forward, and A Scout Troop (Lt Gall) took up the positions they had vacated. B Scout Troop (Lt Burt) came up to the British side of the field and lit the way to the gap. Meanwhile, the Assault Troops had encountered the second enemy minefield. The RE Recce party recce'd it. As soon as a 24-yard gap had been completed in the first field, A Scout Troop escorted the main RE party forward to the second minefield, which they gapped. This operation was directed by Lt Jocker, who carried on from a Jeep although he was badly wounded in the legs. As soon as an eight-yard gap had been made, the Assault Troops advanced 600 yards to the lying-up position from which the attack on the objective NAIRN was to be launched. During this period, both Assault and Scout Troops

were under constant enemy shell, mortar and MG fire. Also, they had by
this time almost caught up with our own barrage, and one of our guns
firing short caused several casualties. A Scout Troop lit the way from the
gap to the lying-up position. As soon as the 24-yard gap had been made
in the second minefield, the tanks went through and formed up ready
for the attack at approximately 0300 hours.[6]

The tanks, from 50th RTR were to 'attack, capture and annihilate' objective
NAIRN. The recce men were in support of the tanks with A Scout Troop to
the right, B to the left and all three Assault Troops accompanying the
tanks; C under Lt Hofman had ridden forward on the tanks. As the tanks
began their attack, enemy fire intensified and the first anti-tank fire
appeared from the right flank. One tank was knocked out by an 88 and the
others withdrew, putting down smoke. As this was happening, A Scout
Troop was working forward on the right flank but, as the wind was
blowing from the right, the smoke drifted behind them, silhouetting them
for the enemy gunners. The German anti-tank crews switched their
attention to the troop's carriers and knocked out four in seconds. When the
smoke cleared the tanks had withdrawn, leaving three behind disabled; B
Scout Troop had lost a carrier and A had only one carrier left.

The wounded were evacuated on that carrier and the squadron retired
to where their most recent attack had started, west of the last enemy
minefield. There they dug in at first light and medical officers of 50 RTR
and 51 Recce (Captain Jolly) did sterling work treating and evacuating
wounded under intermittent shelling.

Early that afternoon the tank regiment commander ordered an officer
and 30 men to support a tank attack; the soldiers were to ride into battle on
the tanks. No further details were given but eventually Lieutenant Roberts
and 30 men accompanied tanks in an assault on German anti-tank guns
and machine-guns at the northern end of the NAIRN area. The armour was
within 250 yards of the objective when the leading six tanks were hit and
immobilised; the others withdrew. Almost all Roberts's men of the
Composite Squadron had been on the leading tanks and they took cover
behind them and engaged the enemy; the crews of the immobilised tanks
continued to shell and machine-gun the enemy positions. This battle
continued for about an hour and distracted German attention from an
attack by Seaforths on the right. The immobilised tanks were being
constantly hit by light anti-tank shells; after an hour their ammunition was
exhausted and, one by one, they stopped firing, their crews making their
way back to the mobile tanks which were out of range of the German guns.
The last tank to stop firing was that of the captain commanding the
squadron; he ordered Roberts and his men to withdraw and covered their
withdrawal with the last of his ammunition before escaping himself.
Lieutenant Roberts and his men returned to their own positions at 6.00pm
from where, half an hour later, the Composite Squadron moved into

reserve.

The reserve position was between two British minefields in the area of Divisional Tactical HQ. The Divisional Commander, Major General Wimberley, was quick to congratulate them on the work they had done. The last days of the month were spent in the line with 154 Brigade. Intermittent shell and machine-gun fire continued until the squadron was relieved by South African troops and returned to Divisional Tactical HQ. One officer and 15 other ranks had been killed and five officers and 50 other ranks wounded.

In early November, as Eighth Army moved forward in the first stages of the pursuit that was to lead to Tunisia, the Composite Squadron was ordered to hold part of the line formerly held by 24th and 28th New Zealand Battalions. The Infantry Squadron now came into the picture: formed from men who had been left out of battle or engaged as PoW escorts, it was commanded by Captain Stratton and moved to relieve the Composite Squadron, which was now assigned to 153 Brigade for its advance to El Daba. The squadron recce'd for the brigade advance which met with no opposition and, with El Daba airfield secured, deployed to cover sappers clearing mines from the coast road between El Daba and Galal. In the meantime the Infantry Squadron had moved with 154 Brigade to Tel El Aqqaqir. On 6 November the Composite Squadron was on the move again, carrying out reconnaissance for 51st Division on the coast road to Fuka. The squadron moved beyond Fuka to a point three miles west of Sidi Haneish, taking 500 prisoners on the way. Most were very demoralised and only the first batch encountered put up a half-hearted fight before surrendering. Beyond Sidi Haneish, 8 NZ Armd Brigade were encountered from whom the squadron learned that the road was clear with only mopping-up to be done to the east.

Squadron HQ was set up five miles west of Fuka where Lt Gen Sir Oliver Leese, commanding XXX Corps, congratulated its personnel on their day's work. The Infantry Squadron had moved up to El Daba and on to Galal where the Composite Squadron and RHQ rejoined on 7 November. A week later the regiment re-organised to a more conventional pattern and moved to Sidi Haneish. From there they expected to move with 51st Division to Tobruk or Benghazi but the order was cancelled. Colonel Grant had gone to GHQ in Cairo and returned with the news that the regiment was to become a motorised infantry battalion and would move to Cairo to re-organise and train.

That news was bad enough; worse was to come: on 14 January 1943 the regiment was redesignated 14th HLI. In spite of its title the HLI was a lowland regiment and conversion to a battalion of such a regiment was the worst fate that could befall a regiment of highlanders. The Jocks' disapproval was voiced at a parade to mark their conversion. In the presence of senior HLI officers and members of the General Staff from Cairo they responded to the call for three cheers "with three hearty boos."

Thus ended the service of 51 Recce. Although the Highland Division would later be given another recce regiment this would be 2nd Derby Yeomanry which was not part of the Recce Corps. The three recce regiments committed to the desert campaign had been sent to fight in conditions entirely unsuited to them. By dint of improvisation they had performed excellent service and although this was hardly in their intended rôle it had shown the qualities of adaptation and courage for which their Corps would become famous.

4

Tunisia - 56 Recce clear the way

Tunisia was the Corps' next area of operations and the first recce regiment to serve there was 56th Reconnaissance Regiment, to which fell also the distinction of being the first regiment of the Corps to serve in a true recce rôle.

Formed from anti-tank companies of 56th (London) Division the regiment's soldiers came, mainly, from the TA battalions which made up the division. The first commanding officer was Lieutenant Colonel N.F.V.Hamilton who held command until May 1942 when he was succeeded by Lieutenant Colonel K.G.F.Chavasse, whose cousin, Captain Noel Chavasse, had won the Victoria Cross and Bar, as well as a Military Cross before his death in the Great War.

When Colonel Chavasse took over, the regiment was at Colchester preparing for overseas service. The "final dispatch of unsuitable personnel"[1] had taken place, these individuals being returned to their own units as they did not meet the standards required in a reconnaissance regiment. By the end of July, 56 Recce had received its complement of eight 2-pounder anti-tank guns and in August it was inspected by Major General E.G.Miles, DSO, MC, commanding 56th (London) Division before moving to Barry Buddon camp in Scotland where the regiment began to prepare for a move to tropical climates.

Shortly after taking over command Colonel Chavasse had an approach from Lord Tweedsmuir, Colonel of The Artists' Rifles, one of the London TA regiments. Tweedsmuir asked if his Regiment would be prepared to accept the identity of the Artists' Rifles as the Artists had been designated an Officer Cadet Training Unit (OCTU) at the beginning of the war and thus would be unable to obtain battle honours; if, however, 56 Recce became 56th (Artists' Rifles) Reconnaissance Regiment then any battle honours obtained might be added to those gained by the Artists in the Great War. The suggestion was discussed by the officers of the 56th and rejected. There were two reasons for this: in common with all Reconnaissance Corps units the Regiment had already adopted cavalry nomenclature and therefore the use of an infantry sub-title would be dissonant; in addition, although many officers of the Regiment were from London TA battalions there were none from the Artists and it was felt that the regiment could not happily become Artists' Rifles. And so the suggestion was rejected, although it would appear that it had gone so far in circles outside 56 Recce that an Army Order permitting it may have been issued: certainly a number of sources indicate this.

Having rejected this offer, 56 Recce decided on a distinction that would be all their own: it was agreed that the officers would wear green berets instead of the standard Reconnaissance Corps khaki. These were purchased while in Scotland but were not worn until the regiment went overseas. Colonel Chavasse had also had his Quartermaster obtain cavalry trumpets to add to the cavalry ethos of the regiment.[2]

That overseas move came in October 1942. By then 56 Recce had said 'goodbye' to 56th Division to become the reconnaissance regiment of the recently-formed 78th Division which was assigned to First Army for Operation TORCH, the landings in French north-west Africa. In October 1942 56 Recce, less A Squadron, left the Clyde in a convoy bound for Algiers. Landing on 8 November C Squadron was joined by RHQ, and HQ and B Squadrons which landed six days later. While transport and equipment was unloaded - one LRC was lost when it was dropped into the harbour during unloading - the regiment encamped in the Botanical Gardens in Algiers. On 16 November 56 Recce left Algiers for the front line. It was soon in action: on the way to Tabarka there was considerable evidence of German bombing with burnt-out vehicles littering the roads; that afternoon soldiers of the regiment had their first encounter with the enemy after a 450 mile drive into Tunisia on the coast road. Lieutenant Graham Wheatley, commanding 15 Troop, C Squadron, believed to be the first British troops into Tunisia, met their first Germans when Wheatley recce'd beyond Djebel Abiod on the road to Bizerta. Unfortunately, his driver overturned his LRC into a ditch while attempting to turn the car around on a narrow road. But the contact was reported to Brigade HQ who sent forward a number of anti-tank guns, several 25-pounder field guns and infantry from 6th Royal West Kents.

The artillery engaged the German armour, knocking out eleven Mark IV panzers for the loss of five 2-pounders and some 25-pounders. In the meantime Wheatley and his crew had taken cover in a culvert whence they intended to make their way back to their regiment when darkness fell. Their plan was thwarted by an Arab boy who told the Germans where they were and they thus became the first members of the regiment to be captured.

Shortly after this episode the regiment's first gallantry award, a Military Medal, was won by Sergeant Crutch, C Squadron, who was on a carrier patrol north of Djebel Abiod. Travelling along the coast road Crutch had been told to obtain details of the strength of a German position on the road. He was within a half mile of the position when a heavy machine-gun opened up from cover of a damaged tank being used as a road block. In spite of the heavy fire Crutch "butted" the tank and got within 400 yards of the German position where he was able to note their strength and dispositions. This valuable information was relayed back to 36 Brigade HQ

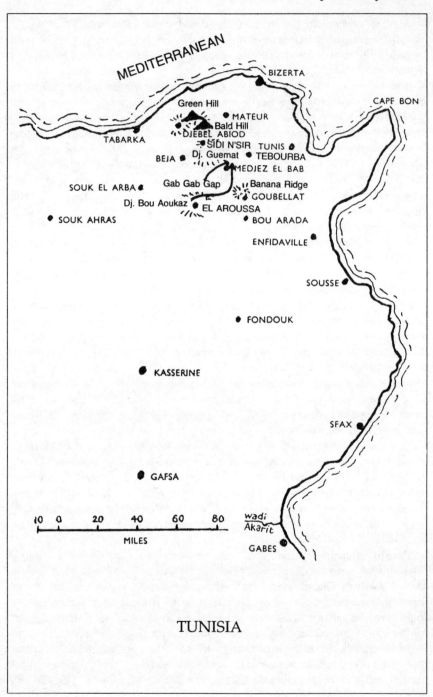

TUNISIA

and, as a result, Crutch was successfully commended for the MM. C
Squadron pushed on past Sedjenane into a valley between scrub-covered
hills. On one hill the scrub petered out part-way up; this was to become
known as Bald Hill while the hill on the other side became Green Hill. At
that point the squadron was recalled to join the regiment for another task:
that recall may have saved it from being thrown into an infantry rôle at the
pass; the Argylls, who got the infantry job there, moved into the mouth of
the pass in the middle of the afternoon of 28 November with a company
spread out in single file on either side of the road, interspersed with the
Bren gun carriers of their carrier platoon. At 3.30, when the leading
companies were in the middle of the pass, the Germans opened up with
scores of machine-guns. Within minutes all the Bren gun carriers were
shattered and for months afterwards the wrecks of eight of them could be
seen spaced out evenly along the road.

The bulk of the regiment, RHQ and B Squadron was assigned to Blade
Force, First Army's spearhead, which was to seize the road between
Tebourba and Mateur. B Squadron was also in action early, resulting in
another MM award. The squadron's assault troop, with the regiment's
anti-tank guns, had been the first elements into El Aroussa village on 22
November where 56 Recce had been told to seize and hold the bridge. One
section occupied a farm on the outskirts of the village, the name of which
was to become depressingly familiar to British troops in Tunisia. Later that
day some French troops arrived to say that enemy forces were
approaching. The enemy turned out to be a motorcycle combination about
a thousand yards away. Presumably a German recce patrol, the
combination withdrew but the farm soon came under heavy machine-gun
fire. Two recce cars were sent out but both were hit and knocked out with
five men of their crews killed and the troop commander, Lieutenant
Robinson, seriously wounded.

The Germans had not finished with the farm for they opened fire on it
again that night, causing further casualties. Although the recce men did not
realise it at the time the enemy were intent on surrounding their position.
Corporal Bob McDonald and two others knocked out a German
machine-gun next morning but a replacement crew soon took over. The
second crew were also knocked out by Bren-gun fire before a grenade
landed near McDonald's position. It was picked up to throw back by Lance
Corporal Harry Thirkettle but exploded, blowing off Thirkettle's hand and
injuring McDonald in the back. As Corporal McDonald attempted to dress
the injured lance-corporal's wrist, Trooper Venables attended to
McDonald's back but the Germans arrived and the trio were taken
prisoner. Their wounds were attended to before being transferred to
hospital in Tunis and then flown to Naples and a PoW camp. It soon
became obvious to Colonel Chavasse that his small force could not hold El

Aroussa and so:

> I tried to get in touch with Blade HQ to give an account of the situation,
> but communications had broken down with it. So I ordered a
> withdrawal off my own bat (wondering what the consequences to me
> would be!). However I was much relieved to receive a signal from Div
> HQ to say that we had reverted to their command and to move
> elsewhere.[3]

And so the remainder of the regiment withdrew from El Aroussa in the
face of heavy enemy fire leaving the village in German hands. The new
task for 56 Recce was the protection of 78th Division's right flank as it
continued its push towards Tunis.

First Army was an army in name only: its total assets on the ground in
Tunisia included two brigades of 78th Division, the ad-hoc Blade Force
battlegroup, and a limited number of divisional troops. General Anderson,
commanding First Army, controlled a force of little over 12,000 while his
counterpart had almost twice that number. Axis forces also had the
advantage of better lines of communication. A similar situation applied in
the air: the Luftwaffe had good all-weather airfields close to the battle area
while the RAF and USAAF all-weather aerodromes were well out of range
and fighters had to rely on makeshift airfields that became unusable as the
weather became wetter. Not surprisingly the Germans soon had control of
the air and for those men who had come through the Dunkirk campaign in
1940 there was a very real sense of deja vu. That air superiority led to
further losses in 56 Recce. B Squadron's carriers had been harboured
around the bridge at Sloughia from which they were ordered to move at
daylight in case of air attack. One carrier slid off the road into a ditch and
struck a batch of French mines which exploded, killing the commander and
badly wounding the driver. As if that were not enough a German fighter
flew over and strafed the area, causing more casualties and destroying a
number of soft-skinned vehicles. The dead carrier commander was buried
by the roadside. Later that day his body was found on top of the ground,
having been dug up and stripped of clothing by Arabs. That barbaric act
caused much anger in B Squadron and increased animosity towards Arabs.

At the time of the attack B Squadron had been under orders to move
into and through Medjez el Bab. However, 5th Northamptons had already
entered the town to find it clear of Germans. The centre span of the town's
Roman bridge had been destroyed but was replaced with a Bailey Bridge
by the Royal Engineers, the first of many to be erected in Tunisia. As soon
as this bridge was in place 56 Recce's men moved across on to the road to
Tebourba which they reached by dusk with no opposition save a single
German fighter plane.

By now 56 Recce was mounting daily patrols and by early December the
regiment had penetrated to within 15 miles of Tunis itself, the Allies' goal.

Opposition was stiffening and patrols were running up against German six-wheeled armoured cars, also performing a recce rôle, and the redoubtable 88mm gun; LRCs and carriers had little chance of survival when faced with such a weapon. But the regiment continued to do its job effectively, sending back regular reports for the divisional commander and all the while improving its own efficiency. Everyone was at full stretch with the crews of LRCs and carriers having little opportunity for rest. Kendal Chavasse had to drive back to divisional HQ each night to report to the divisional commander and return before daylight to issue his orders for the following day.

December was a busy month for the regiment which was now dubbing itself Chavasse's Light Horse. On the 4th they were ordered to extricate personnel of 2nd Para Battalion from Sloughia: the paras had been dropped at Depienne, behind enemy lines, and communication with them had been lost. Sergeant Whatley and Trooper Jones of the Intelligence Section were the first to set off to make contact. Mounted on two motorcycles they had travelled only a few miles when Whatley had a puncture. He took Trooper Jones's machine, leaving him to mend the puncture and went on, avoiding some German tanks, to find some wounded paras in hiding near the village of Depienne. Whatley was able to return to his RHQ and report the positions of those paras; he was later awarded the MM. Trooper Jones, however, was captured by a group of Italian infantry accompanying some German tanks.

C Squadron was given a fighting rôle, to "hunt and destroy enemy in Ksar Tyr" while B Squadron were to "fetch and carry personnel" from the paras. At 11.40 that morning the men of C Squadron made contact with the enemy: there was fierce fighting with heavy enemy armour threatening to prevent the recce men from achieving their objective. West of Medjez el Bab about 150 paras were found and B Squadron managed to extricate 37 of them:

> ...suddenly three armoured cars appeared on the road leading East from Depienne. To our great relief they were friendly and belonged to 56th Recce Regiment. I had not been told to expect any of our own forces in the area so soon and therefore this meeting was very encouraging, even more so because the Troop Commander was most optimistic and trundled on down the road in the direction we would take later on.[4]

The following day, 5 December, C Squadron went out on a joint operation with a US Army recce company. That afternoon there was further fighting with the Germans: another 18 Paras were collected, those located by Sergeant Whatley being among those rescued.

Junkers Ju88s divebombed the regiment two days later and destroyed a number of vehicles, including four LRCs. There was a further air attack, by a Messerschmitt fighter, next day on a troop of C Squadron near Pont du

Fahs. During that day both squadrons were keeping the enemy under observation in no man's land. In the early afternoon of the 9th two Messerschmitts shot up a troop of C Squadron and a patrol of Derbyshire Yeomanry. A troop of B Squadron, going to assist the C Squadron troop, also came under attack and lost three LRCs and three carriers: personnel casualties were limited to slight injuries. Small wonder that one stretch of road earned the nickname 'Messerschmitt Alley.'

Soon after this 56 Recce was withdrawn to Aine Sellam. The move began on the afternoon of 10 December, a day on which Medjez el Bab was under threat from the Germans. Shortly after midnight the regiment arrived in its new area where it had a chance to re-organise and overhaul its vehicles. It was also appraised of its new task, to patrol from Oued Zarga to Medjez el Bab. Patrols were mounted and news received that A Squadron had arrived and would soon be joining the main body of the regiment. Most patrols resulted in 'nil' reports as no enemy troops were sighted.

In this period of comparative calm, a conference was held to consider the lessons of the first weeks of operations. While these would obviously affect the way in which squadrons operated in the future the lessons would also be relayed to the Corps' training element in England so that other regiments could have the benefit of 56's hard-won experience. Among recommendations which Colonel Chavasse sent back to England were the need for a heavier recce car; better, i.e. heavier, armament for that car; and a larger-calibre anti-tank gun to replace the 2-pounder, which was of limited use against most German armour. This same conference also decided that assault troop soldiers should be used for night-time tasks such as observation posts, holding bridges and laying ambushes.

The initial Allied advance to Tunis had come to a standstill on 10 December due to stiffening German opposition and limited counter-attacks as well as ground made heavy by rain. Already the Germans had scored a victory against a joint British-American armoured force at the Chouigoi Pass on 1 December but, on the evening of the 10th, they had an unexpected bonus when panicking soldiers of Combat Command B, 1st US Armoured Division abandoned 18 tanks, 41 guns and 133 other vehicles after bogging down as they tried to retreat along an unreconnoitred track. The Americans had not been the only panickers: General Walter Nehring, commanding XC Corps, had panicked at the thought of Allied troops less than 20 miles from Tunis and in Kesselring's words "drew the blackest of conclusions." Kesselring removed Nehring from his command.

First Army was preparing to renew the offensive with an advance on Tunis in which 56 Recce was to play its part in the spearhead but, at 3 o'clock on the afternoon of 23 December, the operation was cancelled. It had begun to rain heavily and movement became impossible for heavy armour while no air support could be given. Cancellation of the attack meant that the regiment could celebrate Christmas at Aine Sellam: Colonel Chavasse visited each squadron and the divisional padre held a service at RHQ on Christmas morning. The regiment had lost its own padre on 20 November when he was killed by a mine.

Next morning the CO and the IO went to 78th Division's HQ to learn that the regiment was to move to a fresh location at Oued Zarga. By that night the regiment was harboured at its new operational base; some of the equipment losses of recent weeks had been made good with the arrival of twelve replacement LRCs and three carriers, while No 19 wireless sets had been supplied to replace the No 11 sets: the old sets were stripped out of the vehicles and replaced in an overnight operation by the vehicle crews. Those new sets were soon to prove their worth. New faces had also arrived to replace those who had been killed, wounded or taken prisoner since the beginning of the campaign.

On the morning of 27 December Colonel Chavasse and the IO met with officers of 1 Guards and 11 Infantry Brigades to make plans for the regiment's new rôle. That afternoon details were passed on to squadron leaders: B Squadron was to be in support, but would also maintain a wireless set with a company of 1st East Surreys on roads leading from Oued to Oued Zarga; a No 19 set was to be located at the headquarters of 3rd Grenadiers "for liaison and information"; the squadron assault troop was to guard Oued Zarga bridge and one squadron was to be held in reserve.

Patrolling under the new arrangements began almost immediately. The following day A Squadron was ordered to patrol to Naceur and from there to contact a French colonial regiment at Toukabeur. That evening C Squadron went out to patrol the Oued Zarga-Medjez el Bab sector during the night. Supporting the French colonials - an Algerian rifle regiment - A Squadron attacked a supposed enemy strongpoint west of Toukabeur early on the morning of the 30th. There was, however, no opposition. Later that morning the squadron returned to Oued Zarga, leaving an assault troop and mortar detachment under Captain Goode to continue supporting the French.

The year ended with a B Squadron action witnessed by a patrol from A Squadron's assault troop. The latter had taken up OP positions overlooking the Dr Bed valley when they saw B Squadron's patrol being fired on by four 105mm guns. As the patrol withdrew they were followed by three light armoured cars and two motorcycles. Mortars and machine-guns also opened up on the B Squadron men but there were no casualties although one carrier and two motorcycles were written off. The German positions were pinpointed for attention by First Army's gunners.

The first morning of 1943 saw the CO on a recce to Sidi Nsir while B Squadron was laying an ambush in the Dr Bed valley and A Squadron was maintaining its OPs of the previous day. The ambush attempt came to naught as efforts to lure the Germans into it failed. Both A and B Squadrons reported enemy activity in the forms of light signals and vehicles in the mouth of the Dr Bed valley. On 2 January Colonel Chavasse held a squadron leaders' conference at RHQ and explained the three new tasks assigned to the regiment. These were: support of the French garrison at Toukabeur; guarding Oued Zarga bridge; and being prepared to support 2nd Lanacashire Fusiliers at Sidi Nsir. If, however, an enemy attack were to be made on the divisional positions 56 Recce was to have four tasks and would operate from the Monchar area. These were: supporting 2nd Lancashires at Sidi Nsir; supporting forces in the Hunt's Gap area; supporting 5th Northamptons in the Djebel Monchar area; and patrolling the line of the railway south-westwards from Oued Zarga. All likely areas of operations were to be recce'd by squadron leaders and would be allocated after Colonel Chavasse had made his own recce which he did next day, in spite of deteriorating weather.

January was a most difficult month with almost unbelievable weather conditions. Mud, such as few had seen before, sucked at wheels, bogged down two-wheel drive vehicles and threatened to pull boots off. Tracks became slippery messes and keeping dry was almost impossible. But still the war continued with recce patrolling tasks throughout the month. Typical of these were a number of foot patrols carried out by C Squadron around Oued Zarga on the 4th: these patrols reported enemy positions around the village of Heidous and the presence of armoured vehicles, including tanks, infantry and artillery in the Dr Bed valley. A patrol by A Squadron came under fire from mortars at Anserine on the 5th; three days later it was established that Anserine was a base from which the Germans were moving down the Dr Bed valley and establishing positions in farms along the way.

C Squadron was placed under command of the Parachute Brigade on 7 January and operated along the road to Djebel Abiod. German activity in the Dr Bed valley was increasing and, on 12 January, medium and field guns arrived at RHQ for a combined operation against enemy troops in the valley. US artillery officers arrived two days later. Plans were made for an attack on 18 January involving two troops of A Squadron acting as 'live bait' while a regimental OP on Point 667 reported enemy reaction; US artillery 'Long Toms' were to engage the Germans while a French colonial battalion supported by a 56 Recce assault troop and a platoon of Fusiliers made a dawn attack on the Farm du Bed. The operation was a complete success: the farm was cleared while Anserine was still smoking at noon on the 19th from its pounding by the gunners. There was, however, concern that a major German attack was about to be launched with tanks attacking down the Dr Bed valley and paratroopers and gliderborne forces landing behind the Allied lines. Although such an attack never materialised squadron area guards were strengthened as a precaution.

On 21 January the regiment was moved behind the divisional defensive lines with A and B Squadrons attached to 11 Brigade and C Squadron, back from the paras, attached to 36 Brigade, and RHQ at Beja. The regiment had had some cause for celebration with the news, on 12 January, that Colonel Chavasse had been awarded the DSO for his outstanding leadership in the early days of the campaign when his men had been outnumbered and outgunned. Two sergeants, Finn and Mayne, were also awarded the Distinguished Conduct Medal. All three attended a presentation by the GOC, First Army on the 15th and the officers of 56 Recce held a celebratory mess night on the same date. The citation for Kendal Chavasse's decoration noted that:

> Between 25th November and 10th December Lt.Col. Chavasse was in command of his Regt. covering right flank, 78th Div., east of Oued Med Jerga. During this period he successfully prevented German armoured cars and Tank patrols from interfering with our operation. Largely by his personal example, dash and daring, his unit of two weak squadrons, in spite of being outgunned, out armoured and frequently dive-bombed, dominated the area, and throughout the period he obtained valuable information of enemy movement. This officer showed outstanding qualities of leadership. [5]

Patrolling continued with many incidents occurring; squadrons provided much valuable information on artillery and mortar positions and carried out several defensive tasks, including guards against possible airborne attacks. First Army's strength was being built up all the while and, on 30 January, 56 Recce ceased to be the sole reconnaissance regiment in Tunisia with the arrival of 46 Recce as part of 46th Division. This division was to take over 78th Division's operational area which meant yet another change for the recce men. Before the move, however, A Squadron, operating with soldiers of the US 18th Regimental Combat Team, had a skirmish with a German patrol near Goubellat. The squadron lost four men killed and a carrier blown up by a mine but 18 Germans, including an officer, from I/69 PanzerGrenadier Regiment, were captured.

When Colonel Chavasse and his signals officer went to recce their new operational area on 1 February they discovered that plans for their deployment had already been changed. Following a visit by Colonel Chavasse to 1 Guards Brigade the new deployment was put into effect: the Medjez el Bab west sector was handed over by the Guards and 56 Recce moved in. Also in the area were the French colonial 3rd RTA, a company of 2nd Lancashires at Toukabeur, two French regiments at Medjez and 8th Argylls plus a half squadron of 16th/5th Lancers. The commanding formation was 6th Armoured Division.

Once again the patrolling routine was established and determined the pattern of activity for much of February although, towards the middle of the month, A Squadron was sent to the southern part of the Allied line to augment forces in the Thala area. On 14 February the Germans had launched a major attack against the Allies with its main thrust against the American II Corps spread between passes at Gafsa, Faid and Fondouk. The Germans had identified the American troops as a weak link in the Allied line due to their inexperience and Faid fell to 21st Panzer Division. Tactics which had worked successfully against British armour in North Africa before were then brought into play and the armour of II US Corps was enticed into battle, at Sidi bou Zid, against German tanks. The German armour then feinted a withdrawal and, scenting success, the American tankmen pursued the panzers and drove into concealed anti-tank guns, the redoubtable 88mm guns which had been proved so successful against tanks by Rommel in Europe and in Africa. The Americans lost more than 100 tanks and 10th Panzer Division joined 21st to chase the survivors back to Thala.

At Gafsa a detachment of Rommel's Panzerarmee Afrika, drawn from 15th Panzer Division and the Italian Centauro Division, defeated French and American troops and Rommel prepared for a follow-up operation. However disagreement between von Arnim and Rommel, and the absence of their supreme commander, Kesselring, in Berlin, led to the scale of Axis operations being reduced. Even so, the net result was the Battle of Kasserine Pass on 19 February, one of the most humiliating setbacks of the war for the US Army. Against this background, and with the need to stabilise the situation in Tunisia, A Squadron rushed southwards.

With orders from General Alexander to hold the line at all costs, two troops from A Squadron were quickly pushed forward to try to gain a clear picture of events. They were soon joined by a third troop and all three were operating against the stream of American soldiers falling back in confusion and disarray. At least one A Squadron LRC was fitted with a heavy-calibre aircraft cannon retrieved from a crashed Spitfire near Medjez. The weapon was between six and eight feet long and proved extremely effective: its adaptation was carried out by a sergeant who looked "like Desperate Dan" and was able to fire the Boyes anti-tank rifle from the hip.

The reconnoitrers watched a German armoured attack in progress as panzers overran a recently-arrived battalion of Leicesters before being engaged by 25-pounders. The British guns hit a fuel dump behind the panzers which exploded, burst into flames and silhouetted the enemy tanks, thus giving the gunners excellent targets. Eighteen German tanks were knocked out before the enemy withdrew. Despite this victory the situation was still desperate: 17th/21st Lancers and the Lothian and Border Horse could muster only ten tanks which was no match for the German armour. Next morning all ten tanks moved forward into a desperate battle in which seven were knocked out. But what had looked like a suicidal effort on the British side must have appeared to the Germans as the first wave of a much stronger attack and had the effect of causing a German withdrawal, hastened by the arrival of further Allied artillery to join in the bombardment of enemy positions.

A Squadron were ordered to maintain contact. After a 20 mile pursuit they had not met any German troops when one of the two leading LRCs hit a mine and, further down the road, the other came across more mines whereupon the assault troop took to mineclearing and lifted about 100. As sappers came up to clear the minefield, a scout troop moved off across country and quickly came on the enemy. The troop was engaged and all three troops were soon in action which continued until a Guards battalion motored forward to take on the German attack.

As A Squadron disengaged a despatch rider arrived from RHQ with orders to return immediately to Medjez where the regiment, and 46 Recce, was heavily engaged. This battle had begun in the early hours of 26 February when sounds of machine-gun and mortar fire had been heard from positions held by 3rd RTR and the Northamptons. By 6.15am, a German attack was coming in on 11 Brigade's front; ninety minutes later three enemy tanks attacked through what had been B Squadron's harbour area towards Tally-Ho Corner. At Green Belt, 6 Commando was heavily engaged while B Squadron and RHQ were evacuated to Testour under fire. At 8.15 the German thrust turned south towards El Aroussa.

Defensive plans were soon in operation. Colonel Chavasse took command of a composite force at Testour including RHQ and B Squadron, signallers acting as infantry, a light AA battery, a 25-pounder battery and 265 Field Company, RE. C Squadron remained under command of 11 Brigade in a counter-attack rôle. Before noon General Evelegh, the divisional commander, arrived at RHQ and planning for a counter-attack, using tanks, was begun. Concentrated artillery fire was brought down on enemy positions at Tally-Ho Corner and Mayfair Hotel and continued throughout the day. By 7 o'clock that evening the situation around Testour appeared stable but elsewhere matters were still obscure. A B Squadron patrol moved out towards Tally-Ho Corner and encountered a small German patrol. For 6 Commando the situation was still very dangerous: reduced to 250 men the unit was responsible for an area of 75 square miles which it could only hold through a series of strongpoints. One of these came under heavy attack and a desperate battle ensued. The commando had, however, built up close liaison with 56 Recce and Colonel Chavasse sent some of his men to help the beleaguered commandos. The German attack was repulsed and the commanding officer of 6 Commando, Lieutenant-Colonel Mills-Roberts, MC, an Irish Guards officer, was most appreciative of the assistance given by Kendal Chavasse. A tangible token of that appreciation came some time later when Lord Louis Mountbatten, head of Combined Operations, wrote to Kendal Chavasse:

> Dear Colonel,
>
> I have learned with the greatest pleasure from the Officer Commanding No. 6 Commando of the immediate and decisive support which you gave to him during his action with the Hermann Goering Jaeger Battalion.
>
> He tells me that when he was engaged against a very much heavier force, he appealed to you for reinforcements and that your prompt response to this appeal ensured the success of the action and the survival of the unit.
>
> Please accept my warmest thanks, and at the same time my congratulations on the splendid performance of your own Regiment.[6]

That had not been the first instance of co-operation between the two commanding officers for, on 24 February, Chavasse had commanded a seven-hour patrol by a carrier section, and Colonel Mills-Roberts had acted as the bren-gunner on Kendal Chavasse's carrier.

The counter-attack began at 6.30am on 27 February with C Squadron advancing from the north-east with a half-troop of tanks from 17th/21st Lancers. B Squadron was covering operations from high ground overlooking Tally-Ho Corner in the west. Enemy aircraft were active all day and at 2.30pm there was a heavy Stuka attack: although such air attacks held up the operation C Squadron took their objective, a ridge, by 5.30pm. They later withdrew for the night but by then the news had been received that Y Division, an ad-hoc formation under Brigadier Nelson Russell of the Irish Brigade, was pushing the Germans back from El Aroussa. By that time too A Squadron was on its way back from Thala although, at 9.00pm, it was placed under command of 138 Brigade in whose area a new attack appeared to be developing.

Operations recommenced at 6.30 next morning with B Squadron ordered to push on to El Aroussa while C was held in reserve. Before noon A Squadron was in action and lost two LRCs with six soldiers taken prisoner. Shortly after noon C Squadron and RHQ also came under 138 Brigade and moved to the White House area to counter the threat of an enemy thrust down the Dr Bed valley towards Toukabeur. Although enemy activity was reported in the south of the valley and on the approaches to Toukabeur the latter appeared to be in no immediate danger. That evening C Squadron was ordered to hold the ridge north of the Medjez el Bab-El Aroussa road during the night: that ridge was soon dubbed 'Recce Ridge.' A Squadron was to join C at first light and take up position on the latter's left flank.

At 7.30 next morning a force of up to 200 Germans attacked Recce Ridge but were beaten off. Later that morning 10th Rifle Brigade took over the ridge although a troop of C Squadron remained in position there. A Squadron was having a busy day: a patrol to Toukabeur found the Germans had finally taken the position and four vehicles were lost. A Squadron then sent out a night patrol while other elements of the squadron patrolled the left flank of Recce Ridge. B Squadron had been in action at Tally-Ho Corner where they had captured ten prisoners, two tanks and a pair of 88mm guns. By 8.00pm on 1 March, the Tally-Ho Corner-El Aroussa road was clear of enemy and B Squadron had linked up with Y Division.

The major German assault, codenamed Operation Ochsenkopf, had been turned. That attack was probably the high-water mark of German operations in Tunisia and it was time for First Army to go over to the offensive. Some German activity continued in the Dr Bed valley area and around Toukabeur in early-March and 56 Recce's squadrons were busily engaged on observing and reporting such activity. Patrolling, by day and night, remained at a high level throughout the month and was co-ordinated with 46 Recce. OPs were established and a general state of alertness maintained in case of further enemy offensive action. Fighting patrols were also sent out: one from C Squadron on the night of 13 March penetrated enemy positions on Djebel el Ouatiah and brought back a prisoner from 9 Company, 3rd Battalion/756 Mountain Regiment. The patrol suffered no casualties and on its return artillery fire was put down on the German positions it had just visited. Further very wet weather in the middle of the month hampered observation.

On 20 March, 36 Brigade handed over to 24 Guards Brigade of the newly-arrived 1st Division whose arrival also brought another recce regiment into the theatre. By the end of the month 78th Division had handed over its operational area to 1st Division and 1st Reconnaissance Regiment, under Colonel Rea, had relieved 56th Regiment which moved to Ali Bou Abdullah to rest and for maintenance.

Chavasse's Light Horse had led the way for recce regiments in Tunisia. The arrival of 46th and 1st Regiments was a signal that Allied strength in the region was building up. Soon another two recce regiments, 4th and 44th, would arrive for the final phase of operations. As a Royal Irish Fusilier, Colonel Chavasse had had his parent regiment's Gaelic motto, Faugh A Ballagh!, painted across the front of his personal LRC. In English that motto means Clear The Way! and dates from the Battle of Barossa on 5 March 1811 when Sergeant Masterson of the 2nd/87th (Prince of Wales's Irish) Regiment had captured the first French eagle ever taken in battle: as the Irish soldiers charged they had called out Faugh A Ballagh and the regiment gained both its motto and a soubriquet, The Faughs. That motto was most appropriate for 56 Recce for it had cleared the way most effectively in Tunisia.

5
Tunisia - the struggle continues

In early-January 1943 46th Reconnaissance Regiment embarked at Greenock and Liverpool for the voyage to Algeria. Most of the regiment sailed on the *Duchess of Bedford* which was damaged before it left harbour and travelled alone at top speed; the passengers believed that the captain had wanted to do this all along. The result was a rough voyage in heavy seas as the "Drunken Duchess" made her way to Algiers where "the Luftwaffe provided us with a warm reception."[1] RHQ travelled on board HMT *Batory*, on which it provided an anti-aircraft defence party, disembarking at Algiers on 17 January. The whereabouts of the remainder of the regiment was unknown but, as it was understood that C Squadron, with 139 Brigade, had gone forward to the Bone area, RHQ was ordered to move to Bone by sea arriving there on the 21st.

On 30 January Lieutenant Colonel F.H.Cotton, MBE, the CO, with A Squadron's commander and the IO went forward to positions held by C Squadron and visited 56 Recce at the front which 46 was to relieve; by 11 February all three squadrons were at the front and patrolling actively. Their first casualty occurred four days later when Sergeant Hewitt suffered a shrapnel wound in the neck when A Squadron at Munchar was bombed by nine Messerschmitt Bf109s.

On 26 February came the German attack as part of Operation Ochsenkopf, during which the regiment received its battle inoculation. A Squadron deployed to Hunt's Gap with 128 Brigade to protect tanks. B Squadron was described as having the "liveliest" time that day and suffered two fatal casualties with Lieutenant A.L.Brace and Trooper Williams killed in action.

On 1 March A Squadron was still at Hunt's Gap, probing forward and observing enemy positions. The squadron had also mined the Mateur-Beja road after 5th Hampshires had withdrawn along it and the assault troop was still providing protection for tanks. During the night the squadron withdrew to Beja but the assault troop remained to defend the tanks; that night Lieutenant Hill and an assault troop party blew up an abandoned Mk IV tank with gun-cotton slabs. B Squadron was observing the enemy, two battalions of whom had turned off from the main line of the German advance through Hunt's Gap. Subjected to mortaring and machine-gun fire the squadron could not reply since it was outranged by the opposition's weapons. During the night, however, B Squadron brought in two prisoners from II/755 Grenadier Regiment who had given themselves up. C Squadron remained on standby but was not engaged.

'Lively' was the description applied to B Squadron's day on 2 March during which they observed much enemy movement, including infantry, wheeled and horsed transport, and artillery, between Dr Bed valley and the Mateur-Beja road. This task was being shared with a 56 Recce squadron. There were also unfounded rumours of glider landings at Oued Zarga. The squadron took offensive action against a German-held farm in which Major Millen was badly wounded while Trooper Poole was killed; Sergeant Gent and his LRC crew were wounded while Sergeant Thompson and his carrier crew, with the exception of Trooper Ketley, were posted 'missing' but presumed killed. Although A Squadron had had a quieter day they had also had a fatality with Sergeant Brooks killed in a strafing attack by a German aircraft; three assault troop men were injured on a British mine.

There followed a quieter day although B Squadron's sector was still liveliest with shelling, mortar fire and continued rumours of glider landings. Liaison continued with 56 Recce on observing enemy movement in Dr Bed valley; A Squadron was providing communications with the combined remnants of 2nd/4th and 5th Hampshires who were cut off and unable to use normal communications. Two subalterns, Badger and McLay, led patrols northwards with McLay's men going to a point level with, but north of, Sidi Nsir. The following day contact was lost with this patrol and it was presumed lost.

B Squadron and 56 Recce were still co-operating on the flank. During the morning of 5 March a German force at about company strength attacked and drove in one of the OPs before withdrawing. It was believed that this attack was intended to divert attention from the farm where Major Millen had been wounded and which had been shelled by British guns the night before. A Squadron's assault troop was also under attack: in fact, it had been mortared continuously for 36 hours and several men had been wounded. The troop was not finally withdrawn from its position until nightfall on 7 March. The remainder of the squadron was in reserve on the morning of the 5th but that afternoon it was called forward by 128 Brigade to meet a threat from two enemy companies to the north-east; no action ensued and the squadron dispersed in scattered locations for the night. But there was to be no rest for A Squadron as divisional headquarters then assigned it the task of keeping open the road from midway between Beja and Chemical Corner and Khanguet Mine during the night. On 6 March, B Squadron co-ordinated a recce in force by 3rd Grenadier Guards through the valley. A and B Squadrons, which had both been with 128 Brigade, reverted to regimental command but continued to support the brigade. Fighting rumbled on with 10 Troop, C Squadron coming under systematic shelling at Djebel Abiod on the night of the 7th while next day a carrier of B Squadron was destroyed on a mine. Killed in the explosion were Lieutenant G.F.Todd, a "very promising young officer" and Trooper

A.King, an original member of 1st Royal Fusiliers' carrier platoon, who was outstanding at driving and maintenance and was generally regarded as *the* carrier driver of the regiment.

Peace reigned on 9 March and B Squadron returned from Oued Zarga while C Squadron's assault troop left to operate under 1 Commando. Patrolling was the order of the day for the 10th although an OP of A Squadron observed and assisted a shoot by 172nd Field Regiment on a farm in the Zouave Bend area. Two troopers from C Squadron's assault troop returned to base but the remainder of the troop, Lieutenant S.A.E.Burdest and 20 men, were missing. They were still missing two days later when C Squadron recorded slight patrol clashes with no casualties. That same day Corporal Brighton of A Squadron led a patrol of 5th Hampshires to take over an OP at Chemical Corner, but it had been occupied by the enemy who machine-gunned the patrol. The Hants captain commanding the patrol was wounded - he was stripped by Arabs and died from his wounds - while Corporal Brighton was posted as missing. A nearby Arab village was burned to the ground by 5th Hampshires as a reprisal for their officer.

Relative calm returned for a few days but the regiment's CO had been pressing for specific offensive action to dominate the area. This was called for since the regiment had noted that:

> ...the enemy's policy has been gradual encroachment on to all dominating features, however insignificant, so that suddenly one wakes up to find him sitting on a feature dominating some vital position or line of communication lying below... Accordingly we have long been pressing to be allowed to occupy certain dominating points (or for infantry to be detailed to do so where we were not in sufficient strength to do so), and to evacuate Arabs from certain areas.[2]

Arabs had been passing on information to the Germans in the area thus allowing the Germans to take the tactical advantage on a number of occasions:

> We suspected the fellahin played both sides to their advantage, for they held no esteem for the infidels. Quite often we were mortared in concealed positions far from the enemy's prying eyes but not the Bedouin... We dropped the services of all Arabs...[3]

For 46 Recce the main worry, at this stage, was that C Squadron's location at Khanguet Mine had been dominated by the Germans for several days with the threat of the squadron being cut off completely. That would also allow the Germans to dominate the Djebel Abiod-Beja road which passes through a deep, narrow gorge at this point. As a result of the regiment's representations an ad-hoc company of Durham Light Infantry came under command of C Squadron on the 12th; a further DLI company followed two days later. On the 15th these companies occupied Point 520 and then took over the Mine de Si Ahmed, thus denying the Germans good OPs from which to dominate the area, and reducing the danger of C Squadron being cut off.

At Point 226 an OP group from B Squadron saw one of their carriers being driven off "in mysterious circumstances" before blowing up on a nearby bridge. The incident was investigated the next evening by Lieutenant Pierce who braved machine-gun fire to discover that the wrecked carrier contained the body of its driver, Trooper Wheatley, and a dead German. It appeared that the German had been making off with the carrier and that Wheatley was trying to stop him when both were killed as the carrier was blown up.

Several days of patrolling with some mortaring and machine-gunning, followed as well as convoy escort duties. One troop, together with A Squadron's assault troop, assisted 5th Hampshires in clearing a farm of Germans who were believed to be laying mines on the Djebel Abiod road. No Germans were found in the farm but four were seen in the distance while, the previous night, a road patrol from 9 Troop of C Squadron had discovered a new type of mine laid on a bridge. A large beehive-shaped device surrounded by a ring of Teller-mines, it had been removed by REs, who were a standard part of such patrols. Had the mine been detonated it would have destroyed the vehicle that had set it off and probably the bridge as well. It had been discovered because the night road patrols had adopted a formation designed to search for mines: patrols were led by an armoured car using a searchlight, followed by a recce car and an assault troop truck with two RE sappers. The beehive mine would certainly not have been detected by any vehicle other than a searchlight-equipped armoured car.

Captain F.H.Pratt of B Squadron captured two Germans from III/755th Regiment at Y Farm on the 26th and brought in a Swiss civilian who had been with the Germans. In the closing days of the month, squadrons operated with units of 5th Hampshires and a tank squadron in an offensive against the enemy. Early success saw German troops forced to reinforce the Djebel el Beida feature but heavy rain later made it impossible for vehicles to operate; A Squadron returned to Beja for maintenance on the 29th and contact was lost with C Squadron who were under command of the Para Brigade. Next day C Squadron passed to 36 Brigade of 78th Division and, with better conditions in their sector, had a very busy day working in a true recce rôle.

C Squadron had been ordered to recce to Sedjenane for a force of British and French colonial troops; with sappers clearing mines in front of them they moved to within sight of their objective but were prevented from reaching it by a blown bridge just west of Sedjenane. Mines had forced the squadron to advance by road. Bombed and machine-gunned from the air several times on their advance they lost five LRCs, two carriers and a

15-cwt truck, some of which were later recovered. There were a number of casualties. In the early hours of the 31st the assault troop was sent to Sedjenane and the Germans were caught on the hop for the troop took several prisoners and killed many other Germans. C Squadron's commander, Major Preen, his SSM and several others also surrounded and captured a group of 16 Germans, among them a soldier from Witzig's para engineers. The Germans were forced back up the valley to their former positions on Bald and Green Hills and the month ended on a high note for the regiment.

Active patrolling continued in the Sedjenane sector which was reported "fairly quiet" by 6 April. A week later 46 Recce moved to El Aroussa and B Squadron came under command of 9th (US) Division for five days to carry out patrols contacting American standing patrols before returning to 46 Recce on 18 April.

Early April had been busy for the men of 56 Recce. Although B Squadron left the regiment's sector on the 3rd to take over from B Squadron, 46 Recce at Munchar, the remainder of the regiment was preparing for a divisional attack for which, on the afternoon of 5 April, C Squadron moved to Sloughia under 11 Brigade. Operation SWEEP began at 4.00am on the 7th and success had been achieved by 6.45pm with Djebel el Nahel, Djebel el Mahdi and Mergued Chaouch in the hands of 78th Division. Although two troops of A Squadron had tried to move through the Dr Bed valley progress had been impeded by mines on one road and by the damage done to the surface of the only other track by Churchill tanks. C Squadron had had a most successful day with 11 Brigade, taking about a hundred prisoners.

At 6 o'clock on the morning of 8 April, 11 Brigade attacked Point 512 and by 8.08am that feature was firmly in the brigade's possession. Shortly before this two scout troops and an assault troop of A Squadron with a troop of self-propelled 25-pounders had started out for the Dr Bed valley and had crossed Oued Bouneb by 8.45am to make contact with the enemy two miles to the north. Twelve prisoners were taken but less than an hour later Squadron HQ came under shellfire from the north from which direction there were also sounds of machine-gun fire. It was impossible to move forward along the mined track and mineclearing was out of the question due to the enemy fire. The assault troop soldiers under Lieutenant Tony Michelle were pinned down by the Germans and the squadron leader, Major Darsie Murray, went forward on foot to see what was happening. Major Murray was returning to his vehicle when he was killed by a burst of machine-gun fire as were three of his men; six others were wounded. The patrols were pinned down by machine-gun and mortar-fire until 2.35pm when 5th Buffs advanced through them towards Point 667. The Buffs were also pinned down, and Colonel Chavasse came up to see the situation for himself. A Squadron was withdrawn for a time until the infantry brought the situation under control which allowed the recce men to move forward.

Shortly afterwards, enemy tanks held up progress but by 5 o'clock the tanks, having been shelled, began to move northwards and the squadron was able to push on for another mile and a half. The following day B Squadron had a similar experience, being pinned down in much the same location by heavy shelling from the north; they also suffered strafing from the air. Although unable to make further progress the squadron took eight prisoners; two of the crew of an LRC were killed and their car destroyed. By noon on the 10th, RHQ was established in Dr Bed valley, about a mile north of the crossing at Oued Bouneb, from where it moved to Oued Zarga wood two days later.

Seventy-eighth Division was now preparing for an attack on Djebel Tanngoucha and 56 Recce was placed in divisional mobile reserve. Throughout the operation the regiment provided OPs, flank guards and recce patrols; it also provided soldiers to serve in an infantry rôle. One of 78th Division's objectives was the village of Heidous which Sergeant Bradley of A Squadron recce'd during the evening of 18 April and found to be occupied by about 40 Germans. The regiment was moving from command of one brigade to another and back to division while squadrons were also being deployed under various commands, including that of 1st (US) Division to which B Squadron had been assigned on the 17th. Fierce fighting for Tanngoucha and Longstop continued for several more days with a determined German counter-attack on 11 Brigade's front during the night of the 21st/22nd. RHQ came under air attack late on 23 April, during which the 2ic, Major Hartland-Mahon, was among five casualties.

On the left flank of 78th Division an advance by 1st (US) Division in Dr Bed valley had removed any threat from that direction. With that operation complete A Squadron returned to its own regiment. On 78th Division's front the enemy was still holding on to Tanngoucha, Longstop and Heidous. However, on Easter Sunday, 25 April, 1st Royal Irish Fusiliers took the features dubbed Butler's Hill and Point 622, thus unlocking the approach to Tanngoucha where the Germans quickly surrendered to the Inniskillings while the London Irish took Heidous. With the Irish Brigade having cleared Tanngoucha, 36 Brigade was able to capture Longstop.

Operation VULCAN, the final advance to Tunis was now beginning. On Easter Monday 36 Brigade attacked Djebel el Rhar with A Squadron supporting 5th Buffs; the squadron took 36 prisoners on the Medjez el Bab-Tebourba road. Next day C Squadron came under 11 Brigade's command and when 36 Brigade took over the running they had C Squadron under their wing. Shortly after the regiment went into divisional mobile reserve.

During the latter part of April 46 Recce was also engaged on offensive operations. Briefed on their rôle on the morning of 21 April they were to move into position that evening with both A and C Squadrons providing protective screens for gunner regiments as well as the northern flank of 138 Brigade. The Germans upset this planning somewhat by attacking that afternoon and occupying some of the farms the regiment was to use. As German troops also moved on to some of the high ground the move forward was postponed. C Squadron's task of providing a defensive screen for gunners was cancelled and its rôle of flank protection for 138 Brigade was expanded; it was to carry out this job with B Squadron, Derbyshire Yeomanry.

At 4.45 next morning 9 Troop and SHQ, C Squadron together with SHQ and a troop of Derbyshire Yeomanry pushed forward to Apple Blossom Farm. A patrol of 11 Troop reconnoitring the route to Rag el Hir Traifa came under heavy shellfire on the forward slopes of the feature in mid-morning; the troop commander decided to seek an alternative route through dead ground to the east. At much the same time a patrol from 10 Troop was sent to recce a track junction and farm buildings at Bir Abadelia Si Hanida; both locations were reported clear of Germans. However the Derbyshire Yeomanry had spotted German half-tracks towing anti-tank guns as well as a platoon of German infantry who had entered some farm buildings. Orders were sent to 10 Troop not to go any further forward in case of anti-tank guns and the gunners of 162 Battery dropped forty rounds on the farm to good effect. Similar tasks were carried out throughout the day and B Squadron went into night harbour south of Bou Arada ready to provide flank protection for 128 Brigade on the morrow; the squadron was to recce east along the Bou Arada-Pont du Fahs road.

The advance continued on the 22nd; Lieutenant R.W.Challenor and six men were involved in a small battle along the way while two carriers and a recce car were lost to anti-tank fire during the day. By the end of the day the divisional objectives had been taken and the armour was pushing east and north-east above the Sebkret el Kourzia salt lake.

Recce patrols were carried out on the 23rd, including some for units of 19 (French) Corps. For the following day the regiment had orders from divisional headquarters to recce and clear the Djebel Bessioud feature. At Division it was believed that this hill was lightly held but 46 Recce considered it to be held by at least a battalion. A Squadron was sent to investigate and had a very active day although initial progress was slow due to mines. However, patrols from the squadron, under Lieutenants Badger and Borden, worked round the northern and southern approaches to the djebel. The northern patrol made some progress before coming under fire from mortars and machine-guns: a carrier was hit and a trooper killed. The southern patrol got as far as Hir Chelbi before being machine-gunned and mortared, but Corporal Fellows managed to get his LRC to the top of Djebel Bessioud and was followed by two other LRCs. Although strong enemy opposition forced them to withdraw, the action had enabled a gunner FOO on high ground to the west to plot enemy positions on Bessioud. A Squadron's patrols confirmed that the feature was held by at least a battalion and so divisional headquarters decided a full-scale attack with armour was needed to clear it. At dawn on 25 April this attack was launched and Djebel Bessioud was cleared of German troops.

Not being involved the regiment had a quiet day; B Squadron was manning OPs while the other squadrons were in harbour. RHQ moved to a new location on the edge of the Goubellat Plain next day as the routine of patrols, OPs and listening posts was maintained throughout the regiment's sector. A carrier hit by 37mm anti-tank fire on 22 April was recovered, but another carrier and an LRC which had also been hit had been removed by the Germans. On 28 April A Squadron deployed patrols to contact 4 Recce in the Goubellat area.

During that phase two LRCs of B Squadron carried out a search of farm buildings where an enemy patrol was believed to be concealed:

> There was evidence that the Germans had been in occupancy, they had left empty food containers and hordes of voracious blood-hungry fleas that leaped from the floor on to our legs. We beat a hasty retreat ... Rather than advance to the front of the other houses we decided to approach from the rear when we were completely taken by surprise to see two unarmed German soldiers in crouched constitutional mode attending nature's call. They too were totally shocked to see us [and] did not know whether to raise their hands or pull up their pants... At a much later date I could not help but wonder what tale the prisoner would tell his grandchildren [of] how he was captured during the war in North Africa.[4]

The beginning of May found 46 Recce with new masters: the regiment was under command of 1st Armoured Division with 139 Brigade and was charged with patrolling and manning OPs. This attachment lasted for two days and the regiment was back with 46th Division on 3 May. The fall of Tunis was imminent but the regiment was not involved in the advance on the city. It continued its routine in the Goubellat area and heard, on 7 May, that Tunis and Bizerta were in Allied hands. It was also expected that an A Squadron patrol might meet up with elements of 1st Reconnaissance Regiment who were in Tebourba and reported to be pushing down. That evening the regiment, less B Squadron which was with 78th Division, was ordered to support 128 Brigade the following day.

The brigade was advancing towards Tebourba which it reached by 6.30am on the 8th to find infantry of 1st Division already established there. Recce patrols were sent out from A Squadron to make contact with the

Germans but none was found; contact was made with Americans at Chouigoi. The next few days were quiet and, after moving to a divisional concentration area on 10 May, it was expected that there would be at a least a week for rest and so a maintenance programme was started. At 2.00pm on the 11th the regiment was ordered to move to Ain el Asker; although engines had been stripped it arrived by 8 o'clock that evening where B Squadron returned to the regimental fold.

Fifty-six Recce were also left out of the advance to Tunis. This contradicted what Colonel Chavasse had earlier been told:

> When the final battle for Tunis was being planned I was often told that the General hoped to push us forward when the time came, and be the first troops to enter Tunis and certainly get there before the Derbyshire Yeomanry. When the time came someone from Corps HQ had seen some of our admin vehicles and did not like their appearance. I cannot actually remember what was wrong. 78 Div was informed and I was sent for to see the General. He expressed anger and told me we had forfeited our right to enter Tunis first and we were placed under temporary command of 4th Indian Division and were given a mopping-up task of enemy pockets which had been left behind. However, I was told to provide a Light Recce Car to take Randolph Churchill into Tunis, and one of the wheels came off on the outskirts of the city. We did laugh and no-one got it in the neck except from Randolph.[5]

It was a car from Lieutenant Bill Croucher's troop of C Squadron that embarrassingly lost a wheel with the prime minister's son on board. The first infantry to enter Tunis were from 78th Division and it seems logical that their recce regiment should have led them, especially as that regiment had been so close to Tunis almost six months earlier; the pettiness of a corps staff officer, however, put paid to that.

6
Tunisia - race to victory

The status of senior regiment of the Reconnaissance Corps was claimed by 1 Recce, on account of their designation and date of formation.* Although several sources claim the regiment to have been formed from a Hampshires' battalion, this is inaccurate as the regiment formed from the brigade anti-tank companies of 1st Division except the Guards Brigade who refused to transfer men to the new formation although they did provide the RSM. As a result of the Guards' action, men for A Squadron were transferred in from the Hampshires who were not represented in 1st Division; B Squadron came from 2 Brigade which included Loyals, North Staffs and Gordon Highlanders; C Squadron came from 3 Brigade with contingents from the Duke of Wellington's, Sherwood Foresters and KSLI. On 8 January 1942, the regiment celebrated 'Foundation Day' and, on this first anniversary of its birth, the CO wrote in a Special Order of the Day:

> The First Battalion Reconnaissance Corps was formed on 8th January 1941 and is thus the oldest battalion in the Corps. During the coming year it must be our endeavour to ensure that the 1st Battalion remains the first without question. Let us fit ourselves therefore by hard training and an ever-increasing pride in our battalion to deal effectively with the enemy. Let us alone ensure that by our personal bearing and smart appearance we are a credit to the 1st Battalion.[1]

The first CO of 1 Recce was Lt Colonel E.A.B.Murphy, MC, a Royal Ulster Rifles officer; there are shades of that regiment's Rifles Day in 1 Recce's Foundation Day, although Burke Murphy had relinquished command by that time. In April 1942, 1 Recce adopted the title of Regiment some six weeks ahead of the official change of nomenclature throughout the corps. The regiment was now commanded by Lt Colonel S.C.W.W.Rea who took it to Tunisia in March 1943.

By the end of the month, 1 Recce was at the front preparing to relieve 56 Recce, having carried out some patrols and made contact with 46 Recce. April found the regiment holding static defensive positions although C Squadron had been detached to serve with 19 (French) Corps in a recce rôle to contact US troops in the Pichon Fondour area. Difficulties with

---

* *This claim would be strongly contested by 53 (Welsh) Recce which was formed in Belfast on 1 January 1941: the first entry in their war diary is dated that very day whereas 1 Recce's diary does not begin until a week later.[2]

language were noted, although it was not recorded whether those difficulties were with French or American troops. On 9 April the squadron returned to regimental control and static duties.

On the night of 22/23 April, 1 Recce relieved 2nd Sherwood Foresters in the Portigne Ridge area and a scout troop and an assault troop were assigned to 6th Gordon Highlanders to act as flank protection. During the night B Squadron's positions on Banana Ridge were heavily shelled; the bombardment continued into the next day when the commanding officer was wounded and had to be evacuated. Major E A S Brett, another Ulster Rifles officer, took command.

On the 25th, C Squadron moved on to Banana Ridge to close the gap between B Squadron and 1st Loyals. Shelling continued and seemed worst in the regiment's area; very dry tracks gave rise to dust clouds whenever there was movement and this gave away positions. Two days later the regiment moved to Djebel Bou Aoukad in a flank guard rôle. There was to be no respite there: on the 29th RHQ was divebombed and machine-gunned by eight enemy aircraft.

During the morning, A and C Squadrons' locations were constantly bombarded by enemy mortars and at about 4 o'clock that afternoon a German attack was launched with infantry and ten tanks supported by artillery. The shelling was concentrated on B and C Squadrons' positions at Points 212 and 132 at the Gab Gab Gap, but the regiment's vehicles on the reverse slopes also suffered heavily. Four enemy tanks, including a Tiger, overran C Squadron at the Gap and worked their way on to a ledge behind Point 132 where the anti-tank guns were unable to engage them. The artillery were also impotent as their shells could not clear the crest. Six German tanks then rushed the Gap and came in behind 1 Recce's positions, and those of the Irish Guards, at Points 212 and 214. Although Churchill tanks moved up they were soon in trouble from the Tiger at Point 132 while the Germans had also established an artillery OP overlooking the valley which was directing very effective fire.

B and C Squadrons were forced to retire behind A Squadron and the troop on the Irish Guards' right flank. Captain L.C.Ashford maintained his position "with skill and determination and continued to report enemy movement with coolness."[3] Ashford later withdrew his patrol under cover of darkness on orders from RHQ. At Point 212 Sergeant Salt and some of 13 Troop with Irish Guardsmen drove off three enemy attempts to take the position.

At 4.00am on the 29th, as dawn broke, B and C Squadrons re-organised and again the Gab Gab Gap was held. Demands were made for mines to be laid in the Gap but it was two and a half hours before permission was given to do this. This delay had serious consequences later that day for the Gap was again overrun in spite of the efforts of C Squadron. A counter-attack by tanks with support from A Squadron succeeded in stabilising the situation. The troop at Point 212 fought off more German attacks and during the night the Gap was mined and 17-pounder anti-tank guns, capable of dealing with any German tank, moved into position.

Enemy attacks on Points 212 and 214 continued next day but artillery fire, directed by 1 Recce's OP on Point 187 helped break them up. During the night of 29/30 April Lieutenant R.A.Young tried to bring up supplies to Point 212 but was killed only 70 yards short of the position. Sergeant Salt, who had so gallantly and coolly conducted the defence of Point 212 was also killed. The Irish Guards spoke highly of his leadership and bravery.

Recovery of some damaged regimental vehicles was carried out despite continuing mortaring and shelling; two 6-pounders that had been lost were also retrieved. Shelling and mortaring of A Squadron's positions continued throughout the first day of May; on 2 May recce patrols were out by day seeking information on the enemy's positions. One patrol was especially active and, having located Germans at Points 156 to 166, also identified a tank harbour in an olive grove with twenty Mk IV tanks. Enemy infantry were engaged and 20 Germans killed or wounded; the patrol lost three dead and two wounded. Air support was called for and twelve B25 Mitchell bombers attacked the tank park at 5.30pm scoring direct hits on many of the tanks. Artillery fire, called down by the recce men, also wiped out two mortar positions and OPs. Special mention was made of Sergeant Reeves and Corporal Gumber for their leadership and courage during this six-hour patrol. Throughout the night C Squadron's assault troop continued active patrolling in the area covered by the daylight patrol: they discovered that the Germans did not occupy their positions in strength at night and also came across three tanks engaged in minelaying. When the tanks had departed the patrol remained nearby and lifted the mines at dawn. The commander of 1st Division's armour was highly appreciative of the information that 1 Recce had obtained on enemy dispositions and activity.

At 10.40am on 4 May German infantry, with mortar support, attacked Points 187 and 151 but were driven off with many casualties. This was the last serious German attack in the regiment's area and the following day 1 Recce was patrolling to build up a picture of enemy dispositions and strength in preparation for a British attack. That attack began early on the 6th after a three-hour bombardment by 400 guns. C Squadron provided left-flank protection for 4th Indian Division with B Squadron in support and A in reserve. By 6.45pm all objectives had been taken and the Germans were retreating; B and C Squadrons had taken some 800 prisoners and had overrun the enemy anti-tank positions

The advance continued next day with 1 Recce moving forward with all three squadrons up in spite of difficulties with mines, blown bridges and fords mined at El Bathan. A Squadron was ordered to take the river crossings at Djedeida which was held by the Germans. The bridge at Djedeida had been blown and German rearguards were active but the squadron curtained the enemy and took 70 prisoners. During the night and into the next day B Squadron was in contact with Germans. The regiment continued to advance towards Chaouai and, on the 11th, on orders from 4th Indian Division, moved to Djdaou, patrolling as far as the road near St Marie de Zit farm and denying it to the Germans. On 12 May, after heavy fighting and 10,000 prisoners being taken by the division, the campaign came to an end and 1 Recce concentrated at La Mohammedia under the wing of 1st Division.

Two other reconnaissance regiments had been operating in those closing stages of the Tunisian campaign. These were 4th and 44th Regiments: the latter had already seen service in North Africa, having fought at the final battle of El Alamein. Following 44th Division's disbandment, 44 Recce had been given a series of tasks and had been issued with Marmon-Herrington armoured cars to replace the Humber LRCs which had proved unsuited to desert conditions. At the end of February 1943 the regiment became part of 56th (London) Division at Gaza; the 'Black Cats' were without a reconnaissance regiment as 56 Recce had been transferred to the newly-formed 78th Division. It was rumoured that General Montgomery had declared that he did not want recce regiments with his infantry divisions: whatever the truth of that story the fact remains that no proper rôle had been found for such regiments in the desert where recce was assigned to armoured car regiments of the RAC and it therefore seemed logical that 56th Division should move to the Middle East sans reconnaissance regiment. In mid-March the London Division concentrated in the Nile delta to refit before joining Eighth Army in Tunisia.

After the long haul through Egypt and Libya, 44 Recce arrived at Enfidaville on 24 April, days after the town had fallen to Eighth Army. With the campaign almost over the regiment saw little service compared to 56th or 46th Regiments but what it did see was sharp enough. Its intended rôle was to have light recce forces probing forward to observe and report, with the main force some distance behind, but while there was some of this activity, the regiment spent much time sitting on the receiving end of German artillery which was, as ever, very effective.

Patrols from 44 Recce were quite successful and in their short involvement in Tunisia the regiment captured some thirty Germans. A Squadron, operating on the coast, had a number of engagements with enemy troops and repulsed German attacks so effectively that the enemy afterwards admitted thinking that a brigade opposed them on the coastal sector.

From Enfidaville, 44 Recce made the first contact with soldiers of First

Army coming down from the north. The regiment's short spell of fighting ended on 13 May when all hostilities ceased in Tunisia. In June 44 Recce moved to Tripoli in Libya to prepare for its next operational task which would take it to Italy.

The other recce regiment to serve in Tunisia was 4 Recce, formed in January 1941. Under Lt Colonel P.G.C.Preston, of the Lincolns, the regiment had embarked on the *Nea Hellas* at the King George V Dock in Glasgow to sail for Tunisia. The çonvoy left Britain on 16 March 1943 and, at sea, the regiment learned of its destination - part of the convoy was bound for India, the remainder for Algeria. On 23 March the convoy was attacked by German aircraft and the *Windsor Castle*, alongside *Nea Hellas*, was hit by two torpedoes. The scarred convoy arrived in Algiers shortly afterwards and at the beginning of April the regiment moved into Tunisia, travelling 400 miles in three days:

> It was a strange way to motor to battle. The route was lined at frequent intervals by Arabs selling eggs, dates, rings and even watches, while Arab children everywhere begged for Army biscuits and chewing-gum and cigarettes; the Americans had been that way before us.[4]

Several days were spent encamped in the Medjerda river valley waiting for the rest of the vehicles to arrive during which period an advance party went to Beja to recce areas for squadron harbours. The regiment arrived at Beja at 2.45am on the 11th, a little over two hours before zero hour for an attack by 10 Brigade towards Sidi Nsir; as this was mountain fighting the regiment was not required but by 5 o'clock that evening 4 Recce had been deployed to protect the left flank of the advance. Four hours later the regiment had linked northwards with 46 Recce, patrolling the area from Chemical Corner to Zouave Bend; an assault troop was deployed at Zouave Bend and LRC patrols were active. C Squadron had its assault troop defending south of Chemical Corner and its anti-tank guns at the Corner.

Next day was one of patrolling, during which the regiment came under air attack and had its first battle casualty when a mortar-carrier hit a mine near Zouave Bend and the driver was killed. A carrier OP from A Squadron was sent to cover the left flank of 1st/6th Surreys north of Djebel Bendrar the following day while a B Squadron patrol was detailed to check tracks for mines. On 14 April the regiment took its first prisoner: Josef Friegerlus, an Austrian soldier of 5 Company II/755 Grenadier Regiment in 334 Infantry Division. "Complete with waterbottle and blankets" he proved "most talkative and delighted to be out of the war."[5] At 7.30pm contact was made with US patrols to the north; the area between was clear. That afternoon a 10 Brigade attack had been abandoned due to heavy mortar and machine-gun fire and the brigade took up defensive positions across the Sidi Nsir-Beja road. From those positions patrols of 4 Recce moved out next day to try to make contact with the enemy; most found no Germans but a patrol from B Squadron was mortared. Further patrols by day and night on the 16th reported nothing seen. At noon that day the regiment was warned of an impending divisional move to the Medjez el Bab area with the Beja area being handed over to 1st (US) Division.

That move was to take place on the night of the 19th and on 17 April a recce party went to Sloughia to check the new concentration area. Patrolling continued in the Beja area with B Squadron working in the area between 10 and 12 Brigades, especially in two map squares codenamed 'Frankie' and 'Johnnie'; two troops deployed on these patrols. 'Johnnie' was reported clear that afternoon but there were reports of shots north of 'Frankie' although that area was eventually reported clear as well. Patrols from A and C Squadrons had had nothing to report.

American troops began to take over the Beja area on the evening of 18 April, a day on which a foot patrol from 4 Recce under Lt Lancaster had gone missing. The regiment moved to Sloughia where it arrived at 3.00am on the 20th: RHQ and B Squadron were located near Testour with A and C Squadrons near Sloughia and B Echelon near Teborsouk. The commanding officer attended a conference at divisional headquarters that morning at which General Anderson, GOC, First Army, outlined plans for the advance on Tunis and Bizerta.

During the night of the 20th/21st the Germans infiltrated 1st and 4th Divisions' areas, attacking Banana Ridge, Grenadier Hill and Djebel Djaffa. HQ of 4th Division was divebombed and mortared during the course of the morning and several attacking tanks were knocked out. While the battle raged on 10 Brigade's front and near divisional headquarters, A squadron was on stand-by to assist 10 Brigade if necessary; at 10.30pm the squadron was ordered to move and by midnight it was taking up positions on heights north of Djebel Djaffa pass. Patrols recce'd as far as the Goubellat-Medjez el Bab road but by noon Goubellat was reported clear and the patrols were withdrawn.

On the afternoon of St George's Day, A Squadron was again patrolling the Goubellat area and spotted German motorcycles near the village. The patrols were mortared and an LRC hit a mine while trying to avoid mortars; the car caught fire and the crew were presumed killed. The squadron was trying to sweep the road for mines, a task made more hazardous by German fire and the lack of mine-detectors.

Phase II of Operation VULCAN began before first light on 24 April and included an attack by 12 Brigade with 10 Brigade, still with A Squadron under command, patrolling to the south flank. A Squadron was keeping a watch on the road from Goubellat to Delaney's Corner to Peter's Corner and particularly a wadi east of the road. Lt Townley's patrol reached Delaney's Corner and was shelled there; the patrol then advanced on foot to establish an OP. At the same time a carrier patrol went north to observe the road and wadi from high ground but one carrier hit a mine, killing Sergeant Attwood. East and south-east of Delaney's Corner a tank battle had developed and 1st Armoured Division was engaging the enemy. The British tanks were repeatedly divebombed by the Luftwaffe and also found a very strong anti-tank line along the foothills to the east; the tanks had to withdraw in the face of this. Townley's patrol had come into contact with the Germans and a skirmish had developed but the patrol was forced back when German shells and mortars began to fall on them. The strength of the enemy defence in the area was later confirmed by a patrol from the assault troop under Lt Hill who was slightly wounded, as was one of his men.

Townley was again prevented from reaching Peter's Corner next day by equally strong opposition; his patrol left the road and moved to the west to observe German fire. Two LRCs had been hit with one man wounded. Carriers brought up to Delaney's Corner in the afternoon to act as OPs were forced to withdraw in the face of intensive shellfire. That evening the regiment was ordered to be ready to pursue the enemy if 12 Brigade broke through at Peter's Corner and preparations began for this task.

On 26 April Colonel Preston was appointed to command 10 Brigade after its brigadier had been injured in a car accident; Major Fisher assumed command of 4 Recce. For the expected advance C Squadron was to be ready to take the lead with B in reserve; A Squadron was to continue patrolling Delaney's Corner. That patrolling was still being met with determined opposition: an LRC was blown up with one soldier killed and a heavy armoured car that was left as an OP was later hit with two casualties. Patrolling in cars was stopped and superseded by foot patrols. That evening the regiment concentrated between Banana Ridge and Grenadier Hill at one hour's notice to move forward, although A Squadron remained at Goubellat.

A Squadron's patrolling task along the road to Peter's Corner was continuing on the morning of the 27th. There was little opposition to patrols although a tank battle was raging near Peter's Corner. About noon A Squadron, supported by field guns and 3-inch mortars, recce'd the Sidi Bel Halouni area in force. While the carriers drew enemy fire attempts were made to pinpoint German positions: the assault troop approached machine-gun positions on foot but heavy mortar and machine-gun fire made it impossible to close on the positions. The squadron withdrew to prepare for a fresh attack on the German strongpoint for which they requested infantry support to hold the position after its capture. This support was refused but the second attack went in anyway with two heavy armoured cars supporting with their Besas, and an artillery concentration on the German-held area. But, once again, definite positions could not be pinpointed and the attack was called off: two men had been killed, another injured and a carrier had been lost while six men were missing and a motorcycle had been abandoned. Four of the missing men returned by 9 o'clock next morning.

A decision was taken to mount an attack with a company of 2nd Hampshires supporting A Squadron on the night of 28th/29th but this was scaled down to two night recce patrols due to the lack of concrete information on German positions: this was an excellent example of how good the Germans were at camouflage and concealment. During the day A Squadron sent a patrol to recover some important maps abandoned by motorcyclists of IX Corps but, although one of the motorcycles was found, there was no trace of the maps. However, a prisoner was taken from a party investigating an abandoned British lorry. The German, who gave himself up, was from II/Hermann Göring Jäger Regiment: aged 20, his morale was poor but his identification was a valuable piece of information.

The night patrols were sent out, one from A Squadron and one from B; there was little to report although B Squadron's patrol had been fired on. During the morning of 29 April tank and infantry battles raged with attacks and counter-attacks at Sidi Abdullah, Cactus Farm and Argoub Ridge while the recce men waited for the order to advance. In the late-afternoon A and B Squadrons were ordered to take over protecting the division's southern flank from 2nd Hampshires while A Squadron was to remain in the Goubellat area guarding the Mahmoud Gap. At 7.00pm a German penetration of 1st Division's positions was reported causing A Squadron to be redeployed to Banana Ridge ready to repel any attack from the north; 6th Armoured Division moved into position on the southern flank of 4th Division and B Squadron took over A's tasks at Goubellat.

The battle at Peter's Corner continued throughout the 30th and 4 Recce waited for the word to move forward to Tunis; in the meantime patrols continued. By 4 May a new divisional plan of action was being worked out and B Squadron was withdrawn from the south flank which became part of 78th Division's area. The regimental rôle was to protect 4th Division's right flank while 10 and 12 Brigades attacked their objectives in four phases; C Squadron was first of all to seize Point 141 and hold the line of high ground running north and south of it while B passed through to take Point 155 and push patrols out to Frendj and Point 116. At 9.50pm on 5 May, 4th Division's artillery began a twenty-minute bombardment. At zero hour, 3.00am next day, a two-hour bombardment began and C Squadron, followed by B, moved up for the attack.

By 5.15am, C Squadron had reached Hammeda but was heavily mortared. The troop which had gone north to Point 131 had captured it but the bulk of the squadron was under heavy fire from Hammeda and from south of the Tunis road; the squadron leader, Major Mike Burke, was killed and the forward link destroyed. As a result there was confusion and the squadron became scattered. As all but two officers had been wounded the confusion was exacerbated and the squadron had to abandon Hammeda. Major J.D.C.Churchill took over C Squadron and concentrated its troops while B Squadron attacked Point 141 from the north. B Squadron took its objective but could not go on to attack Point 155 as Allied tanks had passed through the regiment and a tank battle was in progress along its front. The squadron eventually took Point 155 at 10.30am but could advance no further due to German tanks south of the Tunis road. By the end of the day the regiment had achieved its objectives and had taken a large number of German prisoners, mostly from 115 PanzerGrenadier Regiment but also from 190 Recce Unit which was fighting as infantry; it seemed that the lot of recce men was similar in both armies. The regiment's losses had been: dead, one officer and eight ORs; wounded, six officers and thirty-seven ORs; missing, one OR: all but one of C Squadron's officers had been wounded. These losses were added to those in April which had been ten dead, eight wounded and seven missing - all from A Squadron.

While tanks cleared the road to Tunis on 7 May, 4 Recce rested in a cornfield; advanced elements of the armoured divisions had reached Tunis by 3.30 that afternoon and hundreds of prisoners were taken. La Mohammedia was the regiment's next destination; it moved there by various routes during the next day and spent the 9th recce'ing foothills south of Hamman Lif and probing hills and passes with foot patrols in the Creteville area. At dusk the regiment moved forward to Nassen and patrols encountered enemy OPs north of Creteville; once engaged the Germans withdrew. Sixth Armoured Division made a breakthrough at Hamman Lif and, on the 10th, A and B Squadrons were ordered off in pursuit of the enemy in front of 10 and 12 Brigades. Crossing the start line at Hamman Lif at noon, B Squadron passed through 6th Armoured Division west of Soliman and came into contact with the retreating enemy just east of there. Blazing vehicles were strewn along the road and the squadron had several brushes with Germans. By 5 o'clock the squadron had reached Beni Kalled from where it pushed on to occupy Korba on the east coast before handing it over to 12 Brigade.

A Squadron's advance in front of 10 Brigade saw them occupy Menzel Bou Zelfa by 6.00pm after much delay from traffic congestion between Hamman Lif and Soliman. During this advance Major Fisher was attached as divisional liaison officer to 6th Armoured Division while Colonel Preston, who had returned to the regiment, and the intelligence officer were with the leading squadrons. On 11 May at 4.00am the leading troop of A Squadron started a northward sweep around the Cape Bon peninsula. An hour later prisoners were coming in in large numbers and the pursuit was so fast that, by 2.00pm, the leading troop had "turned the corner" at Cape Bon and taken El Haouaria, the northernmost village of the peninsula. By 3.30pm patrols from B Squadron met near Menzel Heure on the east coast and Kelibia had been taken. The peninsula had been occupied by the regiment and all resistance had ceased: thousands of prisoners were filling the roads and a steady stream of captured transport was moving them towards Soliman and Tunis.

B Squadron had pushed up slowly from Korba, meeting considerable opposition and one LRC had been lost with its crew as casualties. There was still much mopping up to be done and Germans were still trying to escape by sea on rafts but the war in Tunisia was almost over for 4 Recce. But in the dying gasps of the campaign Sergeant Don 'Smudger' Smith of B Squadron earned an immediate award of the MM:

> At 2130 hrs on 12th May a patrol of light and heavy cars was at road junction 571403 (rd Beni Khalled-Korba) when a German tank knocked out the Troop Commander's Heavy Car (Lieut J.D.Wigham). Light cars came back from the front of the Troop Commander's Car and took back wounded. Sgt Smith dismounted from a light car and took up a forward position with a Bren and a total of 7 men. Four 3-ton lorries of enemy infantry approached, Sgt Smith withholding his fire until they were 100 yards away. He then opened fire, the infantry dismounting and continuing to advance until driven off by further fire from Sgt Smith's Bren gun. Sgt Smith's efforts undoubtedly saved the leading vehicles and their crews from destruction.[6]

Don Smith's own account of the incident differs slightly from the official version on a number of points:

> ...all of a sudden round a bend I saw a blaze and it looked like one of my 'Heavies.' I shouted to my driver to stop but we were going that fast it took him a quarter mile to do so. I grab a TSMG [Thompson submachine-gun] and a couple of mags and ran back down the road. Sam, the driver of the skipper's car, Captain Jack Wigham, MC, (later Major) was running towards me in a terrible state in shock and with blood all over him, and gasped they had been hit by an 88. I told him to go to my car and wait whilst I sorted things out and going farther down the road to the blazing car I heard somebody staggering towards me, and yelled out 'Halt, what gives?' and Jack Wigham recognised my voice [and] identified himself. He was wounded and said Kiper O'Neill was dead. I don't know what happened to the fourth member of the team; looking back they must not have had one. Anyhow I got the captain back and found a carrier and sent him and his driver back to the medics; Jack had only a bit of shrapnel in his backside and [he] was back a few days later.[7]

Such were the mopping up operations carried out by A and B Squadrons on the 12th. On that day the garrison of Kelibia fort surrendered, and after collecting prisoners 4 Recce moved to the Temime area to form dumps of enemy stores and equipment in the coastal strip from Kelibia to Korba.

7
Sicily - short and sharp

The end of the North African campaign allowed the recce regiments an opportunity to relax and recover from their endeavours although they were soon preparing for further battles.

Back in London it had been decided to take a close look at how the Corps had performed in its first major campaign and so Lt Colonel C.J.Luce, a War Office staff officer with responsibility for advising the General Staff on all aspects of the Corps, was sent to Tunisia to study the Corps' performance, to see if its equipment had been up to the job and to look at the tactics employed. Luce looked at every aspect of operations in Tunisia and discussed the actions in which the regiments had been involved, what they thought of the new heavy armoured car, the wireless equipment used, and the various examples of improvisation that had been carried out. As it had the longest experience in Tunisia, 56th Regiment provided Luce with most information and it was on the information and notes that he took back from Tunisia that the training of other regiments was based.

Luce's notes were to be put into effect at the new Recce Training Centre at Catterick which, in August 1943, replaced the two centres at Lockerbie and Scarborough with Colonel W.H.Whitbread, TD as its commandant. Whitbread expended much time and effort to improving training methods and the equipment of the Corps. He was also the Corps' most senior officer after Gen Sir Bernard Paget who had become Colonel-Commandant in June 1943: this appointment seemed to carry with it a mark of approval for the Corps as if it had completed its probation and had become a fully-fledged formation on the Army List.

Not all the other reconnaissance regiments were still in the UK: 2nd, 5th and 45th Regiments had all departed for India which was threatened by the Japanese advance through Burma to the Indian border. Of these three regiments only two were to fight the Japanese - they would be joined by 81st and 82nd (West African) Reconnaissance Regiments - while the other - 5th - would fight in the Mediterranean after a spell in Persia waiting for a German attack.

On 3 February 1941, the recently-formed 3rd Tower Hamlets Rifles became 5th Battalion, The Recce Corps under Lt Colonel N.R.Blockley of the RB. The following month the battalion moved to Loughgall, County Armagh and took part in a valuable series of exercises in Northern Ireland before returning to England in early-1942 to "mobilise for overseas service in a tropical climate." At the end of March the battalion sailed in a convoy from Glasgow to South Africa. While 5th Division took part in operations against the Vichy French in Mozambique the battalion remained on board HMT *Almanzora*. The division then sailed for India, berthing at Bombay on 19 May from where it moved to Ranchi in Bihar province, some 200 miles from Calcutta.

Fifth Division had been intended to "strike immediately at any Japanese force attempting an invasion of Bengal"[1] but its stay in India was short and on 19 August 5 Recce were back at Bombay embarking on HMT *Rohna*: their new destination was Basrah in the Persian Gulf where they disembarked ten days later. Originally the plan had been that the division's vehicles, including the reconnoitrers, would travel overland via the Baluchistan desert but flooding of the Indus cut Quetta off from the rest of India and sea travel became essential.

The move of 5th Division to the Gulf region was a result of fears of a German attack through the Caucacus. The great concern about such an attack was a possible German thrust into India to link up with the Japanese; there was also still a possibility of Rommel's forces breaking through in Egypt and joining up with the thrust through the Caucasus. Such German strategy never developed and 5th Regiment, as it now was, spent some time at Kermansah in Iran, where the new anti-tank battery and the mortar troop were able to do some serious training, before moving to the holy city of Qum. From Qum, 2 Squadron was ordered to Teheran where rioting had broken out but their time there was relatively peaceful. At Christmas the regiment provided an escort of armoured cars for American vehicles travelling from Bandar Shapur on the coast to the Russian border.

In January 1943 came news that the division was to join Eighth Army in North Africa for a new campaign. And so the regiment moved yet again, this time to Syria to prepare for the Sicilian campaign. Heavy armoured cars were received to replace some of the LRCs in the scout troops. However, these were not the Humbers with 37mm guns being issued to other regiments but South African Marmon-Herringtons with turrets adapted for Italian Breda 47mm guns. Although welcome the 'new' cars - they were already well-used - came to the regiment so soon before embarkation that there was no opportunity for tactical training of the scout troops in their use. The Operation HUSKY landings took place on 10 July 1943 with 5th Division in the assaulting force. It was the only British division with a recce regiment - the others were 50th and 51st Divisions who no longer had such regiments - although one squadron had been left behind to follow up later. Trooper Rockliffe of 3 Squadron became 5 Recce's first battle casualty when he was wounded in a German air attack on the beachhead area.

On the morning of 14 July the regiment was given its first operational task, mopping up pockets of Italian resistance south of Augusta during which 3 Squadron took a large number of Italian prisoners. Eighth Army, advancing up the east side of Sicily, ran into German defensive positions soon after the capture of Augusta. The main German defensive line was on the Catania plain where 5th and 51st Divisions were brought to a standstill. Just before the front line hardened around Catania, a scout troop from 5 Recce, sent to reconnoitre a tributary of the Simeto river, ran into a strong German force, part of the defences impeding Eighth Army's advance. In the battle that followed, three reconnoitrers were killed, including the recce section commander, Lt Sutcliffe; another 12, including the troop commander, were captured and most of the vehicles destroyed. In the midst of this Sergeant Fisher rallied the rest of the troop and successfully got them out of their predicament. Fisher then returned alone to note and plot the German positions; he had not forgotten the prime purpose of a recce regiment. He was decorated with the MM.

The German stand meant that 5 Recce was now deployed holding part of the British front line, an experience that other recce regiments had had in North Africa and which others would have in the future. With 2 Squadron still to arrive in Sicily, this task put the regiment under some strain which was eased some days later when that squadron finally arrived. The regiment's defensive stance depended to a large extent on the mobility of its LRCs, armoured cars and carriers, and thus it was a relief when, at much the same time as 2 Squadron arrived, a number of Canadian tanks, an anti-tank battery and a machine-gun company of 7th Cheshires joined it in its sector of some six to seven miles along the dried-up bed of the Gornalunga river.

There were various encounters in no man's land all of which helped the regiment's learning process. By early-August 5 Recce was eager and ready to follow the Germans who were once again on the retreat. This time German defences were anchored on the mountain town of Centuripe but Eighth Army had been strengthened by the arrival of 78th Division, led by 56 Recce. Chavasse's Light Horse was soon at the spearhead, leading 78th Division as it pushed its narrow front forward. As well as probing forward, 56 Recce put patrols out to both flanks to maintain contact with the Canadian and Highland divisions to left and right respectively. On 1 August Catenanuova fell to a Canadian brigade under command of 78th Division. C Squadron had "had a good day's hunting" on the right flank in the Muglia area, inflicting up to 20 casualties on the Germans and forging ahead of the Highland Division. The next objective was Centuripe. The Germans were determined to hold Centuripe for as long as possible for German strategy in Sicily was now based on a complete withdrawal from the island. 'Complete' meant the successful evacuation of men and equipment and orders were issued that any soldier without a rifle would not be evacuated. Once again the British advance stopped as German resistance hardened.

German paratroopers wrote finis to the initial 78th Division plan for the capture of Centuripe but over the August bank holiday weekend an almost incredible attack by the Irish Brigade, with A Squadron under command, took the hilltop town and Eighth Army was on its way again. Ahead lay Bronte and Aderno and the final advance to Randazzo with 56 Recce playing its part in the action. About two kilometres from Aderno, having passed through Biancavilla, C Squadron was held up by mines, machine-guns and mortars and suffered some casualties and damage to vehicles. The next day, 7 August, the squadron moved under command of 36 Brigade with 2nd LF, a battery of self-propelled 25-pdrs, a squadron of tanks from 50 RTR and some sappers to advance towards Bronte. Teller-mines and S-mines caused delays as did craters and isolated German machine-gun positions. B Squadron came under 36 Brigade next day with C Squadron patrolling in front of Bronte which had been captured by 11 Brigade.

On 9 August B Squadron was patrolling the road on the left flank of 36 Brigade to try to contact Seventh (US) Army. Once again the ubiquitous mines, machine-guns, mortars and shellfire slowed progress; the squadron's assault troop was called on to flush out a German machine-gun position in an unexpected location. Contact was finally made with the Americans on the morning of the 11th by Lt Perkins but later that day a soldier of B Squadron was killed and two others injured when the squadron lost two LRCs and an armoured car on the Bronte-Randazzo road from mines and the fire of an 88mm self-propelled gun. B Squadron reached Randazzo on the 13th and the following day the regiment was out of action, its part in the short, bitter Sicilian campaign over.

When the British advance re-started 5 Recce had been patrolling in the same fashion as their comrades of 56th Regiment. Beginning their pursuit of the Germans, 1 Squadron had a close escape on the evening of 3 August:

> ...the regiment was ordered to move into a forward harbour by night. The last two words were the saving of one squadron and RHQ, who ran into an area thickly infested by the Bosche, who had refused to obey the marks on the divisional intelligence map and were still well in front of the proposed harbour. Thinking very quickly, and ordering everyone to fire back everything he had, Colonel Blockley reversed the long line of vehicles through the pitch blackness, helped by the coolness of the wireless operator in the leading car who, under heavy fire and until his vehicle brewed up from tracer bullets, remained at his set reporting the situation to the rear of the column.[2]

Although safely extricated, 1 Squadron had lost several killed and there had been others wounded. Thus began a hectic week for 5 Recce. Patrols nosed towards the foothills of the slumbering volcano, Mount Etna, and the villages beneath. There were many reports of enemy positions to radio back and regular scraps with German units. Twelve Troop, held up by strong enemy opposition, called down an artillery shoot on the Germans and the troop commander, Lieutenant Frank George, calmly directed the shellfire as it sought out the opposition. LRCs from one patrol entered Paterno to find themselves in close contact with the Germans; the contact became much too close when two self-propelled guns were spotted. On the flanks contact was maintained with the neighbouring divisions in the advance.

A patrol was lost when its two cars were hit from behind by an 88. The sound of firing was the regiment's last contact with them and it had to be assumed that their crews had been killed or captured. Their troop commander took a carrier section on a right-flanking move to locate the 88; they came in view of a farmhouse near the incident and almost immediately were machine-gunned from a nearby hill. The troop commander and his sergeant, who had been wounded in the shoulder, ran across open ground and entered the farmhouse to find a German soldier preparing lunch. The cook denied knowing anything about the 88 but suddenly dropped to the ground which prompted his interrogators to do likewise. A shell hit the house but the troop commander had spotted the flash from a camouflage screen about half a mile away. The information was passed to a gunner FOO who had just arrived and the 88 was quickly knocked out.

As the advance continued 5 Recce snapped at the Germans from in front of 50th Division. This task was carried out by two mixed-force columns, each containing a recce element. One column was commanded by Colonel Blockley, and thus called Blockcol; the other was Camcol, under Colonel Cameron of the County of London Yeomanry. Camcol had some small-scale skirmishes but apart from those the two columns had a relatively straightforward job and, on 12 August, after some final patrolling around Etna, 5 Recce was withdrawn to rest and re-organise near Catania.

Another campaign had ended for the Reconnaissance Corps, a campaign not truly suited to the Corps but its representative regiments had, once again, served with distinction and performed admirably every task given to them.

8
Into Italy

The Mediterranean remained the focus for the next phase of Reconnaissance Corps active service. Although the Americans had been anxious to shift the emphasis of operations to north-west Europe with an invasion of France in 1943 they had been persuaded by Churchill and the British Chiefs of Staff of the wisdom of continued operations on the southern flank to 'close the ring' around Germany. During the Sicilian campaign the Americans finally agreed that the next major objective would be the Italian mainland itself and planning began for the invasion of Italy.

The Italian invasion involved three operations: BAYTOWN, a landing on the toe of Italy; SLAPSTICK, a landing at Taranto; and AVALANCHE, a landing at Salerno, south of Naples. The first two operations were the responsibility of Eighth Army under General Sir Bernard Montgomery; AVALANCHE was that of the Allied Fifth Army under General Mark Clark. The first operation to be launched was BAYTOWN with soldiers of Eighth Army crossing the Straits of Messina under air and artillery cover. This operation had two objectives: to secure the straits for Allied shipping and to allow Eighth Army to move up from the toe of Italy to join Fifth Army as soon as possible. To distract the Germans from the Salerno landings, Operation SLAPSTICK was to be launched at the same time. But the German commander, Field Marshal Albert Kesselring quickly identified AVALANCHE as the main threat and the full pressure of German forces in southern Italy was unleashed on Fifth Army soon after a beachhead had been created.

The first wave of Fifth Army was at sea between North Africa and Salerno when Italy's surrender was announced. Hitler had anticipated this and German forces moved to neutralise the Italian army. As leading elements of 46th and 56th British and 36th US Divisions came ashore Kesselring had already deployed von Vietinghoff's Tenth Army to meet them. Resistance was light at first as Vietinghoff held back his forces until he was certain that the Salerno landings were not a feint; then he hit the Allies with two Panzer and two PanzerGrenadier divisions in an attempt to implement Kesselring's order that "the invading army ...must be completely annihilated and ...thrown into the sea."

Two regiments of the Reconnaissance Corps were in the Salerno beachhead: 46 Recce with 46th Division and 44 Recce with 56th Division. Further south, 5 Recce was leading its division through Calabria while on the Adriatic sector 56 Recce was in front of 78th Division. There was a further recce unit in the peninsula also: 1st Airlanding Squadron, part of

1st Airborne Division, had landed from ships at Taranto.

The first regiment to arrive had been 5 Recce. Their landfall had been on the toe of the country but they had not been in the leading elements of 5th Division which, with a Canadian division, was the main body of Eighth Army at that stage. After the first troops ashore in Italy had found the area deserted, the sailing order of the remainder of the force had been changed, putting 5 Recce at the tail of its division rather than the head. After landing in Italy the regiment took two days to get to the head of the division which was already on the move. As they advanced a despatch rider passed on the news of Italy's surrender although no one was too sure of what exactly that meant.

Once established at the front of the division, on 10 September, 5 Recce was ordered to push ahead. It was a pure reconnaissance job, such as that carried out by 56th Regiment in the early days in Tunisia. RHQ, on several occasions, was over a hundred miles ahead of 5th Division while patrols were almost as far ahead of RHQ. Such distances, coupled with the mountainous terrain, meant that wireless sets could not be relied on and the Don Rs, or despatch riders, became some of the regiment's most valued soldiers. The speed of 5 Recce's progress took them off the maps issued to them and they had to make do with two old motoring maps that had been obtained from a "friendly, retired Italian general." On occasions crews and vehicles were stranded for as long as three weeks awaiting recovery; the lack of maps made it impossible to give REME personnel map references of where the breakdowns had occurred.

The capture of Cosenza airfield was assigned to 1 and 2 Squadrons; this involved using the inland roads. The coast road was fairly clear, having been left to the Italians, but the Germans had done a very thorough job of mining and cratering inland roads. By now vehicles had had their floors sandbagged to reduce the danger from blast, but the rugged mountain countryside was almost impassable in places and German demolitions proved very effective. About forty miles from Cosenza, 2 Squadron was held up in this manner and the squadron leader had begun a search for horses on which to patrol when a train whistle was heard. The train was stopped at a tunnel mouth and the crew persuaded to take it back to Cosenza, from where they had come, with the recce men lying on the carriage floor. Having improvised to such an extent, the men of 2 Squadron were chagrined to find a 1 Squadron patrol at Cosenza; their rivals had reached the airfield by another route. Such was the picture as 5 Recce probed its way up the leg of Italy.

Because of the situation at Salerno it was vital that Eighth Army should advance as quickly as possible to help Fifth Army. Fifth Division quickly reached Sapri on the coast, some fifty miles from Salerno, and was then switched inland to move up the centre of Italy and threaten the Germans at

Salerno. One Squadron was detached to make contact with Fifth Army which it did on 17 September when 8 Troop met a reconnaissance party from 36th (US) Division.

The previous day 5 Recce had had its first serious encounter with the Germans in Italy when 3 Squadron bumped the enemy on the approaches to the town of Lagonegro. The squadron was stopped by mortar and small-arms fire. The enemy were strongly positioned and no recce vehicles could get off the road nor move along it after a bridge over a gorge was blown as the leading LRC approached. A gunner FOO tried to locate the concealed German positions but only some targets could be identified. An attack by some of the assault troops also failed as the attackers were scattered by the mountainous terrain and many trees. During the night the Germans withdrew and 5 Recce resumed its normal rôle although progress was now slower and sappers accompanied patrols to search for mines while diversions had to be found for vehicles due to demolitions and cratering.

General Montgomery was anxious that the Germans should be fully aware that Eighth Army was bearing down on them and a staff officer was sent to 1 Squadron's HQ to emphasise the importance of establishing contact with the enemy:

> Luck was with the Squadron as a patrol, under Lieut. "Mouse" Sims, encountered an enemy patrol at one of the "blows". L/Cpl Aitchison personally "collected" a prisoner, and at least two of the enemy party were killed, so General Montgomery's instructions could fairly be said to have been carried out.[1]

As 5th Division and the Canadian division converged, the former fell back to allow the Canadians to take Potenza. The recce men had been kept busy with active patrolling which continued throughout this period. Having regrouped around Vietri, 5th Division began the next stage of its advance with 5 Recce leading through the Canadians at Potenza, to Melfi and on to the main Foggia-Naples road.

When the Canadians reached Campobasso 5th Division moved up to relieve them but, as it was now the start of November and the winter rains had begun, 5 Recce, less 2 Squadron (which, however, soon rejoined), was left behind at Bovino as it was considered to have no proper rôle in the mountains. Instead a training programme was ordered by the divisional commander who believed that the reconnaissance regiment would not be needed until the spring by which time, hopefully, the Allies would be north of Rome.

> On October 8 a strange apparition walked into RHQ Officers' Mess. It appeared that a disreputable Italian tramp had entered the holy-of-holies, but when this extraordinary figure removed its fantastic hat it revealed itself as Major Lewis, last seen in Sicily in command of 1

Italy
First Phase
100 miles

Venice

Ravenna

Bologna

Florence

Rimini

San Marino

Pisa

Arezzo

Ancona

L. Trasimene

Perugia

ROME

HITLER LINE

ADRIATIC SEA

Anzio

Ortona

Cassino

GUSTAV LINE

Foggia

VIKTOR LINE

Barletta

Naples

ITALY

Bari

Brindisi

OPERATION
AVALANCHE
(44 & 46 Recce)

Salerno

Taranto

OPERATION
SLAPSTICK
(56 Recce, 1 A/L
Recce Sqdrn.)

TYRRHENIAN
SEA

Lagonegro

OPERATION
BAYTOWN
(5 Recce)

Cosenza

Reggio

SICILY

Squadron. On the capitulation of Italy he had walked out of his prison camp, near Bologna, just as the Germans had walked in, got on a train... and then made his way through the enemy lines into the Canadian area... He also brought maps and plans which had been entrusted to him by an Allied agent whom he encountered en route.[2]

Lewis left after a few days and not long afterwards the regiment bade farewell to Colonel Blockley who returned to the UK to be second-in-command of the RAC OCTU at Sandhurst and Chief Instructor of the Reconnaissance Wing. He was succeeded in command by Lieutenant-Colonel M.F.Douglas-Pennant, MBE, of the King's Royal Rifle Corps, who had been Brigade Major of the Irish Brigade in Tunisia and Sicily. As a rifleman Colonel Douglas-Pennant (now Lord Penrhyn) was an inspired choice for a regiment which held dear its rifle traditions and customs.

At Taranto the landings had been unopposed; only a mine which blew up a cruiser provided any setback. Unfortunately for 1st Airlanding Squadron their 6-pounder anti-tank guns were lost with the cruiser. Once ashore the squadron was sent forward to find the enemy, reconnoitring along two of three parallel routes; the third route was covered by an SAS unit. The middle route was taken by the main body of the squadron with Major C.F.H.Gough in command; they were to probe along a road that led through Massafra and Mottola to Gioia del Colle. Apart from a trigger-happy Italian farmer there was no opposition until just outside Massafra. Appropriately, perhaps, it was from Fallschirmjäger and was dealt with quickly by flanking fire from one section, under Lieutenant Galbraith, while the bulk of the troop drove their jeeps rapidly into Massafra. The Germans made an equally speedy exit, hastened by the fact that the main body of Brigadier Sean Hackett's 4 Parachute Brigade was almost upon them as well. The next opposition came from the hillside town of Mottola: as the leading jeeps of the squadron rounded a bend just over a mile from Mottola they came under fire; Douglas Galbraith actually felt bullets pass through his clothing. The maroon-bereted reconnoitrers took to the hillside to assess the German strength. There were two defensive lines, one of trenches, and a row of substantial pillboxes on a ridge. The trenches were taken by Gough's men but the pillboxes were a different story causing the recce men to consolidate their positions and await the clearing of the ridge by 156th Parachute Battalion. That was done by the middle of the afternoon after which C Troop entered Mottola to check for Germans; once again the enemy was leaving as the reconnoitrers entered. A patrol subsequently sent out towards San Basilio captured a Luftwaffe officer and two NCOs in a staff car heading for Taranto. There was another contact with Fallschirmjäger on the San Basilio road when a jeep patrol was taken unawares by an armoured car hidden by a German truck convoy. Two men on the jeep were killed; Lieutenant Galbraith then opened fire on the trucks with a Bren, killing or wounding almost 30 Germans.

As Gough's group approached Gioia they ran into heavy machine-gun fire again and once more took to the surrounding countryside where they were pinned down by increasingly accurate mortar fire. The pressure from the German mortars was eased a little by Trooper Jim Taylor, the only unwounded survivor of his group of four, who poured Bren-gun fire at the mortar crews:

> Tpr Taylor was a member of the leading troop in the advance from San Basilio on 11th September, 1943. ...the troop came under heavy fire from 20mm and MGs, two Jeeps were knocked out and the Troop was pinned down on a ridge. It was essential that this position be held as a pivot for a left flank attack by a Para Bn. The Tp Commander, realising that there was dead ground on his left front, reconnoitred an LMG position to cover this area. The post was manned by a L/Sgt and three men, of whom Taylor was one, with two Bren guns. They managed to dig themselves in, but throughout the afternoon they were under continuous and heavy fire from mortars and machine guns. One man was killed and the L/Sgt and another man wounded, leaving Tpr Taylor to man the post alone. He continued to return fire and remained until he was withdrawn by the Tp Commander at a time when the Battalion attack had developed sufficiently to render the enemy positions untenable.

> Throughout the operation Tpr Taylor displayed the highest qualities of courage and determination.[3]

Taylor's courage had allowed 156th Parachute Battalion to carry out a left-flanking approach that spurred the Germans to withdraw.

From San Basilio patrols over the next few days had further encounters with the Germans. However the pace of operations was less frenetic. Gioia was taken by 10th Parachute Battalion on 16 September, thus ending the first phase of operations. Quartered at Gioia, the squadron learned of the fate of B Troop which had advanced on an easterly route via Martina Franca. Just after Martina the troop had been ambushed at a Y-junction and lost three dead and several captured; only a few escaped.

After a few days' rest the squadron was ordered to recce towards Bari which it found to be clear of Germans. As the first Allied troops into Bari 1st Airlanding Squadron naturally took the best accommodation for itself and subsequent patrols from the town saw at least some members return to the comfort of the Imperial Hotel!

Soon the squadron was on its travels again, travelling towards Foggia via Barletta. Asked for a report on the airfield at Foggia, Major Gough not only recce'd the Luftwaffe base but attacked and captured it. Several ground-crew were surprised as they serviced aircraft, and machine-guns from captured Junkers 88s were taken to be mounted in pairs on the squadron's jeeps.

Foggia was the squadron's last operation in Italy; it was then withdrawn to Bari to rest for some weeks before returning to Taranto to re-embark for North Africa. By December the squadron was back in Britain and stationed in Lincolnshire.

Also in action from Taranto up to Foggia had been 56 Recce. Landing at Reggio on 19 September the regiment had motored across to Crotone whence it advanced towards Bari, Barletta and the airfields of the Foggia plain which were wanted by the Allies so that strategic bombers could fly against German targets from the south. As 56 Recce, temporarily commanded by Major Marcus Hartland-Mahon as Colonel Chavasse was recovering from malaria, moved from Crotone on 22 September German opposition was hardening. Their first task was to secure the airfields at Bari and the regimental advance was led by B Squadron; there were pockets of German resistance but within three hours the squadron and RHQ were five miles from Bari with standing patrols operating; the assault troop and anti-tank troop were located at Modugno and Spielo. In the meantime Major Hartland-Mahon had been called to 78th Division's headquarters at Taranto to learn that he was to command a force consisting of B Squadron, 56 Recce, A Squadron, The Royals, a troop of 17th Field Regiment, elements from the airborne division and GHQ Liaison (Phantom) Regiment for an operation to seize and hold crossings over the Ofanto river before going on to occupy Foggia.

On the 23rd, the Royals on the coast road were stopped by enemy opposition about six miles from Barletta which was said to be strongly held by infantry and artillery. B Squadron and Battle HQ had moved forward towards Andrea before meeting opposition some three miles east of the town at about 4.00pm. Two soft-skinned enemy vehicles were destroyed in the skirmish and several casualties inflicted on the Germans with no loss to B Squadron. A prisoner from a Flak regiment claimed that there was a large force in Andrea but the advance continued and at 9 o'clock next morning the force began fording the Ofanto in the face of fierce opposition, including mortar fire which later killed two men of the assault troop and wounded five from that troop and the anti-tank troop. A troop of Shermans from 3rd County of London Yeomanry, placed under Marcus Hartland-Mahon's command, engaged the Germans: one was hit by enemy anti-tank fire and another accidentally damaged. Heavy shelling continued from the German positions and later that day Hartland-Mahon's force passed to the command of Brigadier John Currie's 4 Armoured Brigade to become known as A Force.

B Squadron and Battle HQ were across the Ofanto next day unopposed, although there was opposition later and further strong resistance six miles from Foggia, but patrols of armoured cars and carriers of 56 Recce plus tanks cleared the enemy positions. Foggia was reached at 9.00am on 27

September although the main road party had been delayed by a blown bridge. Patrols from C Squadron reached Lucera from Foggia the following day. At 2.00pm Fallschirmjäger were encountered north of Troia and several Germans were killed and one taken prisoner. The regiment was out of action for a day before resuming operations on the last day of September when Colonel Chavasse returned. On that day forward elements of the regiment, patrolling towards Castelnuova, ran into strong opposition five miles from there. Two patrols were held at different parts of what was believed to be the main German defensive line by machine-guns, mortars and anti-tank guns; the assault troop was also pinned down. Under cover of darkness a successful withdrawal was made.

At a squadron leaders' conference at 2.30 in the morning of 1 October the next objective was outlined: to cross the Fortore river and gain the high ground beyond. The bridge over the Fortore was blown with a wide detour necessary along a route on which a strong German presence was reported. At 5.00am two carrier troops of A Squadron deployed under A Squadron, The Royals on the right of the road while B Squadron and Battle HQ, 3rd County of London Yeomanry and the Kensingtons, the divisional support battalion, moved four miles south of San Puolo. The advancing units came under shellfire and Lieutenant R.C.Courts of 56 Recce was killed by an airburst. By 10.30am the river had been crossed after a long, difficult detour and B Squadron, supported by tanks, led an advance over open country to the outskirts of Serracapriola. Opposition was overcome by artillery fire: an 88 was captured intact although its crew had been killed and a half-track and one other vehicle were found burned out. Serracapriola was captured but the Germans had left many booby traps behind and one recce sergeant was among those killed by these devices.

Recce patrols went out from Serracapriola to check the tracks from the town. Early next morning B and C Squadrons, with Battle HQ and the CLY moved through Serracapriola along diversions built by sappers. A patrol from B Squadron found the going along the tracks on the left flank so hard that they took to their feet. A carrier was blown up on a mine on a diversion around a blown bridge: the driver was killed and an officer wounded. At 8 o'clock that morning enemy aircraft attacked troop concentrations in Serracapriola.

Termoli was the next goal but most bridges en route had been blown thus complicating the advance. C Squadron occupied San Martino where Colonel Chavasse met the brigadiers of 4 Armoured and 11 Infantry Brigades. Heavy rain throughout the day made the going even harder. The next major obstacle before Termoli was the Biferno river which B Squadron and Battle HQ reached on the 3rd "by many and devious detours." No contact was made with the Germans who had left many very effective demolitions in their wake. The Biferno was impassable without bridging equipment and while sappers laboured to put a pontoon bridge across German aircraft bombed the area. It was an hour before midnight before RHQ and B Squadron crossed by pontoon bridge to harbour two miles south of Termoli on a very wet night. During the 4th the squadron moved through Termoli to recce forward to Vasto along the main road and, having motored to just three miles south-east of Petacciato, withdrew to east of Termoli.

During that day a landing had been made at Termoli by a force comprising 3 Commando, 40 (Royal Marine) Commando and the Special Raiding Squadron who had reported the town clear of enemy and moved to secure the approaches, including the Biferno crossings. During the night of 3/4 October, 36 Brigade landed at Termoli to take over the town's southern defences and move on to the high ground at first light. The forces advancing by road were under command of 11 Brigade while the Irish Brigade was to move up by sea later.

After a quiet night B Squadron pushed patrols along the coast road and towards San Giacomo. It was believed that the only Germans in the area were Fallschirmjäger with artillery support and limited armour. The main body of B Squadron had a brief battle at a farm just off the coast road and cleared the farm of Germans, taking one prisoner. Thirty minutes later 11 Troop took another prisoner, a German motorcyclist who was captured as he rode along the road from Petacciato. He turned out to be from 16th Panzer Division which Eighth Army Intelligence had believed to be on the west coast. The prisoner revealed that his division had been travelling towards Termoli for the past two nights. His information put a different complexion on affairs at Termoli where the light force had no armour and would have to wait until tank-supporting bridges had been laid across the Biferno. Mark IV tanks had also been spotted by B Squadron patrols on the coast road.

Before noon the Germans had launched a counter-attack against Termoli at which stage Colonel Chavasse was given command of a force consisting of 3 Commando, an SRS troop, B Squadron and an anti-tank battery with orders to take up position on the high ground overlooking the Simarca river from the sea to the church west of the brickworks, giving right flank and rear protection to 8th Argylls. The Commando was already in position and B Squadron's men, including most of the drivers, were deployed from the main road to the right of the line held by the Argylls. The SRS troop arrived later in the day and was placed between 3 Commando and the sea. At first light next morning an OP was placed in the church west of the brickworks and troops were pulled back from forward slopes.

Following confused mortar and machine-gun fire, RHQ moved forward to the olive grove occupied by B Squadron's vehicles and 3 Commando; the grove dominated the surrounding countryside. German attacks were being made on the perimeter and especially on the Argylls who were forced to pull back. Sappers had been struggling to make a ford across the river in the absence of bridging equipment and six CLY Shermans managed to cross before the ford became so churned up as to be unusable. The tanks were sent to help the Argylls: four were lost before the survivors and the infantry were forced to fall back to the brickworks by 11.00am. Attacking panzers managed to turn the Argylls' right flank, and their CO with two men from 56 Recce manned an anti-tank gun in the ensuing battle: recce men had already joined anti-tank guncrews elsewhere and some had died as the guns fell to stalking panzers. Among the dead was Trooper Ives who had singlehandedly manned an anti-tank gun and taken on several tanks before his gun received a direct hit. The brickworks was also under artillery bombardment with shells falling on it from both sides; British artillery was firing from across the river.

During the afternoon the enemy advance on Termoli continued. Anti-tank gun positions became untenable and the pressure on 3 Commando and the SRS increased as three tanks supported by infantry approached. B Squadron and RHQ were being shelled and Kendal Chavasse ordered the evacuation of all vehicles except the wireless LRCs. On his right flank, the SRS were being overrun by the enemy; a farm south of the main road, overlooking B Squadron's line on the left flank, was also occupied by Germans. The wireless link with B Squadron had been lost when their rear-link vehicle was destroyed and they were then out of touch with their RHQ. The Argylls were ordered to fall back from the brickworks where they had suffered over 160 casualties, including Major Anderson, VC who had been killed; their CO also advised Marcus Hartland-Mahon to withdraw B Squadron. As the Germans attempted to encircle his RHQ, Kendal Chavasse advised his men that they now had "an all round shoot." But the line was now held only by 3 Commando:

> It was getting dark and the voices of enemy infantry could be heard through the shelling. The order to withdraw came to me from Division. I remember walking through the olive grove, with bullets whistling, to contact the C.O. of the Commando to tell him to withdraw. Then came the problem of getting our vehicles out. I got on to Division and asked for as much noise as possible so that the enemy would not hear the engines starting up. I remember the gunner saying he had never been asked for "noise" before! Anyway, they gave it, and plenty of it too, and we slipped away unnoticed to behind the firmer line that had been established behind us.[4]

That firmer line had been established by the Lancashire Fusiliers and the withdrawal was complete by 2.45 on the morning of 6 October by which time the Irish Brigade was landing at Termoli. Later that morning an Irish Brigade attack, supported by Canadian armour, pushed the Germans out of

Termoli. Soon afterwards the brigade also took the Petacciato ridge, clearing the way for a further advance.

Chavasse's Light Horse had performed magnificently at Termoli, playing a significant part in denying the town to the Germans who could then have inflicted even heavier casualties on troops advancing across the Biferno. For his actions at Termoli, Kendal Chavasse was awarded a Bar to the DSO. This was the only Bar to the DSO awarded to the Reconnaissance Corps. The regiment continued to play its part in Eighth Army's slow advance, constantly patrolling and probing as river crossing followed river crossing. Casualties were suffered but much valuable information was brought back and squadrons also took part in fighting at Montecilfore and the capture of Montenero. At one stage eight officers from 6th Lancers (Watson's Horse), 8th Indian Division's reconnaissance regiment, were attached to 56 Recce for instruction and experience. After the San Salvo battle at the beginning of November the regiment again led the way with C Squadron recce'ing as far as Vasto where they fought German troops. At the end of the month 78th Division was fighting its way over the Sangro and A and B Squadrons' carriers were allocated to the Commander, RASC of the division to carry supplies over the river. On 30 November C Squadron crossed the Sangro with 4 Armoured Brigade.

In early December 56 Recce relieved 15 Brigade of 5th Division. RHQ was established at Vastogirardi, B and C Squadron's assault troops were at Capracotta while A Squadron and the anti-tank personnel moved to San Pietro. In those positions the regiment saw out the year as snow fell around them, making movement almost impossible.

On the west coast of Italy, Fifth Army had entered Naples on 1 October but their struggle on the Salerno beaches had been, to paraphrase Wellington, a close-run battle. The two British divisions of X Corps which had been in the first wave of invaders had included recce regiments in their orders of battle. In Fifth Army's situation there was little scope for the normal operations of a reconnaissance regiment and once again it was a case, for 44th and 46th Regiments, of helping to hold a line.

Believing that the Americans were the weak link in Fifth Army, Kesselring tried to drive a wedge between the British and American elements on the beaches. The attackers had the line of the River Sele as their axis of advance for that river marked the inter-Allied boundary in the beachhead.

On D Day, 9 September, elements of both recce regiments had been among the first troops of their divisions ashore. At 4.30pm, B Squadron, 46 Recce, moved into Salerno town. They found very few civilians about and the main streets were blocked by demolitions, so they travelled carefully, ready for ambushes, by side streets to the western edge of Salerno where they met with men of 2 Commando who had landed early that morning and had been fighting for much of the day. Meeting with men of 46th

Division was a morale-booster for the commandos. Moving on through the Vietri defile, B Squadron entered Cava de'Tirreni where the Germans were still manning defensive positions. A prisoner taken in a side street provided the information that twenty-five tanks, with 500 infantry, were only one and a half miles away and preparing to advance. With that information the squadron made its way back to Vietri as darkness descended.

Fifty-sixth Division had landed south of 46th Division with the Tusciano river marking the boundary between them. C Squadron, 44 Recce landed with 167 Brigade while RHQ and B Squadron came in with 169 Brigade. The regiment was soon in action, a squadron going forward with a commando troop to join 41 (RM) Commando at the La Molina defile. Early next morning, the squadron recce'd forward to discover Germans dug in at La Molina in positions overlooking 41 Commando in the valley. The squadron was later withdrawn by 138 Brigade to rejoin the brigade in Salerno. During the morning 41 Commando was machine-gunned and mortared by the Germans above them but at the same time 2 Commando was creating a perimeter in the hills around Vietri.

On 10 September, the regiment was placed on 56th Division's right flank and given two tasks, both of which it carried out successfully. These were to reconnoitre and observe the enemy on that flank, and to establish contact with the American 36th (Texas) Division. However, pressure from von Vietinghoff's Tenth Army soon had the Allies on the defensive and that pressure was to last for almost a week with Vietinghoff at one stage claiming that Allied resistance was collapsing and that his army was "pursuing enemy on wide front."

During that week 44 and 46 Recce deployed as infantry in a situation where every available soldier was put into the line with a rifle or a submachine-gun. The anti-tank guns were busily employed too, and the anti-tank troop commander of 46 Recce later wrote an account of some of the actions involving his guns. They were nicknamed the "Troop with the Shiny Barrels" as they had never fired at German armour in Africa. Salerno presented plenty of opportunities. Their first was against a Mark IV Special, a tank that "looked like a single-decker tram, with a mammoth's head and a trunk stuck on top."[5] That tank was engaged from the side and put out of action after five rounds from a 6-pounder. Shortly afterwards two Mark III Specials were engaged and knocked out but then two Tigers (described in the account as Mark VIs) appeared and the gun detachment tried to get to a better position but the gun stuck in a ditch and had to be destroyed. Then the troop commander realised that he was stuck in the middle of a tank battle. An LRC had to be abandoned and a retreat made on foot; most of the recce men got away although one was missing and Corporal Fletcher's gun detachment had been captured. "Later we heard that it had been a major attack, with tanks and many infantry, calculated to throw our division into the sea."[6]

The breakout from Salerno put three recce regiments - 5, 44 and 46 - on the western sector while 56 was advancing on the Adriatic sector. From Salerno 44 Recce's squadrons operated with the three brigades of the Black Cat Division in following up the retreating Germans. There were several small scale actions and A Squadron was able to surprise a German sapper party preparing to blow a bridge; the sappers were captured and the bridge taken intact.

But there was no possibility of a swift advance up the Italian peninsula. The grain of the country was against the Allies with the Apennine mountains forming a spine and rivers flowing down to either coast. The valleys and hills were custom-made for defence and Albert Kesselring was a master of defensive warfare. As he prepared a winter line across Italy his rearguard units took a heavy toll of the advancing Allies; on the east coast Fifth Army's advance to the Volturno river cost 12,000 casualties, most of them from the British X Corps. As winter set in the Germans established a defensive line across Italy from Gaeta on the Tyrrhenian coast to Ortona on the Adriatic; this was the Gustav Line, whose most famous feature was to be Monte Cassino. Forward of the Gustav Line in the west was the Bernhardt Line anchored on Monte Camino and stretching along part of the Garigliano river near the west coast to the headwaters of the Trigno river which flowed into the Adriatic. Forward defences had also been created in the Adriatic sector along the lines of several of the rivers on Eighth Army's route; the battle at Termoli had pierced the Viktor Line. A new German army had been created in Italy, Fourteenth Army, to stand alongside Tenth Army in Kesselring's Army Group C. The opposing forces were almost evenly balanced. That gave the defenders a distinct advantage.

9
Singapore - first blood

At 6.00pm on 15 February 1942 over 100,000 troops surrendered at Singapore to a Japanese force less than one-third of their strength. That capitulation ended a ten-week campaign in Malaya during which the Japanese had outgeneralled, out-thought and outfought their opponents. To the commander in Malaya, Lieutenant General Arthur Percival, fell the ignominy of capitulating to Lieutenant General Tomoyuki Yamashita of the Imperial Japanese Army in the greatest setback to British arms since the surrender of Yorktown in 1781 during the American rebellion.

Among those who marched into captivity were soldiers of 18th Battalion, The Reconnaissance Corps who had arrived with 18th Division shortly before the surrender. Formed from 5th Loyals at Madeley Heath, Staffordshire on 30 April 1941 the battalion's personnel officially transferred from The Loyal Regiment to The Reconnaissance Corps on 9 May 1941. Training continued through that summer and the issue of tropical kit indicated a move to North Africa. With no Reconnaissance Corps cap badges the battalion made do with Corps flashes,* issued in early June, and with painting Reconnaissance Corps markings in a diamond shape on their helmets.

Following inspection by the King on 22 October the battalion embarked on an odyssey that was to end in the tragedy of Singapore. The first leg took the convoy to Halifax, Nova Scotia where 18 Recce transferred to the US Army transport *Leonard Wood* and sailed from Halifax in a convoy protected by the aircraft carrier, USS *Ranger*. On 18 November *Leonard Wood* was accidentally rammed by *Joseph Dickenson* and its fuelling tanker. Next day the convoy left Port of Spain in Trinidad but *Leonard Wood* soon fell behind, although a destroyer escort was provided. Cape Town was reached on 9 December where, thirteen days later, the Battalion learned that its destination was Bombay. It finally reached India on 27 December and disembarked on the last day of 1941 to move to Ahmednagar. From India 18th Division sailed for Singapore as a result of the worsening situation in the Far East.

Although the main body of the division had landed to join III Indian Corps, 18th Reconnaissance Battalion, together with other divisional troops,

---

*   *This information is taken from the War Diary; the flashes are presumed to be the arm of service strip.

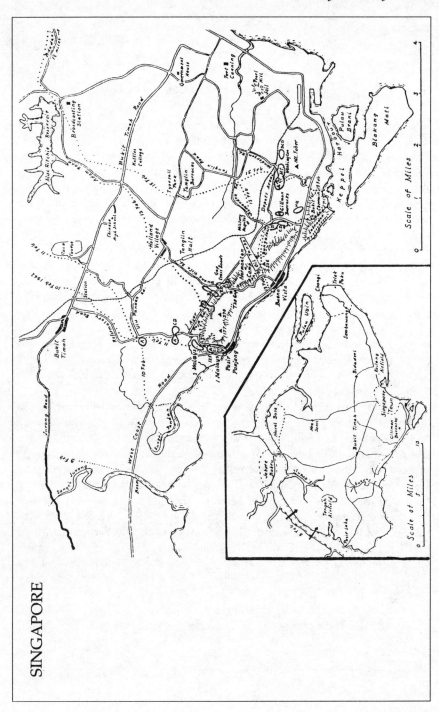

SINGAPORE

did not arrive off Singapore island until the morning of 5 February. It was

> ...a glorious sunny morning, not a cloud in the sky or a ripple on the sea, and the white wake creaming back from the majestic ships ...with just 10 miles to go to reach Singapore, that bastion of the East, with its so-called impregnable defences.

> What a rude awakening was in store for us, the bombers and Zeros came in from every angle and had a field day.[1]

At about 1100 hours, when the leading ships were close to Singapore and the slowest ship, the *Empress of Asia*, was south-west of the Sembilan Islands, the convoy was attacked by enemy dive-bombers. The *Empress of Asia* received several direct hits and soon began to sink.

> ...troops had to take to the water owing to fire on the ship. Some great acts of gallantry were performed, especially by members of the hospital staff. Rescues were quickly effected by the Royal Navy. The loss of life fortunately was small, but nearly all weapons and equipment on board were lost... It thus happened that some of these units landed without their equipment. They were re-equipped as far as possible with small arms and fought thereafter as infantry.[2]

The convoy had actually been attacked the previous day and, although the ship had sustained no damage, the stokers abandoned their posts and *Empress of Asia* fell behind the convoy. The other three ships reached Singapore safely on the morning of 5 February but the *Empress* was attacked about ten miles offshore. Five Japanese divebombers struck at the ship and three bombs hit amidships with an oil bomb exploding in the officers' saloon; Captains R.W.Dixon and A.H.Lawson were killed and Major F.J.Randall fatally injured. The air attacks lasted for about 30 minutes during which soldiers of 18 Recce helped man the ship's anti-aircraft guns in spite of intense heat and blinding smoke. The CO, Lieutenant Colonel H.A.Fitt, took charge of the defences against the Japanese aircraft, although badly burned himself, and inspired all on board by his example; he was later awarded the DSO.

When the attack was broken off the *Empress* was doomed, its upper structure blazing out of control. The order to abandon ship was given and many of 18 Recce's men were taken off by the destroyer, HMS *Yarra*. Others jumped into the sea and were picked up by small craft and taken to Singapore docks. Ashore without weapons or equipment, 18th Reconnaissance Battalion was lorried to billets and, after two days re-equipping, moved to a tented camp near Sembawang at the eastern end of Singapore island to be held in divisional reserve.

The division, less 53 Brigade, was holding the right flank of the northern area of Singapore island. The first Japanese landings on the island took place in the western sector at about 8.45pm on 8 February with about 13,000 troops during the night and another 10,000 after dawn. The heavily-outnumbered Australian defenders had to withdraw during the 9th. On the morning of 10 February elements of 18th Division were sent to assist the Australians and during the course of that day men of 18 Recce moved into front-line positions. Thomforce, an improvised formation under Lieutenant Colonel D.R.Thomas, was ordered to recapture Bukit Timah village which had fallen to the enemy. Thomforce consisted of two battalions of infantry with 18 Recce as its advance guard:

> The advance was led by ten wheeled carriers, which actually succeeded in entering the village; but several of them were then put out of action, either by tanks or anti-tank guns, and their commander, Lieutenant J.M.Wyse, was killed.
>
> The main body of the 18th Reconnaissance Battalion attacked astride the Bukit Timah road, with C Company (Captain A.F.Holt) on the right, and B Company (Captain R.O.Spencer) on the left, while A Company (Captain B.B.Dutton) carried out a left flanking movement. Few ... succeeded in crossing the railway, however, and in the afternoon of the 11th February Thomforce were ordered to withdraw. The three battalions took up a defensive position near the racecourse, north of the Bukit Timah road, about 6 pm.[3]

After further Japanese attacks General Percival ordered a further withdrawal on the 12th following attacks on the racecourse position during which 18 Recce's doctor, Captain J.V.Schofield, and padre, Rev. R.C.Chalk, were killed while tending wounded men. The battalion was withdrawn to Adam Road. The following day the main strength of the Japanese thrust came along the Pasir Panjang Ridge, on the left of the British positions. Eighteenth Recce was ordered into reserve but it was a short respite for, on the morning of the 14th, they took up defensive positions on Mount Pleasant road. On the northern area front 53 Brigade was forced back until, by the evening of the 13th, it was back in line with 18th Division which was holding a five-mile front on which there "had been much mixing of units as a result of the piecemeal way in which they had necessarily been withdrawn from the beach defences."[4]

On the divisional front there had been heavy and consistent Japanese pressure over two days and 1st Cambridgeshire Regiment was especially hard-pressed. In the early evening of the 13th a Japanese attack, supported by tanks and artillery, to the right of the Cambridgeshires succeeded in pushing through almost a mile to create a large salient within the British line. East of the McRitchie Reservoir another enemy attack gained some ground but this was taken back in a counter-attack. Further right, 53 Brigade's left flank was pushed back south of Braddell Road although the right flank held firm north of the road.

During the 14th the municipal water engineer, Mr Nurnane, informed General Percival that water supplies for Singapore were about to fail. Percival met the Governor who emphasised the dangers of the island suddenly losing its water, but Percival stated that he intended to fight on as long as possible. His decision was supported by the Supreme Commander, South-West Pacific who signalled:

> In all places where sufficiency of water exists for troops they must go on fighting.[5]

A later telegram stressed that:

> Your gallant stand is serving purpose and must be continued to limit of endurance.[6]

The water situation began to cause even more worries on the morning of 15 February when the Director General of Civil Defence declared his belief that there was only enough water for about 24 hours. Japanese infantry had infiltrated all sectors of 18th Division's front during the night, obtaining a foothold on Mount Pleasant Ridge where 18 Recce's positions remained intact. All troops were now fully committed to the struggle and, although there was no reserve, spirited counter-attacks, including recce men, pushed the Japanese out of some of their recently-won positions.

But the gallantry of so many of the defending soldiers was to no avail. As General Percival recorded:

> At 09.30 hours the Senior Commanders' Conference met at Fort Canning... A discussion on the general situation followed. The danger of the water situation, particularly as it affected the Indian troops and the vast civil population, was stressed. There was also the danger of a break-through into the crowded Town area if the Japanese delivered another determined attack. It was clearly no good remaining on the defensive as we were. As I viewed the situation, the alternatives were either (a) to counter-attack immediately to regain control of the reservoirs and of the military food depots and to drive back the enemy's artillery with a view to reducing the damage to the water supply system, or (b) to capitulate immediately. Formation commanders were unanimously of the opinion that in the existing circumstances a counter-attack was impracticable.
>
> I could see no immediate solution for the crucial water situation and decided to capitulate. The other members of the conference concurred unanimously with this decision.[7]

And so Singapore fell, to the surprise of many of its defenders who had believed that they would fight on to enable an evacuation to be organised or to gain time for reinforcements to arrive. The men of 18 Recce had played a gallant part in the hopeless defence of Singapore and many had died in the desperate fighting on the island. Survivors felt frustrated and angry at the surrender. One veteran wrote

> My contribution to the defence of Singapore lasted just two days with an

old Ross rifle, 50 rounds of ammo, and an Australian bush hat.

We were caught in heavy mortar fire in [Bukit Timah] road where my arm was rendered useless, and I was incapacitated for about 4 months, but by then we were guests of Nippon and our days of captivity had well and truly begun.[8]

The reconnoitrers marched into a cruel captivity that would claim many more lives than the battle for Singapore itself. By the end of the war 264 members of the regiment had died as prisoners against 55 killed at the time of the surrender of Singapore. Officers and men of 18 Recce were imprisoned in a camp at Changi until November 1942 when those fit to work were moved to Thailand to construct the Bangkok-Rangoon railway which task ceased in mid-1943 after which the prisoners were put to work in labour camps.

10
Turning point at Kohima

While the Italian campaign was bogged down in the mountains and valleys south of Rome, in Burma another enemy, the Japanese, were in the ascendant. In India reconnaissance regiments prepared for operations in Burma. Two regiments had come out from Britain and two from West Africa. Those from Britain were 2nd and 45th Regiments which were to see considerable action in 1944 in different operational rôles.

The 1944 battles to secure India's frontiers involved 2 Recce. Originally 6th Bn, The Loyal Regiment (North Lancs), a TA motorcycle unit, it had converted to recce on 6 May 1941. Under Lieutenant Colonel J.A.L.Powell (4th Hussars) the regiment sailed for India in the spring of 1942, arriving at Bombay at the beginning of June and was soon training at Poona.

Training was interrupted in August by internal security duties in Poona. Aware that the Congress party was planning a mass disobedience campaign, the authorities moved to forestall this by arresting the leaders on 9 August: Mahatma Gandhi was detained in the Aga Khan's palace at Poona and the town thus became a centre of unrest. Widespread rioting led to the equivalent of over 50 battalions being assigned to internal security.

The training programme for 2 Recce resumed in September, continued through into October and included exercises at the Battlecraft School at Ahmednagar. Squadrons were detached on IS duties on a daily basis for the first 12 days of November because of trouble at Yeravda Jail but training continued for the rest of the regiment. There was a further spell on IS duties in December because of dacoit, or bandit, activity at Belgaum where the regiment moved for jungle training in January 1943 by which time it was commanded by Lt Colonel J.M.K.Bradford of the Dorsets.

The pattern of training and IS duties continued into 1943 and 2 Recce returned to Poona in mid-May. June was devoted to combined operations training with B Squadron re-organising as a liaison squadron, with a large increase in wireless equipment. In September several Alligator amphibians were issued to the regiment as well as an amphibious jeep, the latter "for experimental purposes." At Ahmednagar an Alligator squadron was formed from A Squadron and exercises and demonstrations were carried out by the regiment which, by the end of November, had moved to Visapur. Re-organisation led to the creation of D Squadron, formed from the assault troops of A and B Squadrons plus an extra assault troop created from half the Anti-Tank Troop which had been reduced to a 6-gun establishment.

The Alligator was not popular: hard to control it was slow on both land

and water, lacked sufficient power to make headway against a tide and bogged easily on soft ground; two other Alligators were then needed to tow it out. Although it could carry 24 fully-armed men, or 4,500 lbs of cargo, its disadvantages, including its noisiness but most of all its lack of armour, made it unsuitable as a fighting vehicle. The regiment considered that it could not be used where "the element of surprise is required" but might possibly be used to ferry troops across muddy water under supporting fire, or where surprise might be gained by crossing in an unexpected place, or over ground considered impassable. The most suitable use was considered to be that of "an amphibious tractor" following up in advances over swamps and creeks with heavy stores and ammunition, and being available to carry troops over creeks. In spite of this C Squadron was also converted to Alligators in January.

On 22 January 1944, Lord Mountbatten inspected the regiment and, on the same day, A Squadron was assigned to 36th Division and moved to Calcutta to be followed by C Squadron in preparation for an operation in the Arakan. Late in February this operation was cancelled and A and C Squadrons left their Alligators at Calcutta to return to Ahmednagar.

When the Japanese crossed the Chindwin in March A, B and C Squadrons reformed as reconnaissance squadrons and the regiment moved to Dimapur. By then the Japanese were advancing on Kohima in Assam: General Mutaguchi had launched his Operation U GO, which he grandly styled the 'March on Delhi.' Kohima sits on on a ridge about 5,000 feet high and is surrounded by higher hills: the Chin Hills, to the east, are some 3000 feet higher while Mount Pulebadze, to the south-west, is more than 5000 feet higher. The strategic importance of Kohima was its location midway along the road from Dimapur, site of a main supply depot and railhead, to the garrison town of Imphal. High-level decisions had been made that would leave Kohima almost without a garrison but fortunately the Assam Regiment, at great cost, delayed the Japanese advance long enough for those decisions to be reversed and a brigade moved to Kohima in time to meet the Japanese onslaught.

General Slim, commanding Fourteenth Army, considered that the Japanese could be at Kohima by 3 April and might then advance to Dimapur in a week. At Slim's request, India Command agreed to send XXXIII Corps to assist at Imphal and Kohima: the corps consisted of 2nd Division, then based in Western India, under Major General Grover and four independent brigades. By 4 April, after a remarkable operation, leading elements of 2nd Division were arriving at Dimapur and two days later the first major Japanese attack was launched on Kohima. The attackers took Jail Hill and advanced on several tactically important positions, threatening to break through the defending 4th Royal West Kents. The West Kents held on grimly and launched local counter-attacks; by 8 April the Japanese had cut the road from Kohima to Dimapur at Zubza thus effectively isolating the garrison.

It was from near Zubza that the first elements of 2nd Division advanced to Kohima: 5 Brigade moved off on 10 April and were in action the following day. A few days later, 2 Recce moved out of Dimapur and deployed to defend the road to Kohima. While A Squadron under Captain J.F.Hulton was assigned 18 miles of that road, the main body of 2 Recce - still divided into four squadrons plus HQ Squadron - was concentrated into a defensive box at Zubza. A Squadron first came under fire on 18 April when Japanese soldiers fired at vehicles on the road to Kohima but there were no casualties. A week later HQ Squadron moved to Punjab Ridge and D Squadron to Lone Tree Hill.

At the beginning of May the regiment was covering the southern flank at Jotsoma, sending out recce patrols and mortaring enemy positions. May saw many actions involving 2 Recce's men: patrols spotted Japanese troops and found maps on the 4th; wireless sets were found on the 12th and on 27 May patrols from D Squadron assaulted a Japanese position, killing five enemy soldiers who had been surprised while cooking a meal. But the regiment's major activity was to clear the Japanese from Pulebadze ridge and turn the flank of their position on the Aradura Spur. This operation, under the command of Colonel Bradford, began on 11 May, and eventually involved the entire regiment. By that time the arrival of 2nd Division had ended the siege of Kohima; the Royal West Kents, the Assam Regiment and Assam Rifles had held out for 13 days against the full strength of General Sato's 31st Division which had been advancing towards Imphal. Thereafter the Japanese were on the defensive as the battle for Kohima continued.

The Aradura Spur had been held by the Japanese from an early stage in the fighting around Kohima. On and about the Spur, and the nearby GPT Ridge, Sato had deployed an infantry regiment - equivalent to a British brigade - and a mountain artillery battery. Earlier attacks on the Spur, and the effects of attrition generally in the battle, had much reduced the strength of the regiment at Aradura by the time of 2 Recce's attack. Nonetheless, the Japanese fought tenaciously, accepting high casualty levels to hold their positions, but 2 Recce's endeavours were to reap success and turn the Japanese flank although the regiment never actually got on to the Spur itself. Colonel Bradford, who was awarded the DSO for his part in the action, wrote an account of his regiment's endeavours in the battle and described the initial chaos with "two hundred and fifty porters trying to find loads - stores still arriving - and a unit organised to run on petrol trying to control porters."[1] Due to "hopelessly" inaccurate maps the expedition relied on Naga guides - the local tribespeople who remained loyal to Britain - to lead it through dense jungle. The conditions were unbelievable and when the CO "saw what the country was like I revised all

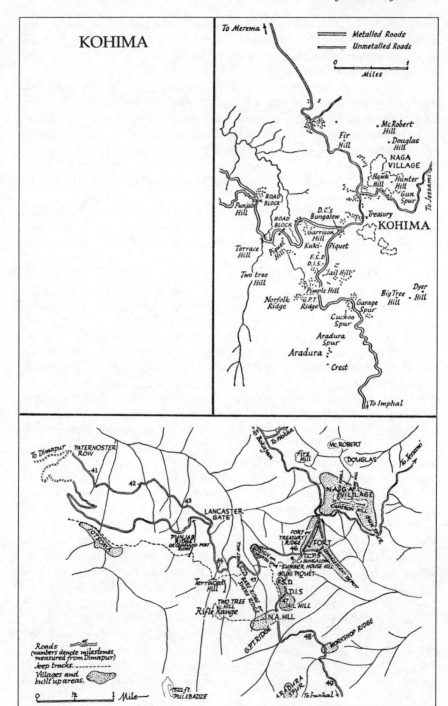

KOHIMA

previous ideas I had had of time."[2] The battle of Kohima was also fought
during the monsoon season: the received wisdom was that operations were
impossible in such conditions but, like the myth that had precluded jungle
warfare training, this also proved untrue.

At first it seemed that the Japanese had no real idea of the strength of 2
Recce: "he probably thought it was just a patrol which would soon go
away."[3] But the Japanese were always aggressive and on 28 May they
attacked at the junction of A and HQ Squadrons and a seven-hour battle
ensued: at the end of it the enemy withdrew leaving seven dead and six
wounded while 2 Recce had lost ten killed and 19 wounded. Next day a
patrol under Lieutenant Henderson killed four Japanese and wounded
three others.

On the last day of the month another battle, lasting from 4.25pm until
9.00pm, left 14 Japanese dead and 23 wounded against 2 Recce's losses of
one dead and four wounded. The battle began when Colonel Bradford and
Major Peter Wells set out to recce a position to which the latter's squadron
was to move the following day to protect the regiment's supply line:

> We walked along the ridge admiring the huge view, east to the Chind
> and Naga Hills and west down into the cloud-covered Brahmaputra
> valley. It was a lovely clear sunny day.
>
> We got to the hill we were going to look at when, crack! - not fifteen
> yards ahead. No doubt about that, the Jap was already there. I had been
> thinking, as I had thought many times before, that this was in every way
> the best place for the Jap to cut our supply route. It had the gentlest way
> up, very steep at that, and it was hidden by trees so we could not see
> movement on it. Sadly, my leading chap [Tpr Bunce] was hit. The burst
> knocked us over, and rolled us down the hill on to a lower track which
> the Jap could not see. We dived into the bushes and further down the
> hill, doubled back a bit on our tracks and lay up.
>
> From then on there was pretty continuous firing all along the ridge. ...I
> thought B Squadron were being heavily attacked a mile and a half away
> across a big valley...[4]

It was after 10 o'clock that night before the CO and his party could get
back to the relative safety of their own positions; both the colonel and Peter
Wells had been wounded but refused evacuation.:

> It was soon clear that the Jap had put in quite a strong attack on the
> whole of our positions. There had been action the whole way round. At
> dusk he again withdrew, except across the ridge at our back. He had
> taken a pretty fair knock - that was clear by the amount of equipment of
> his which was already in our hands. Next day patrols brought in much
> more. The men were in great form and obviously pleased with their
> efforts. Our casualties were practically nil, for which I was very thankful

as, if we had had many stretcher cases, there would have been a most difficult problem to solve.[5]

That same day 2 Recce received orders to withdraw to a location where they could be supplied more easily while continuing to exert pressure on the enemy further south. The withdrawal, over two miles, took some 20 hours, such was the country in which they were operating. Everyone was confident that the Japanese, their 31st Division virtually shattered, would soon have to withdraw from the Kohima area. And so it happened: on 3 June the Battle of Kohima ended. Second Division's commander, Major General Grover, described the battleground as being like the Somme in the Great War; the pleasant hill town of Kohima had been turned into a nightmare scene of destruction, and skeletal trees added to the air of desolation. But the Japanese advance had been fought to a standstill by the defenders of Kohima, and Imphal had been saved; the siege there would be raised three weeks later. General Slim's Fourteenth Army could now move over to the offensive.

In the first ten days of June the intensity of operations reduced for the regiment and squadrons were relieved in turn to rest. The divisional commander wrote to Colonel Bradford to congratulate 2 Recce on its performance:

> I am well aware how severe and testing were the conditions under which your Regiment had to move and operate. The going was... only just possible, and in wet weather almost impossible. Everyone was constantly wet, with little or no shelter, and at times short of supplies and even water.
>
> ...your Regiment stuck determinedly, for some three weeks, to their task... [and] made the most valuable contribution to the operations... by their determined threat to the enemy's weakest flank...
>
> Your Regiment may well be proud of its achievements during their three weeks or so on the Pulebadze Ridge, and I am glad to know that in the end they secured, not only the Pulebadze feature itself, but also the features which form the top of the Aradura Spur and which were their primary objective.[6]

On the 12th, a day after moving to Mao, two troops of B Squadron set out to recce the western slopes of Tarhazu and a stream junction while 9 Troop of D Squadron, under Lieutenant Tarmey (later awarded the MC for his inspiring leadership between 26 April and 15 June), moved off to recce east of Khakhama for an advance by the regiment on Viswema. The proposed route was impassable and the troop returned next morning.

Lieutenant Amos's anti-tank troop tried a westward route around Tarhazu early on the 14th and reached the summit of the ridge without seeing any Japanese. At 8.30 that morning 2 Recce, with a half squadron of Grant tanks from 149 Regiment, RAC, moved off as the advance guard of the division. While one squadron recce'd with the leading tanks the others deployed to clear features to the flanks. Recce patrols were sent to check routes and seek out enemy positions and over the next few days there were a number of skirmishes with Japanese troops; a "very weak" Japanese prisoner was brought in by a patrol under Sergeant Hampson and identified as belonging to 5 Company, 2nd Bn, 124th Regiment. On the 18th A and B Squadrons took over from 1st Royal Welch Fusiliers and headed for Tuphema which they occupied at 10.30am and consolidated. By noon they had been joined by C and D Squadrons and RHQ, and the regiment formed defensive positions at Tuphema sending out patrols, one of which located considerable enemy dumps at West Chabumei. On the 20th 2 Recce moved up the Dimapur-Imphal road and C and D Squadrons set out to patrol the Barak river valley to Karong, intending to seize and hold a bridge to prevent its demolition by the Japanese. Bad weather conditions and extremely difficult terrain led to the operation being abandoned and the squadrons were recalled next morning.

On the morning of 22 June C and D Squadrons, with RHQ, were to move down the road to Imphal, then flank left to rejoin the road but before this could happen 2nd Division and Imphal Force met up; the struggle for Imphal was also over and the Japanese were well and truly on the retreat in Burma. Patrols over the next four days found much evidence of a hasty Japanese withdrawal. At 10.30am on the the 23rd, 17 Troop, D Squadron brought in four prisoners, three of whom were wounded and in very bad condition, and one exhausted. Another five dead enemy soldiers were found with quantities of equipment, including six lorries, three of them in working order. Documents and a marked map were found next day while a patrol from A Squadron discovered four badly-decomposed Japanese bodies west of the road. On three successive days, 24 to 26 June, patrols skirmished with small groups of Japanese; six Japanese were killed, two taken prisoner and one found dead. Active patrolling, sometimes over very difficult country, continued into early July when 2nd Division went into reserve and 2 Recce was withdrawn to rest and refit on the Kohima-Imphal road where it remained for a week before beginning a lengthy training programme. The division was too heavily vehicled to tackle the country between Imphal and the Chindwin as there was no passable road at that time although a new road was being constructed. Training continued in monsoon conditions, with emphasis on the lessons of the fighting during May and June, until early October although there were some squadron deployments in September that did not lead to active operations. This included patrolling:

> ...down to the Chindwin north and south of Homalin. I cannot remember why. Maybe it was either to mislead as to future plans on the crossing of the Chindwin, or to cover possible routes out for the

Chindits.[7]

D Squadron was disbanded on 14 October and its personnel distributed through the other squadrons while the regiment re-organised on a light reconnaissance regiment war establishment. A move to Moreh took place on 25 November followed, a day later, by another move, this time to Yazagyo from where some of the signals troop was detached to V Force until 20 December for long-range penetration patrols. On 21 December the regiment crossed the Chindwin over the longest pontoon bridge yet built and, with C Squadron deployed to defend Mutaik airstrip from the 21st, B Squadron, under 6 Brigade command took Pyingaing unopposed on Christmas Eve.

Two days after Christmas the regiment finally began operating in its true mobile recce rôle. A Squadron passed to 6 Brigade on the 28th to provide flank protection for the brigade's advance towards Kaduma which was reached two days later and, on the last day of 1944, the remainder of the regiment was ordered to Kaduma from where it was to capture Ye-U airstrip. This task was to be undertaken in conjunction with advances by 5 and 6 Brigades, the former to Kabo weir and the latter to Ye-U. In spite of a shortage of vehicles - the regiment was still virtually an infantry battalion - A Squadron had occupied the village near the airstrip by 5.00pm on 3 January 1945 and was joined next day by the remainder of the regiment. It was hoped that 2 Recce would remain at Ye-U until its hoped-for vehicles arrived but only ten scout cars were received, and patrolling was ordered to clear as far as the Mu river, east of the airstrip. A patrol of Lieutenant Hassell, the intelligence officer, and Sergeant Anderson (who commanded an attached platoon of Burma Intelligence Corps) found the area clear and the regiment prepared for its next task which was in the reconnaissance rôle: after the capture of Shwebo a break out to the south was planned, using 2 Recce as the spearhead to regain contact with the retreating enemy.

Shwebo was taken on 10 January and the break out was scheduled for the 14th. As a result of recces it was decided to concentrate south of Shwebo. Under command were two batteries of 99th Field Regiment, a troop of 6-pounders from 100th Light Anti-Aircraft/Anti-Tank Regiment, detachments of RE, RAMC and RASC, the latter providing carriers to move the regiment which had only sufficient vehicles to make one squadron and part of RHQ mobile. This force, dubbed Bradforce after the CO, was to have armoured support from a half squadron of 3rd Dragoon Guards. The main axis of the advance was along the Shwebo-Mandalay road.

All went to plan but with no contact with the Japanese for the first two days. Then, on 16 January, a C Squadron patrol reached Yetwingaung and began to search high, rocky ground, inaccessible to vehicles. Japanese troops were spotted and B Squadron's commander sent a fighting patrol, supported by 3-inch mortars from Kyamingi, to tackle the enemy post. As the country was "very thick," restricting visibility to a few hundred yards, a

patrol from C Squadron under Lieutenant Henderson was to control the
mortar shoot by wireless from the east side of the hill. That involved the
patrol radioing back to the squadron which would then relay the
information via its forward link to the mortars. Although the first round
nearly hit the C Squadron patrol the shoot was successful and the assault
troop was able to get in and occupy the enemy position: one Japanese
soldier was killed in the infantry attack.

The advance resumed on the 17th in spite of difficult terrain which
meant that A Squadron's patrolling was on foot. A Squadron's assault
troop, moving in lorries, chased a Japanese OP party from one hilltop so
quickly that the enemy left their dinner on the boil. Another troop noted
large parties of Japanese moving along the main road to Nandwin and
called in an air strike although the enemy disappeared before the aircraft
arrived. By the end of the day 2 Recce was so heavily committed to
occupying positions due to be handed over to 4 Brigade that no further
offensive action, except by patrols, was possible until the relief took place.

> The Japs were holding the ground lightly with a large backing of
> mortars and artillery. He gave ground as soon as pressure was brought
> to bear. He carried out no counter patrolling. His sole counter measures
> were artillery and mortar fire which he directed on his own vacated
> positions. This has been a particular characteristic in this area.[8]

On 18 January, 2nd Division ordered the regiment to hold Point 547, to
patrol to Kinywa and remain in position until relieved by 100 LAA/A-Tk
Regiment, and to take over responsibility for the area from Point 547 to
Sheinmaga on the Irrawaddy river. These tasks were carried out and the
two batteries of 100th Field Regiment ceased to be under 2 Recce's
command, being replaced by a battery of 10th Field Regiment, 2nd
Manchesters, less two companies, and a troop from 100th AA/A-Tk
Regiment.

From 20 January, for a five-week period, the regiment was "to give the
impression that an effort was to be made to attack the Sagaing Hills from
the north."[9]

> The way we operated was to tow scrubs behind vehicles putting up
> clouds of dust. Our signal network was used to transmit pre-prepared
> coded messages at set times and from set locations.[10]

Active patrolling and artillery fire also entered the equation while
squadrons searched for enemy positions in their areas and harassed the
Japanese with ambush parties. Enemy positions were located at Pagyi,
Padu, Taungyin and on Point 725. At Pagyi on 23 January Lieutenant
Baker's troop from A Squadron struck at the Japanese with 3-inch mortars.
The patrol then withdrew after coming under accurate shellfire from a
ridge to the south. Although the Japanese carried out much shelling over
this period it was largely indiscriminate and unco-ordinated. While such

diversionary activities were being carried out, Ondaw was captured on the 24th. The regiment lost its first two dead of the year when Lieutenant Fitzwater and Sergeant Wolstenholme were killed by booby traps on 22 January.

More active operations came on 28 January when B and C Squadrons attacked Padu and Taungyin respectively. B Squadron approached Padu in carriers, noted the enemy positions and then withdrew to conduct a highly successful mortar shoot. C Squadron sent two recce troops, under Lieutenants Henderson and Kirby, to Taungyin and the south while an assault troop in carriers with 3-inch mortars moved up close behind into the hills:

> On entry of village six Japs ran out to hills. The village was cleared and patrols pushed up towards hills. Meanwhile the Assault Troop (Lieut Johnson) debussed and moved into the area where the Japs had gone. A close quarter fight took place in which 13 Japs were killed. The force withdrew unmolested except for snipers and being chased by shells. Our casualties were one killed, four wounded (including Lieut Johnson). The result of this day's work was that the Japs evacuated Padu and Taungyin except for occasional patrols, and withdrew to other positions outside.[11]

Patrolling continued to the end of the month by which time the units that had been under command of 2 Recce, including the attached RASC vehicles, had departed. At the beginning of February the regiment was still covering 2nd Division's left flank from Point 547 to Sheinmaga on the Irrawaddy to maintain pressure on the Japanese and report any indications of an enemy build up. Further deception activities were carried out during much of the month and the Japanese remained "completely inactive" for many days at a time. The regiment's work was assisted by a number of Burmese interpreters who went out on every patrol and were engaged in some sharp close-quarter battles.

Close liaison with the RAF on Sadaung airstrip led to two pilots joining the regiment on active operations while officers and NCOs of 2 Recce went aloft in Beaufighters on reconnaissance and, on a number of occasions, guided pilots to strafe Japanese locations which they had themselves located on the ground. On 22 February 2nd Division crossed the Irrawaddy and the regiment, less C Squadron, began to move towards the river ready to cross.

At that stage the Japanese became very active in front of C Squadron, which had an infantry company of the Nepalese Mahundra Dal Regiment from 281 Brigade under its command. This enemy activity seemed to be intended to force troops leftward to watch the flank, and to cover the Japanese withdrawal in front of 19th Division, north of Mandalay. On 24 February C Squadron, under Major K.G.Hook, with A Company, Mahundra Dal Regiment, became Hookforce which later reached battalion strength. Hookforce was the only cover for the RAF airstrip at Sadaung and for Corps HQ a little further south. Japanese activity included re-occupying Padu, 'jitter' parties around Hookforce's positions and some recce patrols but, surprisingly, there were no serious offensive operations.

Hookforce, strengthened by 53 Deception Company on 2 March, suffered a number of casualties at the end of February. A patrol under Sergeant Howard moved out for Ywathitkale and Indaung; half a mile from the latter Howard dropped off a half-section with a Bren gun and went forward with four other men and two local guides to observe the village. About twenty minutes later the Bren group heard machine-gun and mortar fire followed by two bursts of Sten-gun fire. A patrol failed to find Howard and his men but spotted a Japanese machine-gun in an ambush position. Local reports that Howard had been killed by mortar fire and that one of the guides had been tied to a tree before being killed were received and the men were presumed dead. Their bodies were found and buried on 8 March. Hookforce remained responsible for the area until 11 March by which time 19th Division had reached Mandalay and Hookforce was disbanded. Throughout the month of March the regiment continued active patrolling. On 27 February it had been ordered to relieve a battalion on Ngazun island but, as a result of 20th Division's rapid advance, orders were changed on 2 March; 2nd Division was to break out eastwards with 2 Recce ordered to regain contact with the enemy and provide information on dispositions and strength between the river and the high east-west ridge from Fort Henry while maintaining contact with 20th Division. Over the next week this area was patrolled aggressively with many engagements with Japanese infantry; the enemy artillery regularly fired on patrols with mortars joining in from time to time. As soon as the infantry brigades were in their jumping-off positions, 2 Recce moved to Fort Henry to be on the divisional right flank although still covering the entire area.

A day before the advance a carrier patrol of B Squadron under Lieutenant Watson reached Nabebin and reported the area clear and 6 Brigade used their route for a long advance the following day. However, other patrols encountered stiff opposition two miles east and south-east of Fort Henry and a patrol under Lieutenant Tarmey had a close-quarter encounter in which they inflicted many casualties on the enemy before Japanese reinforcements caused a withdrawal. Corporal McAleer was awarded the MM for his part in this action and Sergeant Rothwell of A Squadron won the DCM in a series of bitter actions fought by Lieutenant Frank Sutton's troop of A Squadron. The troop had developed the tactic of driving into enemy positions with Brens firing before dismounting and rolling grenades into Japanese bunkers. In spite of the number of actions, and the amount of shellfire, 2 Recce suffered surprisingly few casualties. On 11 March, however, between Tamabin and Letpanbin an A Squadron patrol came under fire from light machine-guns, "extremely accurate" mortars and 75mm guns. A 75mm shell bursting near an LRC claimed the life of the car commander and knocked out the troop commander's car. Next day it was decided to sidestep the opposition as 6 Brigade had got through without contact and 20th Division had also advanced rapidly, bypassing this pocket of opposition. So 2 Recce moved south to tackle the pocket from that direction and protect 20th Division's main line of communication as the division fought outside Mandalay. In the middle of March the regiment spent three days in vehicle and weapon maintenance at Thayetkon before resuming operations under 20th Division on 19 March. Deploying on the left flank of 20th Division, which put it between 2nd and 20th Divisions, the regiment was to cover the latter as it turned south to Kyaukse. There were no contacts until 23 March when Lieutenant Anderson of A Squadron led a patrol to Monbaung and Ywatha where small parties of enemy soldiers were seen running away. Pushing on to Pingya, Anderson's patrol came under fire from three machine-guns on the east bank of the Ziangyi river and from snipers on the west bank. Four recce men were killed and another wounded, but the patrol called for mortar fire on the enemy positions which were rapidly vacated. Some further contacts occurred that same day which proved to be a very hectic one for the regiment.

B Squadron was detached to 5 Brigade to recce for its advance to Myingan and thence to Natogyi. Performing this rôle until 10 April the squadron was actively engaged along 5 Brigade's line of advance, being first to encounter the Japanese on several occasions. On another occasion B Squadron's men recce'd a route to bypass Taungtha which they then occupied until relieved by the brigade, whereupon they again advanced, occupying Kabatywa until relieved. Further recce patrols from Kabatywa found Japanese dug in at Legyi but routes were found around the flanks and when 5 Brigade moved up the squadron was released to return to its regiment.

The remainder of the regiment had been recce'ing in preparation for an advance by 4 Brigade to Natogyi. Its first patrols, on 25 March, found strong Japanese positions south of Myotha and west of Pyinzi. A day later 2 Recce with a troop of 25-pounders, a company of Lancashire Fusiliers, and a machine-gun platoon moved to Pyinzi and sent patrols westward from there. At milestone 30, contact was made with Japanese soldiers covering a bridge but C Squadron's assault troop cleared the bridge before encountering more enemy positions beyond. Northward patrols also encountered enemy troops although those travelling southward found the area clear but were shelled while returning. Over the next few days recce patrols did invaluable work in penetrating behind the Japanese positions and locating their main line of communication as well as locations of concentrations of enemy forces.

By now the battle for Taungtha was over and, on 29 March, contact was made with elements of 268 Brigade advancing south from Myotha against spirited Japanese opposition. It was hoped that the Myingan-Taungtha-Mahlaing-Meiktila road might be open which would allow a column to head for Meiktila and so 4 Brigade was ordered to send a battalion group to Mahlaing. C Squadron was despatched to recce the route to Mahlaing on 30 March. The route was clear and an armoured column moved off next day with C Squadron recce'ing ahead to find that the Meiktila column "was pouring down the road from Taungtha."

Although the Myotha-Pyinzi-Myingan triangle was clear there were still numbers of Japanese troops from 118th Regiment in villages around Nyaungok and for the next week 4 Brigade and 2 Recce patrols cut off and harried these Japanese as they tried to slip out of the net. Many casualties were inflicted on the enemy before the regiment was withdrawn on 7 April, by which time the area was clear. The last operation was fought by B Squadron as it supported 5 Brigade in its capture of Mr Popa.

As ever in Burma the regiment had suffered from deficiencies in its vehicular strength:

> ...the main difficulties were again lack of suitable and operationally sound vehicles. Carriers were taken over from the RASC platoon and driven by Regimental drivers. There were sufficient for only four Carrier Troops. The scout cars were also mechanically unsound, and numbers dropped to ten, sufficient for only two Troops. The result was that the same Troops were continually on patrol. The three Jeep Troops could only be used on certain occasions. In spite of this both carriers and scout cars stood up exceptionally well to all types of fire. The great deficiency was hitting power of a heavy nature. The lack of it was continually felt.[12]

No-one knew it at the time but 2 Recce had finished active operations. During May, when Rangoon fell (sandwiched between the German surrenders in Italy and North-West Europe, this achievement was pushed off the front pages at home and added to Fourteenth Army's sense of isolation, summed up in its self-applied soubriquet of 'the Forgotten Army') the regiment was at Kanchrapara re-organising for an operation which was cancelled. It then moved, for training, to Kamareddi where, in June, it said goodbye to Colonel Bradford, DSO, who was promoted to command 51 Indian Infantry Brigade, being succeeded by Major J.S.Walker.

The war ended in August although there were still clearing-up operations to be carried out. These did not involve 2 Recce which remained in Burma until November before sailing for Malaya. The regiment arrived at Singapore on 23 November and began training at Kanzar Kahang. On 11 December it moved to Selerang Barracks on Singapore island and later in the month helped police deal with civil disturbances. The regiment arrested a number of looters and shot dead two others at the Red Cross stores.

During 1946 2nd Reconnaissance Regiment was reduced in strength and eventually disbanded. The regiment's time in action may have been relatively short but it had the distinction of taking part in one of the decisive battles of the Second World War - and one of its bloodiest - and the inscription on its division's memorial on Garrison Hill at Kohima is eloquent testimony to the men who died there:

> When you go home
> Tell them of us and say
> For your tomorrow
> We gave our today.

11
Jungle green - Burma warriors

While 2 Recce had the longest spell in action of any reconnaissance regiment in Burma they had been preceded into battle by 45 Recce in a rôle totally different from that of a normal Reconnaissance Corps regiment.

In early 1943 Orde Wingate and Mike Calvert had carried out the first Chindit expedition - Operation LONGCLOTH - taking British troops behind Japanese lines into the jungles of central Burma. The operation increased morale among British soldiers in the theatre, proved that the Japanese were not invincible in the jungle and made the Japanese pay more attention to their lines of communication. It also provided several valuable lessons, not least of which was that a sizeable force could be maintained in the jungle by air support; other lessons concerned diet, mule transport and the importance of wireless communication. (LONGCLOTH had also opened Japanese eyes to the possibility of operations in what had been regarded as the impassable terrain of India's eastern frontier and led to Japanese operations in that area in 1944.)

But perhaps the most important effect of the Chindits' operation had been in the mind of Winston Churchill: the concept fired the prime minister's imagination and brought his approval for Wingate's proposal for long range penetration groups; American support was also forthcoming. This led to the 1944 Chindit campaign in which 45 Recce served in a totally unexpected rôle.

In April 1941, 45th Reconnaissance Battalion had been formed from anti-tank companies of 45th (West Country) Division. When 45 Recce sailed to India on board MV *Dominion Monarch* in August 1942 it joined 70th Division which, as 6th Division, had earlier served in North Africa. In late 1942 and early 1943 the regiment participated in exercises that brought home many valuable lessons: the need for camouflage and immediate dispersal at all halts; the need to harbour away from villages to avoid malaria; and the difficulty of maintaining contact over distances as the use of wireless was not permitted, except in cypher, since Japanese wireless operators could read morse. During February 1943, 45 Recce carried out internal security duties due to the condition of Gandhi who was on hunger strike.

The regiment also adopted some distinctive features. At Ranchi on 29 April a topee flash, a vertical yellow arrow on a green diamond, was adopted. Three days after a parade to mark victory in North Africa - Tunisia Day - a divisional sign in the form of a red cloth star on the right shoulder, the badge of the former 6th Division, was issued. And in early June an adaptation was made to the topee for LRC crews: the front brim was removed and a shock-absorbing buffer fitted instead. From Ranchi the regiment went to Bangalore at the beginning of August and took part in Exercise TRUMPET II after which it was highly praised by the corps commander:

> At the Corps Commander's conference on this exercise he didn't stop to give single compliments for the Regiment but handed them out in dozens even going so far as to tell the CO that this Regiment is the only one in the Corps which has any idea of how to use country.[1]

At Bangalore the divisional commander, Major General Symes, told the regiment that 70th Division had been selected for LRPG duties by the Prime Minister. The division was therefore to re-organise as the British element of 3rd Indian Division, or Special Force, the official designation for the Chindits. The recce regiment was given the option of disbanding or converting to Chindits and decided on the latter becoming part of 16 Brigade whose commander, Colonel Bernard Fergusson, then spoke to them on the long range penetration rôle.

By the end of November training for the new rôle was underway. The regiment had re-organised to suit this rôle with C Squadron detached to reinforce a gunner regiment and many operators and drivers transferred to brigade HQ or other units. The CO, Lieutenant Colonel Trotter, his 2ic and the senior squadron leader moved to new appointments and the remnants of A and B Squadrons formed 45 and 54 Columns.

On 6 December, Lance Corporal F.J.Pugh with Troopers P.R.Egbers, J.Fleming, J.W.Laird and F.J.O'Brien were drowned in Gangan reservoir, Pugh and O'Brien while trying to rescue Fleming, but training continued with airdrops, river crossings - by day and night - and punishing marches through jungle carrying heavy packs. It was quite a culture shock for men who had been trained for the recce rôle:

> ...we had to hand in all the vehicles and got mules and ponies - quite a change, footslogging with a 70lb pack on your back, from driving along in a Bren-gun carrier.[2]

Proposals for the operational use of the Chindits in 1944 were still being discussed, as was the overall strategy in Burma. Wingate produced his assessment of events in the theatre in 1944, assuming - correctly - that the Japanese would attack Kohima and Imphal with the intention of breaking through into India. That could allow the Chindits to play a major rôle and his fertile brain produced the 'Stronghold' plan. He envisaged strongholds for operations being established in wild country far enough from roads or railways to hamper Japanese deployment of artillery or tanks against them; re-supply would be by airdrop. Each stronghold would also need clean water and a sufficiently large flat area on which to build an airstrip for C47

Dakotas to bring in supplies and fly out casualties. With Mountbatten's approval, this idea became Operation THURSDAY and details were agreed on 18 January 1944. Fergusson's men would march in to the Indaw area from Ledo and so 16 Brigade moved into Assam in late January; the final phase of their training took place from 10 to 19 January. Mountbatten and Wingate visited the Regiment on the 17th. Men and mules were pronounced "very fit" and ready for operations. There was a final concert on 8 February at Ledo which was "quite enjoyable [with] some lusty community singing."[3]

Two days later Fergusson's brigade set out: the brigade included 1st Queen's Royal Regiment, 2nd Leicesters, and gunners acting as infantry as well as 45 Recce; each unit provided two columns. They were to capture Japanese airfields at Indaw but would also detach two columns from the march to seize the Japanese outpost of Lonkin facing 'Vinegar Joe' Stilwell's Chinese forces. At the end of their march 16 Brigade would reach the stronghold codenamed 'Aberdeen' from which the attacks on Indaw were to be launched. The other two brigades to be committed in the initial phase of THURSDAY, 77 and 111, were to be flown in behind enemy lines; only 16 Brigade was to march in.

The diversion to Lonkin served no real purpose other than delaying the progress of the brigade; 45 and 54 Columns, commanded by Lieutenant Colonel C.R.Cumberlege and Major R.A.G.Varcoe respectively, crossed the Chindwin on 3 and 4 March, helped by inflatable craft dropped by aircraft. RAF liaison officers accompanied columns to co-ordinate the airdrops needed to re-supply the Chindits. On the 4th, light planes landed on a sandbank to evacuate sick and take out mail; two officers were also flown in to rejoin the regiment. On 20 March leading elements of 16 Brigade reached 'Aberdeen,' two weeks behind the timing of the original plan; 45 Recce's two columns were two days further behind, with those columns diverted to Lonkin another eight days behind.

Although the brigade was below strength, Wingate, who met Fergusson at 'Aberdeen' on 20 March, insisted that they attack Indaw immediately to obtain the greatest possible tactical advantage. This was a change from the original plan which had allowed for a period of consolidation before attacking. Fergusson asked for a few days to evacuate men who were either sick or physically worn out; Wingate refused and insisted on the attack. As Robert Hand noted they:

> ...had marched into Burma over mountains [of] 5,000 and 6,000 feet. We had 70 miles of this till we got to the Chindwin river. After we crossed it, the going was better. I think we marched another 380 miles to our objective [the total march was over 400 miles] and then started to fight the Japs, not even a day's rest.[4]

That march itself had been an epic undertaking through an area where even today maps fail to indicate the exact nature of upland areas. Robert Hand and his comrades had marched across two mountain ranges, the Patkai Bum and the Sangpaw Bum, with gradients of one in two, tropical heat in the valleys and freezing cold on the heights. Commando engineers had done an excellent job of cutting steps into slopes, creating traverses and building bridges. Without their efforts the brigade could not have carried out its march.

Wingate's change of plan was a result of the worsening situation at Imphal and Kohima. He believed that 16 Brigade, by attacking immediately, could draw some of the pressure from the defenders of both strongholds. Wingate also obtained permission for another brigade to be flown into 'Aberdeen' as soon as possible and the first unit of 14 Brigade arrived there on 23 March. To Fergusson's chagrin, Brigadier Brodie's formation had no orders to assist 16 Brigade.

By the time 14 Brigade started to arrive, Fergusson's men were on their way to attack Indaw. Unfortunately, because they had been sent forward so soon, no proper reconnaissance had been made and the Queen's and Leicesters columns suffered badly from the absence of water on their route. The recce columns were at Manhton when they received Fergusson's orders to attack Indaw on 22 March. Five Troop were already recce'ing the Maingpok area when 45 Column met the enemy on the 25th at Auktaw. No Japanese sentries had been encountered and so the presence of Japanese troops and men of the Japanese-recruited Burma National Army took the column by surprise. The enemy were equally surprised. Confused fighting began in which Lieutenants Ryley and Dickinson were killed but the arrival of part of 17 Column from the Leicesters to support the recce columns allowed an attack on Auktaw to be launched with the Leicesters clearing the village at bayonet-point.

The brigadier had planned a rendezvous at Auktaw from where the Queen's columns would strike out to the west of Indaw and those from the Leicesters and 45 Recce to the east, moving along the narrow, tree-clad Kyaung ridge. But, once again, plans were changed and 45 Recce was ordered to head instead for Thetkegyin on Lake Indaw's northern shores to obtain water for mules and men since it had been discovered that Auktaw forest in March was like a desert, all streams and lakes having dried up. En route, the columns ran into Japanese defensive positions. At Auktaw, as we have seen, the Japanese were driven out, but Thetkegyin was defended with determination by a small group of Japanese soldiers. A two day battle raged over 26/27 March. Mules carrying 54 Column's flamethrowers were hit by mortars and blazed immediately, setting off ammunition, including grenades and mortar bombs. Although the column inflicted casualties on the enemy, 86 of whom were killed, it also suffered heavily and was forced to withdraw. The action became known as 'the battle of the water bottles:'

As soon as a Jap was killed his water bottle was taken away whenever possible and given to the wounded. Every single approach to water courses was covered by the enemy. About twenty claimed to have shot a Jap officer who had advanced madly in the open with his sword raised. We heard of the machine-gunner [the only member of his crew to survive] who never left his gun for forty-eight hours and stayed in position when the jungle around him was blazing, and the rubber pipe on his gun was melting with the heat; of the others who dug all night long, after fighting two days, for water for the wounded and at last found enough muddy water to ease their thirst. I was shown the bullocks on whom wounded were strapped and brought safely out.[5]

Not until 1 April did 54 Column arrive at Aberdeen; the war diary notes that they were "very tired and exhausted" with 25 wounded being carried on mules. Both recce columns were soon back in action as a single column and, in a series of engagements, lost several casualties killed in action. Colonel Cumberlege was relieved of his command and Major Astell of the Burma Rifles succeeded him.

The first of the Chindit brigades to go into Burma in 1944, Fergusson's was also the first withdrawn. In May the brigade was ordered to abandon Aberdeen by General Joe Lentaigne who had been appointed to command Special Force after Wingate's untimely death in an air crash in March. Sixteen Brigade, having fought off determined Japanese attacks, was flown out and Aberdeen and two other strongholds were abandoned. In a sense this was the end of Chindit operations for Wingate's visionary ethos of long range penetration had gone and the Chindits had been handed over to Stilwell to assist his operations. That was a death sentence for many.

Back in India 45 Recce went to Bangalore to reform. In common with everyone in 16 Brigade the reconnoitrers were exhausted, physically worn and suffering from ill health after their time in the jungle. There was to be no immediate return to operations and the period from June to October 1944 was given over to rehabilitation, leave and re-organisation. There was a message of congratulations from Mike Calvert to Fergusson:

Have been proud to serve with and Command Recce Regt in battle. Their determination and skill and courage in action with the Ghurkhas dealt the enemy heavy blows from which he has not yet recovered. We much regret the losses but enemy losses proved greater.[6]

On 5 September General Lentaigne, visiting the regiment to congratulate them on their achievements, referred to possible further operations. These were not to come about and, instead of reverting to its rôle as a divisional reconnaissance regiment, 45 Recce was disbanded as a Reconnaissance Corps regiment in October, reforming as 2nd South Staffords. Thus its part in the history of the Corps ends there although it is worthy of note that many of its soldiers defiantly continued to wear the Recce badge. Its part in the 1944 Chindit expedition had been marked by a number of gallantry awards, among them a MM and Bar to Trooper M.Flynn. In early 1945 most of the officers and many men volunteered for conversion to the parachute rôle and became 16th Parachute Battalion in which rôle several Recce officers were among those who, in August 1945, volunteered to drop on prisoner-of-war camps holding British personnel. In that last act of the campaign can be seen the spirit of the Reconnaissance Corps.

***

The Chindits of 45 Recce and the men of 2 Recce had been joined in Burma by the recce regiments of 81st and 82nd West African Divisions. Created from independent West African squadrons, both were brought up to strength by transferring Reconnaissance Corps personnel from Britain. The officers and warrant officers in each regiment were British; officers were a mix of Regulars and Territorials from British regiments, and colonial service officers and civilians from Africa. Reconnaissance Corps NCOs were also posted to both West African units.

The main area of operation for the West Africans was Arakan, on the western littoral of Burma. First into action was 81 Recce which had been formed in Nigeria in early 1943 with Lieutenant Colonel Richard N.Cartwright of 5th Royal Inniskilling Dragoon Guards as its CO. Three West African countries provided the squadrons: Nigeria for A Squadron, Gold Coast (present-day Ghana) for B Squadron and Sierra Leone for C Squadron. The regiment embarked on HMT *Johan de Witt* at Lagos in September 1943 with its training incomplete. Training continued, as far as possible, on board ship; there was a change of ship, to HMT *Ormonde*, at Takoradi before sailing for India via Durban. On the voyage two soldiers, Elijah Oeantiaka and Chiaga Naneu, died and were buried at sea.

Training followed disembarkation at Bombay on 6 November before, in mid-December, 81 Recce entrained for Calcutta to sail for Chittagong and then to Chiringa, about 50 miles down the Arakan road, which was reached on Christmas Day.

The regiment was now divorced from its division to serve under 5th Indian Division in XV Corps. The regiment's first task was the defence of the Teknaf peninsula for which a composite squadron of two assault troops and a mortar troop from each of B and C Squadrons was formed under Major Alan McBean, MC, a Rhodesian. By 7 January the composite squadron was established at Teknaf and Mhila. The main task assigned to 81 Recce was that of defending Maungdaw and Colonel Cartwright was ordered to dominate the entire coastal plain of the West Mayu. For this purpose some additional troops were placed under the regiment's command; these were 290 Special Purposes Company, Inland Water Transport; a section of Burma Intelligence Corps; a battery of 4 Field Regiment; 54th Observation Squadron (whose role was to provide

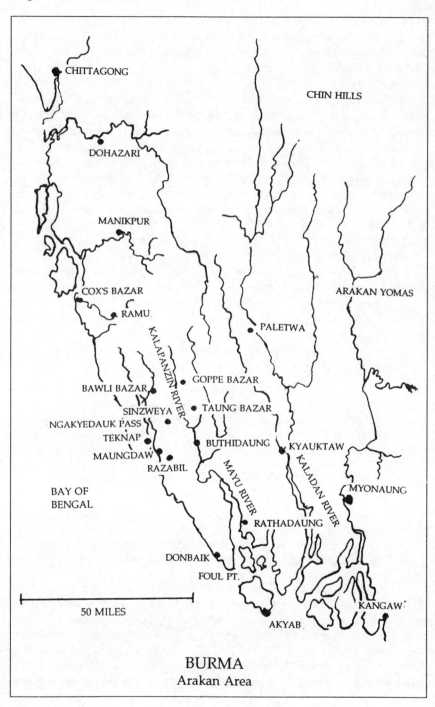

CHITTAGONG

CHIN HILLS

DOHAZARI

MANIKPUR

COX'S BAZAR

RAMU

ARAKAN YOMAS

PALETWA

KALAPANZIN RIVER

BAWLI BAZAR

GOPPE BAZAR

SINZWEYA

TAUNG BAZAR

NGAKYEDAUK PASS

TEKNAP

BUTHIDAUNG

KYAUKTAW

MAUNGDAW

RAZABIL

KALADAN RIVER

MYONAUNG

BAY OF
BENGAL

MAYU RIVER

RATHADAUNG

DONBAIK

FOUL PT.

KANGAW

50 MILES

AKYAB

BURMA
Arakan Area

deception by simulating battle sounds) and a detachment of V Force guides. V Force was an intelligence-gathering organisation, although it had originally been formed for guerrilla activities, and the elements in Arakan operated under Major Denis Holmes, a friend of Cartwright from Sandhurst days.

Richard Cartwright quickly devised plans to dominate the area. Since the coastal plain was so large and his regiment comparatively small he reckoned that the best method of operation was active patrolling and raiding to create the impression that the Japanese faced a much larger force than they did in reality. He also intended to draw the enemy out on to specially prepared 'killing grounds' on which the largest possible number of casualties would be inflicted on the Japanese.

With the able assistance of their V Force guides, the regiment established patrol bases inside enemy-occupied territory and their recce activities allowed them to call down aircraft to strafe and bomb Japanese positions as well as directing artillery shoots. Scout car and carrier patrols operated over a wide area while, thanks to 290 Special Purposes Company and the Royal Indian Navy, the regiment also became waterborne with several river steamers and smaller craft at its disposal; these were used to land raiding parties along the Mayu peninsula as far as its extremity at Foul Point. The activities of the regiment were so successful that they attracted the attention of General Slim, commander of Fourteenth Army: in his memoirs *Defeat into Victory*, Slim wrote:

> Conspicuously successful were the raids behind the enemy lines delivered by the Reconnaissance Regiment of the 81st West African Division. This unit developed to a high degree the technique of small amphibious commando operations. One of its coastal raids in January identified what up till then had been the missing regiment of the Japanese 55th Division which we had thought to be in the Pacific. Its arrival from that theatre was another pointer to enemy intentions in Burma.[7]

During the battle of the Ngakyedauk Pass in February 1944 a detachment from C Squadron, 81 Recce was among the first troops over the Goppe Pass to meet the attacking Japanese; these men carried out intensive patrolling which brought back much valuable information until they returned to the regiment on 14 February.

Detailing the activities of 81 Recce in the Arakan alone would require a volume but two examples of their operations may serve to indicate the nature and extent of the regiment's work. A raid on Dodan on 22 January left four Japanese dead and gained a selection of valuable enemy documents and maps; it also cost the life of the popular Sergeant Avunga who had saved Denis Holmes's life. Major 'Satan' Mooring led a raid on Alethangyaw that had to be aborted due to sea conditions on the 27th but, three days later, Mooring led an attack that overran Alethangyaw and brought the identification of the Japanese unit that had been transferred from the Pacific.[8] Operations in the Mayu area continued until 26 March when 81 Recce, under 26th Indian Division, crossed the Ngakyedauk Pass to consolidate near where the Ngakyedauk Chaung met the Kalapanzin River. But they had moved without Colonel Cartwright who had been promoted on 25 March to take command of 6 (West African) Brigade; his place as CO of 81 Recce was taken by the former 2ic, Major Bernard Shattock of the Queen's Royal Regiment. For his outstanding service between January and March 1944, Colonel Cartwright was awarded the DSO. Tragically, this capable and popular officer died in July 1944 while commanding 6 Brigade.

From its new base the regiment, for almost a month, patrolled the Kalapanzin valley and basin from the east bank of the river to the Arakan Yomas. More than a hundred patrols, mostly on foot, sought out Japanese positions and troop strengths; many patrols lasted for as long as ten days while others were short fighting patrols. On 20 April the regiment re-organised on an infantry basis to rejoin 81st Division which was crossing the Arakan Yomas towards the Ri and Saingdin Chaung areas.

A skeleton RHQ, two assault troops and a composite troop left Taung Bazar on 23 April to join 81st Division at Mazegaung Hkamwe. With the monsoon season about to break the division was preparing to move east of Taung Bazar and 81 Recce deployed to cover the withdrawal and cause as much hindrance as possible to Japanese forces trying to make contact with the division. For the men of 81 Recce that led to a new experience as much of their activity was in unfamiliar and difficult country, the foothills of the Yomas, which proved very gruelling. But they quickly settled in "and soon in fact were more adept than many who had been in with 81 Div from the start."[9]

The regiment joined the main body of 81st Division on 12 May in their new positions east of Taung Bazar. During the following month the main activity for 81 Recce was patrolling forward over the divisional front with two aims: to conceal the division's intentions and the monsoon line, and to find out what the enemy was doing. Several patrol battles occurred but, generally, torrential rain and flooded paddy fields restricted activity. On 6 June the regiment moved back to Chiringa near its location of the previous December. It moved minus C Squadron which rejoined a week later. With the complete division back at Chiringa, intensive training and re-organisation followed although the area was completely cut off by monsoon conditions. When these eased there was an opportunity for leave in India.

During training the regiment was shocked by an order to re-organise on a new war establishment for a West African Reconnaissance Regiment;

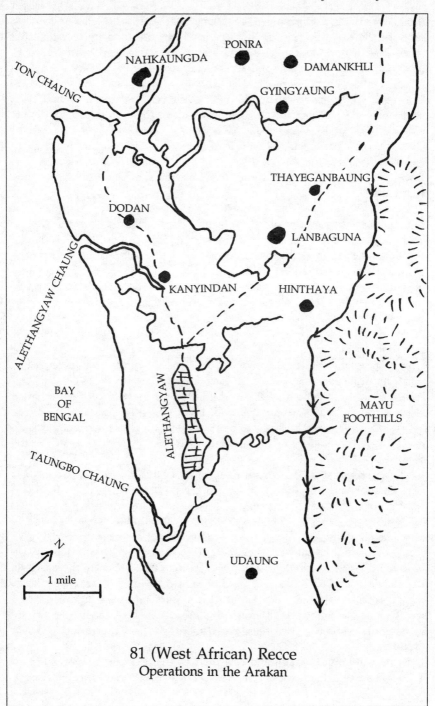

TON CHAUNG

NAHKAUNGDA

PONRA

DAMANKHLI

GYINGYAUNG

THAYEGANBAUNG

DODAN

LANBAGUNA

ALETHANGYAW CHAUNG

KANYINDAN

HINTHAYA

BAY
OF
BENGAL

ALETHANGYAW

MAYU
FOOTHILLS

TAUNGBO CHAUNG

N

1 mile

UDAUNG

81 (West African) Recce
Operations in the Arakan

there was even an element of insult in being referred to as a 'battalion' in the order. This new establishment put the regiment on to a purely infantry basis and it lost all its transport apart from fourteen jeeps for commanders' recces. It seemed that the idea behind the re-organisation was:

> ...to bring us in line with the rest of 81 div and to put us on a headload basis, as it had been decided that we were never again to be separated from our Div as in the good old days at Maungdaw.[10]

Since the division was to resume operations in country unsuitable for vehicles there was no argument against the decision to take away 81 Recce's vehicles. The regiment began infantry training but one other sad aspect of the re-organisation was the loss of a number of top class NCOs and drivers.

> We were supposed to be ready for ops again by 1st Nov., which did not leave a lot of time, but everyone got down to the business of training very wholeheartedly. We found that the basic principles of recce on foot were what we had always known in our Assault Troops; we thought out and perfected some new Battle Drills, and generally made great strides.[11]

Operations began in early October: 81st Division was to advance down the line of the Kaladan river to turn the Japanese right flank before moving to Paletwa and holding a line there until relieved by 82nd Division, which would be fresh, in December. While advancing along the Kaladan the division would protect the left flank of XV Indian Corps.

The forming-up area was near the upper reaches of the Sangu river to which RHQ, A and B Squadrons moved in mid-September. C Squadron was sent south to strike out east of Taung Bazar, deep into the Arakan Yomas, with two tasks: to obtain information on the enemy south of 81st Division's line of advance and east of the main front, and to find tracks which 82nd Division could use for a secret move from their forming-up positions in the Kalapanzin area to Paletwa in the Kaladan valley. Events moved much faster than anticipated, however, and much of this plan was never implemented.

The main advance began with A and B Squadrons assigned to a familiar reconnaissance rôle ahead of the leading brigade of the division. But the main route was along chaungs flowing through thick bamboo jungle and the going was very tough. As squadrons also had to recce side tracks, keeping ahead of the advance, and reconnoitring thoroughly, proved extremely difficult. Nonetheless everything went much as planned during the first month although there was little to report. One episode however deserves to be recorded: led by the commanding officer, Colonel Shattock, A Squadron carried out a sweep that took them south of Paletwa thus blocking the Japanese escape route southwards. The presence of the squadron proved a considerable impediment to the enemy.

In spite of heavy going through the jungle the advance was rapid and, instead of handing over to 82nd Division at Paletwa in December as planned, 81st Division took part in another forward move which took its soldiers down to Kyingri. There 81 Recce was deployed to hold the airstrip which, as the only landing-ground available to the division, was essential for casualty evacuation and re-supply. While RHQ and HQ Squadron sat at Kyingri to guard against attacks by Japanese troops cut off in the advance, 81st Division moved into the hills to the east. In that move squadrons of the regiment in turn held the east end of the Soutcol, the pass over the Yomas popularly known as the 'Gateway to Chittagong,' and linked up with C Squadron whose boundaries included the western end of the Soutcol; the latter squadron was still operating independently.

From Kyingri 81st Division was about to start its last push with Myohaung its objective. The divisional commander, Major General Loftus-Tottenham, decided to use 81 Recce in a diversionary rôle and sent it to the Kanzauk area to simulate as large a force as possible. There the regiment was to link up with 25th Indian Division which was advancing eastwards from Akyab. The speed of advance had increased even more and had in fact become "one long chase." On a number of occasions groups of retreating Japanese were caught in ambushes and engaged by shell or mortar fire.

In spite of the conditions under which they had to work the regiment's wireless operators performed magnificent service and perfect communication was maintained with 81st Division's headquarters some 50 miles away across hills and dense bamboo jungle and with C Squadron which was in much the same area. The regiment's B Echelon was still at Chiringa, over 250 miles in the rear, yet contact was also maintained with it via an old No 22 set.

The regiment returned to amphibious operations as the many watercourses in that part of Burma hindered movement by land. With the aid of outboard motors, dropped by RAF aircraft, a number of vessels were pressed into various rôles including carrying fighting patrols. The naval officer commanding one LCT (landing-craft, tank) decided to attach himself to 81 Recce for two weeks. His attachment was entirely unofficial but his LCT was highly appreciated and carried rations and animals as well as moving fighting patrols.

Myohaung fell to a pincer movement of 81st and 82nd Divisions on 25 January 1945. Its fall marked the end of 81st Division's part in the advance as well as the return of C Squadron. In fact, C Squadron, under Major J.C.Stokes, had "crossed to the Kyingri Loop over the Soutcol route"[12] from where they were been flown in to join the division north of Myohaung. The squadron then led 81st Division's forward brigade on the last bound into

Myohaung. With the capture of Myohaung 81 Recce moved eastwards to mop up stragglers and reached Konbaung where, on 29 January, C Squadron finally rejoined. Although there were rumours that the regiment was to go forward again with 82nd Division these proved unfounded and, after moving as far as Minbya, 81 Recce was withdrawn and travelled by river steamer to Akyab and then by ship to Chittagong and Chiringa. The bulk of 81st Division "had to march for eight days from Myohaung to Buthidaung."[13]

Leave and training were the order of the day at Chiringa, the latter because there were plans for 81st Division to return to Burma. At the beginning of April, 81 Recce moved to Madras where training continued in spite of extremely hot weather that precluded any activity from 1 o'clock to four. Reinforcements were received as many British members of the regiment had been due for repatriation; the new men were preparing for active service when the news came that the division would not be returning to Burma: the speed of the advance there made its presence unnecessary. Then, in July, came further news: 81st Division was to return to Africa; 81 Recce was to be split up in India with its squadrons returning to their parent brigades. RHQ and HQ Squadron were disbanded but the second-in-command, Major J.C.Stokes, and the adjutant, Major Jack Rostron, went to 82nd Reconnaissance Regiment and with them went a number of 81's NCOs. Thus ended the service of 81st (West African) Reconnaissance Regiment.

The "younger brothers" of 81st Regiment were the men of 82nd (West African) Reconnaissance Regiment who moved to the fray after the senior regiment. Their division was committed to the Burma campaign in November 1944 and was engaged in the Arakan from January 1945. Independent reconnaissance companies had been combined in early 1943 to create 82nd Reconnaissance Regiment which arrived in India in mid-1944. The regiment was stationed at Chas in Bihar State where its training began. However, 82 Recce was very much under strength and consisted, in August 1944, of five officers, eight British NCOs and 173 African soldiers who formed the main part of Regimental Headquarters, HQ Squadron and Y Squadron with Lieutenant Colonel R.C.Barron, KSLI, as CO and Captain J.E.T.Kelmsley, Royal Ulster Rifles, commanding HQ Squadron. Some personnel were posted in from 81 Recce.

Training and exercises continued throughout September, October and early-November when a Reconnaissance Training Regiment arrived at Comilla. On 16 November the regiment, still lacking two squadrons "yet to form" entrained for Calcutta where, six days later, it embarked for Chittagong which was reached on the 25th. The following day 82 Recce arrived at Chiringa where it bivouacked.

By 2 December, X Squadron had been formed and RHQ, HQ, X and Y

Squadrons moved to Goppe Bazar to relieve 3rd Bn Gold Coast Regiment as Goppe Keep garrison on the 4th and began sending patrols out the following day. On 6 December the regiment was finally complete with the arrival of Z Squadron.

On 10 December a patrol brought in a number of "suspects" who had tried to run away as the African soldiers approached. The "suspects" turned out to be local villagers and a section of V Force; the question of identity was finally cleared up by the intervention of a local magistrate. The regiment's first real prisoners were taken twelve days later when two members of the renegade Indian National Army, referred to as Japanese Indian Forces, were captured and sent under escort to Corps HQ.

The regiment moved to Taung Bazar and then to Kyingri in January 1945 and, on the 21st, came under command of 6 Brigade of 81st (West African) Division at Chaungchi. Three days later a Y Squadron patrol was ambushed by Japanese at Brukchaung and five men were wounded as well as two of the ambushers. The following day another patrol was fired on at Gangyuan and, on entering the village, found the tracks of a gun and limber as well as empty 75mm shellcases.

On 30 January Colonel Barron accidentally shot himself through the arm and Major McBean, the second in command, took over. Less than three weeks later McBean was hit by a free-dropping load from a Dakota and suffered a broken leg. Lieutenant Colonel Rice of the Suffolks assumed temporary command until succeeded by Lieutenant Colonel A.Hlawaty of the Polish Army in early March. In the meantime the regiment had had a series of minor actions and engagements in which several casualties had been suffered: three men were killed in a Y Squadron encounter with a Japanese company on 16 February; next day five were drowned in another action and several were wounded and an officer killed on the 20th. Against this at least 17 Japanese had been killed in the same encounters. On 27 February another two men were killed in an action at Mechaung village.

Also during February, Sergeant Isa Nupe won the Military Medal. He was commanding two sections returning from a patrol when:

> ...they were ambushed and attacked from three sides with LMG, mortar fire and grenades. Despite being twice wounded, Sgt Isa Nupe repeatedly organised attacks on the LMG positions. By nightfall, nine out of the twelve men were wounded and the Japs were dug in all round.
>
> In the dawn light, Sgt Nupe shot dead two Japs as they showed themselves in preparation for an attack. The attack came in, and was driven off by LMG fire and grenades. Sgt Nupe then ordered a counter-attack. At the head of his little force he broke through the encircling enemy and brought every man safely back to Regimental HQ.[14]

Isa Nupe was later promoted to Squadron Sergeant Major and was one of the Reconnaissance Corps' representatives in the Victory Parade in London on 8 June 1946.

As the Japanese continued to withdraw the regiment harried them throughout March and April until, on 28 April, 82 Recce was withdrawn to monsoon quarters at Kindaungyyi. Its main activity in the Burma campaign had ended for, although it carried out some patrolling from Dalaba in May, it returned to a training routine in June which continued throughout July although there were some patrols against Dacoits. The regiment had received a number of officers and men from 81 Recce but, when the war ended in August, the objective of its training, renewed operations against the Japanese, had been removed.

Until November 82 Recce remained at Kindaungyyi, from where it moved to Letpadin. The final entry in the war diary, for December 1945, reads "nothing to report." Its time at war had been brief but 82nd Reconnaissance Regiment had acquitted itself well.

Finally one other regiment ought to be mentioned in the Burma campaign: 11th (East African) Divisional Regiment, the recce unit of 11th (East African) Division. This was the Kenya Armoured Car Regiment but it was removed from the divisional order of battle in June 1944 just as the division was committed to action in Burma. Two months later 5th King's African Rifles assumed the reconnaissance task for 11th (EA) Division.

As in other theatres the Reconnaissance Corps had done its duty well in Burma, whether as Chindits, raiders, or in the many and varied tasks assigned to the regiments which fought in that uncompromising battleground.

12
Royal Armoured Corps

On 1 January 1944 the Reconnaissance Corps became part of the Royal Armoured Corps. Some staff officers had always maintained that reconnaissance regiments belonged to the Royal Armoured Corps. Since the Reconnaissance Corps assumed the rôle previously performed by divisional cavalry regiments there was logic in that view, but the circumstances of 1940 had shifted the infantry division's recce rôle onto the Director of Infantry at the War Office. When reconnaissance regiments adopted cavalry nomenclature in June 1942 there was an implicit acceptance that the units, although 'of the infantry,' were not infantry. In February 1943 a War Office conference discussed the possibility of transferring the Reconnaissance Corps to the RAC but, although there was support for such a move, the proposal was shelved temporarily.

Once raised, there was a possibility that the transfer proposal would come back again, and that is exactly what happened. In October 1943 a paper "on whether or not the Reconnaissance Corps should be incorporated in the Royal Armoured Corps"[1] was drawn up and a memorandum for the Executive Committee of the Army Council was prepared by Major General James Steele, DSO, MC (Director of Staff Duties) although it was actually attributed to the Deputy Chief of the Imperial General Staff and the Adjutant General. The memorandum was sent to General Sir Bernard Paget, Colonel Commandant of the Reconnaissance Corps for his comment.

The reasons behind the transfer proposal were based on training, administrative and operational factors. It was pointed out that both corps were about to have a joint training depot; that officers for the Reconnaissance Corps were trained at the Royal Armoured Corps OCTU at Sandhurst and that much reconnaissance training already came under the wing of the Major General, Armoured Training. Administratively there were frequent transfers of warrant officers and senior NCOs from the RAC to the Reconnaissance Corps to make up deficiencies; the records office for the Reconnaissance Corps was moving to Barnet where RAC records were held; reinforcements for recce were often supplied by the RAC; there would be more opportunity for promotion within the RAC and it would be possible for soldiers to become Regulars in the RAC which was not possible in the Reconnaissance Corps. Operational similarities in the rôles of both corps were emphasised as was the fact that, outside the RAC, the Reconnaissance Corps was the only armoured car operator.

General Paget indicated that he was in favour of the transfer, provided that the Reconnaissance Corps did not lose its identity. This eliminated one of the two options put forward, that of absorbing all units of the Reconnaissance Corps into the RAC and thus made the second choice the preferred option "by absorbing the Reconnaissance Corps as a complete entity into the Royal Armoured Corps in the same manner as the Royal Tank Corps."[2] Since this latter would mean no change in badges or unit nomenclature for the Reconnaissance Corps it was formally placed before the Army Council for submission to the Secretary of State for his approval and to the King for final sanction.

The change came into effect on 1 January 1944 and regiments then became reconnaissance regiments of the Royal Armoured Corps. They continued, however, to wear their Reconnaissance Corps badges, shoulder titles and arm-of-service strips. The only obvious change was the adoption of the RAC black beret and even that took considerable time as stocks of the old khaki berets had to be used up and there were insufficient black berets to meet the needs of all the recce regiments.

Re-organisation brought another regiment into the Reconnaissance Corps order of battle. When 6th Airborne Division formed in May 1943 a light tank squadron had been included in the divisional troops to carry out the recce rôle. As an armoured unit this squadron had been part of the RAC. On 1 April 1944 the squadron became a regiment with the title 6th Airborne Armoured Reconnaissance Regiment; its recce function had taken it into the reconnaissance arm from 14 January. Equipped with light tanks, carried in Hamilcar gliders, the regiment was to take part in the invasion of Europe, the repelling of the Ardennes offensive and the Rhine crossing. Its tanks bore the Recce 41 as well as the airborne forces' Pegasus badge. To this day a driver of 6th Airborne Armoured Recce probably still holds the world tank speed record achieved involuntarily when his tank crashed through the nose of its Hamilcar - which had landed at too high a speed - and shot forward at about 80mph. The incident occurred at Tarrant Rushton in April 1944 during the British Army's first air landing of tanks.

13
Italy - tough old gut

We left Italy with the Allies bogged down in the southern Apennines against the Gustav Line defences. With little opportunity to carry out their normal duties reconnaissance regiments in Italy found themselves deployed as infantry.

On the east coast Eighth Army's advance had ground to a standstill after a series of strongly-contested river crossings. A Canadian division had relieved 78th Division before the crossing of the River Moro and the Battleaxe Division had been withdrawn; with it went 56 Recce. Before long the division was back in the line, this time in the Apennine mountains holding positions taken in the last advance. Intended to be jumping-off positions for the next advance, these instead became defensive positions. Among the troops deployed to hold them were Chavasse's Light Horse who were responsible for the 15 miles from Vastogirardi through San Pietro to Pescopennataro where 10 Commando (which was composed of men from the occupied countries of Europe) was also based; two recce personnel were attached to the commando for liaison. Nearby also were 6th Inniskillings from the Irish Brigade and D Support Group of 1st Kensingtons. Information from local people enabled an attack by German troops on Pescopennataro to be fought off with the enemy suffering from very accurate artillery fire brought down by the FOO attached to 56 Recce.

A blizzard blew up on 31 December and by late-morning of New Year's Day snow was drifting up to ten feet deep. Colonel Chavasse issued orders to watch for enemy ski patrols and several outposts were withdrawn. Weather also affected communications with wireless sets completely useless for a time. The regiment was snowed in for several weeks during which ski patrolling was started. Captain Tony Michelle, MC was "an expert skier and he taught a number of us and some became sufficiently proficient to go out on ski patrol."[1] Colonel Chavasse "occasionally visited the squadrons on skis, but usually ended on my bottom going downhill!"[2] He also initiated the practice of visiting some of his forward posts at night: travelling alone he caused considerable anxiety in his RHQ where no one wanted to lose a most popular and inspiring CO.

For about three weeks all roads were impassable and the Army Group evening situation report always ended with "56 Recce still snowed up." However, things were not so bad as were believed on the outside:

> ...There was plenty of grub in the village, but we were supplied by air, and a body of Canadian volunteers, who were all expert skiers, visited us with relief supplies, and were surprised that we were not starving.[3]

There was another encounter with Germans, this time a six-man patrol, at Pescopennataro at the end of January. The Germans were forced to withdraw under a hail of mortar bombs and grenades. Heavy snow returned in early February along with Wigforce, a small guerrilla-type unit commanded by Major Wigram of the Buffs. Wigforce attacked Pizzoferrato on the night of 2/3 February but, although the operation was successful, Wigram was killed in the action. At the end of February 56 Recce was finally relieved by the Podolski Lancers, the recce regiment of 3rd Carpathian Division, and moved to Cisterna and Fifth Army's front.

From Cisterna the regiment went to Mignano and began training under 2nd NZ Division, although elements were maintaining forward reconnaissance posts. That training ended with the attack on Cassino on 15 March but this assault proved unsuccessful and 56 Recce, less C Squadron's assault troop who were still manning a reconnaissance post, was sent to the Rapido line south of Cassino to relieve 2nd LF. At the end of March 23rd NZ Battalion relieved 56 Recce who returned to Mignano and another training scheme, this time including hill-climbing.

The regiment played a minor rôle in the run-up to Operation DIADEM, the smashing of the Gustav Line in May 1944. It did, however, provide an ad-hoc squadron to relieve a LF company in the line for most of April. This was X Squadron, made up from A Squadron HQ, an anti-tank battery troop and A and C Squadrons' assault troops. At Mignano the regiment had a portent of things to come when a demonstration of the tactical use of the American M8 Staghound by a recce squadron was laid on by a troop of C Squadron; the Staghound was later to be issued to replace the Humber heavy armoured cars.

***

Earlier efforts had been made to break through the German lines before winter set in with all its severity. Those efforts had involved 56th Division attacking Monte Camino in which operation 44 Recce were given an altogether new rôle, being employed portering supplies to the assaulting infantry battalions of 167 Brigade. On 28 November a Porter Battalion was established around 44 Recce: also included was a company of 6th Cheshires, troops from 100 LAA and 67 A/T Regiments, the defence platoons of 168, 169 and 201 Brigades and 56th Divisional Defence Platoon. A jeep train was also established.

Not all 44 Recce's personnel were involved in portering. Captain Osmond of A Squadron departed the British lines through the forward defended localities of 2nd/5th Queens to carry out a two-day patrol behind the German positions on Monte Camino. On 30 November the divisional commander, Major General Templer, telephoned the CO to say that Osmond had returned with complete and valuable information. He described Osmond's patrol as "an inspiration to every officer in the

Division."[4] Less than a week later Osmond carried out a similar patrol for 167 Brigade; it was equally successful with his singlehandedly clearing 12 Germans from Colle.

On 1 December recce porter parties attacked with the companies for which they were portering. One detachment took ten prisoners but the regiment lost three killed, three wounded and 25 missing. A welcome end to porterage duties took the regiment to San Donata and Falciano to spend Christmas, prior to which announcements were made of the awards of two MCs and four MMs to 44 Recce.

On 8 January 1944 the regiment became the core of Hicksforce which also included two companies of 6th Cheshires, a battery from 67th Anti-Tank Regiment and 56th Division's Defence Platoon. Hicksforce's task was to take over the coastal sector south of the Garigliano river thereby providing a screen for 5th Division's concentration to the rear of the sector. The force operated for a week, during which it carried out extensive patrolling and captured five prisoners. The deployment of Hicksforce had been part of X Corps' plan to cross the Garigliano and on the night of 17 January that crossing began: 5th Division was on the left flank and 56th on the right. During the following day 44 Recce crossed the Garigliano on foot to fill the gap between the two divisions. However, plans were changed almost as soon as the regiment had crossed and, instead of filling in in the centre, 44 Recce deployed with C Squadron on the left sector of the San Salvatito feature, A Squadron continuing the line across the road and B Squadron in reserve.

The Germans still had a number of machine-gun positions on San Salvatito which B Squadron was ordered to clear. During the afternoon of the 19th the squadron cleared those positions and several Germans were killed or wounded with another five taken prisoner. C Squadron inflicted even more casualties on the enemy when it was attacked that night. The squadron's fierce resistance drove off the attackers who left 20 of their number dead, including the company commander. B Squadron was again in action on 20 January when one of its troops, supported by tanks, attacked and took Massa Vezza without loss.

The CO, Lieutenant Colonel K.B.Hicks, attracted the attention of the enemy on the afternoon of 23 January by accidentally setting fire to the chimney of RHQ. The smoke and fire provided a marker for German artillery and shells began to fall around RHQ. Two rounds landed quite close and Colonel Hicks' popularity temporarily diminished.

On 27 January the regiment was relieved, moving back to Montanaro to re-organise on to a jeep, carrier and White scout car establishment. But, once again, plans were changed and 44 Recce returned on foot north of the Garigliano on 1 February to relieve 8th Royal Fusiliers. Its new location was Lorenzo from where it patrolled until relieved by 40 Commando, RM on the 12th. While at Lorenzo the regiment captured a number of prisoners, including an entire six-man patrol (taken by a four-man patrol from A Squadron), a Pole - serving in the German army - and a German in civilian clothing. At the end of this stint the regiment was commended for its work by the commander of 56th Division, the brigadier of 167 Brigade and the CO of 40 Commando. It had also lost a number of men, including two killed when an armour-piercing shell landed on a house being used as a section position on the crossroads at Lorenzo. Eight men were buried of whom two managed to get out and four were dug out before REs advised against further digging due to the dangerous nature of the building.

Forty-four Recce relieved the King's Dragoon Guards on 11 March. They were spectators at the bombing of Monte Cassino and carried out a series of patrols as part of their infantry rôle, enduring shelling and mortaring but intercepting some German patrols before being relieved by Moroccan troops on 28 March. The White scout cars were finally collected at Montagano on 5 April and a training spell began which lasted almost until the end of the month when C Squadron, under command of 5th Grenadier Guards, occupied positions on Point 1190 in the Castel di Sangro area. C Squadron was joined by B Squadron on 9 May but the regiment was relieved a week later and withdrawn with 56th Division to Egypt.

Those other veterans of the Salerno landings, 46 Recce, had been in the Middle East almost two months when 44 Recce arrived in Egypt in early June. Forty-sixth Division had been relieved by 4th Division with 4 Recce taking the place of 46 Recce in Italy at the end of a spell of infantry work in which 46 Recce had suffered considerable casualties.

At the end of 1943 46 Recce was providing flank protection for its division in the San Martino area in front of the Gustav Line. The first days of 1944 saw the regiment in an infantry rôle having relieved 16th DLI; its vehicles were left, for the first time, some four miles behind the forward positions. One squadron was in the line while the other two were held in reserve and, for the front-line squadron, life was a routine of night patrols and watching by day over snow-covered no man's land. OPs were set up, but the lack of equipment for such duties was bemoaned, as was the fact that the level of such work had not been anticipated in the UK.

On 5 January 46 Recce passed to 23 Armoured Brigade for a crossing of the Garigliano river. Patrolling continued and, on 19 January, 12 Troop were heavily engaged by the enemy while crossing a valley mouth: four men were killed and eight wounded. But four days later a patrol from 46 Recce made the first crossing of the Garigliano in their sector since X Corps had reached the river line. OPs were still being maintained and occasionally suffered heavy mortaring from the Germans; casualties, however, were light. By the 26th all three squadrons were on the river line with their vehicles still far behind.

Patrolling, defensive infantry duties and OPs continued along the Garigliano into February while C Squadron crossed the river to relieve a Royal Marine Commando "at a high cost in casualties." On 7 February Cottonforce was formed from elements of 46 Recce, King's Dragoon Guards, a platoon of Vickers machine-guns, a section of 4.2-inch mortars and a composite company of 120 anti-tank gunners. Next day patrols from each squadron crossed the river to check if, as suspected, the Germans had left San Ambroglio. C Squadron's patrol was fired on before it could cross, A Squadron's crossed by ferry but was attacked with grenades and returned while B Squadron's saw no enemy at all. The front settled down for a time although harassing fire continued from the German positions; one man from A Squadron was killed and two others wounded in the San Nicola area by mortar fire on the evening of the 13th.

A change in routine came with a diversionary 'Chinese' attack across the Garigliano on the night of 17/18 February although this produced little enemy reaction. Three nights later, a patrol attempting to cross the river was stopped by the strong current while on the 21st the war diary notes German abuse of the Red Cross with ambulances being used to carry ammunition. As a result orders were issued to shell German ambulances unless it was clear that their rôle was absolutely humanitarian. Patrols sent to establish crossing points along the bank of the river reported nothing of interest; the riverbanks, however, were very steep and up to eight feet high.

The regiment's spell in the front line was drawing to an end and on 27 February came the news that they would be relieved by 2nd/4th Hampshires. Even at this late stage German patrols seemed "keen to establish the identity of 46 Recce."[5] That was almost a pointless exercise for on 29 February the regiment was relieved by the Hampshires and the following day was out of the line and "relieved of all tactical commitments for [the] first time since landing in Italy in September 1943."[6] The war diary noted that B Squadron had been in the line nearly eight weeks with only a two-day break; the other squadrons had fared slightly better with five-week stints in the line.

And so began Operation PITCHFORK, the move out of Italy. Vehicles and equipment were handed over to 4 Recce before travelling to Taranto. There, on 8 March, black RAC berets were issued; the regiment had learned of the Corps transfer to the RAC on 1 February and generally thought it a positive move. By the end of March 46 Recce was in Egypt where leave was granted before going to Palestine for training and a short spell of internal security duties. The regiment would not return to Italy until July.

When 5th Division had crossed the Garigliano it had done so without 5 Recce which was training at Savignano. However, the regiment moved to Falciano in Fifth Army's area on 22 January where, three days later, it received four Humber Mk IV armoured cars and one White scout car, the

Humbers being intended to replace the tired Marmon-Herringtons. On the 30th, the regiment, with two platoons of 7th Cheshires under command, was ordered to relieve 11th King's Royal Rifles.

For 12 days the regiment held the coastal strip between Minturno and the sea, an unpleasant location where slit trenches more than two feet deep soon filled with water. Smoke was used to obscure positions in this flat area, causing everyone to cough and splutter. Squadrons carried out patrols and suffered "some slight shelling" by the Germans before being relieved and returning to Falciano on 11 February although 2 Squadron was left in the line with 201 Guards Brigade. An assault troop was disbanded at this stage, its men and vehicles forming an engineer troop for future operations. At Falciano the regiment received a letter about a distinction it could have done without: it had had the highest VD rate in 5th Division during January and was told to mend its ways.

On 5 March the regiment came under command of the newly-arrived 88th (US) Division. This caused a re-alignment of regimental positions with 2 Squadron permanently on the coast while 1 and 3 Squadrons, with US troops under command, alternately held 88th Division's right flank between the Garigliano river and San Lorenzo village. On a recce patrol to Scauri village during this spell Lieutenant Holloway and Sergeant Britt, of 2 Squadron, located enemy positions:

> ...by the simple expedient of tracking the sound of a Boche relieving himself from the upstairs window of a house. In an attempt to take a prisoner Lieutenant Holloway and his companion, regardless of a German sentry only five yards away, crept into the house and the former climbed upstairs to the third storey in search of his man. When encountered, the Boche had a rifle in his hand, but Lieut. Holloway, disregarding this, tried to persuade him to join them for a walk back to our lines, and when he showed reluctance to do this, shot him. The pair then made rapid tracks for home through a hail of small arms fire and grenades.[7]

Holloway was subsequently awarded an MC while Britt was mentioned in despatches.

On the night of 16/17 March the regiment staged a diversion to distract German attention from the NZ attack on Cassino. The regiment's effort - mounted by 1 Squadron - was planned to last for five hours with a patrol establishing and maintaining contact with the enemy in Castelforte:

> Unfortunately it turned out to be about the wettest and blackest night of the whole Winter and the patrol made its way up the terraced fields into Castelforte with every man holding on to the belt of the man in front of him.
>
> In the dark the patrol blundered into a German sentry... A fire fight developed and Sergeant Butler, with a well-aimed grenade, silenced an

enemy machine-gun which had the Sergeant's section pinned down. ... The patrol then retired into a deep rock fissure and put up a Very light which brought down more pre-arranged artillery fire on the Boche positions. The patrol then emerged and engaged another German position in a fire fight which lasted some considerable time. The patrol's casualties in the night's work were two men wounded.[8]

For his gallantry Sergeant Butler was rewarded with the MM.

The regiment was relieved four nights later and moved to Nocera, near Naples, on the 21st but a further move was occasioned by the rain of volcanic ash from Vesuvius which had just erupted; 5 Recce travelled across country to Termoli and thence to Casoli - in a blizzard - to relieve 6th Lancers (Watson's Horse) on the 25th. Back in the line 5 Recce was soon patrolling, using Italian partisans whose local knowledge proved useful but who were a mixed blessing otherwise. There were several spirited actions during one of which three men, including a partisan, were killed and further gallantry awards earned.

On 5 April the regiment came under command of D-force, commanded by Colonel Dawnay of 23 Armoured Brigade, with which it operated until the 13th when RHQ was ordered to Perano. There 5 Recce was told to provide two squadrons, a tactical HQ and mortar sections - a total of 290 men - as an infantry force for Anzio; this force was to arrive at Anzio on the 21st.

Rear detachments of 5 Recce stayed at Villa Equesne south of Naples although 2 Squadron continued to operate with D-Force at Casoli and the anti-tank battery was acting as demonstration battery at the divisional tactical school.

A detachment from the regiment - a recce section of 8 Troop, 1 Squadron - had already joined 5th Division HQ in the Anzio beachhead where it had arrived on 9 March. That detachment had had a very active time in the beachhead by the time its fellows arrived, with patrols, shelling of the HQ, and several air raids. On 20 March the divisional HQ area had been shelled and one round had landed in the RE stores which, fortunately, had been unoccupied. The shell was a 17cm and it shook dugouts many yards away as well as an armoured car in which Trooper Campbell was operating the radio set.

> Anzio was our next stopping place. Battered, bloody Anzio. We were just behind the front line and had our headquarters in a wood on the edge of one of the deep wadis so well known to all who took part in that weary, grim siege.
>
> All the time Jerry pounded away with his mortars and artillery. Cruel splinters of jagged steel whining through the air while you perforce bit the dust. Brain jarring explosions firing the sun-baked grass, until you were burnt and suffocated by the stinging smoke. You scarcely dared

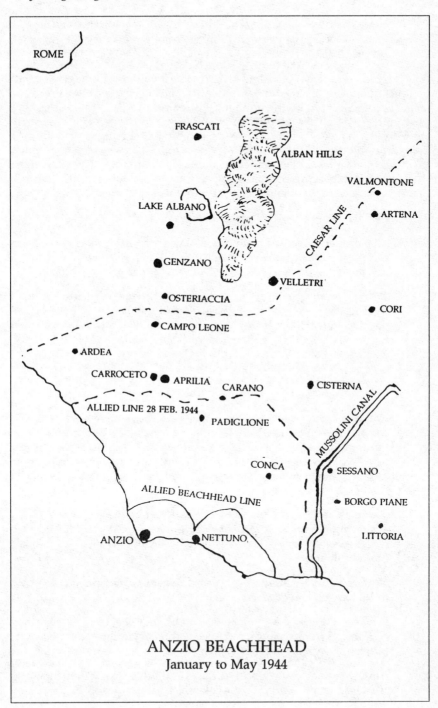

ROME

FRASCATI

ALBAN HILLS

VALMONTONE

ARTENA

LAKE ALBANO

CAESAR LINE

GENZANO

VELLETRI

OSTERIACCIA

CORI

CAMPO LEONE

ARDEA

CARROCETO APRILIA

CARANO

CISTERNA

ALLIED LINE 28 FEB. 1944

PADIGLIONE

MUSSOLINI CANAL

CONCA

SESSANO

ALLIED BEACHHEAD LINE

BORGO PIANE

ANZIO NETTUNO

LITTORIA

ANZIO BEACHHEAD
January to May 1944

move an inch out of the foxhole by day in which you were huddled. The foxhole that was bedroom and dining-room, yes, and even at the worst, latrine as well.[9]

During May additional elements of 5 Recce arrived and the regiment was ready to play its full part in Operation BUFFALO, the breakout from the beachhead. Meanwhile it continued to patrol, to suffer shelling and discomfort, and all the other frustrations of life in the beleaguered Anzio sector. Typical of its patrols was a seven-man fighting patrol from 1 Squadron on the night of 26/27 May under Lance-Sergeant Skinner. Skinner's patrol lasted just under two hours, moving out at 11.00pm with the twin intentions of ascertaining if an enemy section position was still occupied and, if so, to obtain identification of its occupants:

2300hrs: patrol left own lines by patrol path.

2320hrs: patrol reached point about 40 yds from left bank of Fosso Della Moletta. Patrol leader established half patrol in position to give covering fire and went forward with other half to search by probing for mines.

2330hrs: Probing party had just started work when an unusually loud challenge was heard from a German sentry apparently on the section position at 764310 itself. Reply was not heard. Patrol froze and listened for sounds of relief but only whispering was heard.

2335hrs: Noise of heavy lorry heard starting up from direction of road junction 758324. Vehicle moved off in NW direction. Patrol remained listening and observing enemy position.

0005hrs: Patrol leader and one man was about to move forward to reconnoitre enemy position when red verey light was put up apparently by own troops right rear from approx 775309. This was immediately followed by red verey light from a German position not far east of the section position under observation. Spent light fell about 15 yards in front of patrol position.

0015hrs: Patrol leader and one man crossed river bank to recce line of approach from far bank to German section position. Just at this time the moon went down making observation difficult. No suitable approach could be found.

0040hrs: Patrol leader and OR rejoined remainder of patrol and returned to Squadron lines without incident.

Between 2315hrs and 0010hrs sounds of shovelling and sandbagging were heard from enemy section position on about three occasions as if position were being improved.[10]

The Germans regularly shelled the troops in the beachhead but they also received plenty of retribution, some of which came from 5 Recce. Using their 2-inch and 3-inch mortars the recce men harassed their opponents and on occasions, such as the afternoon of 28 May, returned more than they received: that afternoon the 3-inch mortars of 1 Squadron fired three bombs for every one put down by the enemy. The regiment's PIATs were also used very effectively as mortars.

At one stage men began to disappear mysteriously at night "as though they had been swallowed up into the earth."[11] There seemed no explanation for men vanishing who had earlier been seen only a few hundred yards from their own positions but the mystery was solved when one missing man returned and explained what had happened to him:

> He had been out with a party putting a standing patrol in position. It was quite dark, and half a dozen men were working alongside a road not far from one of the outposts. Jerry was quite a long way off and everyone felt reasonably safe. Our man went across the road for something and promptly vanished! ... the others searched for him, called to him but he was gone as completely as though he had been spirited away. Here with a logical explanation to follow it, the whole affair seems rather insignificant. Out there in the dark, where death was commonplace, and where nerves were under constant tension, the thing seemed tremendous. You caught yourself glancing over your shoulder at every real or imagined sound. ... Imagine then, the relief when the missing man turned up again after three weeks, unharmed, and with the solution of the mystery. When he had crossed the road, and was still only a few feet from the remainder of the party, two figures had suddenly materialized at his side out of the blackness. One said, quite politely and in perfect English: "Please come with us."
>
> The man quite naturally imagined them to be members of a patrol from the neighbouring unit making a routine security patrol, and he went along, peaceably enough. Needless to say, we played the same game ourselves after that, with sufficient success to discourage the Boche from continuing his night marauding activities.[12]

The regimental historian described the time at Anzio as a "nerve-wracking and rather eerie experience."[13] With no movement in forward areas in daylight there was the feeling of being cooped up under the gaze of the enemy with only the sea behind. Anxiously awaited indeed was the advance from the south which would allow the Anzio force to break out.

That breakout came almost unexpectedly. With the smashing of the Gustav Line and the fall of Monte Cassino the German armies around Rome were in danger of being routed completely by General Alexander's armies. Part of Alexander's plan had been the breakout from Anzio with VI Corps linking up with Fifth and Eighth Armies to destroy the German forces before they could withdraw north of Rome. When the men of 5 Recce heard one strangely quiet morning that the Germans had pulled out overnight they were overjoyed at the end of their ordeal and delighted to learn that they would be pursuing the fleeing enemy. One squadron took the coastal route, another drove through the low foothills and "everyone was in high spirits at the sudden action after weeks of static warfare. We were Recce in the true sense of the word, and it was going to take quite a lot to stop us."[14]

The pursuit, on 2 June, took them along roads littered with the detritus of war - burnt-out vehicles, craters on and alongside the road and trees blasted by explosions. Prisoners were already coming back and there were numerous blown bridges and mines left by the Germans to slow the chase. Stops were usually short, however, as detours were recce'd but there were casualties from ambushes and mines: one carrier ran over five Teller mines and completely disappeared. By the time 5 Recce reached the Tiber it had accounted for large numbers of enemy soldiers, including two companies of the elite Italian Folgore parachute division who were still fighting for the Germans.

On 5 June RHQ was at Ostia Antica where the regiment heard that it was to be withdrawn to Egypt. It left Naples a few days later on board HMT *Derbyshire* and arrived at Alexandria from where it moved to Mena and took over 44 Recce's equipment in early July before moving to Palestine. The regiment's part in the Italian campaign was over.

***

While 5 Recce was leaving the fighting in Italy behind, 1 Recce, which had also been engaged at Anzio, was still in the peninsula. At the end of the Tunisian campaign 1 Recce had remained in North Africa where, for a time, elements of B Squadron had been involved in searches for German troops and equipment believed to be in the area. Refitting and training absorbed most of the time until November when preparations began for a move to Italy.

Landing at Naples on 9 December, 1 Recce moved to Taranto and then to Cotignola under command of Eighth Army with orders to relieve 8th Indian Division. That order was cancelled and 1st Division moved instead to Salerno under Fifth Army command; 1 Recce HQ was established at Torre del Greco. Re-organisation of the regiment created an LOB (left out of battle) squadron and Bakerforce. The latter, under Lieutenant J.S.Baker of A Squadron, consisted of 4, 6 and 13 Troops with armoured cars, LRCs, 3-inch mortars in White scout cars and two 6-pounder anti-tank guns and its task was to protect 2 Brigade's left flank. Bakerforce moved to Salerno for embarkation on 18 January and arrived at Anzio in Operation SHINGLE four days later by which time the rest of 1 Recce was preparing for embarkation.

The landing at Anzio was part of a plan to break the Gustav Line south of Rome. As the landing took place attacks were being made on the Gustav

Line itself and the intention was that those in Anzio would be joined by the main body of Allied forces smashing through the Gustav Line to send the Germans reeling. Such was the intention: the reality was very different with only limited success in the attacks on the Gustav Line and no prospect at all of the anticipated breakthrough.

Bakerforce's first task, having landed at H plus 90 minutes, was to move at dawn on 22 January to cover the demolition of the bridge over the Moletta river after which it would provide a recce screen on 2 Brigade's left flank. The force met no opposition until the bridge where a German armoured car was engaged by the leading armoured car of Bakerforce; the Germans withdrew, losing a second car in the process. The bridge guard was captured and the sappers found the bridge already prepared for blowing. However, the armoured cars, which had crossed the bridge, were lost as one bogged down in soft ground and the other also bogged as it tried to tow the first car clear. Both were stripped of guns, wireless sets and other equipment before the crews withdrew. All this took place under enemy fire but the Germans were themselves engaged by Bakerforce's anti-tank guns, firing HE shells, and mortars. Bakerforce remained in position at the bridge that day but was ordered to withdraw behind the infantry after dusk when strong German patrols began probing forward.

Bakerforce carried out 1 Recce's first patrols in the Anzio beachhead that night and the following afternoon. Then, on 24 January, the bridgehead was enlarged as the infantry advanced to the Moletta.

When the main body of 1 Recce landed at Anzio next day the Germans had already realised that the American corps commander in the beachhead was not prepared to push his troops out too far and too soon. Countermeasures were put into action in the form of air raids and shelling while German troops were moving into positions that would create a state of siege in the beachhead.

By the 27th, B and A Squadrons had disembarked with the former moving forward of 2 Brigade to protect the left flank of 24 Guards Brigade which was directed on Carroceto crossroads while tactical HQ was established with the Guards HQ. A patrol of an armoured car and an LRC from 11 Troop with the assault troop and a section of anti-tank guns pushed forward to the Buonriposa feature where the assault troop and guns got into position while the cars moved on to the next feature:

> This patrol crossed the Buonriposa feature and passing Carroceto Station reached the road junction 851339 without much trouble, though fired on by machine guns and mortars from the north west. An enemy observation post party was successfully shot up and an SP gun engaged, the crew being killed and the gun badly damaged by the 37mm Besa. The patrol carried on up the track to the road-railway bridge 875364 where an enemy engineer party occupied in preparing the bridge for

demolition was destroyed by Besa fire, and the covering party successfully engaged by the supporting car of the patrol. A second patrol now joined the first and had a happy hour engaging enemy targets to the north west. Anything that moved was shot down and the enemy were quickly discouraged from attempting to interfere with the patrols.[15]

By dusk the squadron had accounted for about 50 to 60 Germans killed, an SP gun destroyed and four machine-guns captured; only three members of the squadron had been injured.

The Anzio force was still moving forward although enemy resistance was hardening and, on 29 January, A Squadron, which had relieved B on the Guards' flank, lost one dead and four wounded, with an armoured car destroyed and an LRC badly damaged, without making any headway. The remainder of the regiment had relieved American troops on the right flank of 1st Division; the two squadrons took over from 1,800 American paratroopers and Rangers on a 3,600 yard long front.

On 30 January 3 Brigade carried out an attack which was stopped short of its objective. Next day 88mm fire stopped all forward movement and A Squadron moved into defensive positions. The attack continued on 1 February and an Assault Squadron was formed under Captain L.C.Ashford from three assault troops to make a night attack which began at 2.00am on the 2nd. The first objective was reached by 2.15 but the attacking troops were then engaged by heavy machine-gun fire. One house was cleared with grenades but fire from a second house pinned down the attackers. German reinforcements were fought off by the second assault troop, while the third troop moved into phase two of the attack. But opposition proved too heavy and the squadron was eventually forced to withdraw, disengaging under cover of smoke at 4.30am. Five men had been killed; another five had been wounded and 15 were missing.

In the small hours of 4 February the long-expected German counter-attack was launched. The Germans hit 6th Gordons from the east and B Squadron's left flank was engaged; two companies of Gordons were overrun and 3 Brigade was cut off. During the day the German left flank was engaged by A and B Squadrons. By last light the Germans had consolidated in the nearby wood and during that night all squadrons put out patrols. At noon next day a company of Germans was still in position and throughout that day A and B Squadrons subjected the enemy to heavy fire. At 6.00pm, 1st London Irish Rifles relieved A Squadron and a counter-attack by the London Scottish on the axis of the main road succeeded in extricating the remnants of 3 Brigade. C Squadron was heavily engaged throughout the 7th while 17 Troop inflicted casualties on the enemy in front of the squadron sector. Their holding out against this attack put the regiment on to the front pages of the national press with the description of 'the thin red line' being applied to them. *The Times* correspondent wrote:

> ...a 'British thin red line' was strung out along two miles of the
> perimeter defences. The 172 men who manned this line held off at least
> two enemy battalions and by aggressive night patrolling caused chaos
> and confusion in the enemy camp. These were the men of the 1st British
> Reconnaissance Regiment, the Reconnaissance Corps. Their spirited
> interpretation of their defensive role proved a decisive factor in
> countering the enemy's first testing thrust against the beach-head.[16]

The firepower of a recce regiment had played no small part in that battle as
had the training which encouraged recce men to think aggressively and use
their initiative.

Attacks and counter-attacks - another major German attack was beaten
off on the 16th and 17th during which one scout troop held off attackers,
including tanks, for over five hours - patrolling, shelling, mortaring and
machine-gunning continued day after day with occasional air raids thrown
in for good measure. This was the pattern of activity in the beachhead until
the end of February, a pattern familiar to all who served there and which
could never be forgotten. In March the regiment deployed as infantry, a
move the CO, Paddy Brett, objected to as it caused 'rustiness' when a
return had to be made to mobile operations; it also caused a reduction in
levels of vehicle maintenance. Throughout it all, however, 1 Recce
performed sterling service and the morale of the soldiers remained high.

One factor in that high morale was the leadership of the CO, Colonel
Brett. Another, which stemmed from the latter, was the feeling that the
regiment's officers cared for the welfare of their troops. This was
demonstrated by the issue of rum in the beachhead:

> ...one of the most serious offences in the Army was any fiddling with the
> rum, which was held by the QM for issue when directed. No issue to the
> troops could be made by the Regiment; instructions for any issue had to
> come from Div HQ. During most of the time we were in Italy our
> Division was under US command, comprising part of the US 5th Army.
> The US Army was 'dry' and it seemed obvious that the lack of any
> instructions for us to make a rum issue in the appalling conditions faced
> by most of our chaps in the forward positions at Anzio was no doubt a
> feeling among the top brass that it would be too sensitive a decision
> when under US command. Frank Unwin, our QM, was most concerned
> and one day he quite exploded when discussing the situation with me,
> exclaiming that it was absolutely outrageous that we could not make a
> rum issue to the chaps. At that time I was a sergeant with the QM and
> as the RQMS was back at base in the Naples area, I was acting as RQMS
> on the beachhead, and I was fully in agreement with Frank Unwin and
> wondered whether we could arrange an 'accident' with our supplies.

However, salvation was at hand! Shortly afterwards one of the

divisional infantry battalions had a shell on their stores and their QM
came along to ask whether we could loan him some stores. Our QM
called me over and told me to fix them up and then took the other QM
on one side. He told me afterwards he had suggested that the rum issue
had been lost and after some considerable persuasion the unit's QM
decided this was the case, and he would indent for fresh supplies. But,
of course, Frank Unwin knew his man; he was, as I well knew, very
good at weighing others up. The outcome was that a few days later this
QM came along to us in a panic: he and his Bn QMS, on the arrival of
the additional rum, suddenly realised what an offence they had
committed. So then our QM played his trump card by quietly offering to
take over this rum. The offer was immediately accepted and the QM
told me to take a truck and collect the rum. The truck was quickly
loaded by the unit's QM and Bn QMS and the latter asked what we
were going to do with the rum. I laughed and said, "The QM and I are
going to have a bloody bath in it."

Frank Unwin immediately advised the CO we had this extra and a rum
issue was promptly made. RHQ and the QM's were close together in the
woods but it was arranged that, if RHQ was forward and the QM felt
the conditions justified a rum issue, we would send a message forward
to say the weather was lousy; if we had a reply 'Yes', then we made a
rum issue. I can definitely state that every rum issue made on Anzio and
later in those equally appalling conditions in Northern Italy was from
our unofficial supply. No instructions were received from above to make
an issue. But Frank Unwin was never satisfied as he felt more should
have been available. However, those supplies were well used and by the
time the Regiment handed over when moved to Palestine in January
1945 only a few drops remained. During this period the only worry we
had was that someone in our Regiment might mention rum to someone
in another unit and thus 'spill the beans', but we got away with it; no
doubt our own secrecy helped - only the CO, QM and myself were
aware of the truth.[17]

Fred Whybrow of 1 Recce recorded his feelings throughout January and
into those tense days of early February in a diary. His comments cover
patrols, listening posts, attacks, casualties, conditions - all the horrific
atmosphere of Anzio:

3rd Thursday [February]. Hear that Assault Sqn suffered badly. Had
about four letters from Grace... I will be pleased when I am again able to
write to her. 'Stood to' at 23.30 hrs. Seems to be an enemy attack on the
left of us. A few shots in our sector but nothing serious.

4th Friday. ...a little shelling. On listening post at night. It rained all the
time and I was soaked to the skin. About 23.00 hrs we were fired on by
machine-guns and had to withdraw to the road. Frozen all night. Never
was dawn so welcome.

5th Saturday. Good sleep today. On No 1 post at night. A lot of shells in our area, two landed at Sqn HQ. Ratford and some Loyals injured and two killed. Received two Daily Mirrors from home.

6th Sunday. Weapon maintenance and sleep. Reserve section at night. Fairly quiet.

7th Monday. On OP all day. Plenty of shelling. On listening post at night. At 22.00 hrs enemy salvo round my post followed by intense mortaring. Shelling continued all night.

8th Tuesday. 0300 hrs. Large enemy patrol tried to break through in this sector. We had to withdraw to the wadi. At 07.30 hrs two men of 16 Troop came to us and said 16 Troop had been surrounded and all were prisoners. Jerry left a lot of snipers behind last night and they were shooting all over the place. The Gordons on the left are prisoners. The last we saw of 16 Troop the enemy had them digging trenches. We managed to withdraw and now at 12.45 hrs we are in a position about a mile back. We are in a bit of a state though, as we have no food, and we are soaked to the skin from fording the river. Sam managed to salvage the mail though and there was one from Grace. I wonder what she would have thought if she could have seen me when I was reading it - just chased from one hole and cowering in another to avoid the shells and machine-gun fire. Still, I suppose it's all in a day's work. We start to dig new positions. At night we are ordered to attack and retake the positions we had lost. We get as far as the blown bridge and were just forming up when five mortar bombs dropped in the middle of us. There were not many of us left on our feet. Sanderson, Thacker, Foakes and Lytton were killed and ten more injured. There are four missing. After we got the injured back, we dug in by the DLI and acted as a reserve line, but there were only twelve of us left. It poured with rain all night.

9th Wednesday. Stayed in position all day. At night we were withdrawn out of the line. On the way back we saw heaps of US infantry and tanks going to take our place. We get to rear HQ and all our vehicles are bogged. We eventually reach A Ech. Then food, tea, rum and sleep. Just what we needed.

10th Thursday. I feel a lot better today as I didn't wake until twelve. General sorting out and we get our tent fixed up a little.

11th Friday. Checking of missing kit and weapons.

12th Saturday. We get a lot of reinforcements. My troop is up to strength again but short of NCOs. We get a new officer.

13th Sunday. Very heavy air raids here last night, but not much to do today but I feel pretty awful. I do hope a couple of aspirins tonight will make me feel a lot better. We hear that Cpl Jones and Murray were

definitely killed last Tuesday night. Air attack at night, one HE bomb ten
feet from my tent and my ankle is shattered. God - but it hurts. Cotton
has come up and put a splint on it, and it's not too bad.[18]

So ended Fred Whybrow's war. He was evacuated by hospital ship to
Naples and then to Algiers from where he sailed home to the UK, arriving
in Bristol on 11 April 1944 while his comrades were still enduring the
rigours of the Anzio beachhead.

The deeds of 1 Recce in the Anzio beachhead would fill a volume and
their time there ranks as one of the Corps' greatest achievements. They
remained at Anzio until the end when VI Corps broke out in Operation
BUFFALO. And in that breakout 1 Recce once again played a spectacular
part.

In the days following the smashing of the Gustav Line, the troops at
Anzio waited for the order to link up with the main body of General
Alexander's forces. For 1 Recce that order came on 21 May when Brettforce
was created: as well as RHQ and B Squadron the force included an
additional troop, sections from two other troops, 156 Field Regiment, plus
US elements in the form of Company A, 805 Tank Destroyer (TD) Battalion,
detachments from three companies of 894 TD Battalion and 3rd Bn, 36th
Engineer Combat Regiment (less a company). Brettforce's task was to break
out of the beachhead on the coastal sector west of Littorio and link up with
the main Fifth Army forces from the south; alternatively the force was to
link with a US parachute drop in the Sezza area east of Highway 7. At the
same time C Squadron was to support 18 Brigade in a breakout rôle.

On 23 May Brettforce fought against strong German opposition
including 88mm anti-tank guns being used with their usual devastating
effect. The formation went forward again at midnight on the 24th/25th,
almost immediately suffering casualties from Allied mines. Now under
command of Fifth Army, contact was made with that Army at Borgo
Grappo at 8.36am. Littorio was occupied without incident just after noon
and less than four hours later Brettforce met a US reconnaissance regiment
on Highway 7. By 7.00pm the force was consolidating and an hour later it
reverted to 1st Division command.

The following day Brettforce moved into a regimental harbour; three
days later an A Squadron patrol reached Ardea and shot their way through
the town. Another patrol met strong opposition from south of Ardea and
came under heavy fire. The intelligence officer, Lieutenant R.V.Jeffrey,
attempting to make contact with the patrol, also met heavy fire, bailed out
and was reported missing. On the evening of the following day a patrol
from B Squadron, recce'ing forward of 5th Division, found his body.

In the opening days of June the junction between VI Corps and Fifth
Army was complete and 1 Recce's job was successfully concluded. German
troops were on the retreat but the opportunity to perhaps cut off that

retreat and possibly end the Italian campaign was lost when General Mark Clark directed Fifth Army on Rome instead of, as Alexander had planned, towards cutting off the Germans.

The next phase of the Italian campaign was to bring some very quick operations and the opportunity for reconnaissance regiments to shine.

14
The Normandy Invasion

While reconnaissance regiments fought in the Mediterranean and Far East, others continued training in Britain itself for the long-anticipated invasion of France and the liberation of occupied Europe. Thus far, 13 regiments, plus 1st Airlanding Squadron, had seen active service. NW Europe would involve another nine regiments, plus 2nd Derby Yeomanry and 1st Airborne Recce Squadron (formerly 1st Airlanding) while 5 Recce would finish its meanderings by taking part in the final thrust into Germany.

The regiments which fought their way from the channel coast to the German plains had prepared long and hard for their endeavours and had enjoyed the benefit of the hard-won experience of those regiments already committed to battle:

> In the same way that all the previous fighting had been in a sense preparation for this moment, so had all the fighting so far done by the Reconnaissance Corps in Africa, Sicily and Italy been a prelude to the Corps' role in the campaign across north-west Europe. This was the test, the final justification. The lessons had been learnt, the equipment devised and mastered, the drills and tactics rehearsed to perfection.[1]

The British element of the Allied Expeditionary Force, the British Liberation Army (BLA), included Second (British) and First (Canadian) Armies, thus accounting for the nomenclature of 21 Army Group. In the first wave of Second Army, which provided the assault force for Operation OVERLORD on 6 June 1944, were I and XXX Corps, each represented by a complete infantry division, I Corps by 3rd Division (it also contained 3rd Canadian Division) and XXX Corps by 50th Division. The recce regiments of those divisions were the spearhead of the Recce Corps in North-West Europe. Leading elements of 6th Airborne Division landed in France during the night of 5/6 June with the remainder of the division, including the reconnaissance regiment, arriving on the evening of D Day.

***

One of the earliest recce battalions had been created by the transfer of 8th Royal Northumberland Fusiliers, a motorcycle battalion. The Fusiliers became recce in April 1941 but held tenaciously to their earlier identity: they always described themselves as 3rd Reconnaissance Regiment (NF) and wore on their steel helmets the Roman numeral V, thus proudly proclaiming the precedence of the Northumberlands in the Infantry of the

Line as the 5th Foot.

The Northumberlands also provided 50th Division's original recce battalion. However, 50 Recce had been smashed in Libya in 1942 and was never re-formed in the Reconnaissance Corps, although the battalion from which it had been created, 4th Royal Northumberland Fusiliers, was re-formed in 1943. Without a recce regiment as it trained for the invasion, 50th Division attracted the attention of the CO of 61st Reconnaissance Regiment who had been bitterly disappointed in 1943 when 61st Division was transferred from the BLA to Home Forces. That transfer meant the loss of many of the best men of 61 Recce but it also set Lieutenant Colonel Sir William Mount, Bt, TD off on a mission of his own and after "a number of swift trips to London" 61 Recce found itself "chosen to fill the vacancy"[2] in 50th Division. In January 1944 the regiment moved from coastal defence duties in Kent to join 50th (Northumbrian) Division in Norfolk:

> Only those who have experienced it can know the inferiority an unblooded regiment feels when surrounded by battle-scarred heroes. But the 50th Division made us so welcome, and refrained so carefully from flinging their blood and sand into our eyes, that we soon felt at home in what must have been the happiest of divisions in spite of all its casualties.[3]

As preparations for OVERLORD moved into top gear these two regiments learned of their rôle in the opening phase of the invasion. There would be no initial demand for reconnaissance but reconnoitrers' skills would be needed and so 3rd and 61st Regiments were to provide Contact Detachments for a communications network in the beachhead. In addition 3 Recce was to supply a Beach Traffic Control Group to ensure the smooth flow of traffic through the exits off the beaches on D Day; 61 Recce would also land a skeleton reconnaissance regiment.

For both regiments these tasks involved re-organising regimental structures and training. In the case of 3 Recce each of the groups consisted of about 100 officers and men; 61st's Contact Detachments were of similar strength, composed of C Squadron personnel, while the other two squadrons and RHQ provided the skeleton assault reconnaissance regiment with about 40% of their strength. This skeleton regiment, due to land from H plus 4 onwards, was allowed to choose its own equipment and thus acquired a good number of half-tracks plus very many bicycles. On landing the skeleton 61st Regiment was to concentrate with a composite force of 8 Armoured Brigade, an infantry battalion and a RASC element. Landing beaches assigned for the British and Canadian troops were codenamed Gold, Sword and Juno: 3rd Division was to land on Sword beach in the east, just north of the city of Caen, while 50th Division was to go ashore on Gold beach in the western sector.

At 7.25am on 6 June 1944 mineclearing tanks of 22nd Dragoons landed

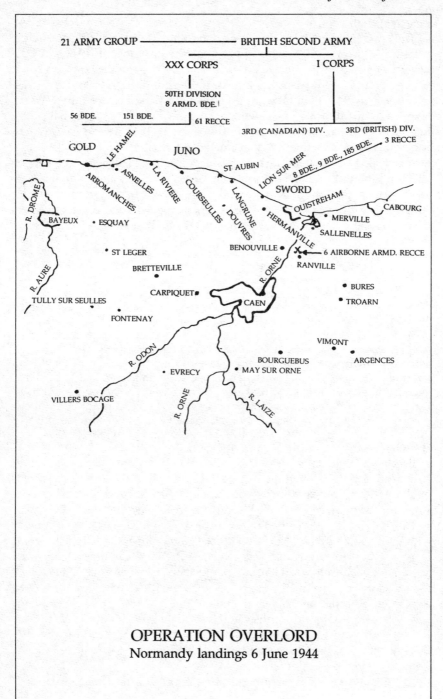

21 ARMY GROUP ———————————— BRITISH SECOND ARMY

XXX CORPS   I CORPS

50TH DIVISION
8 ARMD. BDE.

56 BDE.   151 BDE.
                              61 RECCE

                              3RD (CANADIAN) DIV.   3RD (BRITISH) DIV.
                                                              3 RECCE

GOLD   LE HAMEL   JUNO   8 BDE., 9 BDE., 185 BDE.
                                        ST AUBIN
                          LA RIVIERE   LION SUR MER   SWORD
          ARROMANCHES   ASNELLES   OUISTREHAM
R. DROME   COURSEULLES   LANGRUNE   CABOURG
          BAYEUX   ESQUAY   DOUVRES   HERMANVILLE   MERVILLE
                                                                  SALLENELLES
R. AURE   ST LEGER   BENOUVILLE
                                                              6 AIRBORNE ARMD. RECCE
                  BRETTEVILLE   RANVILLE
                                    R. ORNE
TULLY SUR SEULLES   CARPIQUET   BURES
                                        CAEN   TROARN
          FONTENAY

                  R. ODON   VIMONT
                              EVRECY   BOURGUEBUS   ARGENCES
                                    MAY SUR ORNE
          VILLERS BOCAGE   R. ORNE   R. LAIZE

OPERATION OVERLORD
Normandy landings 6 June 1944

on Sword beach to begin flailing the sand with their rotating chains. With them came REs; 30 minutes later the first infantrymen, 2nd East Yorks and 1st South Lancs of 8 Brigade, came ashore. Throughout the morning landing craft deposited more and more soldiers and equipment on the beach including the Beach Contact Detachments from 3 Recce. Numbers 1 and 2 Detachments under Major Gaskell were attached to divisional headquarters; Numbers 3, 4, 5 and 6 Detachments to 8 Brigade and its three battalions; No 7 Detachment to 9 Brigade HQ; No 8 Detachment to 2nd RUR and Numbers 9, 10, 11 and 12 Detachments to 185 Brigade and its three battalions. Also ashore was the Beach Traffic Control Group under Major Gill who was wounded during the Group's first hours on the beach.

The Beach Control Group did an excellent job, often under heavy shellfire, in establishing a traffic flow forward from the beach exits. The Group displayed initiative and the Beach Exit Officers, Captain Stevens and Lieutenants Brogan, Brough and Farnworth, were firm in their handling of traffic, thus ensuring that vehicles were cleared from the heavily congested beach in the initial critical hours of the invasion. Control of beach traffic in the early stages of the landing had been recognised as a key factor in subsequent success and "the fact that the flow of traffic forward from the beach exits went relatively smoothly must be largely attributed to Major Gill and his men."[4] That "relatively smoothly" is a masterly piece of the understatement so typical of British officers' reports for there was a massive traffic jam on Sword beach which created critical delays. The jam was caused by a tide much higher than usual due to strong onshore winds reducing the distance between waterline and beach exits to 30 feet rather than the anticipated 30 yards. In addition too many non-essential vehicles were brought ashore in the first hours. The Beach Control Group had their work cut out as they sought to impose order. Even after clearing the beach, vehicles could only move very slowly along a narrow road between minefields; that added to the problems on the beach. The Staffordshire Yeomanry's tanks were static for an hour before the Beach Control Group could get them moving; having cleared the exit the Staffords then entered a nose-to-tail queue that delayed them even more and put plans for the deployment of the regiment well behind schedule.

As further troops and armour came ashore over the next few days the Beach Control Group continued in its important, if unglamorous, task, finally relinquishing it on D plus 4 to return to England and rejoin the main body of 3 Recce who were awaiting the call forward to France.

The contact detachments were also busily engaged throughout D Day and beyond remaining with the formations and units to which they were attached until the rest of the regiment arrived from England. For much of that first day in France the contact detachments were the principal providers of wireless communications between battalions and brigades and at times were the only links available. Their work ensured that divisional headquarters was kept informed of the course of the battle throughout the day. Accounts written by two detachment commanders show how difficult and dangerous were the conditions under which they worked. Lieutenant Forrest was in command of No 7 Detachment with 9 Brigade Headquarters:

> [Landed] At 1200 hrs at Lion-sur-Mer and immediately get stuck on an obstruction in the sand. Dig ourselves out and proceed inshore. We have a little trouble with snipers, but soon link up with Bde HQ. Dig in furiously and prepare for anything. At approx 1300 hrs mortar bombs fall around Bde HQ, injuring Brig Cunningham, the IO, the G3, a LO and killing several HQ personnel. This is a great blow, but the Bde carry on under "Swazzie" Waller, the Bde Major. We move on from here to a cornfield and get mortared all afternoon. A further move to Colville towards evening makes us realise that the operation is not going quite to plan. Dig again furiously in an orchard and find ourselves right next door to the SP guns which give us no rest whatsoever.
>
> About 1800 hrs we witness the finest sight so far, the landing of the Airborne Div., which puts new heart into everyone. Forward troops at this time on a ridge beyond Hermanville. Stay the night at Colville.[5]

Meanwhile, No 8 Detachment, under Lieutenant Beck, was working with battalion HQ of 2nd Royal Ulster Rifles, also in 9 Brigade:

> After rough crossing... Lieut Beck plus 2 ORs with 68 set, landed one mile east of Lion-sur-Mer. Jeep with Sgt Benetts plus 1 OR and 22 set landed later, and married up just north of Hermanville. Heavy mortaring and shelling all afternoon - shovels and picks well to the fore. 12 Ju88s bombed beach on D-Night but RAF downed four near us. It was a great sight to see Airborne troops coming in during the evening. Spent night on Hermanville Ridge.[6]

The detachments continued their vital rôle for almost two weeks until they were withdrawn to await the arrival of the regiment. Constantly close to, or in the thick of, the action they had a number of casualties although not as many as might have been expected. The bulk of 3 Recce, less C Squadron, began landing at Courseulles-sur-Mer from Tilbury on 19 June. Two LSTs discharged their loads but another did not and by the morning of 20 June a storm was preventing it from beaching. Two-thirds of the regiment was ashore; by 5.00pm on the 19th, B Squadron was patrolling in the areas of 8, 9 and 185 Brigades to watch the minefield area from Beauville to Cazelle. The squadron's first casualty came at noon on 22 June when its harbour area was shelled, killing one soldier and wounding three others. Based on Periers-sur-le-Dan, B Squadron carried out its minefield-watching task for ten days while the rest of the regiment remained in reserve near Colville; the last third of the group embarked at Tilbury managed to get ashore on the 22nd but C Squadron had yet to arrive.

During its training for the invasion 3 Recce had been constantly reminded by its CO, Lieutenant Colonel Hugh Merriman, MC, Queen's Royal Regiment, of the need to be ready for any eventuality. The lessons learnt by other reconnaissance regiments had not been lost on Colonel Merriman who had conducted a rigorous training regime that gave his regiment a high level of professionalism, confidence and morale. As they took part in the battle for Normandy those qualities and the effectiveness of that training were to be put to the most severe of all tests, that of combat where death was the only umpire.

On 26 June A Squadron, with an anti-tank troop, was assigned to 3rd Division's left flank, taking over from a reinforced company of 1st Norfolks. At this stage the divisional front around Colville was overlooked by the Germans at Lebisey and on the high ground around Epron and La Lande. Opposing the division was 21st Panzer Division with an SS formation on its left flank. A Squadron's task on the left flank was to block the Caen-Blainville road and hold the ridge running west from the road just south of Blainville. Listening patrols pushed forward to the Beauregard area and the regiment began to get its first lessons in the holding of ground on an extended front, a task that was to become very familiar to 3 Recce as the campaign developed.

At 6 o'clock in the evening of 27 June, B Squadron's assault troops took up defensive positions forward of Le Mesnil wood with RHQ inside a walled garden at Mathieu. Both squadrons suffered enemy shelling and mortaring and when another anti-tank troop took up position at Cambes it too found itself on the receiving end of German artillery. In the closing days of June attempts were made to push the divisional front further forward but these were fiercely resisted and heavy casualties were inflicted on the attackers; 8 Brigade suffered 350 casualties in the fighting for Le Chateau de la Lande on the 28th. Clearly the breakthrough would not now come on 3rd Division's front and 3 Recce "kept an eye cocked the whole time over to the West where it looked as if 12 Corps and 30 Corps might be on the big thing between the Onde and the Orne."[7] That thrust had lost momentum by 1 July when a possible German counter-attack on 3rd Division's front was rumoured. Preparations to repel any such attack included 17 Field Coy, RE, coming under command of 3 Recce at Blainville.

On 3 July C Squadron landed on Juno beach and moved to the Mathieu area where it was joined next day by A Squadron which had been placed in reserve. The regiment was getting ready for its part in Operation CHARNWOOD, the first phase of which was to be the capture of Lebisey by 185 Brigade, followed by a divisional attack on Caen, spearheaded by 9 Brigade.

In this operation 3 Recce was restricted to providing contact detachments once again with most of the regiment in divisional reserve. On

7 July RHQ moved back to Colville to be near divisional HQ for the operation and that evening the regiment watched the awesome spectacle of RAF Halifax and Lancaster bombers pounding Caen in preparation for the attack. Early on the morning of the 8th the attack went in on Lebisey; 185 Brigade was successful and the contact patrols did their job well after a difficult start. The next day all of Caen west of the Orne fell to I Corps and contact detachments from 3 Recce, under Lieutenants Darrell and Lewis, were among the first British infantry to enter the city. In spite of being in reserve the remainder of the regiment had a number of casualties, including two killed, from enemy shelling of its positions.

With the capture of Caen came a fresh task: 3 Recce became responsible for 3rd Division's left flank along the Orne from Blainville to Herouville. When the division was drawn back to rest the regiment took over the full divisional front although this was essentially the same sector of the Orne: B Squadron held Blainville and the Shipyard island, A Squadron held Herouville, under the gaze of Germans on the factory chimneys at Colombelles, and C Squadron was in reserve at Beauregard although it later relieved A at Blainville, where RHQ was also sited. The regiment remained in those positions for eight days until 17 July when 2nd Derby Yeomanry - 51st Division's reconnaissance regiment - relieved them.

While along the Orne 3 Recce patrolled on Shipyard island and into no man's land in addition to holding large areas of ground. The mortars were also brought together several times to produce battery fire, including a very successful shoot on Colombelles on the afternoon of 12 July. Following their relief the regiment moved back to Hermanville for a well-earned rest although B Squadron was left for a time to guard Pegasus Bridge over the Orne.

The rest came to a sudden end on 18 July. That morning, east of Caen, Second British Army launched Operation GOODWOOD in which all three British armoured divisions, under command of VIII Corps, were to attack along a corridor cleared by massive bombing to seize Bourguébus Ridge, before the Germans had recovered from the bombing, and then drive for Falaise. As VIII Corps carried out its task, II (Canadian) Corps was to strike out from Caen to secure the rest of the city while I and XII Corps launched infantry attacks, supported by independent armoured brigades, on the flanks. Initially 3 Recce had no rôle in the operation; 3rd Division's task was the secondary one of protecting the left flank of the advance by capturing the villages from its jumping-off point to and including Troarn. However, GOODWOOD appeared to be going well in the first hours and divisional headquarters called 3 Recce forward to the Escoville area where RHQ was machine-gunned and "showered with anti-personnel bombs" many of which, fortunately, failed to explode.

Operation GOODWOOD soon bogged down, however; 3 Recce found

themselves holding a second-line position behind 8 and 9 Brigades with A Squadron in Sannerville, C Squadron in Toufreville and B Squadron in reserve at Escoville with RHQ. B Squadron tried to recce forward to Emieville and south-west of Troarn on the 19th but met stiff opposition and were pulled back. Heavy rain, which lasted for three days, began that same day and helped bog down GOODWOOD, although it has to be said that the operation was flawed from the start, relying too heavily on surprise when 8,000 tanks and other armoured vehicles had to cross the Orne to their assembly areas. As well as the rain, heavy bombing of Sannerville and Banneville-la-Campagne made roads virtually impassable.

The regiment remained static until 27 July, suffering frequent shelling, mortaring and bombing with several casualties. Patrols liaised with flanking units: on the night of the 24th one patrol from A Squadron was knocked out while trying to contact the Suffolks in Banneville-la-Campagne. Two men were killed and another wounded as the patrol was hit by shells and mortar bombs. On the 27th the regiment, less B Squadron - which had relieved A Squadron in Sannerville the day before - moved into reserve at Colleville. B Squadron had the task of holding Toufreville for 8 Brigade with its assault troops while its armoured car troops were held back in Escoville. The squadron stayed with 8 Brigade until 31 July when it rejoined the regiment just as 3rd Division was crossing to the west of the Orne into 21 Army Group tactical reserve "awaiting [a] special task."

For the first few days of August the regiment prepared for the next phase of operations, buoyed by news that the Americans were dashing around Carentin and that VIII Corps' push through Caumont was also going well; it looked as if mobile warfare, the recce speciality, was about to begin. By 5 August 3 Recce was in the Carville area with C Squadron further south, near Montisanger, with elements of 11th Armoured Division, under command of which 185 Brigade had been operating for several days.

On 6 August the other brigades of 3rd Division were ordered to occupy high ground east of Vire in readiness for advances on Tinchebrai and Flers. The Fallschirmjäger holding the high ground were expected to withdraw rapidly as the overall battle was moving quickly, and so B and C Squadrons pushed out ahead of 9 Brigade to seize and hold that high ground while A Squadron maintained contact with the Americans heading for Vire on the right. But the Fallschirmjäger were not disposed to moving off their commanding positions quite so easily and fought fiercely to hold their ground: B Squadron, who had to cross a river to reach the high ground, were mercilessly mortared by the paras. Although bridges had been destroyed the squadron managed to get some elements across only to be pinned down on the far side by even heavier fire.

To the left C Squadron made better initial progress with Lieutenant Turner's carrier troop across the river while Lieutenant Snelling's armoured car troop had flanked left to cross at Burcy. Both troops pressed forward determinedly but ran up against a strongly-held defensive position and were forced to withdraw; Lieutenant Turner was missing. Two other troops under Lieutenants Davies and Anderson (carrier and armoured car respectively) later made another left-flanking move but again ran into stiff opposition that forced a withdrawal, leaving the armoured car troop to hold the bridge at Burcy. Snelling was later awarded the MC.

With the reconnaissance squadrons stopped by German resistance, 9 Brigade mounted an infantry attack which overcame the Fallschirmjäger. The regiment's other task, that of maintaining flank contact and liaison with the Americans had been going particularly well, and a close friendship had blossomed with 102 Mechanised Cavalry Group, an American reconnaissance unit who were most co-operative although "not always too accurate with their information."[8]

The next phase of fighting, from 8 to 11 August, was scrappy. Vire was taken by the Americans while British troops took Yaudry and Viessoix from which 3 Recce probed south-easterly. Eastwards from Viessoix opposition became stronger. B and C Squadrons in succession had a flank protection rôle in the Viessoix area and there were several probes along the Vire-Tinchebrai road, along which the Germans were said to be withdrawing. However, the optimistic reports indicated a faster rate of withdrawal than was the case, which led to some difficult moments for 3 Recce's squadrons. A Squadron ran into some determined Germans and the squadron leader, Captain Gardner, was wounded while Lieutenant Nundy earned an MC. That was followed on a subsequent day by B Squadron having three armoured cars knocked out and a troop commander, Lieutenant Whitelaw, wounded.

After a short spell when 3rd Division was supposed to hold its ground A Squadron, now under Major Greenall, was sent ahead of 8 Brigade in the late afternoon of 12 August. That evening the brigade passed through A Squadron on its way to Tinchebrai but 185 Brigade, moving along a parallel axis, left of 8 Brigade, was unable to make much progress and so, by dawn on the 13th, 8 Brigade had to be pulled back almost to its start line. A Squadron then deployed behind the leading elements of the brigade; the rest of 3 Recce was backed up along the Vire road ready to move forward in exploitation of any break on 3rd Division's axis. A squadron of the Household Cavalry Regiment was to be under command on the right flank but there was no exploitation as the Americans in the area were in close contact with the Germans and the Household Cavalry squadron could not be released.

By now 21 Army Group was creating a ring around Falaise and bringing heavy pressure to bear on the Germans; it seemed as if the front had to loosen up at last. This time those expectations were well-founded: on the evening of 14 August a two-squadron advance on Tinchebrai and Montsecret was ordered with further exploitation if possible. The squadrons moved off with C on the right and B on the left. Having negotiated mines, C Squadron moved quickly over the last mile to Tinchebrai beating 102 Mechanised Cavalry there by ten minutes; the colonel of the American regiment was not held to the wager of a Staghound armoured car if 3 Recce won the race for Tinchebrai. However, a blown bridge and a rearguard party then delayed C Squadron for a time.

B Squadron had a relatively fast run to Montsecret but their approach route left them exposed to observation from nearby high ground and when the squadron reached the bridge at Montsecret they were subjected to heavy fire from the Germans; by 3.00pm it was clear that their advance had been held on the river line. During the fighting at Montsecret, Major Gaskell, B Squadron leader, was fatally wounded. The regimental advance was over for the day as RHQ moved north of Tinchebrai and orders for the morrow were awaited.

Those orders were for the regiment, with two squadrons of Household Cavalry, to pursue the retreating enemy towards Flers as the infantry had lost contact with the Germans. Here was a pure recce job and so, at 10 o'clock on the morning of 16 August, 3 Recce began its "last, and best, battle in France." The two Household Cavalry squadrons were deployed well out on the right flank and met little opposition up to the Flers river; C Squadron went down the main Tinchebrai-Flers road, the divisional centre-line, and A Squadron used a circuitous route via Montsecret while B Squadron was in reserve.

Both A and C Squadrons had speedy advances and captured many prisoners, although the latter had the bigger haul. The regiment had been ordered to stop on the outskirts of Flers which was 11th Armoured Division's objective. Since 3 Recce had got there so quickly, however, permission was sought to move on and capture the town. This was granted and C Squadron pushed ahead and deployed with an anti-tank troop in the town centre. Although there was still some enemy resistance on the eastern outskirts the Germans withdrew during the night and 3 Recce had the distinction of having liberated Flers. It was a distinction not appreciated by the Northamptonshire Yeomanry of 11th Armoured Division who expressed themselves displeased with 3 Recce for having taken their prize. Major Norton, commanding C Squadron, mollified the Northamptons by handing the town over to them before its capture was announced by the BBC.

The regiment had taken almost 100 prisoners over two days, captured two towns and covered a long stretch of ground. There was satisfaction at these achievements and pleasure that the frustrations of earlier weeks had been left behind. Congratulations came from the divisional commander -

who authorised a rum ration - and from the corps commander, General O'Connor, who visited the regiment to thank them for their work.

> So ended our part in the battle of France. It had not taken exactly the form which we had expected - there had been more holding and less mobile work than we had hoped for. But the principles laid down by the Colonel early in the summer of 1943 that we must be flexibly minded and prepared to take on any jobs given to us were amply justified.[9]

The other regiment ashore on 6 June, 61 Recce, had also fought its way through the battle of Normandy. On that first day in France 61st's Contact Detachments set up the first signals links for 50th Division on the beaches. Contact patrols were probably the best tasks the Corps could do in such a situation and both regiments "had done well by the Corps badge, time and again beating the normal channels with information of importance."[10] However, the price paid by 61st Regiment was much higher than that of 3 Recce: nearly half the contact patrols of 61st with the assaulting infantry were killed or wounded, either on the beaches or before reaching them. Nonetheless the survivors carried on while some patrols, whose wireless sets had been shot up, performed sterling service as infantrymen.

The other element of 61 Recce disembarking that morning was a skeleton, or assault, reconnaissance regiment made up of RHQ, A and B Squadrons, all at about 40% normal strength. Landing from H-hour plus 4 onwards the skeleton regiment concentrated with 8 Armoured Brigade, an infantry battalion and some RASC in a composite force which was to break out of the beachhead that evening, advance ten miles to Tessel Bretteville wood where it would spend the night and then, next morning, seize the high ground near Villers Bocage. That high ground overlooked the country for miles around and the composite force was to hold on there for four or five days until relieved by the main body of Second Army. Behind this plan was the memory of the failure to exploit the initial success of Operation SHINGLE at Anzio and a resolution that such failure would not be repeated in Normandy.

But weather conditions conspired against the plan: rough seas caused a number of the Rhino ferries that were to carry the regiment from the LSTs to the shore to break away and just over half the regiment was ferried to land on D-Day; the remainder stayed aboard the LSTs about three hundred yards offshore. On the morning of 7 June the 2ic, Major Philip Brownrigg, who was still aboard an LST contacted Colonel Mount by wireless:

> He gave me a new rendezvous for the rest of the Regiment; then he ordered A Squadron to move there. As the rendezvous was well within the bridgehead, I was slightly disturbed a few minutes later to hear the Squadron Leader report that he was held up by heavy machine-gun fire. This penetrated the armour of several of the carriers, but Corporal Billingham, although wounded, drove on into the middle of the enemy

position, throwing grenades, until he collapsed with a wound in the head. Soon afterwards I called up the Commanding Officer again, but he cut me short: "Get off the air; I'm shooting Boches."[11]

In fact, most "Boches" in the area were Russian and not of particularly high morale. During the 7th the rest of 61 Recce got ashore and the regiment spent "an uneasy night." That day Colonel Mount had taken out a patrol which returned with nine prisoners. Next morning a less ambitious version of the original Villers Bocage plan was begun: at 9.30am A Squadron and a tank squadron from 24th Lancers advanced to take some high ground about two miles outside the bridgehead perimeter in the general direction of Villers Bocage. Although a stormy German reaction to any move forward was expected, the advancing squadrons passed through the foremost Allied positions without hindrance. The trouble began when A Squadron had advanced about half a mile to Le Bas d'Audrieu where it was held up by isolated parties of Germans and much sniping. The hold up was reported to brigade headquarters whose response was to tell A Squadron to "use your big friends [the tanks] and push on."[12] Determined to encourage his men, Colonel Mount went forward in a carrier to join A Squadron. Once there he stood up in his carrier to encourage his troops and give orders to the tanks. Over six feet tall, Mount was an inspiring leader but he also made a good target and he was shot through the thigh at short range some 30 minutes after his arrival at the scene of the action. Major Brownrigg quickly assumed command, receiving detailed orders from his wounded predecessor, in spite of the latter's pain.

The rest of 8 Armoured Brigade had been advancing along a parallel road but with no more success; the brigadier, therefore, decided to switch them to the route taken by A Squadron and 24th Lancers. As a result A Squadron was relieved by an armoured regiment but not before two carrier sections had been sent on a flanking move to clear a village from the rear. A recall message reached only one section and the armoured regiment was heading for the same village - in the opposite direction. As the armour entered the village firing in all directions "the other section of carriers motored straight through the fire, from the opposite direction, with the officer standing up in the leading carrier and looking distinctly surprised."[13] Fortunately no one was hurt, although the situation had all the ingredients of a ghastly tragedy.

From that operation the skeleton regiment moved onto normal reconnaissance work for about a week. Every day patrols found enemy resistance stiffening. One squadron, sent along the same road to recce the same ground on five successive days, found Germans waiting for them daily at the same spot. On the sixth day brigade headquarters heard a rumour that the Germans had pulled out and the squadron leader was told to send an armoured car patrol down the road yet again; the cars were to beat up any enemy who might be left. Both armoured cars were knocked out by a German tank, waiting in the usual place.

As resistance intensified there was less scope for reconnaissance patrols and 61 Recce found itself holding part of the British line. At first squadrons were used in a 'long stop' rôle, with their armoured cars as machine-gun posts, before being put into the line as infantry. Their first spell in an infantry battalion position was at Briquessard, near Caumont, where they relieved an American unit.

> For the rest of the campaign we used to judge all "black spots" by references to Briquessard. Anything described as "worse than Briquessard" stank. It wasn't that our casualties were heavy there - they were comparatively light, seeing that it was an obvious position on a forward slope and had at least its fair share of missiles. The trouble was that for the first time we had to abandon every appearance of reconnaissance. We parked all our vehicles about two miles back, re-formed our squadrons of seven troops into companies of three platoons, and occupied an almost continuous trench system, with some very large gaps in which concertina wire had to do the job of men. We were amused to find that some of our prisoners were converted German reconnaissance troops, and very disgruntled at doing infantry work. Although we didn't appreciate it at the time, our fortnight in the line at Briquessard was first-class training. But I think if we had been there much longer our scout troops might have lost some of their dash, which they were to need again shortly. Whenever our General visited us he was most upset about our casualties. "This isn't really your job," he said, "I want you for recce'ing the crossings over the Seine."[14]

Soon afterwards the Allies were fighting their way out of Normandy and 61 Recce was back to its true rôle, passing through Briquessard where German corpses were testimony to the work of the regiment's mortars and the Essex Yeomanry's guns. From there B Squadron, led by Lieutenant Truman's carrier troop, carried out a classic reconnaissance into Amaye-sur-Seulles. About a mile before the village were strong defensive locations but the squadron by-passed these and came in from a flank, taking the Germans totally by surprise. That was the first of a series of actions, usually at about troop strength as room for manoeuvre was still restricted. One of these was another classic operation, carried out in the shadow of Mount Pinçon, and watched by the divisional commander and an infantry unit. Lieutenant Truman was again the recce officer in the heat of things: he and the infantry commanding officer had discussed who should clear up an enemy strongpoint ahead and Truman had suggested that the infantry leave it to recce. With supporting machine-gun fire from an armoured-car troop, he took his carriers on a left-flanking move that broke the Germans. As Truman returned to make his report the infantrymen who had witnessed his action broke into spontaneous applause.

Near Le Plessis-Grimault, Lieutenant Flint won the MC "in a brilliant patrol with his gunner, chasing Boches in and out of houses."[15] A little

1. Early recce cars on exercise with 5 Recce in Northern Ireland, October 1941. The cars were improvised from trucks as airfield defence vehicles for the RAF and were pressed into service with Reconnaissance Corps units.

2. Ironsides, armoured car based on Bedford 3-ton lorry chassis. 1941. Known in 15 Recce (to whom these examples belonged) as a 'meat safe'

3. WO I Bill Harrison of the Grenadier Guards was the RSM at the Recce Training Centre for much of the war and was "one of the straightest, most honest and soldierly men that I ever met" - John Fairley.

4. Assault troops in training, 1941. Perhaps this is where the BBC got its perception of the Corps from?

5. Moving in Red: carriers of a reconnaissance regiment probe forward in Tunisia, 1943.

6. Men of 1 Recce fording the stream at El Batham, south of Tebourba, May 1943. The bridge had been blown by the retreating enemy.

7. Cpls. Thomas & Heard, 17 Troop, C Sqdn., 56 Recce range their 2-inch mortar in the Sangro area, southern Italy, 1943.

8. Members of 56 Recce decorated for service in Tunisia (l-r) Tpr. C. Reid; Sgt. H.Dean; Sgt. B. Mayne; Lt. Col. Chavasse; Major J.Forshaw; Lt. E.A.Edwards.

Men of 2 Recce near Sadaung ⸱dy a map as they plan their next ⸱trol. Note the mixture of ⸱adgear, including khaki beret, ⸱ck berets & bush hats.

10. Lt. C.R.Beale MC of 1 Recce meets Lt. Leroy R. Weil of Chicago as Fifth Army forces meet with the breakout force from Anzio.

11. The northern Appennines in the winter of 1944-45 when recce units held the line here as infantry.

12. A Humber heavy armoured car of 46 Recce in training in Palestine in the summer of 1944.

13. Armoured cars of 15 Recce leading the advance to Belgium: on the road to Lille, early September 1944.

14. Monty decorates Sgt. R.Millroy, 15 Recce, with the DCM in December 1944. Note the divisional emblem in the background which is emblazoned with 'battle honours' from Normandy onwards.

15. A soldier pays tribute to a fallen comrade of 1st Airborne Recce Squadron at Arnhem, September 1944.

16. Advancing into the low countries a Daimler armoured car of 2nd Derbyshire Yeomanry lends its support to the infantry of 51st (Highland) Division.

17. A Humber armoured car of 3 Recce firing its Besa outside Goch as 3rd Division operates south of Goch, February 1945.

18. 5 Troop, A Sqdn., 81 Recce (which includes the recipients of an MC, a DCM, two MMs, a Certificate for Gallantry and three mentions in despatches).

20. Bren-gun carriers of 49 Recce are cheered as they drive through the Choorstraat to Utrecht town hall.

21. Humber light recce car 'retired' to the Tank Museum in Brussels. It has been restored to represent Kendal Chavasse's 'Faugh A Ballagh.'

22. The lightning flash seemed appropriate for a reconnaissance unit. This flag was captured from an Italian recce unit at El Alamein.

further on Lieutenant Williams came on some armoured cars "of a rival regiment" which had stopped short of several suspicious-looking clods of earth in the road. In response to a "we can't get on - mines," Williams dismounted, lifted the clods, threw them off the road and drove on.

***

As the first arrivals of 3 and 61 Recce carried out their tasks on the Normandy beaches on 6 June the men of 6 Armoured Airborne Recce were boarding gliders at Tarrant Rushton and Brize Norton for the flight to France. That evening the regiment arrived in Normandy although the 2ic's glider had been forced to land in England. Some mortarfire met them on the landing zone at Ranville and a tank was damaged when a Hamilcar landed and struck it.

By the early morning of 7 June recce patrols were operating over a wide area and the regiment had its first engagement when a patrol met a German armoured car; a recce jeep blew up after being hit by an incendiary round but no one was injured. The crew of a light tank were posted missing after their tank struck a mine while another tank was hit by anti-tank fire and one man injured. By the end of the day patrols had reported enemy movements in the Toufreville and Sannerville areas and had identified the presence of 192 Panzergrenadier Regiment.

Patrols continued over the next few days and the regiment brought back much valuable information on enemy troop locations and identifications of enemy formations. Engagements were fought with German troops, casualties inflicted and a number of prisoners taken. The War Diary illustrates a typical day on 11 June:

0115: Elements of 153 Inf Bde passed through posn.

0600: Recce patrols to same area.

0630/0930: SP Guns, 3 Mk 4 Tanks and Half-Tracks seen moving into Sannerville. Armd cars seen in [map square] 1269.

1030/1130: SP Guns seen at 109696, 115685

1130 on: Under Cmd 153 Inf Bde. One Recce patrol operating from 1369, during the afternoon penetrated Touffreville E of Sannerville, and to Bdg 142083 without opposition.

1800/1900: 4 SP Guns in 1208 seen firing on area X-Rds 140708.

2200: Attack by 1 Gordon on Touffreville. Touffreville and Northern part Sannerville occupied. To deal with threatened counter-attack on 1 Gordons from Cuverville 2 Light Tank Troops and 1 Recce Troop were sent to Escoville which was found empty. It being too dark for tanks to fire, Troops returned at 2330.[16]

So the pattern of operations continued with the regiment reverting to command of 6th Airborne Division on the 13th. From Ranville, squadrons supported a range of offensive and defensive divisional tasks during June and July. August saw the mortar troop particularly active with 840 HE rounds fired between 11 and 15 August; they were credited with the destruction of at least one enemy mortar position. By now the Allies were breaking out of Normandy and the regiment, with some Cromwell heavy tanks in use, was recce'ing for the advance. On 21 August patrols contacted 49 Recce and two days later a troop of 6 Airborne Armoured Recce assisted infantry in Honfleur.

With a Belgian recce squadron under command the regiment carried infantry on its tanks and other vehicles in a dash to Pont Audemer on the morning of the 26th to cut off enemy troops falling back on the town. The forward elements were in Pont Audemer by 8.30 that morning to find the bridges blown. The task was handed to the infantry as 6th Airborne Division was withdrawn from battle to return to Britain, their job in Normandy over. But the men of 3 and 61 Recce were still engaged as the Allies broke out of Normandy that August.

And so the first two reconnaissance regiments to arrive in France were heading for the Seine. They had long ceased to be the only representatives of the Reconnaissance Corps in France having been joined in Normandy by several other regiments. These included 15th (Scottish); 43rd (Wessex); 49th (West Riding); 53rd (Welsh) and 59th Regiments: 2nd Derbyshire Yeomanry, honorary members of the Corps, had also arrived with 51st (Highland) Division. With the exception of 59th and 61st Regiments, both to be disbanded, these regiments would fight through to the final German surrender being joined by 52nd (Lowland) and, finally, by 5th Regiment which would travel up from southern France.

15
Battle for Normandy

As Allied forces consolidated the bridgehead, further formations arrived to strengthen 12 (US) and 21 (British) Army Groups. Among them was 49th (West Riding) Division, originally an assault division for OVERLORD until replaced by 50th Division. Nonetheless, 49th Division was an early arrival in France with elements of 49 Recce landing on 13 June. A Squadron was first ashore, followed four days later by RHQ, B Squadron and part of HQ Squadron; C Squadron and the balance of HQ Squadron arrived on 2 July. Formed in September 1942 from independent reconnaissance squadrons 49th (West Riding) Reconnaissance Regiment was one of those to adopt a specific regimental distinction: a small White Rose of York superimposed on the Corps badge.

Coming ashore in the early stages of the invasion gave 49 Recce a series of experiences similar to those of 3rd and 61st Regiments with patrolling playing a lesser part than holding stretches of line as infantry. For the first five weeks, 49 Recce had a purely infantry rôle as it protected 49th Division's left flank and covered the gap between the division and formations from I, and later XII, Corps. Based initially on Le Hamel, squadrons had to cover and patrol into a long cornfield stretching out some three kilometres from Le Hamel.

When 49th Division opened its attack on Fontenay and Rauray, 49 Recce made several sweeps through the cornfield using its carriers and assault troops. Many casualties were inflicted on the enemy although the recce men were subjected to heavy fire from 88mm guns on high ground east of Rauray. In the advance B Squadron, with a troop of the regiment's anti-tank guns, deployed to provide left flank protection. On the outskirts of Fontenay the anti-tank gunners spotted and engaged four Panther tanks coming out of a wood about 50 yards away: "the first three were disposed of by one gun in four shots."[1] The fourth "fell to a PIAT handled by a lance corporal who is a silk-hatted bank messenger at a London branch of the Midland Bank in civil life."[2]

There was little movement during the first three weeks of July with squadrons in long-stop positions behind the infantry or holding various parts of the line. It seemed that this routine might end when 49th Division was transferred from XXX Corps' area to that of I Corps, north and north-east of Caen. But there too the rôle was that of infantry and not until mid-August did any forward movement occur. Patrol reports on the night of 14/15 August indicated a German withdrawal from 49th Division's front to high ground about Argences and, on the 15th, the regiment advanced to reconnoitre in front of the division.

For two days 49 Recce advanced rapidly although the Germans had blown bridges and left many mines behind; the only real resistance came at Mezidon on the river Dives. Thus the scene was set for the regiment's dash to the Seine during the next two weeks:

> During this time we advanced approximately 50 miles and took 600 Prisoners of War; the enemy had destroyed all the bridges over all the rivers, but rarely put up any resistance except at those river obstacles, so that each day resolved itself into a rapid advance from a bridgehead secured by the infantry to the next obstacle where the process of examining the bridges and locating the enemy defences was repeated; by the time infantry came up we were able to give them a complete picture of the state of the obstacle and the positions held by the enemy so that they were able rapidly to cross the river and secure a foothold on the far bank for us once more to pass through.[3]

As 49th Division battled for Le Havre the main Allied force was racing across France and Belgium. Now well behind the mainstream of that advance, 49th Division rested for a few days which 49 Recce spent near Guerville before beginning its travels again on 21 September. The first phase of the regiment's progress towards Germany had ended with the last days of the summer of 1944 but other reconnaissance regiments were still at the spearhead of the advance.

***

One of the regiments surging through France and Belgium was 15th (Scottish) Recce, formed in February 1943 and therefore one of the youngest recce regiments. Under Lieutenant Colonel J.A. Grant Peterkin, 15 Recce was an amalgamation of 15th, 45th and 54th Independent Recce Squadrons: the latter two, with 76th Squadron, had been created when 54th Recce Battalion was split up in November 1941. To bring it up to full establishment, 15 Recce had also received a draft of some 300 men from 162 Regiment, RAC, previously 9th RWK. This mixed force quickly welded together to form a very effective regiment for a division that had been upgraded from a drafting formation to a 'higher establishment' formation in late-1942.

Colonel Grant Peterkin, a Cameron Highlander who had earlier commanded the Reconnaissance Training Centre at Scarborough, took the regiment to war in summer 1944. Sailing from Gosport on 27 June, the regiment's LSTs and LCTs landed their passengers and cargoes at Arromanches later that day to set off for St Gabriel. By then 15th (Scottish) Division had been in Normandy for more than a week and was engaged in Operation EPSOM which, as a result of their contribution, was dubbed the battle of the Scottish Corridor.

The division's reconnoitrers did not have long to wait before being committed to battle with A and C Squadrons taking part in the final stages of EPSOM. Filling in between 15th and 49th Divisions on 30 June, C Squadron was first in action to be followed by A next day: the latter closed a gap on the right flank of C Squadron and the KOSB who had lost contact with 49 Recce, the XXX Corps unit to their right. Both squadrons deployed as infantry but so wide was the gap that A Squadron never made contact with 49 Recce. The tasks set A and C Squadrons saw them fight off German tanks and some casualties were suffered by both. That afternoon the regiment's anti-tank guns came into action on both squadron fronts; the night was quiet as was the following day, during which 15th (Scottish) Division was relieved by 53rd (Welsh) Division. The two recce squadrons were relieved by 53 Recce and retired to Secqueville en Bessin.

The regiment's next task was to provide a squadron to assist 46 Brigade clearing the area west of Caen and Carpiquet on 9 July; this assignment, a recce job, was given to A Squadron. Just short of Verson the squadron harboured for the night and next morning set out for the river Orne, travelling through Eterville and Maltot; the latter was about a half mile short of the river. Although it had been thought that the area was clear of Germans there was considerable resistance at Eterville with enemy troops dug in on reverse slopes behind the village while, on the approach to Eterville, German aircraft attacked the squadron. Firing a Bren-gun, Sergeant Robinson of 1 Troop shot one attacker down in flames.

A battalion from 43rd (Wessex) Division was to take Eterville after which 9th Cameronians, led by A Squadron, would pass through to seize the high ground overlooking the river. But the Wessexmen failed to take the village and the task fell to the Cameronians. The Scottish infantry were already fighting when three recce troops of A Squadron were sent forward, with 2 Troop leading from 3 and 1 Troops. The village church had fallen across the road through Eterville, and burning vehicles also blocked it, so 2 Troop under Lieutenant Blair made its way through a field and a farmyard to the Louvigny area and into action against some German infantry. Having crossed the main road from Caen, 3 Troop also met enemy infantry and the troop commander, Lieutenant John Arundel, called his carriers forward to support the armoured cars in pursuit of the Germans who had fled into cornfields. It was Arundel's intention to cut through the enemy to reach the river but the situation was quite dangerous as there were a number of well-concealed enemy troops:

> ...the whole troop was perched on the top of a hill, from which we could see the opposite bank of the river. The Brens in the carriers and the Besas in the armoured cars were firing at the enemy snipers, who would pop up, fire and dive back into the corn. My carrier commander, Sgt Munton, told me to keep their heads down with bursts from my Bren. I did. ...but ...[m]y gun slipped... and fired through the front of the carrier

above the driver's head; my head was bleeding slightly, and for a moment I thought that the holes in the carrier had been caused by German bullets.[4]

The situation became more dangerous when a smokescreen on the right cleared to reveal five German tanks which opened fire on 3 Troop, forcing it to disperse and knocking out the two leading armoured cars. Lieutenant Arundel and Trooper Griffiths, his driver, became the regiment's first fatalities in action when their armoured car took a direct hit. As the action developed the squadron leader, Major W.L.Rowlands, was seriously injured and his driver, Trooper Ballard, killed when their recce car was also hit by a tank shell. Lieutenant Blair's troop had met up with Canadian troops near Caen but their return route had been blocked: Blair recce'd another route which added to the information that A Squadron was able to amass that day for 46 Brigade. But the cost had been 20 casualties, including four dead.

A Squadron went into night harbour south of Verson that evening but found little respite with a bombing attack and persistent mortaring. The following day the squadron was back in action, securing the flank of 214 Brigade, which was trying to recapture the dominating Point 112.

Operation GREENLINE was the regiment's next major action; this was intended to deepen the bridgehead and draw German troops away from First US Army on the right. For this operation 15 Recce's major task was traffic control on five routes approaching and crossing the Odon; this was to be carried out by RHQ, with elements of HQ and A Squadrons, while A Squadron's carriers were to convey wounded over ground impassable to ambulances; two LRCs were loaned to the commanders of 44 and 227 Brigades.

The operation started on the evening of 15 July under artificial moonlight provided by searchlight batteries and 15 Recce was involved until the night of the 17th when its division was relieved by 53rd (Welsh). In that period the regiment suffered further casualties with several dead, including Lieutenant Blair, fatally wounded by a mortar bomb at his traffic point; the commanding officer, Colonel Grant Peterkin, was fortunate to escape uninjured when a shell burst close to him in an orchard. C Squadron, which was to have gone into action under 227 Brigade, was withdrawn after enduring a bombardment between Baron and Gournay.

Even in the regimental harbour, south of Cheux, no one was safe: on the night of the relief German aircraft attacked and two men were killed and a number of vehicles, including two ammunition trucks, were set on fire. B Squadron finally joined the regiment in the bridgehead on 19 July and, two days later, the three assault troops combined to form Macforce, under Major MacDiarmuid, to assist 7th Seaforth Highlanders in the Le Baltru area. Macforce had an unpleasant task in an unpleasant location:

It rained like hell for the first two days and we were mortared. The infantry were down to eight men to a platoon and were very tired. They rested while we manned forward posts and patrolled. One of the posts, right down in the wooded valley, was periodically cut off. We had German patrols coming and looking at us. A party of three men from each troop was sent out on reconnaissance, down through the valley and up the other side, and as it was crossing a field it saw that the hedge in front was lined with German machine guns. These opened up when the patrol was backing out, but everybody except Trooper W.J.Pugh, of C Squadron, who was killed, managed to get back. Another patrol, looking for the Germans in the blackness of a rainy night, was nearly shelled by our guns. During a burst of German gunfire one member of Macforce mistook a latrine for a slit trench in his dive to avoid a shell which killed two infantrymen in a slit trench nearby.[5]

On 23 July a secret move took 15th (Scottish) Division to the extreme right of Second Army to relieve 5th US Division in the Caumont sector, south of Balleroy, a change described as "like going from the bustle of Oxford Street into the tranquillity of Hyde Park."[6] C Squadron moved immediately into the line in the La Chavetiere-Le Bisson area of the Bocage while the rest of 15 Recce was in reserve near Balleroy. C Squadron was to be the link between 15th Division and the Americans to the right. As the squadron patrolled forward, VIII Corps was preparing for an offensive onto the plain beyond the Caumont ridge.

This fresh onslaught was Operation BLUECOAT which began at 7.00am on 30 July without a preliminary bombardment but with the attention of some 1500 aircraft which bombed pre-arranged targets in two strikes. By the end of the day a six-mile deep wedge had been driven into the enemy lines. A and B Squadrons advanced with 227 Brigade and tanks from 3rd Scots Guards. The two squadrons mopped up pockets of German resistance along the way but it was a difficult advance with hedges, woods and the inevitable mines to hamper movement.

During the afternoon the rest of the regiment followed up the advance and C Squadron, which was told that it would lead Second Army's break-out from the Normandy bridgehead, was given an unusual evening reconnaissance task. Two troops, under Lieutenants Gray and Royle, were sent to find a way past St Martin which was still in German hands. The town was eventually cleared by 11th Armoured Division on 31 July after C Squadron's patrols reported that only the road through St Martin could take the advance.

Next day, 1 August, the Guards Armoured Division and 44 Brigade cleared the Bois du Homme after intense fighting around Quarry Hill and contact was made with 43rd Wessex Division to the left. The King's Own Scottish Borderers fought with roses in their helmets to mark Minden Day when their predecessors, the 25th Foot, had decorated their hats in similar fashion at the Battle of Minden in 1759. That evening B Squadron helped 46 Brigade battalions clear the area around Galet and La Mancelliere; several casualties were sustained, including Lieutenant G.H.L.Carey and Sergeant E.P.Thompson who were killed by machine-gun fire as Carey led his carrier troop on foot across a cornfield. Of the men wounded in the action one, Trooper M.H.Lawn, was later killed when the hospital ship on which he was being evacuated was sunk.

The regiment continued to move forward over the next two days while providing flank protection for the division and, on 3rd August, Lieutenant Gray won the regiment's first Military Cross when he took a patrol forward under heavy shell and mortar fire to surprise an enemy patrol and bring back valuable information. There was general delight at the rate of progress and 15th Scottish Division received congratulations from the commanders of VIII Corps and Second Army on their contribution to that progress. The regiment's advance began again on the morning of 6 August with B Squadron moving towards Le Codmet with 46 Brigade; Le Codmet fell without opposition but thereafter German resistance stiffened and the squadron was unable to reach Vassy. C Squadron, with a Grenadier Guards tank squadron, had been delayed when the Grenadiers had to deal with German tanks which had broken through near the start line while, on the Estry route, Lieutenant Royle's troop found the town strongly held by 9th SS Panzer Division, and the road to Le Theil mined and guarded by tanks and machine-guns. Some patrols entered Estry and, although forced to withdraw, continued harassing the Germans and providing information for their brigade which had been held up by the determined resistance:

> At Estry Cpl H.J.Higginson and Tpr H.L.Roberts were killed, and Sgt W.McMinn and Tpr J.Bunker won the Military Medal. Sgt McMinn, commanding a carrier section in support of the armoured cars, saw that the leading car had been knocked out, left his carrier and went forward on foot for about 250 yards under machine-gun fire to some houses, from which he could see the car and discover what was happening in the village. He climbed to the top of a house overlooking an enemy machine gun post. The Germans shelled the building and it collapsed, but he extricated himself and reconnoitred the village street, discovering the positions of machine guns and a tank. This information he gave to the infantry.[7]

Such was the intensity of action in which squadrons found themselves. A minefield on the Vassy road accounted for two vehicles of 10 Troop and the crews had to make their way back on foot while the crossroads at La Caverie where C Squadron was located was shelled intensively. That evening B and C Squadrons were withdrawn and the infantry also withdrew to better positions. But the end was near for the Germans in Normandy: while SS Panzers held the area around Estry, the Wessex Division took Mount Pinçon to one side and the Americans captured Vire on the other flank.

A and B Squadrons carried out flank protection rôles between 15th and 43rd Divisions during which several casualties were suffered and, on one occasion, a patrol from 43 Recce opened fire by mistake on positions held by 1 Troop of 15 Recce. Then, on 10 August, B Squadron was relieved by the Inns of Court Regiment who completed the relief of all 15 Recce two days later. Only after that relief did Estry fall to 8th Royal Scots, leaving the Inns of Court Regiment to lead the dash through Vassy to link up with the Americans and close the trap around the Germans in Normandy. When 15 Recce next moved into the line it would be to carry out the rôle for which it had trained for so long: reconnaissance at speed in front of its division.

***

Wales had also been represented in the battles to extend the bridgehead with 53rd (Welsh) Division which had concentrated in Normandy by the end of June. The division included 53rd Reconnaissance Regiment, created in January 1941 from anti-tank companies. At that time 53rd Division had been stationed in Northern Ireland where it had been joined by 61st and, later, 5th Divisions carrying out internal security and anti-invasion duties. The division had moved to the Welsh border counties in late 1941, but its time in Northern Ireland had been put to good purpose and it was by then a well-trained division. Training continued in Britain, resolving into preparation for operations in north-west Europe.

For the Welsh Division, part of XII Corps which had a follow-up rôle, those operations began at the end of June. Hardly had the division concentrated than it was placed under Lieutenant General Sir Richard O'Connor's VIII Corps to relieve 15th (Scottish) Division in the bridgehead over the river Odon near Baron. In the subsequent operations 53 Recce played a rôle familiar to other reconnaissance regiments deployed in the bridgehead. However, at that stage, the only part of the regiment deployed in France was B Squadron under Major Sir H.J.D'Avigdor Goldsmit supplemented by an anti-tank troop. The first night in France was spent near Bayeux from where the squadron carried out traffic control tasks for 53rd Division before relieving A Squadron, 15 Recce in the line near Cheux. Further traffic control duties - at Mondrainville on the dusty road from Caen to Villers Bocage - followed before news came that the main body of the regiment had arrived. B Squadron's experience was fairly limited and was described as being confined to "the art of digging trenches that were of real use and in the inevitable familiarity with the sights and smells of a battle area." They had also endured shelling and mortaring and had their first battle casualty when Corporal Owen, a wireless operator, was killed by shrapnel. Moving back to join the rest of the regiment west of Carpiquet the squadron took "a dozen young chickens and a couple of tame rabbits in the back of the fitters' truck, though Bessie the cow and her calf had to be left regretfully behind."[8]

Towards the end of July the entire regiment was blooded when it took "over from infantry in dug-in positions on high ground, a salutary reminder that our Regiment would not spend all its time patrolling in vehicles or carrying out deep reconnaissance."[9]

That deployment took place on 27 July: B Squadron relieved elements of 158 Brigade at Eterville; the other squadrons relieved 1st Oxfordshire & Bucks LI of 71 Brigade in cornfields beyond the Odon river south and east of Baron and Gavrus. Recce troops were left behind as the assault and carrier troops of the three squadrons each took over about 300 yards of front. The lie of the land was such that little could be done in daylight but night patrols went out to gather information on the enemy's dispositions. A crossroads near the hamlet of Le Bon Repos was an objective for several night patrols, the first of which was led by Lieutenant P.J.Nolan of A Squadron. Nolan, later to win an MC, was accompanied by Corporals J.Hills, later to win the MM, and Briddon and Lance-Corporal Hartley.

Constant mortaring was endured throughout this period in the line but this began to decrease in early August. Not until the night of 3/4 August did the enemy finally pull back from the crossroads at Le Bon Repos. The news of that withdrawal was brought back by a patrol under Sergeant R.W.Robinson. With him were Corporal Hills and a trooper and their objective was to check if a German Mk IV tank was still dug in near the crossroads. Having passed the gunner forward OP, and given the sergeant there the password, the patrol crawled along parallel to, but about 25 yards away from, the road:

> We passed by a number of tanks and armoured vehicles [both British and German] which had been knocked out previous to our taking our position on the Ridge... We passed by an orchard. The forward German fox holes were approximately 40 yds to the rear of the orchard. (I knew this to be correct as this was my third patrol from the Ridge.) Moving on we now had a reasonably good view of the crossroads; there was no Mk 4 tank there. When passing by the orchard we had heard muffled noises of vehicles moving [behind] Le Bon Repos. I moved forward cautiously and, as I had previously arranged, the Cpl and Trooper covered me from a distance of about 10 yds. I was able to ascertain that the forward and secondary line of the German foxholes were not manned and were quite empty.[10]

As a result of Sergeant Robinson's information a recce patrol was sent out on the 4th to the crossroads and over the hill; in LRCs and armoured cars the patrol was to draw fire or capture prisoners for information. An account of the patrol was written by Corporal May, the gunner on the LRC chosen to lead the patrol:

> The Troop Sergeant was to be in command and with Trooper Crosier,

my driver, we crept over the brow of the hill at zero hour to see a large open expanse of shell-pitted ground with many knocked-out tanks and vehicles scattered about... my first thought was whether my car would add to this collection. Then I distinctly remember praying that I should do my best whatever happened for I had never felt quite so frightened before. Our progress was slow but we edged down the narrow road, dodging a partly-demolished carrier and bumping over shell-holes. Still, nothing happened to us and I felt easier. Then I observed a kind of road barrier some 300 yards ahead which I kept well covered with my Bren. Suddenly Crosier applied his brakes and said that he thought he saw traces of mines in the road only a matter of a few yards in front. Our Commander dismounted and was confirming these suspicions when a dirty piece of material was waved from the barrier by an equally dirty individual who later became our first prisoner. We felt proud to have accomplished at least one of our missions.

But at this time the Squadron suffered some casualties. The Assault Troop had come up to clear a passage for us through the mines when one man trod on one and was rather badly wounded. However I felt a lot better now and we continued again through the now harmless minefield and past the barrier into the shell-torn village of Esquay. I wirelessed back that we had reached the first objective and we moved on keeping a constant watch on the ruins for snipers.[11]

Sergeant Robinson had been with the assault troop foot patrol which had helped clear the way for the vehicles. The troop commander, Lieutenant Nolan had gone back to Squadron HQ with the prisoner, leaving Sergeant Robinson in command of 7 Troop:

...we received orders to pass on through Esquay and take the road to Evrecy. We advanced through Esquay and continued for about a half mile, No 7 Troop leading with the two cars eighty yards behind. When 7 Troop came abreast of a large field of ripening corn, two small tanks and three armoured troop-carrying half-tracks came dashing out of a small copse some 300 yds away, making for the road we were on. As we had no A/T weapons with us (left in the White's half-track in the valley below the Ridge) I yelled for the Troop to take cover in the cornfield. They needed no second invitation and in a matter of seconds had disappeared in the corn. Both cars loosed off a few rounds and then they realised they were outnumbered and outgunned, and withdrew, making for the village of Esquay. From the cornfield we had a good all round view and could see some Churchill tanks coming over the Ridge with A Sqn's recce cars and carriers in front. Jerry also could see what was happening and decided to apply that well-known axiom: 'He that fights and runs away lives to fight another day'. Our White's half-tracks had now joined us, so we became a mobile Assault Troop once more.[12]

B Squadron moved from Eterville, where they had been heavily shelled, to Hill 112 above Esquay from where, for the first time, they witnessed an infantry attack. For nearly a week an OP was maintained ahead of the line, the occupants of which moved only at night and silently observed the enemy by day.

Fifty-third was now on its way to Evrecy, the Orne and beyond. C Squadron advanced on A Squadron's right and the Orne was reached on 4 August at Pont de Coudray. Following a rest spell at Le Hom, near Evrecy, the regiment crossed the Orne on 12 August to head for Falaise.

***

Also engaged in the salient before the Baron Ridge had been the Wessexmen of 43rd Division who fielded a Gloucestershire Regiment Territorial battalion in the reconnaissance rôle. In June 1941 5th Glosters had become 48th Division's recce battalion, transferring to the Reconnaissance Corps on 14 October; the battalion moved to 43rd Division in January 1942, renumbering as it did so. The title of 43rd Reconnaissance Regiment came into use in April that year. When it went to war in the summer of 1944 43 Recce was commanded by Lieutenant Colonel F.Lane-Fox.

The Wessex Division had taken part in the bloody battles of Operation EPSOM in the course of which they had suffered heavily, and their commander, Major General G.I.Thomas, had earned the nickname of 'Butcher' from his troops. But 43 Recce had suffered severe casualties before coming ashore in France. The ship carrying the Regiment, the *Derry Cunihy*, had been lying offshore overnight when German bombers dropped acoustic mines:

> Early on the morning of June 24th, before reveille... a landing craft came alongside with orders for the *Derry Cunihy* to steam to another and safer beach to unload. Nearly all were still asleep, the men in the holds or on deck and the officers either in the cabins beneath the bridge or on the boat deck. The ship's engines started up and with the first throb there was a violent explosion which split the ship in two between the engine room and number four hold. The stern half began to sink rapidly, and in a matter of seconds, number five hold was under water... The men of A Squadron and HQ Squadron in number five hold had very little chance of escape. The fortunate were thrown clear, although few of these understand how they escaped.[13]

A total of 180 men were lost while another 150 were injured. This tragedy cost the Regiment the equivalent of more than a squadron in dead and missing. As a result of the disaster 43 Recce was held at Pouligny to re-form and re-equip during July while 43rd Division fought to take and hold Hill 112. To bring the regiment back to strength a complete squadron from 161 (Green Howards) Recce was sent to France to become the new A Squadron, 43 Recce. The Green Howards squadron arrived the day after 43 had left Pouligny and joined the regiment near Bayeux.

On the morning of 1 August, A and C Squadrons took over infantry positions in the Livry-Briquessard area, a rôle with which B Squadron was already familiar having been committed to just such a task early in July. Having landed fit for battle, B Squadron had passed under divisional command to hold reserve positions in the Verson-Mouen area. Although sustaining some casualties from mortaring the squadron had had no other contact with the enemy. As A and C Squadrons relieved infantry units for the advance on the Bois du Homme, south of Caumont, B waited in immediate reserve to exploit any break-through by the infantry.

Just after taking over the line, C Squadron took the regiment's first prisoners, three "rather frightened enemy stragglers" who wandered into the squadron positions. A and C Squadrons had a quiet time although Sergeant Midgeley of 11 Troop was badly injured during a patrol when he trod on a mine. After just over a day in their positions, both squadrons were relieved by 61 Recce and 43 Recce concentrated near La Lande on the morning of 3 August:

> A violent battle had been fought over the fields in which we harboured and the ground was littered with dead - British and German. Arriving in darkness, with a German air raid in progress near by, several of the men settled down for the night by their vehicles to discover in the morning that they had been lying beside corpses. One corporal mistook a body for a sleeping comrade whom he needed for a job and made some attempt to rouse him.[14]

The regiment had received orders for its first true reconnaissance task in France: B and C Squadrons were to pass through the infantry and advance on two axes, B Squadron on the line Jurques-Ondefontaine and C Squadron Jurques-Le Mesnil Auzouf-La Tautainerie. B Squadron's move was delayed by Tiger tanks on high ground overlooking the road from Jurques to Le Mesnil. As the Tigers would have pounded the recce vehicles to scrap, the advance was postponed until RAF Typhoon fighter-bombers had dealt with the tanks. The Typhoons went in with rockets but a subsequent recce patrol under Lieutenant Balsdon of 6 Troop found the tanks still in position.

An infantry attack supported by tanks on the high ground was repulsed next morning and B Squadron was forced to return to harbour which was being shelled by the Germans. During the night of 4/5 August, 5th DCLI reached the top of the hill and the way was clear for B Squadron to set off. As it did so it came under attack from Typhoons which came close to hitting the assault troop's half-tracks; fortunately there were no casualties. C Squadron had departed on the afternoon of the 4th, its orders amended to take it west through the Bois du Homme from where it was to find a route back to the original axis, rejoining it at Le Mesnil Auzouf, thus by-passing the Tiger threat. An alternative route was found and, from Le Mesnil Auzouf, the squadron moved down the road to Montcharivel. A short distance from there a sniper opened fire on them, wounding Trooper Smith, a despatch rider, as he directed 9 Troop round a corner. Although shot in the chest Smith returned fire with his SMG and the troop sergeant, Sergeant Verinder, spotted the sniper in a tree and brought him down with a burst of Bren-gun fire. The carriers were continuing on their way when mortar shells began to fall. With the carriers forming a firm base the cars began probing into Montcharivel but met heavy fire from Spandaus and mortars and, as the light began to fail, were pinned down. However, they were able to withdraw when four Churchill tanks and some infantry arrived and provided covering fire.

Lieutenant Davies had taken 10 Troop past La Tautainerie but, just short of Vory, they too were mortared. The troop took up positions in farm buildings and an orchard and tried to locate the mortars. Meanwhile the squadron assault troop were also being heavily mortared at the crossroads at La Tautainerie which they had taken over. The troop commander, Lieutenant Richardson, was wounded and the position subsequently had to be abandoned. Lieutenant Davies' 10 Troop was also forced to withdraw under cover of darkness and "drove back over the crossroads with houses blazing around them and bullets whistling by."[15]

B Squadron's leading troop met up with part of C Squadron's assault troop just short of La Tautainerie at the end of the squadron's run that day. The squadron had engaged the enemy on a number of occasions; one troop was attacked by two Panther tanks which had pounced as the troop was in ambush positions - the intended victims turned out to be British infantry - and the troop's carriers and an armoured car had to be abandoned. Sergeant Jones, the car commander, was lucky to escape with his crew as they were subjected to Spandau fire from the moment they bailed out of their vehicle. It was 6 Troop, under Lieutenant Scarr, which, having secured a junction on the road to Le Mesnil Auzouf, moved on until it contacted C Squadron's assault troop. As darkness was falling the leading troops were withdrawn for the night. So ended 43 Recce's first day in action.

The following day the regiment resumed its forward movement and encounters with the enemy cost the lives of 7 Troop's commander, Lieutenant Banks, and his 2ic, Lieutenant Vacha. For the next week 43 Recce was kept constantly busy. On 9 August Mont Pinçon was in 43rd Division's hands and the noose was tightening on the Germans as the Americans swept from Brittany towards Paris and the rear of the enemy troops facing the British and Canadian armies. With Mont Pinçon taken, 43 Recce was ordered to move again and reconnaissance tasks, dissolving into small, and not-so-small, skirmishes with German units occupied the next few days until the regiment - less 3 Troop - was withdrawn on the night of 12/13 August. Two days comparative rest followed at the foot of Mont

Pinçon. Those eight August days had been exhausting for the men of 43 Recce. Lieutenant D.E.R.Scarr later wrote an account which gives an insight into how the reconnoitrers lived during that month:

> ...the days were long and the nights were short and one did not reckon so much in terms of daylight and dusk but rather in terms of being "up" or in reserve. Usually a troop was in reserve one day out of four, although this was by no means rigid. Even so, when the troop was committed, there were few of its members who did not look forward to the respite which a few hours of darkness would bring, and as the day wore on, provided nothing too distracting was happening, eyes would search discreetly for signs of lengthening shadows and ears would strain to catch the sound of those ever welcome words on the air: "Hullo Peter two, you may close now and R.V. at my location."

> Then the tense atmosphere would lift as if by magic and without a care in the world everyone would bundle into their vehicles and set off for "home". ...in those summer days it was past ten o'clock as everyone surveyed their quarters for the night, normally an orchard or an open field. ...there were many things to be done before rest could be thought of, and no one escaped his share of those tedious but essential tasks.

> The guard for the night was detailed and several weary troopers would curse their fate... Next came the problem of digging. Perhaps a shallow ditch would be improved or a hole would be scratched out of the ground to get the sleeper below ground level... Sometimes, but very rarely, a man would be too weary to dig and would crawl under, or into, his vehicle to sleep. However, the drone of the nightly German raiders soon dispelled carelessness in this respect. The whine of a shell going the wrong way had much the same effect and then no one was too tired, or too proud to dig.[16]

On the night of 7 August First Canadian Army launched Operation TOTALIZE towards Falaise; the operation began with a massive bombing mission involving 1,000 aircraft. Second Army's Operation BLUECOAT had ended the day before while Third US Army was striking out into Brittany. A German counter-attack had been swiftly reacted to by General Omar Bradley, commanding 12 Army Group, and 21 Army Group was moving to close the Falaise Gap and seal the fate of Field Marshal Günther von Kluge's force of some 100,000 men. The Wessex Division had taken Mont Pinçon, the highest point in Normandy, by the time the Canadians moved off; Crerar's Canadians were in Falaise on 15 August and the Battle of Normandy was over. Although the German high command called for a counter-attack von Kluge declined to issue such an order. Instead he instructed his forces to withdraw. He was relieved of his command and ordered to return to Germany to explain himself to Hitler. On the way he committed suicide by swallowing a cyanide capsule. Such was the price of failure for a marshal of Hitler's armies.

16
The Break Out

By 21 August the Battle of Normandy was over. Since 6 June 21 Army Group had suffered 83,000 casualties, including 16,000 dead. Despite much soulsearching in the Allied high command Montgomery had remained confident that the Germans would crumble and the breakout would follow. And now Monty's army group was heading for the Rhine. Directed north of the Ardennes, British and Canadian forces struck out for Germany. Second Army, under Dempsey, crossed the Seine on 25 August, was in Amiens six days later and entered Brussels on 3 September, five years to the day from Britain's declaration of war on Germany. By mid-September Dempsey's forces had reached the Meuse-Escaut canal. Crerar's First Canadian Army, operating on the left flank of the British force with I (British) Corps under its command, was to clear the coast and capture ports to improve the logistic support of the Allied armies. On 1 September Eisenhower assumed overall control of the army groups from Montgomery, who had taken them out of the beachhead and Normandy.

The rapid advance through France following the breakout provided conditions in which recce regiments were in their element. Here, at last, was the job for which they had trained and at which they excelled - fast, mobile warfare, probing forward to establish contact with the enemy, and reporting back to divisions so that the big picture could be constructed from all the snippets of information provided by Recce.

But this period of the war also spelt the end for one regiment as calls on British infantry manpower brought the break-up of 59th Division and the disbandment of 59th Recce. Neither the division nor 59 Recce had the opportunity to take part in the race across France. Having come ashore on 24 July 59 Recce fought in the beachhead for a month before the division was broken up to provide reinforcements for other formations.

The regiment had been formed in January 1942 as an improvised recce battalion for 59th Division; it became a regiment of the Recce Corps on 15 July 1942. An identity had been quickly established with special regimental bugle calls being introduced on 1 May 1943 when 59 Recce was stationed in Northern Ireland: routine calls were preceded by the Regimental Call, "Listen my lads, the Recce call." Another distinction was that troops were numbered within squadrons rather than regimentally.[1]

A high state of training had been reached when 59 Recce sailed for Normandy in late July. First to arrive were C Squadron who were patrolling the Rauray area with carrier and assault troop patrols by night when the rest of the regiment arrived to be quickly committed to infantry tasks as squadrons took over sectors of line from battalions of South Staffords. The CO, Lieutenant Colonel J.A.Talbot-Ponsonby, decided not to dismount his armoured crews and to allow only the assault troops to patrol. As the squadrons moved into the line their positions were subject to intermittent, and occasionally intensive, mortaring.

As the division began its advance out of the bridgehead at the beginning of August, 59 Recce took up its natural rôle with recce patrols on the roads south of the Noyers-Villers-Bocage road. Less A Squadron, the regiment advanced on two lines in front of 59th Division towards the Orne where 53 Recce was contacted at 9.00am on 5 August:

> The Sqns continued to try to mop up enemy resistance throughout the day but this is impossible. If the infantry battalions had co-operated the question would have been settled immediately, but the infantry was concerned much more with crossing the river.[2]

The regiment continued to be critical of the infantry and morale was not helped when two squadron leaders and the officer commanding HQ Squadron were relieved of their duties following a visit to the divisional commander on 7 August.

Three days later, the regiment crossed the Orne with A and B Squadrons moving out some eight miles. A Squadron was pinned down in front of Forge-a-Cambro-Espins but B patrolled more freely; one armoured car patrol under Lieutenant Knowles-Bolton remained out through the night taking ten prisoners.

As the division advanced towards Falaise, 59 Recce provided right flank cover, searching all roads up to the right divisional boundary. Elements of the regiment penetrated to the centre of Thierry Harcourt on the 11th although infantry support was needed to secure the town. The regiment's rôle changed on 14 August when it was ordered to deny the roads and bridge in the Pont d'Ouilly area to the enemy after 197 Brigade had established itself on the line Mont de Perc-Point 308. As C Squadron moved onto Pont d'Ouilly next day they met opposition and withdrew from the bridge but patrolled into the town with support from B Squadron.

The regiment's rôle in this advance continued until 18 August and once again 59 Recce was highly critical of the infantry who failed to follow up and take over from the regiment. "It would appear that the infantry are not aware of the rôle of a reconnaissance regiment," noted the War Diary.[3] It commented that co-operation had been better in training than in action and suggested that replacements for heavy casualties had much to do with this sad state of affairs. On 20 August 59 Recce went into Army Reserve with the exception of A Squadron which was to recce, and mop up, to the Falaise-Argentan road. In what was the regiment's last action, A Squadron lost two men killed and eleven wounded, one of whom later died.

On 21 August came the announcement that the regiment was to

disband. Three days later the divisional commander spoke to all ranks at RHQ when he explained that to attain a quicker result, ie, to end the war in weeks rather than months, General Montgomery had decided that 59th Division would be broken up for reinforcements "because it was a wartime formation and the most junior division in France and not because of any deficiency."[4] That same day the chaplain, the Reverend D. Stuart-Fox, held a memorial service for 59 Recce's dead. The regiment itself was now dead and as it passed into history the men of 59 Recce became reinforcements to be posted to other regiments of the Reconnaissance Corps.

***

Other recce veterans of Normandy were now advancing with their divisions. And to the West Country men of 43 Recce went the distinction of being the first British troops to reach the Seine. But 43 Recce had several more days of fierce action before the final closing of the Falaise Gap. Moving off from near Caulville on 14 August B Squadron and later C Squadron recce'd ahead of the division and made contact with the enemy at several points that day; Lieutenant Lindsay Baker of 7 Troop earned praise for his aggressive leadership on his first day commanding a troop in action. But a number of casualties were suffered before A Squadron took over the advance next day. Much time was spent mineclearing which hampered the advance but the Germans were pulling back and, on the 19th, 43 Recce was south of the Noireau river, ready for orders to strike for the Seine.

The Wessex Division was given the task of leading XXX Corps' advance to the Seine and 43 Recce's move started on 22 August with A Squadron in a flank-protection rôle for the corps. Pushing out through the Falaise Gap, and the horror of roads choked with dead enemy troops, the bodies of horses and the wreckage of vehicles, the regiment began recce'ing towards the Seine on the 24th when 9 Troop, C Squadron, probed towards Pacy sur Eure to see if the bridge there was intact. The crossing had been demolished and sappers, British and American, began work on a new bridge the next morning over which C Squadron passed to move westward to cover 43rd Division's left flank. B Squadron followed: their task was to reach Vernon, recce a crossing for the division and identify approach routes for the DUKWs that would ferry the infantry across the river:

> B Squadron were warned not to allow themselves to be seen on the river bank. The Squadron moved towards Vernon with three troops up... a party of Royal Engineers was travelling with Squadron H.Q. Major Carter pushed his troops forward at full speed and the river was reached without contacting the enemy. During the day, Divisional recce parties came forward and the assault plans were completed. Towards evening, 129 Brigade arrived in Vernon, having travelled 120 miles in DUKWs, and the crossing began within a few hours of their arrival.[5]

A smokescreen covered the beginning of the brigade crossing which continued that night. Strong German opposition, and weeds fouling the DUKWs' propellers, hindered the operation but, by morning on 26 August, two battalions were across with a third crossing. Bridgebuilding was hindered by artillery and machine-gun fire and it was early evening before a bridge was complete; 43 Recce was "to cross immediately... and then pass through the infantry and to extend the bridgehead in all directions."[6] In an attempt to assist the infantry Lieutenants Jackson and Scarr tried to ferry two cars across but their efforts came to naught when one car bogged down; they had to await the completion of the sappers' exertions. Nonetheless, they were the first members of 43 Recce to cross the river on the morning of the 27th, being followed by B Squadron, A Squadron and RHQ. Shelling had intensified around the bridge area and the CO and General Thomas had a narrow escape when RHQ was bombarded. One trooper of A Squadron was killed and five others injured.

General Thomas ordered cars to support the infantry advance in the centre of the divisional front while recces were to be carried out in both directions along the Seine. B Squadron probed westwards, A Squadron eastwards and other elements backed up the infantry. In the latter rôle, 5 Troop was engaged by enemy tanks and one car was knocked out by a Tiger; only one crewman was slightly injured. Both A and B Squadron's recce patrols were also engaged, Lieutenant Edge of 2 Troop being killed by a sniper near Giverny. Trooper Dow earned the MM for killing the sniper and retrieving Edge's body.

B Squadron's recce achieved the liberation of the village of Notre Dame de L'Isle in which Germans were holding out against 43rd Division. On the evening of 27 August Lieutenant Lindsay Baker studied the lay of the land from the infantry positions and next morning led an advance to the village. After a skilful flanking advance which caused the Germans to retreat towards the river, Baker dismounted and, covered by his car which was moving behind him, moved on foot, alone, along the riverbank:

> Suddenly, rounding a small bend, he came upon four Germans who opened fire and threw grenades. Unharmed, he returned fire with his Sten, killing one German, wounding another and capturing the other two. Some of the enemy had been killed when the carriers and cars entered the village and the others were killed or captured, when they attempted to escape... by the carriers, sent round to cut off their retreat. In this action, fifty Germans were killed, wounded or captured without loss to the Troop and, for his magnificent handling of his troop and his great personal bravery, Lt Baker was awarded the Military Cross.[7]

On 29 August the regiment stood down and moved to woods near Vernonet where they would remain until 14 September although C Squadron was detached to provide local protection for Tactical HQ, Second Army, in early September. On 7 September, C Squadron crossed into Belgium and, two days later, passed through Brussels to Perk where it remained for some days with Second Army's Tactical HQ. During that time several long recce patrols were carried out by armoured cars to gather information for Second Army's commander, General Sir Miles Dempsey. Another spot of liberating was indulged in when a troop cleared part of the town of St Nicholas, south of Antwerp.

***

On 24 August 15 (Scottish) Recce finally got the chance for which its troopers had been waiting when the regiment was ordered to recce at speed in front of the division. Caen and Falaise were left behind as armoured cars, LRCs and scout cars raced for the Seine. Royal Engineers' armoured vehicles were in support, including bulldozers to clear the debris of von Kluge's army from the roads. Quickly squadrons made their way through Le Sap, Vimoutiers, Bernay, Orbec, Beaumont le Roger, Le Neubourg and Barquet to re-form in the area of Louviers. Patrols probing forward to reach the banks of the Seine itself were greeted with wild enthusiasm, flowers, wine, cheers and kisses from the local populace, delighted at this evidence of liberation.

Elaborate crossing preparations had been made as the Germans were expected to use the Seine as a delaying line. Patrols from 15 Recce set out to determine German strength in the St Pierre du Vouvray sector. As the far bank had the advantage of hills and woods to provide cover, efforts were made to draw enemy fire but no serious opposition could be identified. To confirm this lack of opposition, Lieutenants Wheeler and Shirley of C Squadron took patrols across the river, thus becoming the first members of the division to cross the Seine. Wheeler's men were first across, rowing to Herqueville in a boat found at Portjoie:

> After my patrol of four carriers had moved up and down the west bank without drawing fire, I got together a small patrol, and, taking one of the FFI (French resistance) with us, we rowed straight across the river... On reaching the other side I left the Bren gunner in the boat and the rest of us went off to explore. I saw a group of French women and children outside a farm. I managed to attract their attention, and they immediately put their fingers to their lips and pointed up the road. We took cover and I sent the French guide round the back of the farm to get information. When he came back he told us that three Germans had just left the farm and were only round the corner when we got there. One of them had just gone back to bring up reinforcements. I decided that we had all the information we needed... so we returned to our boat. Before we reached our side of the river again the Germans started firing single shots at us with a machine gun. As soon as we landed we made for what little cover there was, but Corporal Dove was wounded in the chest.[8]

Lieutenant Shirley, with some of his troop, crossed by assault boat to an island opposite Muids and kept the village under close observation, reporting sightings back to RHQ and thence to divisional headquarters.

The information from 15 Recce meant that none of the elaborate preparations earlier envisaged had to be used; 15th Division was able to cross the river on 28/29 August. First over were battalions of 227 Brigade who met stiff opposition just south of St Pierre du Vouvray. When they had established a firm bridgehead, 44 Brigade crossed near Portjoie and, next morning, 46 Brigade crossed in the Muids area.

Armoured car patrols of A and B Squadrons were rafted across with A Squadron on the right in the Fretteville area to enlarge 46 Brigade's bridgehead. The leading car of 1 Troop was fired on by machine-guns and mortars on the edge of Fretteville but the commander, Corporal Whiting, silenced some of the guns and the patrol tacked to its left where a further pocket of strong opposition was encountered. Whiting's car was blown up but, although told to abandon it, he worked for 45 minutes under fire to direct its successful recovery. That done, Corporal Whiting patrolled in the car the rest of the day despite damaged steering, jammed turret, and a useless gun mounting. The car was later written off as a total loss. Whiting was awarded the DCM while Lieutenant Blount, who went to help him when his car was disabled, received the MC. Blount also led patrols, both foot and mobile, that stopped German reinforcements reaching Le Thuit where Lieutenant Kerridge's patrol fought the defenders for eight hours and eventually took some 30 prisoners. Kerridge had deployed so well that the Germans never appreciated that he had only three cars; he too received the MC. Other equally tough little actions were fought by other troops.

B Squadron was on the left, advancing, with C Squadron, to Ecouis. There, too, were several pockets of determined German resistance. One patrol, however, had a spectacular run near Les Andelys:

> Owing to slight error in map reading and the unexpected appearance of the A Squadron cars, Sgt Litton's party had failed to recognise the forward infantry positions, and driving on, had realised too late that its support was no longer close behind. Soon the cars came under machine-gun and anti-tank fire, but their speed carried them through it. The road was too narrow for them to reverse out of danger or to turn round. There was only one way open - forward. Both cars increased speed.

> Going round a bend in the road, the light reconnaissance car, leading, was confronted by a large anti-tank gun. One gunner was resting against the gun shield, the others were gathered round a stationary truck on the other side of the road. The Bren in the light reconnaissance car was fired at the truck and the gun crew, and a quick shot from the heavy car's 37mm hit the German gun. The crew dived underneath the truck, which, however, was driven off at high speed. In this chaos the two B Squadron cars were able to turn round and race for home, after

looking down into Les Andelys and seeing that the town was full of enemy.

The way back was under the heavy fire of Germans who were by now very much on the alert. The light car, with one of its front wheels shot off, wobbled the last hundred yards to A Squadron on three flat tyres and a brake drum, and the heavy lurched in with three flat tyres, all riddled. The crews were safe.[9]

This little adventure came to be known within the regiment as the Charge of the Litton Brigade.

Remaining pockets of resistance were soon flushed out and the bridgehead over the Seine was firm. On 29 August the regiment continued to recce in front of 15th Division, A Squadron fighting actions at Fretteville and Le Thuit. Learning that the Germans were abandoning Les Andelys, Lieutenant Blount's troop raced the infantry to the town; Blount's arrival before the foot soldiers earned his squadron leader, Major MacDiarmuid, a bottle of whiskey to add to the MC he had already won. Probing beyond Les Andelys, A Squadron met a patrol from 43 Recce while another patrol, probing outside 15th Division's boundaries, was fired on by troops of 11th Armoured Division.

B Squadron reached Houville and Bacqueville that morning and were in Ecouis in the early afternoon where some stragglers were captured. A patrol from C Squadron, recce'ing beyond Ecouis, ran into a strong German rearguard. One car was knocked out and its commander killed. Having failed to by-pass the Germans the squadron was withdrawn and the regiment concentrated near Ecouis while 7th Armoured and 53rd Divisions took up the running into northern France.

Colonel Grant Peterkin, issued a Special Order of the Day on 30 August:

Since 27 Aug, when the Regiment for the first time was able to get on its proper role, 15 (S) Division has advanced over 50 miles, crossed the major obstacle in France, the River Seine, and driven the enemy back much faster than he wished...

A great deal of the credit for this rapid advance is due to the excellent information obtained by the patrols of the Regiment.

The Commanding Officer has received the following letter from Major-General C M Barber, DSO, GOC 15 (S) Inf Div:

"I should like to congratulate you very much on the excellent work done by your Regiment during the past few days and on the excellent and valuable reports sent in. They have been very highly commended to me verbally by the Corps Commander. Will you please convey to all ranks my appreciation of all their very good work done in foul roads for very long hours in pretty wet weather."

The congratulations of the whole Regiment are due to the Patrol Commanders and their crews, particularly those whose reports hastened very materially the crossing of the River Seine, and the subsequent rapid advance of the British Second Army.[10]

Wessexmen and Scots were across the Seine with the Germans retreating rapidly before the Allies. Also following up were 53 (Welsh) Recce whose division had been ordered to break through to Falaise and link up with American troops advancing due east from Avranches.

On 14 August C Squadron was heavily engaged against SS troops at St Logis farm in Martainville at the beginning of a week during which the regiment suffered its heaviest casualties of the campaign. That August morning:

...was very misty and when the mist lifted it left us exposed to Jerry's artillery and mortars which had ranged perfectly on the road. We eventually put in a recce down a slope through a big wheatfield until we were stopped by 88mm guns. They hit the carriers on either side of mine and I don't know how they missed me. Shells were exploding all round and I dodged back into the wheatfield where we had to stay for the rest of the morning.[11]

The 88s claimed a fearful toll from 5 Troop: Lieutenant 'Timber' Wood, the troop leader, and three men were dead, two others were wounded and three missing. The latter trio had been wounded and captured but were recovered when the German hospital where they were being treated was taken soon afterwards. St Logis farm was taken by 2nd Monmouths after the reconnoitrers had been repulsed:

Our infantry eventually attacked and re-captured them [the missing wounded] and all the Jerries as well. It was magnificent to watch our infantry going in. They came right through our positions in extended order preceded by a mortar barrage. But Jerry was holding out in strength and only 18 of that company returned.[12]

Over the next few days the German forces were pushed into the area between Falaise, Argentan and Trun and heavily bombarded and attacked from the air. On 15 August 53rd Division was told to block all roads from the south and south west into Falaise. The Welsh Reconnaissance Regiment was sent ahead and, after some nocturnal confusion for 2 and 5 Troops of C Squadron and shelling from Allied artillery, the regiment made the first junction with Canadian troops coming into Falaise from the north. Unfortunately there were casualties, including the regiment's popular padre, Harry Smith, who was killed. German rearguards were met over the next few days: C Squadron ran into further trouble with 4 and 5 Troops encountering enemy anti-tank guns which knocked out three carriers. The recce troops also had problems: one driver, Trooper Cox, was fortunate to survive a direct hit on his Humber HAC, the second such incident he had suffered that week.

A Squadron under Major Graesser found itself "being shelled by the Yanks, Canadians and British, not to mention Jerry"[13] as it recce'd from Falaise to Trun. But it also took over 2,000 German prisoners, overran a German hospital and liberated some of the regiment's own men.

> On 21 August this Troop [No 7] of A Squadron was rewarded by making history, for near Trun they linked up with the Americans, the first British troops to do so, and thus, technically speaking, closed the gap.[14]

By the end of that day the regiment's haul of prisoners was almost 5,000, a distinction that featured on the BBC news.

On 30 August, 53 Recce crossed the Seine, having already experienced a foretaste of the fast forward movement that would come later. They had also passed through the killing ground of the Falaise Gap:

> We passed quite five miles of this continuous destruction. There was a horrible smell pervading the whole place. The devastation of men and material was past anything that I can describe to you, huge tanks just knocked off the side of the road and black from burning; dozens of them with crews hanging half-in, half-out of turrets and escape hatches. Men lying dead everywhere. Horses dead, swollen and smelling hideously... Perhaps it is as well that the fullness of such a scene cannot be fully given. It was sickening even to those who were now hardened to the sights of war.[15]

From the Seine 53 Recce passed through 15 (Scottish) to head for the Somme. En route they cleared some enemy resistance near Les Andelys and suffered casualties before coming under command of 7th Armoured Division, the Desert Rats. On 1 September the regiment had its longest single-day move when it covered 55 miles through villages "where all the inhabitants, mad with joy at their liberation, thronged the streets, climbing on to our vehicles and pelting us with flowers and fruit and even bottles of cognac and kisses."[16] Then came the Somme crossing next day after which the advance slowed as more resistance was met. Only after several hours of fighting, and help from machine-guns of the Manchesters, was B Squadron able to push through the village of Flixecourt.

Several days were spent liberating villages and fighting intense small actions with determined German opponents around St Pol and at the bridge in Blangy. The reconnoitrers had always to be on the alert but there were few incidents quite as strange as that involving Sergeant Robbie Robinson near St Pol:

> As leading car (White half-track) commander of A Squadron on patrol on a second-class road, an unusual sight confronted me. A hundred and fifty yards away sitting in an old armchair, in the middle of the road, was an old man sucking a broken-stemmed clay-pipe. I dismounted and

approached the old man and in my best grammar school French asked him why he was sitting there. He got to his feet and pointed under the chair, and I saw a pile of horse manure. I moved his chair and the manure and underneath was a Mk 7 Teller mine. He told me he had been sitting there for three hours.

I noted his pipe was empty, so I took off my steel helmet and passed it around 7 Troop who filled the hat to overflowing with cigarettes and the old Frenchman was soon puffing large clouds of smoke. We removed the mine - disarmed it and thanked the old man, and back to business once again. We all thought he was a brave old boy.[17]

By the evening of 5 September the regiment had reached Lille and formed a ring around the city to block all entrances. B Squadron patrolled to Tourcoing and Roubaix, to the north-west, and reported them clear "thus completing a task which it was thought might need the whole Division."[18]

From Lille 53 Recce entered Belgium on 7 September. But the regiment had lost a troop to German deception: on 6 September a message had been received that a German general with 500 men wanted to surrender and a patrol under Lieutenant A.A.Pounder was sent to take the surrender; they were not seen until after the war, having themselves been made prisoners by their intended captives.

A and B Squadrons fought to secure the small town of Moorsele which had been reported abandoned by the enemy. A Squadron was almost through the town when they were fired on; B Squadron was soon engaged also. Their opponents were doughty but, towards midday, the battle was swinging in favour of 53 Recce supported by guns from 340 SP Battery which had been with them from Normandy. Captain Grey-Jones also brought his 3-inch mortars into play in an unorthodox shoot and by "teatime Moorsele was finally cleared by the combined Assault Troops of A and B Squadrons..."[19] Some 100 enemy dead and wounded were accounted for. Escapees - mainly teenage Hitlerjugend troops for whom their battle at Moorsele appeared to have been quite enough of war - were rounded up by C Squadron next day.

Returning to 53rd (Welsh) Division on 9 September the regiment began to move again, this time towards Antwerp. That night A and C Squadrons harboured at Sinay, ahead of forward patrols of 11th Hussars, and surrounded by enemy, although both were blissfully unaware of each other's presence. On 10 September the regiment concentrated near Antwerp and, for a few days, sent squadron patrols out to check the divisional flank along the Escaut canal before setting off towards the Netherlands on 16 September.

✳✳✳

Also heading for the Netherlands were 61 Recce with 50th Division. After

the Normandy campaign the regiment had advanced for the Seine and
beyond:

> ...the most exhilarating days of the campaign. Our task was to protect
> the left flank of XXX Corps in their armoured dash to the Somme and
> beyond. We were on our own on a virgin route, anything up to seventy
> miles ahead of Divisional Headquarters. One beautiful morning we
> drove forty miles before breakfast. There were several engagements,
> some of them quite sharp, and we collected an enormous number of
> prisoners. There was a pause on the Somme, then C Squadron went over
> a small bridge, and continued to work their way forward on the left
> flank against fairly stiff opposition. Here Lieutenant Laing's troop of
> armoured cars was caught on a long, open road by a Panther which put
> a round through the mudguard of his second car.[20]

Armoured cars versus a Panther would be a battle with a predictable
outcome. Understandably it was not one in which Laing intended to
indulge: instead he ordered his vehicles to put out a smokescreen and to
fire all weapons. Although this was intended to cover a withdrawal by the
cars the Panther withdrew instead. It could very easily have wiped out the
car patrol, the firepower of which would have made little impression on
the German's armour. With the tank out of the way, Laing moved forward
into the nearby village where he took 40 prisoners. As it was evening, and
he had to return to his squadron, he handed the prisoners over to the local
French people. Then occurred one of those tragedies of war that result from
communication difficulties. Laing, a Scot with a strong accent, told the
locals to "Hang on to them for me, I'll collect them in the morning." The
colloquialism was a death warrant for the enemy soldiers for, when Laing
returned next day, he found that the French had hanged all 40 of them.
Remonstration was in vain: the French simply commented, "That's what
you told us, wasn't it?"[21]

From there to the Lille area was a relatively easy passage with only the
"occasional stray enemy" and the experience of liberation, flags and kisses.
From a stopping point 20 miles short of Lille, 61 Recce drove to that city on
a route so difficult it might have been chosen for a map-reading exercise:

> The advance had outrun the supply of maps from England, and all we
> had were a few half-inch maps which scarcely marked the side roads we
> were supposed to use. However, we managed to borrow a German map,
> with which we guided ourselves to Houplin, a village short of Lille.[22]

Outside Houplin, A Squadron's leading troop commander, "with his mind
possibly more on map reading than on the enemy,"[23] was advancing
towards the bridge. About 100 yards short of it his aerial was taken away
by an anti-tank shell. As his map showed what looked like a bridge to his
right he veered off, found it passable, and led his troop into the village. But
opposition was very strong and it was not simply a matter of chasing the
Germans out. Fighting for the village continued for three days and

involved all A Squadron. Before the enemy could be winkled out a battalion of infantry, plus tanks, had to be committed to the struggle.

B Squadron also met opposition which they overcame before going off the air for a time but that night "a faint but cheerful voice came up on the radio to say that they had crossed into Belgium,"[24] the first elements of the regiment to do so:

> The next day the rest of the Regiment, less A squadron, caught them up as their anti-tank guns were knocking out soft vehicles at long range on their left flank, and a carrier troop was beating-up an enemy party that had come to blow a bridge on our route.[25]

Considerable numbers of Germans on the left flank were causing concern at Corps headquarters. Since XXX Corps was making for Alost at some speed, the worry was that enemy forces might try to cut the Corps route behind the tanks. As a result 61 Recce moved into a holding rôle on the Escaut canal from Ghent to a bridge south of Oudenarde. This 35 mile stretch of canal had more bridges than the regiment had troops and for a time, until it was relieved to the south, 61 Recce covered 50 miles with two squadrons.

In the north, C Squadron made forays over the canal to take on isolated detachments of enemy troops; one troop even penetrated the outskirts of Ghent. During the brisk battle that followed a Belgian official hailed the troop leader and led him behind some houses to interview the German commander and tell the latter to surrender. The German refused and the battle restarted. This was not a unique occurrence:

> Just north of Oudenarde a party of twenty B Squadron were holding the bridge at Eyne, with a section of carriers, two armoured cars and one anti-tank gun. In the cold half-light of the September morning they heard shooting on the far side of the canal. Then from the mist there emerged a half-track, a 75-mm self-propelled gun, two more half-tracks, and about a company of infantry. When they were just short of the bridge a German officer got out of the leading half-track and tested the bridge. Sergeant Atkinson, who was in charge of our one anti-tank gun, waited until all four vehicles were closed up. Then with four shots he "brewed-up" all four; changing to high explosive, he attacked the infantry while the rest of the detachment let loose with everything they had. At 1300 hrs. an officer came under a Red Cross flag to collect the wounded. Most of them were evacuated by us. About sixty dead and wounded were counted against no casualties on our side. B Squadron Leader harangued the officer in fluent German, telling him to surrender what was left of his force. The officer agreed to ask his commander, but he returned after an hour to say that he'd had instructions to carry on, as his force was bigger than ours, and so battle was joined again. But they gave no more trouble.[26]

Another engagement followed at the Gheel bridgehead where C Squadron was to cross a bridge and recce forward several miles. But, as they crossed, they came under heavy fire from machine-guns and 20mm weapons. The squadron headquarters vehicles were all holed by the fire. During the night the enemy had been reinforced and the bridgehead was only some 300 yards deep. Later the bridge itself was broken. Durham Light Infantry battalions in the bridgehead had been constantly counter-attacked and were delighted to see the armoured cars of 61 Recce. The cars "fought their way forward like tanks throughout the day, shooting off all their ammunition. The whole squadron did a great day's work, but the casualties were heavy."[27]

In their advance into Belgium 61 Recce had taken about 4,000 prisoners, the handling of whom was a constant problem as no PoW camps had been set up and there was no spare transport to take prisoners back to divisional headquarters. It was a problem that had to be dealt with by improvising as the regiment continued its progress.

***

Those other veterans of the D Day landings, 3 Recce, were resting as the Allied armies broke out of Normandy and surged towards the Seine. No one could grudge them that rest for 3rd Division, in almost continuous action since 6 June, had seen some of the toughest and closest of the Normandy fighting. As most of 3 Recce rested near Les Andelys on the Seine, C Squadron came under direct command of Second Army for the protection of Army HQ, a task which engaged them for some two weeks:

> They had an interesting time with scares of attacks on Army HQ by Panzer Divs, plenty of movement and the holding of some very extended river lines. Their surroundings were very congenial and the Belgians extremely enthusiastic. Perhaps Lt Forrest's Tp HQ at Alost in a brewery with civilian telephone system and lovely female operators was not wholly typical of the operation. But to us left behind in France the stories that percolated back of the Sqn's activities in the forward areas made their job sound a good one. We remained constantly in touch with them, opening up at various times of the day. This was no mean feat on the part of the Regimental Signals, as the distance to be covered went up to 290 miles.[28]

Meanwhile the regiment had begun a training programme that emphasised that there were few new lessons to learn, only old ones to be polished up. Gunner co-operation was one important area of study, as was liaison with sappers and there were many tactical exercises, including mortar and PIAT shoots, in one of which PIAT bombs crashed down on some French factory buildings which, fortunately, were unoccupied. One important change was the replacement of the regiment's Humber armoured cars by Daimlers. Instruction in driving and maintenance of the new vehicles was given by Household Cavalry Regiment personnel.

The regiment finally moved on 16/17 September, making its way into

Belgium and providing a traffic control group for 3rd Division's assault across the Escaut canal. During this operation Captain Brough frequently crossed the canal in a rubber boat while a German 20mm flak cannon swept the crossing area. The divisional bridgehead was well-established by 20 September when A Squadron passed through the infantry and into the Hamont area, almost immediately running into enemy rearguards.

Most of the regiment was across the Dutch border that very day. The following two days were spent pushing into the area bordered by canals around Weert and Nederweert and cleaning up opposition. A small pocket of strong resistance in the Weert area was eliminated by an 8 Brigade attack on the 22nd and 3 Recce then held the line of the canals until the 25th when, less C Squadron, the regiment moved to the Sommeren area. A Squadron had an active few days under 185 Brigade as right-flank protection towards Meijel; one close-quarter battle in a house saw Corporal Morris dispose of an SS sergeant.

On the 28th the regiment began a move to Bakel where concentration was complete two days later. The regiment was to be ready to move north when 3rd Division crossed the Maas for the Nijmegen area.

By now the first signs of winter's approach were being seen and felt:

> Whereas in the palmy days of Normandy one had found that a slit trench and tent had made a most comfortable residence, now such an abode was definitely "chill o' nights" and such alternative accommodation as chicken houses had come into play as we wondered vaguely what sort of an enemy General Winter would be in this part of Europe.[29]

***

As the regiments which had fought in Normandy made their way across France and into Belgium another reconnaissance regiment arrived on the continent. This was 52nd (Lowland) Reconnaissance Regiment, formed in 1941 from the brigade reconnaissance groups of 52nd (Lowland) Division. These Scottish lowlanders were among those recce regiments which pre-empted the change of nomenclature by adopting cavalry titles in March 1942. Despite the division's Lowland title it was trained in mountain warfare and its reconnaissance regiment had a squadron of Valentine tanks included in its order of battle for a time. But the exigencies of war meant that the regiment's first theatre of war would be the low countries of Europe and it would never fight as a mountain regiment. (Its projected theatre of operations had been Norway but plans for a campaign there were abandoned.) The division then found itself training for an air-portable rôle, although a seaborne echelon based on 157 Brigade was created. This 'brigade group' - two of the infantry battalions had been removed - included 52 Recce as well as 6th HLI, 79th Field Regiment and supporting elements.

On 31 August 52 Recce embarked at Tilbury, divided among four vessels. Disembarkation was complete at Arromanches on 6 September and the regiment set off to cross the Seine at Les Andelys and then drove to Lens on the Belgian border. Alost was the next stop where 52nd Division came under command of XXX Corps which was pushing north over the Albert canal and creating a corridor to Nijmegen and Arnhem. In mid-September, 52 Recce moved to Heusden where, for four nights, orders were awaited. There the regiment had its first fatal casualty on active service: the IO, Eric Slatter, was killed by a German patrol while visiting the leading units at Grave. On the night of 20 September the regiment moved out of Heusden to join the stream of units moving north "to the sound of the guns."

The regiment's first action was to be Operation MARKET GARDEN, the attempt to take the bridges over the lower Rhine, Maas and Waal by combined airborne and ground assaults. That operation would involve several reconnaissance units, the most distinguished of which was 1st Airborne Reconnaissance Squadron, last encountered in this narrative as 1st Airlanding Squadron in Italy.

17
Operation Market Garden

When the Allied armies landed in France all ground forces - 12 (US) and 21 (British) Army Groups - were commanded by General Sir Bernard Montgomery. As those armies broke out from Normandy towards the Seine, General Dwight Eisenhower assumed overall command with the move of his headquarters from England to France. Montgomery regarded Eisenhower as a good political general but not a man with a sound strategic sense; differences on strategy were inevitable between them.

Allied troops, looking at the destruction of the Falaise Gap, felt that the end had to be near. It was a feeling shared by German troops: von Rundstedt later stated that a strong Allied striking force could have "torn in pieces" the German defences and given not just Berlin but Prague to the western Allies ahead of the Soviets. And Montgomery had argued for just such a strong striking force, "a solid mass of some 40 divisions," to cut into the industrial heartland of Germany. Eisenhower, however, decided to separate the two army groups, sending them on different axes of advance. Such strategy meant, as Field Marshal Sir Alan Brooke noted, that the war would last several months longer. The vestiges of Montgomery's ideal strategy can be seen in the ground/airborne assault designed to strike into the Ruhr and the north German plain while dealing with V2 bases in western Holland. Since such an operation would make use of First Allied Airborne Army, Eisenhower's sole strategic reserve, it appealed to the American chiefs and drew their blessing. The plan was given the twin code names of MARKET GARDEN, MARKET being the airborne element and GARDEN the ground attack.

Distilled to its simplest, the plan called for First Airborne Army - 82nd and 101st US and 1st British Airborne Divisions, plus the Polish Parachute Brigade Group, to seize the bridges over the Maas, Waal and Neder Rijn at Grave, Nijmegen and Arnhem respectively, while ground troops - Horrocks' XXX Corps - would advance along a land corridor to Arnhem, whence into Germany outflanking the northern limits of the Siegfried Line.

As the plan was refined, 1st Airborne Division was assigned the task of taking the furthest bridge, that at Arnhem: the divisional commander, Major General Roy Urquhart was told simply: "Arnhem Bridge and hold it." With his division due to go in on 17 September he had only seven days for planning. His freedom of operation was restricted by reports of strong flak concentrations at Arnhem bridge and Deelen airfield which dictated that the division could not be dropped on or near the bridge. In addition, the RAF had insufficient aircraft to carry the division in one 'lift' and it would have to go in in three lifts over several days:

> ...the Divisional plan was basically flawed from the outset. Inevitably, the element of surprise, so significant in airborne operations, was initially in danger of becoming lost for the want of an opportunity to hit the main objective immediately after the landing. Nor was this in any degree compensated for by the strength of numbers, since the arrangement for piecemeal delivery of the force not only imposed an overall limitation on the total number to be taken on the first lift, but also ensured that something like one half of them would be tied up for the first vital twenty-four hours in the non-productive role of defending the landing and dropping zones.[1]

With his force landing some miles away from its objective, Urquhart decided to take Arnhem with a small, mobile and heavily-armed group which would hold it until the main body of the division arrived. This was to be the task of Major Freddie Gough's 1st Airborne Reconnaissance Squadron. Gough was not pleased with this idea at all: such a task, although within its capabilities, was not a reconnaissance unit's normal rôle. Instead Gough believed that each of the three elements of the division advancing on Arnhem should be led by a troop of his squadron so that the best approach might be established.

> Gough's reasoning was that the function of any Reconnaissance unit, irrespective of how it was transported to battle, was the provision of information on whatever enemy dispositions and resources might lie in the way of the advancing division. He did not dispute the wisdom of a coup de main so much as the fact that it had been allocated to his force whose greatest military capability lay in the execution of a true reconnaissance role. ... With the benefit of hindsight, it is now possible to say that if Gough had had his way, such forward-placed elements of his own unit as he suggested might precede each battalion of the 1st Parachute Brigade could have provided information in such a way as to compensate in part for the disastrous communications breakdown which subsequently afflicted the entire Division.[2]

Once he had accepted the overall plan and his squadron's part therein, Freddie Gough did his best to reduce the tactical drawbacks that he foresaw. His squadron used jeeps armed with Vickers K-guns which were only available on a basis of one per jeep and Gough's efforts to have, at least, a twin-mounting per jeep were in vain, as was his request to have three Hamilcar gliders assigned to 1st Airborne Recce to carry a reinforcing troop of Tetrarch light tanks from 6th Airborne Armoured Reconnaissance Regiment. Gough believed that no serious effort was made to enlist 6 Armoured Recce's help although he felt that they would have been keen to assist.

And so Gough's squadron went to war again, this time by glider and Dakota. Jeeps, trailers, spare fuel, mortar bombs and other heavier items were carried in Horsa gliders of which all but two arrived in the correct landing zone; the men dropped from Dakotas and, although there were some injuries, the squadron was soon ready to head for Arnhem bridge. They were, however, without 9 Field Company, RE who never managed to link up with the recce men. (One glider carrying 21 men of 9 Field Company crashed in Somerset killing all on board.)

Someone called out the Reconnaissance Corps battle cry of 'Bash on Recce' as the jeeps raced for their objective following the standard leapfrogging operational practice. But, alongside the railway line, near Wolfheze junction, Lieutenant Peter Bucknall's 8 Section drove into an ambush laid by 16th SS Panzer Grenadier and Depot Battalion. Arthur Barlow was lucky to survive the ambush: as Bucknall's wireless operator he should have been in the leading jeep but the first jeep to arrive at the rendezvous was the No 2 vehicle which had no wireless:

> So keen was Lieut Bucknall to get on his way to the bridge after the long delay that I was instructed to wait for the wireless jeep and to catch up with him as soon as possible.

> He went off with Troopers Goulding, Brumwell and Gorringe, Ted Gorringe having taken my place on the jeep. This last minute change over of a crew member was later to save my life.

> As Lieut Bucknall's jeep disappeared round a bend in the road the No 1 jeep with the wireless set arrived. The crew now comprising Sgt McGregor, L/Cpl Thomas and Troopers Minns, Hasler, Pierce and myself clambered aboard and made off in the direction Bucknall had taken. After a short while we left the main road at Wolfheze railway crossing and were travelling on a rough road parallel to the railway embankment when heavy firing was heard up ahead of us. At the same time we were fired on from the front up the road and on the right from the top of the railway embankment. Reg Hasler was driving and immediately stopped the jeep which had taken a direct burst of machine-gun fire across the front radiator.[3]

Sergeant Tom McGregor ordered his crew to dismount and take up firing positions. But it was an uneven struggle: McGregor was killed and the others wounded and forced to surrender. (Arthur Barlow was struck by one round in the thigh while another bent the cocking handle of his Sten which he had been holding to his shoulder.) Later, the bodies of Bucknall and his crew were found. It was believed in the squadron that, having surrendered, they had been shot in the back by SS as their bodies, with all equipment removed, were found in a straight line, each about a yard apart. However, in his book, *Remember Arnhem*, John Fairley suggests that Bucknall's jeep was travelling so fast that it overshot the ambush point and the Germans then fired from behind; the jeep was destroyed, possibly as a result of the fuel tank igniting and exploding. The removal of equipment from the bodies would have been in character for the SS officer commanding the ambush as it would have assisted an intelligence assessment of the British force. Certainly, the others of Bucknall's section who were captured were treated well and, although at a later stage in the battle some SS did carry out a cold-blooded atrocity against Gough's men, in the case of Bucknall's section the evidence remains inconclusive.

One thing was certain: the presence of SS Panzer Grenadiers was now confirmed. And they were not alone: two SS Panzer divisions were nearby resting and re-organising after the Normandy battles. They were to have a pivotal rôle in the subsequent battle for Arnhem, for their presence had not been included in intelligence reports to 1st Airborne Division.

As it raced for the bridge, 1st Airborne Recce had several engagements with the enemy and suffered many casualties. It was clearly not a case of a fast run to the objective and a brief holding exercise until the main body of the division arrived. And matters were not helped by communications problems: Urquhart had lost contact with both Gough and 1 Parachute Brigade; Gough, in fact, had spent much time trying to find the general who, he had been told, wanted to see him. One reason for the difficulties was the effect of the many trees in the area on the wireless sets with their simple rod aerials. Such problems led to rumours gaining credence: Urquhart had sent for Gough because he had heard that most of the gliders carrying the recce squadron had failed to arrive and he wanted confirmation, or otherwise, of this story.

By nightfall on Sunday, 17 September, the northern end of Arnhem bridge was in British hands but held only by part of Colonel John Frost's 2nd Parachute Battalion and some other troops, including men of Gough's squadron. The Germans continued to hold the southern end. Gough's men had arrived, still searching for Urquhart, by the lower road which was the only practical way to enter Arnhem, and had "established... Squadron HQ in [a] building overlooking [the] bridge (north end)."[4]

When day broke on Monday, Frost had about 500 men and four 6-pounder anti-tank guns. They expected relief by units of XXX Corps by lunchtime on Tuesday as planned. Meanwhile the rest of 1st Airborne Division was due to arrive and elements of 52nd (Lowland) Division, in an air-portable rôle, were to land at Deelen airfield when it was secured. For the recce men at the bridge "sniper fire from Germans [was] making life difficult. Setting up wireless communications with rest of Squadron; this because of terrain not successful."[5]

Next day German tanks joined the battle and, although communications were established with XXX Corps, Horrocks' men were bogged down at Nijmegen. For those at Arnhem it was a:

> ...hard battle using all weapons with numerous German armoured vehicles and tanks attempting to cross bridge from South to North. We won this one.

20 Sep: Building now badly damaged and burning. Wounded placed in cellar.

Late Wednesday: Wounded evacuated with German assistance, followed shortly by evacuation of all remaining troops into outside prepared slit-trenches. Approaching midnight, trenches over-run by German infantry. I was a prisoner. Many of my colleagues were not.[6]

Instead of being speedily relieved, 1st Airborne Division suffered siege in Arnhem for the next week. Their story is one of the most heroic of the war. Often portrayed as heroic failure, this is to confuse the strategic failure of the operation with the success of the men on the ground. For 1st Airborne Division held Arnhem bridge almost twice as long as had been planned - and those plans did not take into account the presence of two enemy armoured divisions. It had also created a bridgehead at Oosterbeek which could have been exploited by Second Army: that this did not happen was no fault of the division's soldiers.

Throughout the struggle at Arnhem, Freddie Gough's men acquitted themselves highly. Lieutenant John Stevenson's diary gives a clear insight into events within the bridgehead:

I went by glider with A Troop vehicles. We got down about ten minutes before the parachute party. Our glider had a rough landing and finished with her tail in the air. It took us four and a half hours to unload...

Monday, September 18th: The next day, as a troop, we moved south to the main Heelsum-Arnhem road and began to move tactically towards Oosterbeek and Arnhem. We got about one and a half miles down the road... when the preceding troop told us that the road was under sniper fire and we couldn't get any further.

The remainder of that day was spent in recce-ing, by foot patrols, to the north of the road where we soon found the enemy was in strength.[7]

The following day Stevenson and his men recce'd towards Heelsum. At Wek crossroads, near Oosterbeek, they took up a defensive position and, at noon, ambushed a group of five Germans cycling along the road. The men were Panzer Grenadiers who had been attending an NCOs' training course at The Hague and had been sent to help at Arnhem. The five victims, following behind the main body of their group, had missed a turning. After this skirmish Stevenson's section turned their attention to re-supply which was coming down. "There was a hell of a lot of opposition from the ground and ack-ack fire seemed to come from all round."

Wednesday, September 20th: The trouble started today. About nine o'clock we were ordered to go and make a recce of a railway crossing in the northern suburb of the town. We hadn't gone very far when, coming over the crest of a hill, we saw a Jerry SP gun smack in the middle of the

> road, sited to fire down it. We promptly moved off the road.
>
> The SP gun then gave trouble by shooting up the houses among which we had moved for shelter. We decided we had to get out of the suburbs which we did without serious casualties.
>
> We were then ordered to leave our vehicles entirely and, taking as much ammunition as we could carry, to hold several houses as strong points in the northern part of Oosterbeek. ...At about four o'clock we moved on foot to take up these positions in the houses and for the rest of the day we weren't troubled much.[8]

It was quiet until late next morning when the area was mortared heavily. John Stevenson's house took a direct hit which removed the front part of the roof but this provided a better view:

> After this we got our first sight of Jerry infantry on the move. They were going in and out of the houses on the other side of the cross-roads towards a bakery which was the largest house in our defensive area. As fast as they came we knocked them down.
>
> We had three men and a machine gun in the bakery. [The Germans] set it on fire with incendiary bullets and our chaps had to get out.
>
> ...uncertain whether they had got into the bakery themselves and, since the building dominated out other positions, we thought it best to knock it down completely. We turned the Piat on it from fifty yards range which knocked a great hole in the wall and must have made things most uncomfortable for anybody inside. We made sure by patrolling to the house and lobbing grenades into what was left of it until we were sure there was no one there.
>
> They more or less left us alone for the rest of the day, leaving behind their dead and wounded. By then we had killed a lot of Jerries.[9]

Friday morning brought little sign of German infantry but enemy mortars and artillery more than made up for the apparent absence of foot soldiers. Self-propelled guns hit every house in the troop's area at least once and at very short range. Their arrival was announced by the creaking of their tracks which unpleasant sound came to be dreaded:

> In fact, we decided we must do something about it, so one NCO and a trooper were put in a slit trench at the cross-roads to wait for the next SP gun. About half an hour had gone by when one came creaking up again. The trooper let fly and hit it first shot from about seventy yards. Unfortunately the shot immobilised the vehicle but not its guns. The crew must have recovered very quickly and they brought machine gun fire to bear on the slit trenches killing and wounding two glider pilots who were in the next trench to our chaps.[10]

The two recce men escaped unhurt but the situation worsened as the day wore on and more shells tore into the houses forcing a move back to a house about one hundred yards in the rear. That withdrawal was carried out about 4 o'clock that afternoon but casualties were sustained including the troop leader, Captain Grubb. Although the rest of the day passed relatively quietly the food and water situation had become serious, even though rations had been augmented by the addition of German biscuits.

By that evening the troop was down to two officers and seventeen men from its original strength of four and thirty-eight. While many had been killed or wounded, others had been separated in the confusion; some of these later rejoined the squadron.

Saturday morning was quiet until 7.00 when a severe mortar bombardment began. After raining down on the forward positions the bombardment lifted 300 yards to the rear, "smack on Sqn. HQ."

> SP guns came up again and began systematically destroying every house which might give shelter. All this time, in the cellars of almost every house, were Dutch civilians, women and children, who had been caught by the battle.

> By now we were losing count of time. More SP guns and some shell fire. The night as usual was quiet.[11]

Sunday morning brought a counter-stroke against the German guns and mortars as RAF Typhoons strafed and rocketed the Germans. As a result there was a welcome respite from shelling for the defenders; it was only a temporary lull:

> Soon, however, we were under the old heavy mortar fire, while sniping had increased. At this stage the enemy held houses as little as fifty yards from our positions.

> One incident, among many, sticks in my mind from this day. Not a particularly nice incident and hardly worth remembering, but it happened and was part of the picture. An SS tough had been wounded in the street and was kicking up a hell of a row about it. Our chaps couldn't get to him because of sniper fire so they gave him a lullaby of Lili Marlene through the window - the sort of mad thing people were doing.[12]

The food situation had also worsened: the troop were living on fruit, having had no rations since moving into the houses in Oosterbeek the previous Tuesday. However, there was no weakening through lack of sustenance; the main complaint was the absence of cigarettes.

The Typhoons were back again on Monday morning, 25 September, forcing German mortarmen and gunners to keep their heads down. But by 3.00pm the intensity of mortar fire and sniping made the squadron's positions untenable and, with many casualties to be considered, it was decided to pull further back. As the recce men began their move they were caught in the open by SP gun fire but, nevertheless, managed to reach new positions near divisional headquarters at about 5.00pm. There they learned that a withdrawal was being planned with a crossing of the Neder Rijn secured by 43rd Division; 1st Airborne Recce Squadron would be one of the first units to move.

The withdrawal, Operation BERLIN, was not easy. German mortars, artillery and machine-guns harassed the troops as they tried to make their escape.

> A fair spraying of bullets came down the [Heelsum-Arnhem] road at intervals, so we ran across singly or in pairs. ... The night was black and wet making it impossible to see the helmet or body of the man in front.

> Then about 2130 hours a clatter of mortar bombs came down - lighting the woods and road with a queer blue light. The men scattered like demons in a pantomime. I was lifted off my feet with the blast of one bomb and came to lying against the foot of a tree.[13]

The river crossing that followed brought more casualties with boats overturning and men drowning. Many opted to swim across: those who removed uniforms, equipment and boots found the river no great obstacle but even strong swimmers who tried to swim across with uniform, equipment and weapons had little chance of survival. For those who crossed by boat there were many scares on the way as most boats left the shore overloaded:

> Shortly after I contacted Capt. Allsop [second-in-command of the Squadron] who was wounded in the left thigh. We got into the same boat together - squatting near the bow. Half way across water lapped over the bow. We shouted to the others to move down and the night was saved.[14]

To add to the dangers of overloaded craft, the river was swept by machine-gun fire and there was a further threat from fragments of mortar bombs and artillery shells. The crossing took but a few minutes; it seemed like an eternity to those making the journey. Evacuees continued to cross the Neder Rijn into the small hours of Tuesday morning. On the south side they were met by men of 43rd Division who had secured the area for them. And for at least one airborne reconnoitrer there was the pleasant surprise of being helped ashore by former Airborne Recce Squadron members who were now serving with 43 Recce.

Among those who did not get out was Freddie Gough. In April 1945 he escaped from his PoW camp and later met up with two American and about 50 French escapees hiding in a village called Geisenfeld, occupied by Hungarian SS. When the Hungarians withdrew, the mayor of Geisenfeld sought out Gough and surrendered the village to him. The two Americans decided to rename it Goughenfeld. Gough's motley group held the village, recce style, until the Black Hawk Division of General Patton's army arrived.

Some who failed to get out managed to stay on the run from the Germans. Others who had been captured died as prisoners of war. Tony Platt, HQ Troop leader, and Trevor McNabb, the intelligence officer, were murdered by SS men after two other officers had escaped from the lorry carrying them to Zutphen from Arnhem. Four British officers, and war correspondent and novelist Anthony Cotterill, were victims of the barbarous behaviour of a group of young SS soldiers in the village of Brummen. Fortunately a Wehrmacht intelligence officer arrived on the scene before the SS men could murder the rest of the prisoners as they intended to do.

The plan to turn the flank of the Siegfried Line had failed. But the failure was not solely attributable to the presence of strong German forces in the Arnhem area. Operation GARDEN, the ground element, had not gone according to plan, having fallen behind schedule for a number of reasons. Not least of these was the narrow front on which XXX Corps was operating and the fact that the Germans were able to attack the flanks of the advancing troops. Among the units involved in GARDEN were 52nd and 43rd Reconnaissance Regiments.

The lowlanders of 52nd Division had, as we have seen, been converted to an air-portable rôle as part of First Allied Airborne Army. The air-portable bulk of the division was to have landed in the Arnhem bridgehead at Deelen airfield while the remainder, including 52 Recce, advanced with XXX Corps to relieve the airborne soldiers. However, the division's part in MARKET had been cancelled with the failure to take the airfield. That left the 'marching' element of the division carrying out a ground rôle and, on the evening of 21 September, 52 Recce arrived in Son on the Wilhelmina canal to come under command of 101st (US) Airborne Division which had dropped along the road from St Odenrode to Grave. C Squadron were to protect canal bridges against counter-attack while RHQ moved to St Odenrode. As the recce men wore airborne windproof smocks they had an almost German appearance in poor light while the Americans looked German to the recce men, due to the shape of their helmets. Fortunately no tragic incidents resulted from this confusion.

On the 22nd, C Squadron moved to the right of the divisional corridor to protect that flank, occupying Beek and Donk and observing the Germans on the other side of the Uitwaterings canal. The squadron had mortar and anti-tank detachments as had A Squadron which reinforced them next day. John Hathway, A Squadron's second in command, became its first battle casualty when his Dingo scout car left the road and hit a tree.

Then came an order for 52 Recce to move north to the Grave area to deploy on the north-west tip of the salient. The relief of A and C Squadrons was slow and the rest of the regiment preceded them to Schaik, a village just east of s'Hertogenbosch. Then, as A and C Squadrons were moving to Schaik, the enemy launched a strong counter-attack from Schijndel with a force of about twenty tanks or SP guns and 2,000 infantry:

> They broke through the corridor from east to west just below Veghel and established a position astride our line of communications. George Rogerson commanding the two squadrons moving north was aware of enemy shell-fire and a slowing down and eventual stoppage of traffic. Going forward to investigate he met the Corps Commander [General Horrocks] who put him and his force under the local commander of the American Airborne troops. It was getting dark at this stage and it was decided that no effective measures could be taken that evening to restore the lines of communications. Our force was therefore ordered to hold a defensive position across the road to prevent any southern advance by the enemy during the night.[15]

Offensive action was launched by 52 Recce before dawn when an anti-tank gun, which had been manhandled forward, opened fire on a German SP gun moving out of woods to the left. The SP was illuminated by mortar flares and two of the four rounds fired scored direct hits. By dawn an attack to clear the corridor was ready with a battalion of airborne troops, the two recce squadrons and some tanks from St Odenrode.

Two infantry companies advanced on either side of the road with the tanks and anti-tank guns on the road itself. A recce troop was placed under command of each company; the reconnoitrers were to fight mounted if possible:

> The enemy fire was heavy; there was incessant shell and mortar fire and the closeness of the country was cleverly used by snipers. The advance went well for about six hundred yards and eventually stopped. It must be remembered that all this time we were without artillery support. For all that the enemy suffered heavy casualties. The brunt of the fighting amongst our troops was borne by those under Jerry Leonard and George Hauger. New to the game as they were they did exceptionally well. One NCO, Lance-sergeant Finlayson, worked forward with a Bren until he found a position from which he could fire enfilade on a line of enemy slit trenches. He was wounded in doing so but he must have accounted for twenty of the enemy. His friend, Sergeant Parkes, was killed when his Dingo had a direct hit.[16]

The Germans were pushed back later that day when more infantry joined the attack and tanks from Guards Armoured Division threatened them from the rear. As a result the enemy withdrew to Schijndel and 52 Recce moved to Reek with squadrons rotating on duty in the Heesch-Schaik-Oss line. The Germans continued to cut the corridor frequently which caused a shortage of rations. However, there was a food store and a gin factory at Oss and, as fighting there swung to and fro, the comic situation developed of the food storeman issuing food to the Germans on three days a week and to the British on the other days; the British had most of the gin.

Watching a fleet of Dakotas and gliders heading for Arnhem the men on the ground assumed this to be the main body of 52nd Division arriving but this was not so; the aircraft were carrying out re-supply. German aircraft paid some attention to 52 Recce's area which contained large amounts of military equipment and material as well as large troop concentrations. Luftwaffe jet aircraft carried out sneak raids and one such attack occasioned casualties in 52 Recce from strafing and anti-personnel bombs.

***

In this operation Scotland was also represented by 15 Recce which entered The Netherlands on 21 September. A Squadron led across the Wilhelmina canal into a 46 Brigade bridgehead. It had been hoped that there would be a speedy advance to s'Hertogenbosch and Tilburg but strong opposition along the railway at Best and in woods north of the Best-St Odenrode road put paid to that prospect. The reconnoitrers deployed as infantry to clear the woods.

Infantry attacks on the woods failed and for over a week 15 Recce protected the road which was a vital supply route for the troops at Nijmegen and Arnhem. The regiment held positions as infantry, patrolled into German-held territory and maintained contact with the American airborne troops. Then, on 2 October, the division was relieved by 51st (Highland) Division for its first official rest since landing in Normandy one hundred days earlier.

***

Although a move forward to Arnhem never came for 52 Recce their comrades of 43 Recce got much closer to the beleaguered town. The Guards Armoured Division was leading XXX Corps' advance with 43rd Division behind, ready to take over if infantry were needed; the division was also prepared to assault any river crossings not secured by airborne troops:

> The Regiment was ordered to lead the Division, move through the Airborne bridgehead at Arnhem and then swing Eastward to capture the crossings over the River Ijsell at Deventer, Zutphen and Deesburg. The Regiment was given the 12/60th Kings Royal Rifles under command...[17]

On the night of 16/17 September an aerial and artillery bombardment blasted the way for the attacking units of XXX Corps which reached Eindhoven three days later. Eindhoven had been one of the objectives of 101st (US) Airborne Division whose task had been described by Montgomery as laying a 'carpet' to assist the advance of the ground forces;

82nd (US) and 1st Airborne Divisions were, in Monty's analogy, to put down "two large dining-room carpets." As XXX Corps advanced over 101st Division's 'carpet' that division came under Horrocks' command.

The Guards were in the lead with 43rd Division following up as planned but, when the Wessexmen reached Eindhoven, 43 Recce, with 12th KRRC, were diverted eastward as defence against possible counter-attacks. None materialised; the Guards reached Nijmegen where the bridge over the Waal had been seized intact and, on the night of 21/22 September, 43 Recce moved to south-west of Nijmegen:

> Enemy forces were close to the route in many places and tracer fire split the darkness from time to time, but the Regiment trundled on, phlegmatically, intent only on keeping its vehicles from straying in the blackness of the night. At dawn, we streamed over the great bridge at Grave and into our harbour area where the fields were bright with coloured parachutes discarded by the [82nd] US Airborne Division which had dropped there.[18]

The regiment was now on the first of Monty's dining-room carpets but it had become clear that Arnhem bridge "would not be taken without a hard fight."[19] In the 'Island' area, between Nijmegen and Arnhem, roads were narrow, open, and bordered by marshy ground. It was unsuitable country for tanks and the Guards were held up at Elst by determined resistance and 43rd Division was called upon to clear the enemy with 43 Recce protecting the divisional left flank between the Waal and Neder Rijn rivers while gaining as much ground as possible. Leading elements of 43rd Division crossed the Waal on the evening of the 22nd adding their support to the Guards at Elst. That same evening A Squadron, 43 Recce crossed Nijmegen bridge under fire to be followed, later that night, by the rest of the regiment. By dawn the regiment was "in the dreary flat fields bordering the dyke road near Oosterhout."[20]

With German defenders still holding out at Elst an alternative route to the south bank of the Neder Rijn was needed. A battlegroup of 13th/18th Hussars and Duke of Cornwall's Light Infantry was to flank leftward by this route but first the crossroads at Slijk Ewijk had to be taken; this task fell to 43 Recce. Lieutenant Wood, commanding the assault troops of A and C Squadrons with some carrier sections, advanced towards Slijk Ewijk under mortar fire. Dismounting from their vehicles, Wood and his men made their final approach on foot to discover that the enemy had abandoned the crossroads as the attackers approached. A Squadron then moved forward and quickly consolidated the position.

Patrolling continued next morning as the regiment continued its advance with A Squadron moving towards De Hulk and thence to Andelst, Zetten and Randwijk on the Neder Rijn which was reached by 1 Troop. C Squadron followed A's route to Andelst: 10 Troop occupied the railway station; 9 and 11 Troops patrolled towards Hien and had several brushes with enemy units. However, these were generally older Luftwaffe personnel who willingly surrendered. By evening B Squadron was also committed with Squadron HQ at Zetten and two troops clearing the area north of Slijk Ewijk.

On the 25th and 26th patrolling continued with several skirmishes. Lieutenant Scarr of B Squadron spotted about sixty Germans digging and called down an artillery strike which scattered them. Minutes later an explosion cratered the road where the Germans had been working: it was assumed that they had been preparing a demolition. An enemy group which attempted to assault Scarr's OP was beaten off by machine-gun fire.

In Slijk Ewijk, RHQ was strafed by two German aircraft which were markedly ineffectual. The regimental historian commented that this might have been due to Captain Ellis who:

> ...mindful of his early 'Aircraft Action' drill, lay on his back and sprayed the 'planes with a Sten gun. Doubtless dismayed by this display of belligerency the marauders flew off without having inflicted damage to men or material.[21]

A Squadron, manning OPs overlooking the northern bank of the Neder Rijn, found the covert nature of their operation most frustrating when a German staff car appeared on the far bank and a general climbed out!

Ten Troop of C Squadron was patrolling towards Opheusden. The KRRC had moved into the area east of the village with the squadron's assault troop under command; 10 Troop moved through them on to a narrow, exposed dyke road. Without warning an anti-tank gun opened fire hitting the troop commander's car. Lance Corporal Hawes, the driver, was injured as was the commander, Lieutenant Davies. Although the former was pulled from the car he died from his wounds; Davies was only slightly injured. Unable to withdraw, the two leading cars moved into cover behind a house; the crews dismounted just before the anti-tank gun fired through the building, destroying both cars. Trooper Higgins earned the MM for returning under fire to his vehicle to report the situation to his squadron HQ by wireless.

There was little change in the overall situation on the 26th although news was received that XXX Corps' supply route from Eindhoven to the 'Island' had been cut. This caused no worry in 43 Recce as several days' reserve rations were held and everyone was confident that the Quartermaster, Major Vigrass, would somehow provide, no matter what the circumstances.

A Squadron foiled a German attack that night when listening posts reported activity from enemy troops. An attack towards Elst at battalion strength was underway but the enemy had been unaware of the squadron's presence with its armoured cars. The result was a battle in which A Squadron took a heavy toll of the attackers. By dawn the squadron leader, Major Scott-Plummer, had his men containing the enemy by fire in the orchards flanking the dyke road, an armoured car patrol was harassing the German centre and other cars were firing down another section of road to prevent further enemy movement into the orchards. One car was knocked out in a sharp encounter with troops armed with Panzerfausten; the crew were captured.

Although the recce men could contain the enemy battalion they lacked the strength to drive them back but this was later accomplished by an attack from 8 Armoured Brigade.

On the morning of 29 September, a 10 Troop post spotted German frogmen leaving the river nearby. These frogmen had swum down the Waal to place explosives on the road and rail bridges at Nijmegen, damaging the former and destroying the latter. But the Germans miscalculated the distance to their own positions at Ochten and emerged too soon. Near Hien they were spotted:

> ...clad in their grotesque grey rubber suits flapping across the fields... Our men opened fire with Brens, and one of the enemy surrendered at once, while the others took to the water and swam to the far bank of the river, where Dutch Resistance troops picked them up and returned them to C Squadron. Five more were captured by B Squadron men further along the dyke bank.[22]

***

By now plans to relieve 1st Airborne Division in Arnhem had gone by the board and 43rd Division had instead sent a small force from 130 Brigade - 4th Dorsets with some 43 Recce troopers - across the Neder Rijn to enable some of the airborne, including men of 1st Airborne Recce, to escape.

Since the war there has been much debate about the Arnhem operation and 43rd Division, in particular, has been criticised for being too slow in its advance to relieve the airborne. It has even been suggested that its commander was too concerned about the lives of his own men to take risks to help the men at Arnhem. This argument cannot be sustained in view of Thomas's reputation as a fighting commander who drove his men hard and whose division had sustained the heaviest casualties in Normandy.

No matter what the criticism of their division, 43 Recce acquitted themselves with distinction in Operation MARKET GARDEN, remaining on the 'Island' until early-October and relief by American troops of 101st Airborne. On the regiment's last night there a patrol fought a fierce encounter with German posts during which Trooper Sandell earned the Military Medal. The 'Island' was also to be home to other recce units before the winter was out: 52 Recce was, of course, already there while A Squadron, 61 Recce arrived on the evening of Sunday, 24 September.

18
Into The Low Countries

After the dash across France into the Low Countries and the Arnhem operation the closing months of 1944 brought a change of pace but, with troops along the Rhine, the Allies were poised to invade the Fatherland itself. On the northern flank Montgomery's 21 Army Group had a salient across the Waal but the British forces had Germans not only in front but also on their left flank, for enemy troops still occupied a strip of Dutch territory from the Zuider Zee to the Scheldt; south of the Scheldt the Germans held ground along the Leopold canal eastwards from Zeebrugge. This continuing enemy presence on the Dutch coast denied the Allies the strategically important port of Antwerp which could shorten their logistic tail.

The priorities of 21 Army Group were therefore re-assessed: Montgomery ordered First Canadian Army to clear the Scheldt and then to push north on Second Army's flank towards s'Hertogenbosch. Second Army's task was to "tap" eastwards against that part of the Ruhr west of the Rhine. But, by October, the Germans had gained their second wind and were stabilising a line with von Rundstedt in command. Although the German front was weak, the Allies were stretched to the limits of their support and the German effort was sufficient to check the advance for the winter.

The Canadians cleared the Scheldt area with I (British) Corps under First Canadian Army and 49th (Yorkshire) and 52nd (Lowland) Divisions in its order of battle. Here, as 52 Recce discovered, was some of the most unpleasant country in Europe in which to campaign. Their brigade group moved into the Leopold canal line:

> At first we held the position with two squadrons but the ground was deeply flooded, only the raised roadways, so common in Holland, being above water and they were always heavily mined and covered by intense fire from the enemy. Later our responsibilities were doubled and so on the left A Squadron and a special "Inches Force" from HQ Squadron under the TO were given a new stretch of the line. We had a bridgehead over the canal but the going was very rough. The scene was one of greater desolation than anyone of us had ever witnessed before. There were no houses standing, there was no vegetation visible, and sticking up out of the flood waters were numbers of dead.[1]

With 3rd Canadian Division pushing from the east, 52 Recce's line shortened, enabling B Squadron to move northwards through A. The Canadians gradually eliminated the German pocket and 52 Recce returned to its own division which was about to enter battle for the first time. The task given 52nd Division was part of an amphibious operation to clear North and South Beveland and Walcheren. Within this operation, 52 Recce was to cut the German escape route across North Beveland and Schouwen. C Squadron therefore moved to North Beveland while B Squadron was assigned a stretch of north coast and A protected lock gates on the canal on the east of the peninsula:

> The German troops moving across the island were quickly rounded up and they began to use this escape route less and less. There was always the chance that they might counter-attack and we had to patrol continuously. Through our glasses we could see them across in Zierikezee, the chief town on Schouwen. We were certain they had a V-2 launching site somewhere in Schouwen. Night after night we saw their trails in the sky.[2]

Seemingly anticipating an Allied advance northwards from island to island the Germans sent a raiding party to assess preparations and carry out demolitions. The officer commanding was killed and the remainder of the party, about 30 men, taken prisoner; no damage was done:

> This achievement was largely the work of the troops under command of Peter Evans and Jack Hargreaves. On one of the prisoners was found a document revealing all the signalling arrangements for communicating with the boat that was to come and take them off. A plot was hatched to entice this boat, if it should come, close inshore and if possible induce some of its crew to come ashore. That night we lay in wait and the boat actually appeared off-shore. Tom Galloway, the Divisional IO, enticed two of the crew to come ashore in a small boat; one of these was killed and one captured. The larger boat was raked with fire but managed to get out from the shore and disappeared in the darkness.[3]

After almost a month on Beveland, 52 Recce moved with its division to Bergen-op-Zoom at the end of November to rest and re-fit. This gave 52 Recce "the nearest thing to a rest since landing," but it was a short break. The regiment was on its travels again on 5 December when a move to Schinnen, east of the Maas, began; A Squadron was detached to Brussels in an internal security rôle in case of political riots.

The regiment remained at Schinnen for some two weeks, waiting to take part in XXX Corps' Operation SHEARS, designed to take all the ground south west of the Roer river and west of the Maas to their confluence at Nijmegen. Frosty weather was essential so that the ground could bear the weight of tanks but a thaw brought a postponement of the offensive. When the Germans launched their attack through the Ardennes, SHEARS was cancelled and 52 Recce took over the extreme right of Second Army's line where it met Ninth (US) Army.

With Dutch army liaison staff, the regiment deployed near Schinveld with a squadron, plus mortar and anti-tank gun detachments, at

Bruggerhof, some five miles east of Geilenkirchen. This was an unpleasant location, overlooked by the enemy and constantly under shellfire. Both sides carried out intensive night patrolling with regular clashes, during one of which Lance Corporal Murphy of B Squadron, although wounded himself, won the MM for rescuing wounded under shellfire.

Another location on the Gangelt-Geilenkirchen road was equally unpleasant as it, too, was under constant observation. As the area was heavily mined, mine clearing became a regular task that gained popularity when detectors indicated a series of mines which turned out to be wireless sets and champagne. A further German offensive in this sector was expected as:

> A quick push would not have very far to go to Maastricht, and above Maastricht there was only one bridge over the Maas, that beyond Sittard. The Germans must have felt sure that their Ardennes success would have drawn off reserves from our front. They tried it and we never thought of giving up that bridgehead. Our defence of Schinveld was planned to the last detail; it was to be a "last man and last round" stand and all sorts of normally unwarlike technicians like the LAD, R Section and the cooks were drilled in their defensive positions. Nerves were very much on edge at night and there were one or two cases of "trigger-itch". One night Alan de Rusett was fired on by a nervous RASC driver; Alan emptied his pistol by way of reply but luckily the night was dark and Alan was very short of pistol practice.[4]

The defensive stance was maintained through Christmas, although squadrons were able to celebrate in turn. On New Year's Day there was an air raid during which small-arms fire at Bruggerhof brought down one aircraft. The regiment moved to Valkenburg on 11 January, thoughts of a rest being quickly dispelled when 52nd Division was transferred to XII Corps under General Neil Ritchie, a former Eighth Army commander, for Operation BLACKCOCK, a revision of SHEARS intended to push the Germans back across the Roer.

***

The White Rose of Yorkshire was also prominent on that left flank of the advance in the closing months of 1944 as 49th (West Riding) Division pushed through the Low Countries. We last met 49 Recce as they took part in their division's capture of Le Havre in September. Following up the main Allied force the West Riding Division moved through Brussels to Herenthout, reaching there on 21 September to relieve 7th Armoured Division and, two days later, crossed the Albert canal, liberating Herentals - where B Squadron, 49 Recce built a bridge to assist their own advance. The Turnhout canal was reached on the 24th but, although Turnhout was liberated that day, no further progress could be made by 49 Recce as all bridges had been destroyed; not until the infantry secured a bridgehead and sappers had provided a bridge could the advance resume.

September's dying days brought fierce fighting with little progress as Allied forces attempted to extend their bridgehead over the Turnhout canal to the north east, north and west. But the Germans fought ferociously and only to the west was any significant progress made. St Leonard was captured, allowing 2nd (Canadian) Division to pass through; Ryckevorsel, to the north, was then liberated and became 49 Recce's base. With a Canadian armoured squadron the squadrons:

> made a series of sweeps [through enemy-held territory] which, though they showed little result in territorial gains, succeeded in inflicting considerable casualties on the enemy; during the last seven days of the month well over 300 prisoners of war were taken and many enemy killed.[5]

At the beginning of October the main thrust of 49th Division's advance was brought to bear on the Turnhout area. A Squadron led 146 Brigade north on the Tilburg road and, on 5 October, engaged enemy troops near Aerle; two troops accounted for two 88mm guns and three 20mm guns as well as taking ten prisoners and killing several more. The spearhead of the advance was assumed by C Squadron next day; they were attacked by German paratroopers but the attack was beaten off and severe casualties inflicted on the Germans.

No offensive operations took place between 7 and 18 October when 49 Recce, as part of Bobforce, held a line from Bolk to St Leonard through Ryckevorsel. Many prisoners were taken in the course of patrolling by the reconnaissance squadrons before, on 18 October, 49 Recce left Bobforce to join Clarkeforce, an armoured group under 34 Tank Brigade's commander. Also including 107 Regiment, RAC, Clarkeforce advanced about 25 miles from Ryckevorsel to Kruisland, north of Antwerp, between 20 and 30 October "inflicting great damage on the enemy."

> Throughout the advance squadrons of the Regiment led the tanks into action, and had to fight their way forward against stubborn opposition from enemy infantry, paratroops and self propelled guns. The line taken was via Brecht, Wustwesel, Nieuwmoer, Esschen and Wouw to Kruisland which was reached after the enemy had withdrawn from Roosendaal behind the Mark canal. During this advance most of the work had to be done on foot because of the extreme difficulty and open nature of the country; nevertheless progress was quite rapid and upwards of 150 prisoners of war were taken during the operation. In addition 30 more were taken when A Squadron swept the wood south of Nieuwmoer which had been by-passed and still contained enemy who had succeeded in capturing a considerable number of the Division's vehicles and men. During a three day lull at Nieuwmoer, C Squadron did some excellent patrolling north east of that village and directed our artillery on to many targets, while B Sqn were engaged in bitter fighting

with enemy paratroopers north of the village.[6]

So tenacious was the German defence of the Mark canal line that a full scale infantry attack was needed to crack the line. Once again, as at Le Havre, 49 Recce provided a 'Phantom' wireless net to cover the battle. Apart from two days when A Squadron took over the Klundert area from 104th (US) Division, the regiment had no operational commitments in early November; on 13 November it moved to XII Corps near Schaft for Operation CHESTER, intended to clear the Germans from the east bank of the Maas and to take Blerick, near Venlo, on the German border.

On 18 November 49 Recce passed through 51st Division's bridgehead over the Zig canal. Now under command of 4 Armoured Brigade the regiment led the brigade advance over difficult terrain:

> progress was slow with the enemy hotly contesting every inch of ground and causing some damage with his self-propelled guns. However, the Regiment worked forward via Beringen, Panningen, Maasbree and Sevenum to the railway at [map square] 8315, whence Squadrons, pressing forward, reached Grubbenvorst on 25 November and the outskirts of Blerick on the same day, having covered 12 miles in the preceding week; very few prisoners of war were taken during this operation. The main problems during the advance were blown bridges, mines and considerable shell and mortar fire, and nearly all the work had to be done on foot.[7]

At the end of the month 15th (Scottish) Division took over the Blerick area to allow 49th Division to move north and replace 50th Division on the 'Island' north of Nijmegen; the latter division was to be broken up to provide reinforcements. For a time it appeared as if 49 Recce might be deployed to deal with civil unrest in Belgium but it was eventually decided that the regiment was not needed for this purpose. One squadron then moved to Hien on the 'Island' on 7 December; the rest of the regiment moved to Druten on 14 December.

The Germans had flooded the 'Island' thus compelling the troops there to withdraw into a smaller bridgehead. On 17 December the regiment, less the squadron at Hien, took over from 7th Canadian Reconnaissance Regiment on the south bank of the Waal between Druten and Wamel. This task was carried out by a single squadron with the third squadron being held in reserve near Leeuwen. Both squadron fronts were relatively quiet although there were frequent patrol clashes, with casualties to both sides, and attacks by the enemy on 49 Recce posts. Gradually, however, the reconnoitrers achieved dominance in the area where the regiment saw out 1944.

The disbandment of 50th Division had threatened 61 Recce with the axe also with the regiment withdrawn from the line to be broken up. But the commanding officer managed to gain a last-minute reprieve for a regiment which had already distinguished itself from the beaches of Normandy to the German border. A Squadron had taken the van in the regiment's advance towards Arnhem, being first to reach the Nijmegen bridge, while the bulk of 61 Recce had, for a time, been cut in two as German tanks cut the sole road northward. Then, after Arnhem, the regiment had been engaged in a long spell of line holding, "sometimes watching long stretches of river or very open ground, for which our mobility and communications were ideally suited."[8]. Support had been given to 101st (US) Airborne Division before, in November, the regiment deployed in a series of infantry positions in the 'Island':

> By the time that floods drove us out of our forward positions with water washing the hubs of our vehicles, we had held the line on the extreme west of the "Island", on the extreme north overlooked by the high ground by Arnhem, and on the extreme east. At other times we had been in reserve in the middle. We did not have many casualties on the "Island," but it was a miserable place, and one's heart sank every time one crossed the Nijmegen bridge going north. We started by taking over a battalion position, and finished by relieving a brigade.[9]

Colonel Brownrigg decided to try to have the disbandment of his regiment cancelled and drove to XXX Corps HQ where General Horrocks listened to his appeal over lunch and quizzed him on the situation on the 'Island'.

> He [Horrocks] then told his ADC to get Monty on the telephone. Word came back that Monty was having lunch - was it urgent? 'Yes' said Horrocks.
>
> A few moments later I heard Horrocks start "I have Brownrigg with me." Not surprisingly this didn't ring a bell with Monty, but Horrocks explained and told him that 61 Recce was to be broken up and "they would be worth a brigade to me." Monty apparently said that he'd see what could be done, "but you - Horrocks - won't get them."[10]

And so 61 Recce was saved from disbandment but the reprieve was only temporary for, after holding parts of the line for 49th and 53rd Divisions, the regiment was ordered back to Iseghem in Belgium where, just before Christmas, it began handing in vehicles, equipment and stores. But the German Ardennes offensive brought another stay of execution for, at 11.00am on 21 December, the regiment was ordered to mobilise and move. Having worked throughout that day and night 61 Recce was on the move by 9.00am on the 22nd:

> We joined the armoured brigades of 11th Armoured Division in the Ardennes, first sitting along the length of the Meuse [Maas] from Namur to Givet, and then gradually patrolling farther forward, until towards the end of the campaign we had a battleground of our own with a front of twenty miles between the Americans and the rest of the British. Day

after day the armoured cars set out to find and kill as many enemy as they could, and daily they met anti-tank guns and tanks. And when the armoured cars could not get on, the assault troops penetrated deep into the enemy territory.[11]

Towards the end of the Ardennes offensive vehicle movement became almost impossible due to frost, mines and demolished bridges. One officer of 61 Recce took to horseback:

> We were asked to investigate St Hubert which was strictly in the American boundary. Lieutenant Spreag, on his first operation as a troop leader, started by carrier. When that was blown up on a mine he transferred himself to a horse (first time on horseback). With two Belgian woodmen he rode to the outskirts of St Hubert, then straight through it. The Boches had just left. That night the BBC reported that British armoured cars had entered St Hubert, and the next morning the Corps Commander sent a liaison officer to congratulate us on being the first to enter St Hubert, and would we please never go there again, as the Americans were not pleased.[12]

Spreag had not finished his wanderings: the following day, with Lieutenant Abercrombie, he walked some 20 miles through mine-infested country to contact the British divisions to the north. Reaching the brigadier of an airborne brigade the two men were offered jobs with the airborne! In two days they covered a total of 50 miles on foot.

But once again the axe fell on 61 Recce. This time it was irrevocable "and we returned on our last convoy along the ice-bound roads to Iseghem to start disbanding again."[13]

In its short active history 61 Recce had gained a DSO, eight MCs - plus one to their Belgian liaison officer - a DCM, five MMs, three Croix de Guerre and three MBEs; two additional MCs were gazetted after disbandment. Tribute was paid to the regiment by Major General D.A.H.Graham, commander of 50th Division, when he wrote to Colonel Philip Brownrigg:

> They have been simply magnificent, and although their battle history is not as long as time goes it has been a glorious one, and every one of you can feel justifiably proud of all you have achieved. When much that has happened in this war is forgotten, the memory of your deeds will remain. My heartfelt thanks to you one and all.[14]

***

The pattern of operations in those dreary closing months of 1944 when the optimism for an early end to the war engendered by the dash through France gave way to the resignation of more battles and more casualties was similar for all of the reconnaissance regiments. "Hard and often dangerous work" was how the historian of 3 Recce described that regiment's vigil along the Maas from early October 1944 to 8 February 1945. Initially the regiment held the northern part of the river line based on Haps, then, as 3rd Division took Overloon and Venray, 3 Recce swung south and held Vierlingsbeek, Groeningen and Vortum and kept watch on the Fallschirmjäger across the Molenbeek.

OPs were maintained, from one of which, at St Agatha, the regiment "had a magnificent view onto the enemy holding the Middelaar area:"

> From it we watched the unsuccessful attack by an American Airborne Div onto Middelaar and the activity and confusion that this caused behind the German line. Our gunners (33 Field Regt whose representative at RHQ, Major Edwards, was an indefatigable harasser of Huns) had some excellent shooting from here and said that it was the best shooting they had had since D-Day.[15]

During the divisional offensive against Overloon and Venray 3 Recce became part of a mobile force - also including the Household Cavalry Regiment and two squadrons of the Inns of Court Regiment - which deployed to protect the left flank of the advance by holding the river line to Vierlingsbeek. B Squadron, 3 Recce captured that village at what proved to the tougher end of the line.

Vierlingsbeek proved a troublesome location; a German pocket on the Allied side of the Maas in the Den Bosch area allowed the enemy to patrol readily with Vierlingsbeek a frequent objective:

> On one night a large patrol of about platoon strength tried to break its way into Vierlingsbeek Station area which was at that time held by two carrier troops under... Lieutenant Rogerson. The patrol was, however, well seen off and for his part in this action Lieutenant Rogerson was awarded the MC.[16]

OPs ensured that maximum artillery and mortar fire was put down on any enemy activity and on all known enemy locations; at times light anti-aircraft guns, with little to fire at in the skies, were included in the harassing of the Germans. By early December the regiment was withdrawn to the Meerselo-Venray area, allowing Christmas to be celebrated in style - although B Squadron moved into a back-stop position behind Vierlingsbeek just before Christmas - and a party was organised for local children. The rest came to an end on 2 January 1945 and 3 Recce moved back into the line although they relinquished Vierlingsbeek and took responsibility for Sambeck instead.

At Christmas 15 (Scottish) Recce also organised festivities, although one squadron was in the line. Since October the regiment had taken part in a number of dashes. Returning to the Vleut-Best area as infantry on 19 October they held positions so close to the Germans that every movement could be heard. Thus, on the morning of the 24th, Major Gordon's report that "I hear no coughing this morning" indicated a German withdrawal and "began an advance which liberated a city."[17] Within hours the regiment had reverted to its recce rôle to lead an advance through Dirschot and Moergestel to Tilburg. Supported by units of the Guards Armoured Division, 15 Recce eliminated several pockets of resistance, suffering a number of casualties in the process, including Major Gaddum of A Squadron who died of his wounds:

> A Squadron patrols raced the Highland Division to Boxtel. B Squadron was given the main centre line, followed by tanks and infantry towards Tilburg. C Squadron searched the woodland tracks and was then switched to the left flank in search for a bridge over the canal. Late on the 25th October B Squadron seized a bridge over the canal and a vital bridgehead formed. The following morning B Squadron patrols made a dash for Tilburg, with infantry following on both sides and amongst great scenes of jubilation, by 3 pm the liberation of Tilburg was complete.[18]

A German counter-attack east of Helmond brought orders for 15th Division to return there to reinforce the heavily-outnumbered 7th (US) Armoured Division. When the division arrived in the sector the Germans had penetrated the line and threatened Helmond.

Patrols from 15 Recce went out to assess the situation on the morning of 30 October. A Squadron recce'd the area Asten-Deurne-Leisel, B Squadron linked up with 7th (US) Armoured and C took the centre line along the Heusden-Meijel road. The deployment of 15th Division along the main routes of the enemy advance brought that advance to an end. Although there were some further German attacks British and US troops assumed the offensive and began pushing the Germans back.

Two weeks of hard fighting followed; the enemy were steadily worn down and effective US artillery fire hastened their defeat. Although a fierce rearguard action was fought by German troops at Meijel, patrols from 15 Recce reported the town clear on 11 November. There followed an attack on Blerick by 44 (Lowland) Brigade in which 15 Recce carried out flank protection and traffic control. By the 20th the regiment was clearing Germans from the area between the Deurne canal and the Maas which brought further tough fighting against rearguards in a sea of mud with numerous mines, craters and demolitions to impede the attackers:

> Just as B Squadron had its glorious hour on the roads to Tilburg, so now with C Squadron on the centre line, "Skye Route" to Sevenum. The quagmire was such that their leading patrols could only be supplied by Weasels (light broad tracked vehicles). They pushed on regardless and at times isolated, cut off from any form of support. A Squadron on the left took the line of the Deurne-America-Venlo railway. B Squadron supported C Squadron and made what possible use it could of the waterlogged tracks on the left. Wireless messages to HQ were

> continuous - "Trees felled and verges mined - Bridge blown - track
> impassable owing to flooding etc."[19]

The regiment raced from Horst to Grubbenvorst on 26 November and three
days later 15th Division relieved 49th Division to attack Blerick. The
operation was spearheaded by the Lowland Brigade; after a very effective
deception from the north, the main attack went in from the west and
Blerick fell on 3 December. General Sir Richard O'Connor, commanding
VIII Corps, commented on 15 Recce's achievements:

> Many congratulations on magnificent work carried out by all your
> troops and particularly your Recce Regt. and Engineers in these
> appalling weather conditions - very well done. [20]

The capture of Blerick took 15 Recce into static operations along the Maas,
first north of Blerick around Anna Hoeve and then, when that area was
handed over to infantry, to Hout Blerick, south of the town. The routine in
both areas was identical: one squadron forward, with a series of listening
posts, near the river and the rest of the regiment in reserve. It was a busy
time for the signallers who had to maintain a network of field telephone
cables from RHQ to the forward squadron HQ and thence to the listening
posts:

> The weather became colder to well below freezing point and when the
> snow fell, white overalls were issued to those manning the forward
> positions - some of which were only one to two hundred yards from the
> river bank, from where the enemy positions could be clearly seen by day
> and during the agony of the cold nights (relieved only by a rum ration)
> a strict watch had to be maintained against frequent enemy patrols from
> the far bank.[21]

At Zomeren on 13 December Field Marshal Montgomery decorated 12
members of 15 Recce and commented that "in this fighting no Division has
done better."[22]

Most of the regiment celebrated Christmas in some style with the
regimental concert party, the Tam o'Shanters, presenting Dick Whittington
at Zomeren. C Squadron had celebrated early for it was their lot to be in
the line on Christmas Day:

> It proved to be an uncanny experience: at dawn the daily barrage of
> guns ceased and the only sound came from German festivities echoing
> from the far bank. It was a clear sunny day and the snow glistened on
> the ground. In the circumstances it was hard to believe. The Colonel and
> Padre visited the Squadron and a short service was held. At dusk the
> Germans deemed Christmas was over and were first to restart the gun
> barrage and the reality of the situation returned.[23]

A Luftwaffe attack on New Year's Day caused only minor casualties. This
low-level attack, which was made against other recce units, was believed to

be a fringe element of the offensive in the Ardennes to the south. For 15 Recce their watch along the Maas lasted until 20 January when the regiment withdrew to Belgium to prepare for the assault on Germany itself.

***

The Wessexmen of 43 Recce and their Welsh counterparts of 53 Recce had also been kept busy during the dying months of 1944. After a week on the southern bank of the Waal opposite Ochten and Tiel, 43 Recce deployed to protect Nijmegen to the west and on 13 October took over positions from 61 Recce. The regiment's line stretched for 15 kilometres with a battery of SP guns from the Essex Yeomanry under command. Listening posts were established, patrols sent out and the regiment became responsible for about 200 Dutch resistance men (some turned out to be Nazi sympathisers who gave details of locations to the enemy thus ensuring frequent and accurate shelling of A Squadron's HQ at Dreumel).

OPs in various locations, including church towers at Dreumel and Wamel, allowed the artillery to harass the enemy regularly although German artillery gradually demolished the OP in the Dreumel tower. The regiment's anti-tank 6-pounders were used "for the first and only time" to fire across the river at barges and boats. Finally, on 10 November, 43 Recce handed over to a Canadian reconnaissance regiment and moved south through Eindhoven to Sittard, north of Aachen, as part of a XXX Corps redeployment.

A fresh offensive was planned with XXX Corps on Second British Army's right as the Allies thrust for Cologne. The Corps' first objective was Geilenkirchen, to help Ninth (US) Army's advance to the Rhine. While 43rd Division was to flank left around Geilenkirchen US forces worked eastwards around it; when the link had been made 43 Recce was to pass through to reconnoitre roads northwards towards Heinsberg. The divisional assault began on 18 December when A and C Squadrons were, unexpectedly, given the task of holding a lay-back line behind the infantry and forward of the gun line. At dawn next day both squadrons moved into Germany - the first elements of their regiment, and the Reconnaissance Corps, to do so. Positions were taken up in Grotenrath "and the stay there was practically devoid of incident." Although 43rd Division's operation was successful, and the link with US units achieved, deteriorating weather ruled out further advance as rain made roads and fields almost impassable and German troops began a series of effective counter-attacks.

With no further operational rôle 43 Recce withdrew to Heerlen in the Netherlands but, on 25 November, B Squadron was moved back to the front to defend the road from Geilenkirchen to Randerath. Two days later A Squadron relieved them and, almost immediately, suffered heavy shelling in which Trooper Badman died. Further fatalities were sustained when a party relieving a forward listening post were shelled. Squadron reliefs were carried out every three days:

> and three days was a long period in this unpleasant position. There was
> no water, and all drinking water had to be carried to the posts. As a
> result it was impossible to wash and shave. ... The nights seemed very
> long, for it was rarely light enough to stand down before half past eight
> in the mornings. During that period the posts had to be constantly on
> the alert to prevent German patrols creeping up on them. Nearly every
> night the assault troops sent out a patrol in front of the carrier
> positions.[24]

Further plans to advance were cancelled and XXX Corps withdrew to the
Tilburg area to prepare for an operation in January. On 18 December
elements of 52 Recce took over 43 Recce's forward commitment and the
Wessexmen began moving to Tilburg next day. But that night the move
was stopped and the regiment ordered south. The German offensive
through the Ardennes had begun.

All of XXX Corps was diverted to the line of the Maas to hold that river
and provide a counter-attack force. There was some initial confusion within
43 Recce's area with duplication of tasks with US troops but this was
sorted out with the Americans taking responsibility for Liége and 43 Recce
the line from Huy to Visé. Although the regiment was called on to provide
information for 43rd Division and for Corps HQ it saw no action and A
and C Squadrons were able to celebrate Christmas with the Americans. On
27 December 43rd Division came under XII Corps command and moved to
the Roer front with 43 Recce returning to Heerlen where they would
remain until February.

The 'Island' experience had also been shared by 53 (Welsh) Recce who
had arrived there on 7 October after some notable actions in Noord
Brabant: in one Major Goldsmid led two troops in an attack on Hoogeloon,
taking 200 prisoners and killing or wounding 60 enemy. On the 'Island' the
regiment relieved 61 Recce and, some days later, came under command of
101st (US) Airborne Division. Reek was the next destination, reached on 18
October, where 53 Recce learned of its rôle in the forthcoming Operation
ALAN, a XII Corps attack through s'Hertogenbosch, Tilburg and Breda to
clear the Scheldt and open Antwerp for Allied shipping.

On 22 October 53 Recce, supported by their old friends 340 SP Battery
and 1st East Lancs in Kangaroos, moved into action and A Squadron was
soon at Kruisstraat where resistance was met but quelled with the aid of
340 Battery and the East Lancs. During the next two days 53rd Division
fought its way into the city while A and B Squadrons, 53 Recce, having
relieved 11th Hussars of the right flank recce task, patrolled the marshes
up to the Maas.

By early November XII Corps had taken Tilburg, Breda and Roosendaal,
thus removing any immediate threat to Antwerp but an enemy

counter-attack towards the corridor brought another redeployment with 53 Recce moving to "the extreme north-eastern tip of the Belgian province of Limburg on the Division's new right flank."[25] No further enemy advance took place and once again the regiment was on its travels, moving into the Netherlands at Weert. At the end of the month a static spell began with squadrons deployed along the Maas downstream from Maeseyck. Training courses were organised although these were interrupted by Operation WIND UP on 6 December. This was an artillery programme planned "to cause the enemy the maximum casualties and discomfort in his positions on the east bank of the Maas by bringing at irregular intervals concentrated fire from all guns in the Division."[26] This included 53 Recce's mortars while the anti-tank guns fired in anger for the first time to the great delight of their gunners.

The Inns of Court Regiment relieved 53 Recce on 18 December and the Welsh reconnoitrers moved to Herentals in Belgium from where, rather rapidly, they left for the line of the River Dyle as a result of the German attack in the Ardennes. On Christmas Day the regiment deployed along the Maas from Dinant to Namur under command of 6th Airborne Division whose Armoured Recce Regiment had also arrived. The Germans were stopped at Ciney and only a few patrols ventured near the Maas near Dinant. "For us the remaining week of the year was spent static but observant on the west bank of the Meuse [Maas]."[27]

And so 1944 ended with the Allies poised on the borders of Germany itself but with the German army still showing the ability to mount major counter offensives and to defend as fiercely as ever. The war would drag on into 1945 and the reconnaissance regiments in north-west Europe would play their part with distinction in its final months.

19
Another Italian Winter

By December 1944 the Italian front was once again bogged down with the Allies locked against Kesselring's Gothic Line. And yet, after the breaking of the Gustav Line, the breakout from Anzio and the fall of Rome it had looked as if the campaign might end that summer. That was not to be as German defensive skills were abetted by the withdrawal of large numbers of Allied troops, including the excellent French Expeditionary Corps, for Operation ANVIL, the invasion of southern France. Before that happened, 56 Recce had a spectacular race from Rome to Lake Trasimene where German resistance stiffened and brought the Allied advance to a bloody stop.

As the Germans pulled back from central Italy, Fifth and Eighth Armies launched a parallel pursuit which was to last through the following twelve weeks. This "classical manoeuvre" was occasionally checked, but never held for long, and gave reconnaissance regiments an ideal opportunity to show their mettle.

Having participated in the advance into central Italy, 56 Recce found itself in the Frosinone area as May ended. On 1 June, as A Squadron, supported by tanks, advanced from Frosinone they encountered enemy troops; in the ensuing skirmish two Germans were killed and six taken prisoner. The enemy appeared to have been knocked off balance by the speed of A Squadron's advance as bridges were still intact and trees that had been prepared for demolition were still standing. Early next morning the regiment continued operations along the Alatri road but no opposition was met; the Germans had withdrawn during the night.

By 10 June 56 Recce was in the Civita Castellana area with instructions to recce for crossings of the river Tiber suitable for 78th Division. Those orders led to the creation of Chavasseforce with Colonel Chavasse commanding an all-arms battlegroup of 56 Recce, a squadron of Warwickshire Yeomanry tanks, a company from 1st Royal Irish Fusiliers, a battery of 17th Field Regiment, two troops from 315 Anti-Tank Battery and a field squadron of RE. The infantry element was later augmented by the remainder of 1st RIrF. This was a happy combination as the Irish Fusiliers, the Faughs, were Kendal Chavasse's parent regiment. Chavasseforce's principal task was to protect 6th SA Armoured Division's flank as it advanced along the Tiber.[1]

The advance over the next few days was rapid. Starting from Orvieto on 12 June Chavasseforce arrived on the shores of Lake Trasimene on the 21st. Along the way there had been many encounters with the enemy in which various elements of Chavasseforce had all played their part: recce troops had probed forward; assault troops had set up strongpoints; tanks, gunners and sappers had all contributed their support and the Faughs had attacked German positions; in one short but savage battle a company of Faughs, supported by 56 Recce's mortars, had defeated a small German force leaving 25 of the enemy dead. At the end of the run, Chavasseforce had killed 145 Germans, taken 121 prisoners, captured or destroyed some 30 guns and mortars, more than 30 vehicles - including a lorry loaded with French brandy and sweets - 56 machine-guns and six 2-man tanks; a German cinema unit had also been captured.[2] The capture of Castella di Montelara by D Company, 1st Faughs marked the end of Chavasseforce's run and the beginning of a phase of brutal fighting to crumble the German defences anchored on Lake Trasimene.

That fighting was largely the work of infantry battalions supported by armour and gunners, but the reconnoitrers played their part by locating enemy positions and strengths; B Squadron's assault troop discovered, from prisoners, that 15th Panzergrenadier Division had relieved 334th Division.[3] Patrols also cleared mines, provided OPs and harassed the Germans where possible. As the fighting continued news came that the regiment would be relieved by 4 Recce: 78th Division was to be withdrawn to Egypt to rest, refit and train and 4th Division was to relieve it; but the battle of Lake Trasimene had first to be won.

The battle came to an end in the dying days of June and 78th Division began handing over to 4th Division. By 4 July, 56 Recce had been relieved by 4 Recce and was beginning the journey to Taranto but not before B Squadron had liberated the town of Cortona. On 18 July the regiment sailed on HMT *Empire Pride*, landing in Alexandria four days later and thence to Qassasin.

The regiment which relieved 56 Recce, 4th Reconnaissance Regiment, was last met in this narrative in Tunisia. It had been in Italy since early 1944, having remained in North Africa after the Tunisian campaign. Arriving in Italy in winter conditions, 4 Recce's first task was as infantry holding part of the Allied winter line.

Moving up from Naples, the regiment relieved 46 Recce in the Garigliano sector where troops were billeted in the homes of local people:

> First impressions were of snow, mud, cold and extreme poverty and the low standard of living of the population.[4]

From 46 Recce the regiment inherited a 3-tonner converted as an orderly room, a small horsebox trailer as an office, and an Italian carabiniere interpreter, Carmelo Minuto, popularly known as Charles.[5] The regiment's first infantry task was to relieve 2nd/4th Hampshires on the night of 10/11 March on Monte Camino's western slopes, east of the Garigliano. Until 4 Recce's arrival this stretch of line had been held by Hermanforce which

included the King's Dragoon Guards, under Colonel Herman, plus the
Hampshires' battalion, less a company; on the night of 12/13 March
Colonel Preston of 4 Recce took over from Colonel Herman and the force
became Prestonforce with 44 Recce, which relieved Herman's regiment,
also under command.

Over the next few nights there were regular clashes: the regiment was
very active in night patrolling, searching both for enemy patrols and for
mine-carrying dogs. On 15 March Monte Cassino monastery was bombed
in preparation for an attack but, although ready to cross the Garigliano that
night if a New Zealanders' attack on Cassino was successful, the regiment
returned to "vigorous patrolling" of the river banks when this plan was
cancelled. Towards the end of the month 4th Division was relieved by 4th
French Mountain Division, 3rd Moroccan Spahi Regiment taking over 4
Recce's sector.

In early April Prestonforce took over from 9th and 11th Tabors of
Goums; the force also included an Italian battalion, a platoon of 4.2-inch
mortars from 3 Support Group and 2nd RNF; 30th Field Regiment was in
support. Prestonforce was to dominate no man's land and keep the sector
quiet so that, if necessary, it could be held later by a smaller force. The
Italian Bafile Battalion proved a mixed blessing: dealing with Italian
ammunition, rations and stores caused headaches that were exacerbated by
lack of co-operation from the Italian troops. Nor did the fact that half the
Italian troops who were to join C Squadron managed to lose themselves
and arrive 24 hours late help matters. Then, as if to crown it all, two Italian
patrols clashed, leaving one man dead and another very seriously injured.

On 12/13 April Canadian troops of the Westminster Regiment relieved 4
Recce; Prestonforce became Corbauldforce and the regiment moved to
Vairano for its next task.

Fourth Division moved south of Cassino and 4 Recce was given two
rôles: C Squadron was to hold Castle Hill with two troops from 30 April to
4 May under 12 Brigade, whose battalions would be east of the town; B
Squadron was to supply a minelifting troop for training under 10 Brigade.
A further task was added when A Squadron relieved 5th Royal West Kents
in the area of Cassino station on 3/4 May:

> We saw the Monastery being bombed several times, being close enough
> to watch the bombs leave the planes and follow their flight right down
> to impact. We gloried then. Now, I don't want to see it again.[6]

As the squadrons moved to their new areas C Squadron was shelled and
lost five dead and 15 wounded, of whom one later died. Then, on 4 May, A
Squadron had one killed and eight wounded in mortaring of Cassino
station:

> There is a dim period for me here. We patrolled, I know, but the
> outstanding [memory] was not a patrol, but a defensive position in

Cassino Station, through one window the Baron's Castle, from the next - not window but dug-out under the wall - the Monastery, with the road zigzagging right in front of us up to the top and the "hill" to the right... At night, and we [No 2 Troop] stayed three whole days living under the floor with just enough room to sit up, the fire flies. I'll never forget the sight of them, little red sparks glowing and hovering everywhere.

I got my closest shave... here. We were stretching our legs and moving about the passageway above ground one midday. Someone pushed his camera through a hole in the wall and took a photograph of the Baron's Castle. A minute later there was a sharp ping behind me, and there was a bullet with the tracer just dying, resting amongst the tickets of the ticket board inches from my backside... Nobody took any more snaps, I can tell you.[7]

Much of May was frustrating as the regiment prepared for operations that were later cancelled. Insult was added when a staff officer from Eighth Army examined the stores on 30 May for items that might be surplus to war establishment: the result was the loss of some of 46 Recce's "treasured legacies."

In early June the regiment took part in the advance towards Rome along Route 6, cutting Route 4 on the way. Some minor clashes occurred; two heavy armoured cars were lost but without casualties. On 11 June 4 Recce passed through Rome before spending several days near Riano while 6th SA Armoured Division took over the running. On 22 June the regiment moved to Citta della Pieve and then to La Costa where 56 Recce was relieved of front-line positions. This put 4 Recce into the heart of the Trasimene battle: A Squadron patrols moved forward but a squadron advance on 24 June proved premature when Germans were encountered and replied with heavy shellfire that destroyed two LRCs and three carriers, leaving eight dead and one missing. The regiment was then "ordered to stay put until there were definite signs of an enemy withdrawal."[8]

Recce patrols were carried out over the next two days: on the 27th A Squadron pushed forward beyond Porto and Puntoni against stiff opposition; one man was killed, another wounded and two LRCs were knocked out. Two days later A Squadron was relieved by 2nd King's Regiment and, on the 30th, B Squadron patrolled through Pozzuolo only to be held up south of Petrignano. RHQ's command group moved up to direct operations and set up in Villa Paolozzi where, at 3.30 that afternoon, "a delayed mine or charge blew up the house, incl[uding] the HQ, and many men of the Regiment, the RAF and 11 civilians were buried in the debris. Some were rescued alive."[9] Casualties were seven dead and four wounded, one of whom died later. All RHQ's maps and papers were destroyed. The regiment returned to Porto and B Squadron went into reserve and a day's rest was had before the advance continued. During the month 4 Recce had lost 22 killed in action or died of wounds.

The divisional advance continued in July with 4 Recce moving to Ciggiano from where A and B Squadrons patrolled through Cornia, Civitella and Badia Agnano, a difficult journey for wheeled vehicles due to mines, blocks and demolitions en route. After some days in divisional reserve C Squadron relieved 2nd Bedfords in a protection rôle for a 10 Brigade advance to Montevarchi on Route 69, a task which lasted for five days until 25 July. Until the end of the month the regiment was patrolling towards Figline where A Squadron relieved C to continue the advance while B Squadron pushed on through San Martino. The regiment had a new commanding officer in Major A.C.S.Delmage, MC, as Colonel Preston left to command 28 Brigade on the 28th.

Fourth Division's advance along the Arno valley continued in early August with A Squadron probing along Route 69, B on the high ground to the left and C on the division's extreme left to work with 12 Brigade in case of a breakthrough to Florence. A and B met much rough going as well as obstinate, doughty resistance. On 4 August a special patrol of B Squadron, under 28 Brigade, operated south-east of Florence when the break finally came and the patrol reached Bagno a Ripoli less than a mile from the Arno. Over the next three days A and C Squadrons reached the last enemy line of resistance south of the Arno before being held up for several days.

On 8 August 4 Recce's self-propelled guns fired for the first time as 2nd Duke of Cornwall's Light Infantry took the monastery at Incontro and 2nd Bedfords put in unsuccessful attacks at Castellonchio. The Germans withdrew that night; 4 Recce moved forward on the 9th, occupying the heights overlooking the Arno a day later:

> Following the enemy withdrawal, A and C Sqns pushed forward along very bad, narrow, dangerous roads, as usual well-cratered and well-mined. One LRC of C Sqn went up on a mine, but the crew, though shaken, were unhurt. (This same LRC and crew were shot up two days ago by a 75mm and the crew are still unscathed). An HAC got stuck on an important but extremely narrow road, and was last heard of hanging half-over the edge blocking the road. By now it has probably been pushed over to make way for traffic following behind.
>
> By this evening [9 August] our patrols had reached Pt 255 (9564), Torri 9465 and North of Castellonchio 9265.[10]

Its task complete, 4th Division handed over to 1st Division with 1 Recce relieving 4 Recce who, after seven weeks in operations, moved back to Foligno. For the rest of the month, the regiment remained in the divisional area; entertainments were organised, rest camps opened and leave granted while training occupied those not on leave.

The regiment returned to active operations in early September in the Adriatic sector where Eighth Army's advance as part of Operation OLIVE was underway. Not until 15 September did 4 Recce see action when B Squadron was assigned to 28 Brigade with the assault troops of A and C Squadrons protecting 59 Company, RE on the brigade front. By the end of the month the regiment was concentrated at Ospedaletto where it remained until late October when it took over the right of the divisional sector.

During November 4 Recce carried out various tasks as well as patrolling to recce approaches to, and crossings of, rivers as the infantry prepared for assault crossings. With a bridgehead over the Ronco established the three assault troops were placed under command of 1st/6th East Surreys and distinguished themselves by holding a pivotal sector. Their performance brought a special note from the commander of 10 Brigade:

> Your Assault Troops with the Surreys were magnificent and their patrolling, initiative and offensive action were quite exceptional. They were a decisive factor in our ability to hold that very small and tenuous bridgehead. I would be most grateful if you would inform [Captain K.C.P.Ives, 2 i/c A Sqn] and his men of my thanks and appreciation.[11]

The Surreys' CO also commented that Ives and his men had completely shown up his battalion over patrolling.

After 12th Lancers capture of Forli, C Squadron, with a troop of tanks, attacked the Montone - Canale Nuova line and forced the Germans to pull back over the Montone in haste, leaving several anti-tank guns and a Mark IV tank behind. On 26 November 4 Recce concentrated at Forli under V Corps command.

On 10 December the regiment, under 43 Gurkha Brigade, moved forward with A and B Squadrons occupying defensive positions on the Lamone river line which they continued to hold when the brigade was relieved. Then, under 56th Division, the regiment stayed in the line until 9th Royal Fusiliers took over on the morning of the 19th. The squadrons then moved to Forli to be ready for the road to Taranto next day. By the end of the year most of 4 Recce was in Greece.

***

As 56 Recce left Italy for Egypt 46 Recce was returning to the peninsula. As well as training and re-organising, the regiment had been engaged for a short time on internal security duties in Palestine before travelling to Egypt on the first leg of the journey back to Italy. Arriving at Taranto on 3 July the regiment moved to Villa Volturno where new vehicles were received and the 6-pounder anti-tank guns were replaced by 75mm self-propelled weapons. On 25 July 46 Recce paraded at Perugia airfield to welcome King George VI on a visit to Eighth Army; by then the regiment was preparing for Operation OLIVE.

OLIVE was Alexander's plan to break through the Gothic Line and into the plain of Lombardy; it was scheduled to begin at midnight on 25/26

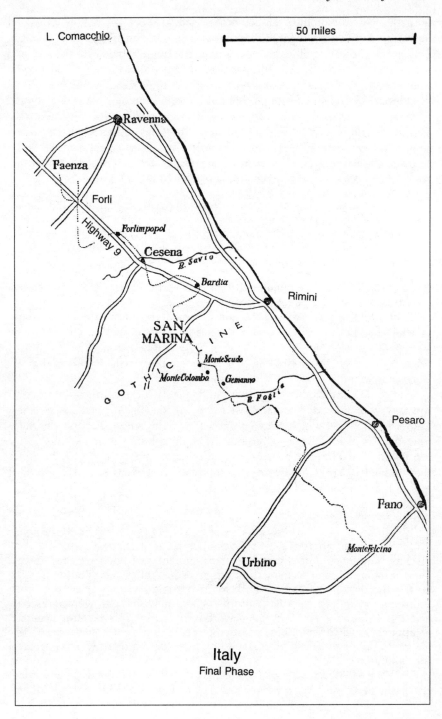

L. Comacchio

50 miles

Ravenna

Faenza

Forli

Highway 9

Forlimpopol

Cesena

R. Savio

Bardia

Rimini

SAN MARINA

GOTHIC LINE

MonteScudo

MonteColombo

Gemanno

R. Foglia

Pesaro

Fano

Montefelcino

Urbino

Italy
Final Phase

August 1944. At 11.00pm on the 25th, A Squadron foot patrols set out to recce crossings of the Metauro river. The patrols returned by 4.50am and, at first light, 1 and 2 Troops went forward to cross the river. On 2 Troop's axis of advance there was heavy going while 1 Troop ran into mines; a heavy armoured car had a wheel blown off. A Squadron was in action throughout the morning.

At noon the divisional commander asked for two good crossing places on the regimental front: the recce to meet this request was undertaken by 2 and 3 Troops. At 3.30pm 2 Troop was engaged by Germans on Monte Bianco. After mortaring the enemy position, the troop attacked and drove the Germans out. A subsequent counter-attack was fought off and the position held until the reconnoitrers were relieved by 5th Sherwood Foresters.

On 27 August the regiment, spearheading 139 Brigade, was continuing its advance along the road north-westward through Isola del Piano. Two Troop was sent forward but, when a carrier overturned killing Lieutenant R.L.J.Rogan, 3 Troop took over the running. They found the going difficult because of blown bridges and mines but took three prisoners from 191 Grenadier Regiment before further progress became impossible. Under constant shellfire throughout the day, 46 Recce suffered thirteen wounded as well as having two heavy armoured cars, an LRC and a 15cwt truck damaged.

A Squadron continued to recce 139 Brigade's axis of advance next morning with 1 Troop pushing forward in spite of craters and demolitions until C Squadron relieved them in mid-morning. Another river obstacle loomed on the 29th when 46 Recce was warned to be ready to take over 128 Brigade's area, the main feature of which was Monte Gaudio which 1st/4th Hampshires had captured the previous day; the regiment was to protect the division's right flank and report on the Foglia river on the regimental front. The plan was for 46th Division to attack across the Foglia with B and C Squadrons holding the high ground and patrolling forward and A Squadron in reserve ready to move to Ripi at short notice.

That afternoon B and C Squadrons sent out patrols to find crossings for infantry, AFVs and other vehicles and to report on mining in the area. By 3 o'clock next morning C Squadron had reported neither crossings nor mines in its area. B Squadron was unable to reach the river due to the distance involved but brought back the valuable information that the road from Ripi to the ford was not mined; C reported the river banks to be some 12 to 15 feet high with the river fast flowing.

Further recce'ing of the Foglia was carried out that day and a crossing point eventually found. Although the Germans had been shelling constantly, it was learned that the Gothic Line defences north of the Foglia were not as strong as had been thought and had been penetrated. A mobile force was therefore formed to exploit that penetration: the force included 46 Recce; 142 Regiment, RAC; 142nd Field Regiment; 272 Field Company; 152 SP A/T Battery; Recce Troop, North Irish Horse and 5th Hampshires in lorries. This force was to cross the Foglia, advance and seize crossings over the Ventena river with 46 Recce leading; A Squadron, in the van, would recce three crossings.

Events did not go as planned: one crossing was not available to the force when it moved off at 5.40am on the 31st. As 2 Troop approached its assigned crossing German soldiers were spotted in the open and engaged by Bren and Besa fire; about twelve Germans were seen to fall. But the troop then came under such intensive fire from mortars, machine-guns and artillery that forward movement became impossible. On the right, 3 Troop was trying to construct a ford but could not do so even with help from sappers. A modified plan, for a modified force, had therefore to be implemented: the force would seize one crossing with B Squadron covering its right flank.

The crossing was made on the morning of 1 September with 1 Troop, A Squadron assisting 142 Regiment, RAC in supporting an attack by 6th Lincolns. At 2.30pm 6 Troop crossed the Foglia and headed north on the right of the brigade axis. The troop came under fire from four 88s at 1000 yards' range but, although an armoured car was hit, there was only one slight casualty.

Flank protection was B Squadron's task next day as 138 Brigade advanced; the squadron also maintained contact with the Canadians on the right. Throughout the day there was considerable opposition to the forward troops and the CO ordered C Squadron to move up on B's right flank; matters were not helped by bad communications. During the course of the day Colonel Cotton was wounded and Major J.H.Preen took command. Against strong opposition, 138 Brigade had made good progress and further plans were made for 46 Recce to cross the Ventena and Conca rivers and provide a flank guard for an advance to San Clemente.

On 3 September the regiment was stunned by the news that Colonel Cotton had died of his wounds. Struck by a shell splinter which penetrated his skull "he died shortly after leaving the Field Ambulance without regaining consciousness."[12]

During the morning of the 3rd, B Squadron seized crossings over both the Ventena and Conca rivers. With these secure, C Squadron passed through B and took up the lead of 138 Brigade's advance, with 9 Troop in front:

> They encountered almost continuous shellfire, especially from enemy SP guns, but continued to press on, until they were finally held up by strong enemy positions on a ridge at [map reference] 910863. During the day they suffered eight casualties wounded, while B Squadron had one

killed and two wounded.[13]

Next day the regiment was to move further west on to the San Clemente-Coriano road which C Squadron was to recce; the ultimate objective was to seize three bridges over the Marano river. These orders were modified to the capture of one bridge, at Ospedaletto, as 128 Brigade had broken a strong German rearguard position and were crossing the Marano to form a west-facing flank to protect 1st British Armoured Division.

C Squadron got moving after some initial difficulty from traffic congestion and 10 Troop finally pushed forward through the York and Lancs' positions and along the San Clemente-Coriano road. But 10 Troop's advance was stopped when the bridge at Castelleale was blown up as they approached; the troop then came under sustained mortar and machine-gun fire from three sides. For most of that day they stayed in position returning fire with their 37mm and Besa guns until ammunition was virtually exhausted and they were forced to withdraw to San Clemente. Nine Troop had also been held up after detouring westward: two armoured cars had been blown up on mines and, although the troop later advanced by another route, they ran into very heavy shellfire at Il Trebbio and had to withdraw. C Squadron HQ at San Clemente had also been shelled and forced to move.

Finally, at 5.30pm, the regiment was told to stand fast in its positions while 1st Armoured Division took over the advance; next day 46th Division was withdrawn for a rest during which heavy rainfall threatened to leave vehicles stranded in muddy conditions in the squadron areas.

On 9 September the CO gathered all officers and troop NCOs at RHQ to pay tribute to Colonel Cotton and to point to lessons from the recent advance which, from the Metauro to the Conca through the Gothic Line, had been:

> achieved more by infiltration tactics than by the set-piece attack; this method required special emphasis on three principles; Direction by Intention; the maintenance of Intercommunication and the frequent passing back of information and the necessity for Commanders to be well forward.[14]

The CO also pointed out that the division might well have to break German defensive positions about Coriano and Monte Colombo to allow the armour to smash through into the Po valley. B and C Squadrons were to move to sites more accessible to the main road lest worsening weather should prevent a speedy move out of harbour. As 46 Recce looked forward on this day it also looked back: all 46th Division personnel wore oak leaves in their cap badges to mark the anniversary of the Salerno landings.

Orders to move came on the 10th with A Squadron having the task of protecting 138 Brigade's left flank. To do this 1 and 4 Troops were to relieve 2nd/5th Queens of 169 Brigade on high ground at Farneto at last light while the squadron formed a stop at the head of the nearby valley. Reaching the high ground as planned, the leading elements of A Squadron found it still occupied by the enemy; the Queens were on a knoll lower in the valley which became the troop position. This was subjected to considerable shelling and mortaring but with no casualties.

Over the next few days 46 Recce carried out holding operations, manned OPs, sent out recce and contact patrols and suffered considerable shelling and mortaring which left five dead and many more wounded. Some forward movement was made when the Germans abandoned Farneto and the ridge was occupied by the Lincolns. By the evening of the 13th, B and C Squadrons were dug in on the Il Tribbio-Farneto spur, securing 138 Brigade's left flank and maintaining contact with 4th Indian Division. As the positions were overlooked by German OPs on Points 311 and 402, any movement at all brought down mortars and shells; two of the regiment's fatalities were incurred on the spur. During the night of 13/14 September 2nd Camerons relieved 46 Recce which was pulled back into divisional reserve to be ready "to take to its feet" for a prolonged infantry rôle to allow infantry battalions to be released for rest. The regiment was not asked to take to its feet for C Squadron was back in action next day assisting units of 128 Brigade and maintaining contact with 56th Division to the right. Once again heavy shelling was endured and casualties sustained. C Squadron assisted 6th Lincolns in capturing Monte Lupo on the 17th, although the squadron's part was limited to the anti-tank battery firing on enemy OPs and machine-gun posts.

On 19 September the regiment was given a recce rôle for a divisional advance as the Germans were withdrawing to a line from San Marino to Verucchio. The regimental task was to recce the Domagnano-Borgo Maggiore-Monte Ventosa-Verucchio road for 128 Brigade, covering the brigade's left flank and contacting 4th Indian Division in the Borgo Maggiore area.

B Squadron advanced through open and undulating country towards Borgo Maggiore, the main town of the Republic of San Marino. The Republic itself, set on a precipitous rock feature, was being used by the enemy for OPs:

> As the leading patrols advanced down the road they came under small arms and anti-tank fire from the town and a ridge to the west of their axis. The second patrol commander's armoured car was hit by anti-tank fire and the wireless put out of action though the crew were unhurt. The leading patrol was last observed at the cross-roads 756852 coming under fire from Pt 433 and though Besa fire was heard for some time afterwards the patrol did not return and was reported missing at nightfall.[15]

Squadron patrols established that Borgo Maggiore was held in strength with German infantry in houses supported by SP guns. Information passed back enabled an artillery bombardment to be brought down on the enemy positions by 172nd Field Regiment and 5th Medium Regiment; B Squadron also took seven prisoners. However, the enemy were still in the town when patrols went out next morning. Contact with 4th Indian Division brought the news that the Indians would attack Borgo Maggiore that afternoon and thus 46 Recce's operations were restricted to lifting mines and maintaining contact with the Indians who took the town as planned.

At midnight the weather broke with rain so heavy that off-road vehicular movement became almost impossible; the roads were unable to handle all the traffic being placed on them. Using the foul weather to best advantage, the Germans withdrew to the Marecchia river before dawn. Patrols from A Squadron nosed forward, taking some prisoners from 3 Company, 992 Grenadier Regiment, but meeting no opposition. Contact patrols were also out and, that afternoon, A Squadron led 5th Sherwood Foresters in an attack on Verucchio which was found to be unoccupied.

Heavy resistance was met on the morning of the 22nd when A Squadron, operating as infantry, crossed the Marecchia. Although the first wave of troops crossed the gravel riverbed unimpeded, the second wave was bombarded by heavy mortar and machine-gun fire, forcing the squadron to take cover in irrigation channels. When a self-propelled gun joined in progress became impossible; the squadron was pinned down for the entire day, withdrawing at dusk as 2nd/5th Leicesters crossed the river to continue the advance.

In the next phase of operations Allied forces pursued the slowly-retreating Germans to the Rubicon river. Although 46 Recce was to advance as infantry within 46th Division, the regiment instead took over forward divisional positions. C Squadron relieved 16th DLI of three positions, one of which was particularly close to the enemy; B Squadron relieved 5th Foresters on Point 160 and sent a fighting patrol forward to a spur where they found Germans occupying a house; in the ensuing skirmish two men of 6 Troop were killed.

On the morning of the 28th C Squadron's positions came under threat of counter-attack and B Squadron were mortared heavily. One C Squadron position, codenamed 'Jonson,' faced German troops in another house only thirty yards away. 'Jonson' was held by the thirty men of 9 and 12 Troops and when a fierce counter-attack, at about company strength, supported by a Mark IV Special tank, was launched the defenders had little chance of holding out. Nonetheless, they fought stubbornly against heavy odds. Their house was blasted by the tank, grenades were fired into the ruins and German infantry worked round the flanks. The officer commanding 'Jonson,' Lieutenant Talbot, was killed by a mortar bomb and the position was eventually surrounded. Twenty-two men were captured, although three were able to get away; another two wounded were treated by German medical orderlies and left in the house until it was retaken by British troops. The loss of 'Jonson' meant the loss of the Il Poggetto spur but the Germans had suffered considerable casualties and advanced no further.

Heavy artillery and mortar fire was brought down on Il Poggetto but a recce patrol from C Squadron reported it still held by the Germans at 4.30 next morning. The regiment continued to receive harassing fire from the enemy and there were also problems in supplying the squadrons as fords on the Rubicon became impassable; at one time B Squadron's rations could only be delivered by porters wading through three feet of water.

At 128 Brigade's request, extensive patrols were sent out on the last night of September to maintain contact with the enemy. One patrol task was to find out if Il Poggetto and Villa Ribano were still occupied by German troops. While the former was reported clear, a C Squadron patrol made contact at Villa Ribano:

> The patrol had moved along the road from Il Poggetto without contact and 4 Troop had established a firm base at the road junction 707992 while Lieutenant Crack and Sergeant Fisk approached the house. They saw no enemy around it and found part of the house unoccupied. They were in fact on the point of reporting it clear when Sergeant Fisk found a room full of Germans, some sleeping and others talking round a candle. One of the enemy opened fire with a machine-pistol and gave the alarm; sentries outside started firing rifles wildly in all directions and others rushed to fire machine-guns on fixed lines. Lieutenant Crack and Sergeant Fisk kept out of the way of the fire and at the same time used their own weapons to good effect in accounting for several of the enemy. 4 Troop however decided to withdraw through Il Poggetto back to the Squadron positions, and the enemy unfortunately took advantage of this move to send out their own fighting patrol which re-occupied Il Poggetto at approx 0730 hrs. No casualties were suffered by our own troops in this action, though during the day further casualties were sustained by A Squadron through heavy shelling on their area.[16]

The new German position on Il Poggetto was shelled heavily as was Villa Ribano. A C Squadron patrol reported Il Poggetto clear at 11.20am; the wounded men left by the Germans two days earlier were then brought back. At Villa Ribano there were still some Germans and a troop from C Squadron occupied a house there throughout the day. During the afternoon came news that 2nd Hampshires were to pass through C Squadron after dark and that 46 Recce would be relieved of its front-line commitments by noon on 1 October.

The relief completed, the regiment moved to a concentration area to re-organise in its normal rôle. Greyhound armoured cars were received for the scout troops who familiarised themselves with the new vehicles over the next week. There was no return to operations until 8 October when A Squadron moved to protect 128 Brigade's right flank and B Squadron and C Squadron to help repel German attacks on 1st/4th Hampshires. Flank protection tasks continued over the next few days with the regiment moving to Canonica on the 10th to protect the divisional right flank. That move was difficult with bad going on the roads: on the 12th the second-in-command, Major Walmsley, was killed when his jeep hit a mine; an 8 Troop patrol probing towards Calisese also lost one dead and four wounded.

On 15 October a recce patrol of a sergeant and four men of B Squadron with a REs' officer came under fire from a jam factory as they moved along the road to Calisese. Two troopers made their own way back, the sergeant and the sapper officer continued to Calisese to find the Germans in strength while the other pair of soldiers were reported missing. Calisese was cleared that afternoon with 6 Troop, later joined by 5 Troop, assisting in the operation. Further patrols were out: A Squadron found Germans on the Palazzo Rognoni ridge which was cleared by tanks from The Bays, infantry from the King's Own Yorkshire Light Infantry and A Squadron.

Next day the regiment provided cover for sappers working on a Bailey bridge until 2nd/4th KOYLI went forward that afternoon. That brought another spell of intensive operations to an end as the regiment moved back to Serravalie the following day, remaining there until the 23rd when it moved north of Urbino.

On the divisional front Eighth Army was still moving forward which brought a new task for 46 Recce - providing carrier patrols to help sappers in route recces, mine clearance and 'special tasks.' Six patrols, each of two carriers with a No 19 set and a despatch rider, were assigned to sapper support on 28 October. And a new principle of patrolling was also established: if a recce patrol reported an objective clear it was to remain in position while the rest of the troop moved forward to assist consolidation.

The road recce patrols left on 2 November and, four days later, A Squadron again undertook flank protection for 128 Brigade on a ridge west of Ravaldino while RHQ, A and B Squadrons moved up on the 6th to take over 1,200 yards of a ridge overlooking the Rabbi river. A recce patrol reported a bridge intact at Fiumana while a German recce patrol was spotted on the Allied side of the Rabbi. A Squadron was subsequently asked to simulate an attack on the bridge over the Rabbi to assist a 128 Brigade attack; harassing fire from mortars, 75s and field guns was laid down on information from Italian partisans.

As the advance continued the regiment provided recce patrols, contact patrols with the Polish Corps, and assisted in knocking out enemy positions, while continuing with flank-guard duties. From 10 November traffic control duties were added; the road recce patrols under the sappers were still out thus giving 46 Recce probably its widest-ever range of duties. That range was widened on the 21st when the SP Battery and the Mortar Troop joined the MMGs of 9th Manchesters in a harassing fire programme to support a 139 Brigade attack.

That night a fighting patrol of B Squadron, under Lieutenant J.F.Carver, approached a house at Casa Casina where they heard voices and movement. The patrol was unseen until it was virtually at the door of the house. Carver and some of his men rushed into the yard of the house and into a close-quarter battle with well dug-in German defenders. Firing machine-guns and throwing grenades Carver's group killed two Germans and wounded another two before withdrawing with no casualties to themselves. On the night of 22/23 November 6 Troop captured Casa Casina, taking five prisoners and killing one other German.

The special skills of a reconnaissance regiment were called upon once again when a road recce party under Captain Doug Waugh was attached to divisional tactical HQ on the 25th to recce crossings of the Lamone river forward of the leading infantry; no easy crossings were found and the party returned after two days. Then, on the 28th, long range patrols were again out to recce the lateral roads between the Marzeno and Lamone rivers and any possible vehicle routes to Brisighella. The patrols, which were still operating on 30 November, found the going very bad: most work was done on foot and a 240-foot gap was reported in the bridge over the Lamone at Brisighella.

The attack over the Lamone involved 46 Recce's SP Battery which, under 169 Brigade, provided harassing fire in the Faenza area. A call for porterage parties was cancelled and the bulk of the regiment was resting and carrying out maintenance at Forli in early December. The long range recce patrols were still out as were A Squadron's traffic control parties which returned on 20 December. By then the regiment was at Montefiore where it ended the year. Early in January 46 Recce was withdrawn for operations in Greece: its part in the Italian campaign was over.

By mid-August 1 Recce was back in action, taking over from 4 Recce while the latter was in contact with the enemy. The regiment's assault troop had been re-equipped with M3 White half-tracks and eight 75mm guns allowing self-propelled close support. The war diary commented that "This will fill a long felt want of immediate fire support during recce tasks."[17]

On 15 August the regiment moved, under XIII Corps, to the Florence area where, on the 23rd, an armoured car carried out street patrols for 2 Brigade against German snipers and street-fighting patrols. Patrolling in the northern area of Florence and in the outskirts at Rinaldi continued for several days; an 88mm gun was destroyed and 20 prisoners taken for the loss of a Humber Mk IV and one LRC. However, the regiment's senior officers considered its deployment "tactically unsound and inevitably leads to trouble."[18] By the end of the month the regiment was patrolling in support of Operation OLIVE setting the pattern for the coming months.

The impetus of OLIVE had died by the autumn and by early October 1 Recce was based at Borgo San Lorenzo which was 'home' for some time before a move to San Benedetto. There the mortars and SP Battery became part of 26 Armoured Brigade Group for operations. Patrolling was still a normal part of life as the Allied armies pushed against the German line and there were skirmishes such as that on 28 October when the leading troop of C Squadron was pinned down for thirty minutes by mortar and Spandau fire; one man was wounded before the troop was extricated. At the end of the month a Polish regiment relieved 1 Recce which returned to Borgo San Lorenzo for rest, training and refitting. That break lasted almost two weeks before, first, A Squadron and then RHQ moved to San Clemente.

A Squadron, with a mortar section and a troop of the SP Battery, took over the Rignano feature on 16 November. Although the war diary recorded the sector as "very quiet", concern about possible enemy attacks led to the creation of Brettforce on the 18th. Composed of 1 Recce with a battalion-sized grouping of gunners and sappers as infantry, Brettforce was intended "to hold Rignano feature in event of Monte Grande being overrun."[19] but the remainder of November passed with no serious incidents.

The beginning of December brought much activity, including increased enemy shelling while artificial moonlight was used in the regiment's sector for the first time. Suspicion was aroused on the 5th by a "blanket of 'un-natural fog' seen by B Sqn in the Sopra valley extending right back into enemy territory."[20] This "un-natural fog" turned out to be perfectly natural! During the month infantry duties continued while the mortars were active in suppressing German machine-gun fire from Il Sopra and Broglio. There was a disparaging comment in the war diary about their American neighbours on the 19th:

> ...the usual American patrol to Broglio went through the Ambush Post a little way, fired a lot of ammunition and returned.[21]

Throughout the month the regiment endured regular German shelling, mortaring and machine-gun fire; a "record number" of reports of machine-gunning were noted on 23 December but, after mortaring until 2.30am, Christmas Day was quiet. By the end of the year 1 Recce was wondering if a new German unit had moved in to the line as "of late the enemy has become very careless on regimental front and shows himself quite frequently."[22]

Similar infantry rôles were the lot of 44 and 56 Recce at the end of 1944. The former had returned from Egypt in July and moved to Sassaferreto at the end of August. C Squadron was first in action with 7 Armoured Brigade and in a series of actions throughout September the regiment suffered nine killed, including Lieutenant N.A.Smith who was mistaken for a German by a soldier of 2nd/7th Queen's; another twenty were wounded.

October brought a similar pattern of recce patrols, listening posts and OPs. On 5 October the CO, Lieutenant-Colonel M.A.A.Little, was visiting A Squadron when a shell hit the house where he was standing. Seriously wounded, Colonel Little died in the field ambulance 30 minutes later. Major Langley took over command. Several other casualties were sustained from shelling before the Canadian Hastings and Essex Regiments took over on 11 October and 44 Recce moved back to Treia.

The regiment remained at Treia until mid-November although a small composite force, Senforce, under Captain L.R.Symonds was called on for active operations for several days and a signals detachment went to 56th Division. In mid-November 44 Recce moved to Forli and, from then until the end of the month, the regiment was heavily engaged on patrolling with numerous skirmishes with the Germans. A further relief at the beginning of December took them to Cesena from where they went back into action at Faenza. Now under the command of Lieutenant-Colonel C.R.Spencer, the regiment spent much of the month as infantry although they were able to celebrate Christmas out of the line at Forli. The end of the year once more saw them in action along the Naviglio canal under command of 56th (London) Division.

Returning to Italy from Egypt in September 56 Recce had been issued with M8 Greyhound armoured cars to replace their Humber heavy armoured cars before moving north to Fano and into the line as infantry in the mountains. Fortunately they had received their full allotment of kit for the first time since leaving the UK which was most welcome in the coming winter. There was little shelter in those mountain positions and great reliance on mules for re-supply. As the weather worsened, winter kit was issued and a mobile bath unit was later provided. There were of course skirmishes with the Germans but, for much of the time, General Winter was the worst enemy.

20
The end in Italy
Greek interlude

The new year of 1945 saw the reconnaissance regiments in north-west Europe poised for the final strike into Germany while those in Italy waited for spring and weather that would allow the Allied armies to thrust into the plain of Lombardy.

In Italy four reconnaissance regiments were committed to the front line in those opening days of 1945. These were 1, 44, 46 and 56 Recce. Of these, 44 and 56 had the longest fighting records: 44 Recce had seen action in the Western Desert before El Alamein while 56 Recce had had little respite since its first days in Tunisia. All held positions in the northern Apennines in that grim winter as the Germans held on to the remains of the crumbling Gothic Line.

But for 1 Recce relief was near. Conditions had worsened in early January with heavy snow on the 6th that drifted up to eight feet deep. While the soldiers cleared snow the squadron headquarters were visited by General Lucian Truscott, commander of Fifth Army, on 9 January and two days later 337 Regiment, US Army began relieving the reconnoitrers. The takeover complete, 1 Recce moved back to Bergo San Lorenzo near Perugia from where it took the road to Taranto to leave Italy for Palestine in early February.

Four Recce had departed from Italy to join its division which had been hurriedly shipped to Greece as part of the force sent to that country to prevent a communist takeover in the wake of German withdrawal; 46 Recce also moved to Greece and although the regiment returned to Italy before hostilities ended it arrived at the front after the German surrender. Thus 44th and 56th Regiments were the final representatives of their Corps in the Italian campaign.

As 1945 dawned 56 Recce, with headquarters at San Apollinare, was operating in an infantry rôle. In reserve on New Year's Day the regiment moved into the line three days later to relieve 1st Royal Fusiliers at Casone from where regular patrols were sent out. During this time in the line the regiment endured the heavy snowstorm of early January. A rest spell at Castro San Martino was followed by a return to Casone. A patrolling routine was again established while a forward post at Casa Salara - about three quarters of a mile in front of the main positions - was held by a troop. On 22 January the troop at Casa Salara spotted a German patrol in snow camouflage and called down artillery and mortar fire on them, causing the Germans to withdraw. But once again the main enemy was the weather: so cold were conditions that 78th Division's full supply of olive oil was issued to 56 Recce to test as anti-frostbite protection.

Casa Salara was the scene of an engagement with the enemy in early February. This occurred, according to Tom Blease of B Squadron, on the evening of 5 February (although the war diary records it as 8 February) when the outpost was attacked. As the Germans approached they called out in English, "A Company, Two Section, don't shoot!" However, some defenders heard German being spoken and opened fire. The Germans retaliated with mortarfire and several bombs hit the house:

> When they had finished their mortaring they fired a long burst of Spandau... I lay in the rubble and watched the tracers hit the softer stones on the inside of the building...
>
> Everything went quiet for some seconds [then] a voice in English shouted "Right boys, out of the house with your hands up." This to me was a bloody insult so I ran up the rubble and gave him half a magazine - there were two of them. After this he fired a Panzerfaust at our position and I remember seeing a vivid green flash - what a lovely shade of green it was; it blew me up in the air and I landed in the rubble.[1]

The round had demolished a wall onto the LMG ammunition but the Germans, from 10 Company, 3rd Fallschirmjäger Regiment, were driven off by artillery, mortars and machine-gun fire. There was a touch of slapstick with the English-speaking Germans exchanging verbal abuse with the defenders: one German taunt was for the recce men to "come out and fight." The skirmish left two Germans dead while B Squadron had one officer, Lieutenant Pickard, and four men wounded.

Shortly after this 78th Division was relieved by an Indian division. There was delight at being out of the hills as 56 Recce moved to Castiglione di Ravenna "to settle down for a period and get ourselves back into much cleaner state."[2] But that delight was overshadowed by the news that the regiment was losing its revered CO: Kendal Chavasse was promoted to a staff position at Fifth Army Headquarters and his regiment paraded to say goodbye to him on 6 March. Colonel Chavasse visited his squadrons to thank them for their work and to wish them well; there were many who felt bereaved at the loss of a superlative leader. His standing among his men was marked by the farewell gifts presented to him: a silver hunting horn inscribed "Gone Away" from his officers and a subscription from all ranks to purchase a set of saddles and bridles as well as a trumpet and the green and yellow recce pennant which he had flown from his car when escorting King George VI on his visit to 78th Division at the end of the North African campaign; the pennant, also flown in Sicily and Italy, was mounted in a wooden frame.

I was deeply touched by this highly illegal and highly irregular subscription from all ranks and have never heard of such a thing happening before in the British Army.[3]

The men of 56 Recce were pleased to learn that Colonel Chavasse's successor would be Major Marcus Hartland-Mahon, another Irishman and a 56 Recce officer who had served with the regiment through all its active service. After three weeks at Castiglione di Ravenna it was back to the front line but this time the regiment relieved 44 Recce on the river Senio.

The Senio sector was very different from anything the regiment had experienced before for the front lines were based on the river's floodbanks and were very close together. From those who had held the sector before, the newcomers learned that there would be large-scale use of small arms of all descriptions and much digging, either to create tunnels or prepare earthworks near the floodbank tops. Each floodbank had its own distinct character: crossing the plain every mile or so they were up to 20 feet high and about ten feet wide at the top. The Senio itself was under 20 feet wide and only three or four feet deep although the floodbanks were a certain indication that things could be very different in winter. In this sector 56 Recce came under the Irish Brigade, deploying, yet again, as infantry.

The Irish Brigade front was held with three units forward - 56 Recce to the right, 1st Royal Irish Fusiliers in the centre and 2nd Royal Inniskilling Fusiliers to the left. The right sector was narrower, with only two positions on the floodbank, but was held in depth; it was also overlooked by German positions at Cotignola which made daylight movement impossible. All in all, the Senio line was very much akin to the trench warfare of the Great War, especially as trench raiding was part of life there.

The first such raid on 56 Recce occurred within an hour of taking over a position from 44 Recce. German infantry attacked with grenades and sub machine-guns while mortars rained down on the centre troop position. Shortlived though the raid was it left three dead, four wounded and five captured. Three days later A Squadron was shelled and mortared heavily but fortunately there was only one slight injury and retaliatory fire in the form of an AGRA shoot soon silenced the enemy gunners. There was yet another attack, involving about 25 to 30 enemy troops, on 19 March during which one man was killed and six wounded. A troop HQ collapsed and Sergeant Cronin earned the DCM for re-establishing contact with Squadron Headquarters; Lance-Corporal Duffy earned the MM for rescuing wounded under fire.

There were no regrets at leaving the Senio when 1st East Surreys relieved 56 Recce on 27 March. The regiment moved back to train for its last operations in Italy:

The move back from the Senio was a welcome change even though it meant another bout of training, the infantry to get used to being carried in Kangaroos (a Sherman tank chassis equipped to carry troops) and having to work with flamethrowing Crocodile tanks, special tanks for bridge building etc. Once the advance started there were to be no halts at nightfall as it had been learnt in the past that this gave the enemy the chance to get himself organised with rearguard parties. Towns and villages on the main route were to be by-passed and subsequently cut off, gridded maps were issued to gunners thus enabling them to work out river widths etc. [And] the RHA had been equipped with some self-propelled 25-pounders.[4]

Training was intensive as 78th Division prepared for Operation BUCKLAND, the objective of which was the defeat of the German forces south of the river Po; for 56 Recce the training lasted from 1 to 9 April. By the latter date BUCKLAND had already begun. The rôle of V Corps had been divided into three distinct phases: in the first 8th Indian and 2nd NZ Divisions were to attack across the Senio; in phase two those same divisions would create a bridgehead across the Santerno, some eight miles further on; in phase three, 78th and 56th Divisions would break out through that bridgehead and cut through the German defences around Argenta:

> It was a rôle that [78th] Division had played successfully before at the Sangro, and again in the Liri Valley. It was not surprising, therefore, that it should have been chosen for the same important task in the final, triumphant phase.[5]

On 10 April the regiment moved to its forming-up area and, next day, made its way to the "wedding areas" where units under 78th Division's command that were to co-operate in battle would meet up. The Indians and New Zealanders had been in action since the 5th and the bridgehead over the Santerno had been established; at 2.00pm on 12 April, C Squadron, 56 Recce was ordered to move with 36 Brigade, plus tanks, to cross and extend the Indians' bridgehead. The remainder of the regiment was to observe and mop up in the area east of the Santerno and south of Reno as well as protecting 36 Brigade's right flank and prevent any Germans in their area from escaping; it was also to move forward to conform with the Irish Brigade advance:

> Events then moved quickly and the Recce Sqdn with 36 Bde together with the tanks were given the job of capturing a group of houses known as Tre Casa, 1,000 yards beyond the most forward infantry of the Indian Div. Once they reached this objective they were to push on towards the village of Conselice, but this village proved to be a tough nut and subsequently had to be taken by infantry.[6]

Almost immediately the reconnoitrers were involved in hard fighting; breaking through the Argenta Gap was to provide the regiment with one of its toughest operations. In the course of heavy fighting on the 14th one 56

Recce M8 Greyhound armoured car was blown up with three men killed. Three days later the regiment passed under direct command of V Corps and over the next two days its squadrons were heavily engaged; 56 Recce took 57 prisoners, destroyed four tanks - and shared the destruction of another - and knocked out numerous anti-tank guns; 12 Germans had also been killed in action.

As the Allies surged towards the Po di Volano, B Squadron had its own bitter struggle to clear the town of Portomaggiore. The squadron was between the Kangaroo Army of 2nd London Irish, who had just reached the Bolognese and di Porto canals to the west of the town, and 1st Royal Irish Fusiliers who had secured a firm right flank for 78th Division. With some Sherman tanks from 4th Hussars, B Squadron was trying to cross the two canals in Portomaggiore itself but a German strongpoint at Croatia, which commanded the northern exits from the town, "was holding out with such obstinacy that no progress was possible beyond the second canal, and the squadron was confined to the difficult, rubble-strewn area of the town's western outskirts."[7]

However, patrols from 56 Recce, moving west through Consandolo, were able to establish that resistance covered only roads running northward and west of Route 16; the Germans did not threaten Route 16 itself which was to be 6th Armoured Division's main axis of advance. As the advance continued B Squadron was still having difficulty at Croatia; during the afternoon of the 18th the reconnoitrers and the Hussars' tanks were reinforced by a company of infantry but still the Germans, with two SPGs, held out. The strongpoint was finally overcome during the morning of the 19th.

By now the Irish Brigade was extending the bridgehead over the San Nicolo canal so that the Kangaroo Army could be pushed forward again. To exploit the confusion that the Kangaroo Army would cause, 56 Recce was ordered to occupy Voghenza while 36 Brigade made for the Po di Volano, west of Cona. In this advance the regiment returned to a flank protection rôle with A Squadron performing that task for 2 Armoured Brigade on the 21st by which time it had taken Voghenza. Passing under command of 11 Brigade on 22 April the regiment headed for its next task, to cross the Diversivo canal and the Po di Volano.

That afternoon considerable resistance was met in the Contrapo area. Infantry of 2nd LF were brought up to clear the area, as were men from the Northamptons but the opposition stiffened along the front. Strong pressure, including UNCLE shoots from the artillery, had, by that evening, compressed the enemy into a bend of the Po di Volano near Contrapo.

At this time C Squadron was given the task of "fanning out inland." Lieutenant Yates, who had been told that he was to be in Naples in three days time to commence home leave, volunteered to go out with his troop to relieve Bill Croucher's troop which had been leading the advance for three days. Yates was seriously injured shortly afterwards and, although he received speedy medical attention, subsequently died of his wounds. His troop was out of contact and 6th Armoured Division was to pass through the area that evening to strike towards Ferrara:

> In an effort to contact Lt Yates' men Lt Croucher plus a pillion passenger from his own Troop went out on a motor cycle and having progressed along the route taken by the other Troop they themselves came under artillery fire ...both were slightly wounded but as soon as the firing ceased recovered the motor cycle and returned to the Squadron HQ. and later Lt Yates' Troop also returned.[8]

On 23 April 11 Brigade crossed the Po di Volano. That evening 56 Recce and 2nd Lancashire Fusiliers pushed into the bulge west of the river while Irish Brigade units were attacking in the direction of the main river Po. Although plans had been made for 78th Division to cross the Po with 36 Brigade in the lead these were suddenly abandoned:

> The landscape was ablaze with burning houses and vehicles and farther north the RAF were dropping flares and bombing the roads and railways beyond the River Po. As dawn approached on the morning of the 25th April it became evident that organised defence was at an end and the Irish Brigade entered Zocca and Ruina to find an incredible scene of devastation.

> Packed in the fields, queued up in lanes, cast in ditches, in farmyards and woods everywhere, even in the river itself, lay the remains of transport and equipment of the 76th Panzer Corps.[9]

In the aftermath of this collapse 56 Recce's squadrons were given the tasks of overlooking the river with each squadron assigned to a brigade area. Then, on 25 April, 78th Division finally disengaged after three weeks of mobile battle in which 56 Recce had lost seven dead and seventeen wounded - comparatively light casualties in relation to the amount of action that the regiment had seen. A week later, on 2 May, German forces in Italy surrendered and 56 Recce's war was over, although there were many tasks still to be carried out in the early days of peace.

Also there at the end in Italy was 44 Recce. Their division - 56th - had gone through the final phase of fighting alongside 78th Division so that the two regiments were never far apart, although 44 Recce saw nowhere near as much action as 56 in those last days of war. The men of 44 Recce had begun 1945 carrying out infantry duties on the eastern side of the Apennines along the Senio:

> We... were kept very busy, sitting most of the time along the Spandau and rocket infested Senio River. From Christmas until our Army was unleashed for its final battle in April, our job was that of an infantry battalion. We held long stretches of the winter line through the dreary

Italian months of rain and snow. At times the Regiment spent as much as five weeks in the line, with each Squadron more than two weeks up and one in reserve...

The enemy did not give us a quiet time and tried all combinations of raids, rockets, Spandaus and shells to drive us from our positions. We stayed all right, replying in hearty fashion with spirited patrol clashes and by throwing back as much ammunition as we were permitted to expend.[10]

At the beginning of January the regiment was on the Naviglio canal between 6th Cheshires and 1st London Scottish with C Squadron to the right, A to the left and B in reserve. As the canal banks were quite low and the forward positions close to the enemy, the area was lively. During the night of 3/4 January, Princess Patricia's Canadian Light Infantry attacked through C Squadron's positions to cross the canal and hook left to take Granarola. The operation was successful and many prisoners were taken; this was followed by 56th Division's Operation CYGNET which cleared pockets of Germans between the Naviglio and the Senio.

On 10 January the regiment moved into positions on the Senio itself, relieving 1st London Scottish:

The Senio River had banks up to thirty feet in height. The river course has been straightened in the past leaving loops or bends which are empty of water but still retain their high banks. There were three of the loops on the Regimental front.

The enemy had prepared his positions in some detail on the western banks and to a lesser degree on the eastern. Most of the houses near the eastern bank had been demolished and fields of fire had been cleared to a depth in places of some hundreds of yards eastwards from the banks.[11]

Some German positions on the Allied side of the Senio had not been mopped up in Operation CYGNET. These gave the Germans the ability to dominate 44 Recce's forward positions by observation and fire and the regiment spent much time preparing defences against a possible attack. Until 13/14 February 44 Recce was responsible for the section taken over from the London Scottish. In that time fighting patrols engaged the Germans on several occasions, inflicting many casualties while the regiment's positions suffered heavy shelling and mortaring. On 20 January there was "unusually heavy shelling" all day while, eight days later, an A Squadron troop position at San Severo crossroads was hit by rocketfire, wounding the squadron leader, Major Hammond, and five others; the position had to be abandoned.

On 5 February a small German force, of about 20 men, attacked one of 44 Recce's forward positions:

About 10 enemy seen approaching from the left. Bren gunner opened up and scattered enemy. Enemy positions on river bank gave good covering fire to the attacking force. Enemy then approached from the right killing the sentry in the right hand position. The officer who was leading the enemy patrol then approached the house shouting "Come out Tommy, you've had it." The reply was a long burst of TMC which killed the German officer. Some further troops then approached the house and threw grenades into the room and fired Schmeisser on the men inside. Sgt Watts took the [brunt] of the attack and was killed. L/Cpl Chapman and Tpr Eddy fired TMC at the enemy approaching the house [who] subsequently withdrew. Afterwards they put down a heavy mortar stonk which demolished half the house, killing one and wounding two other men. A patrol from the troop at Maneresi was sent forward to contact the section. It was decided to abandon the fact [sic] and after digging out the men who had been buried and burying the four dead Germans [this] was carried out.[12]

Relieved by 1st London Scottish on the night of 13/14 February, 44 Recce moved back across the Lamone river to its billeting area where the soldiers had the opportunity for some rest, as well as "a general [regimental] clean up and a sort out after so many weeks of activity."[13] Then, on 3 March, it was back to the line, to relieve 2nd/5th Queens south-west of Cotignola.

This was a new area for the regiment which now had responsibility for a frontage of about 1,000 yards into which all three squadrons put troops:

Each Squadron had positions actually dug in the home side river-bank, and with tunnels dug through so that enemy movement on the river could be observed and sniped. Cotignola was a nuisance as it afforded good enemy OPs and snipers' posts which overlooked the greater part of the forward area.[14]

This section was held for a week until 56 Recce took over. Apart from some Nebelwerfer stonks the regiment had a quiet time in the sector with its snipers claiming a number of victims. The final night, as the advance party of 56 Recce arrived, was described as "the quietest night so far." Although an attack had been expected on the centre of the regiment's front, held by C Squadron, this did not materialise, probably due to heavy concentrations of fire on the Germans. An attack was, however, launched on 56 Recce almost as soon as they moved in, as we have already seen.

On the 11th 44 Recce concentrated near Cesena to rest and refit and while this was happening the CO, Colonel Spencer, left for the UK on leave; command devolved on Major O.G.Longley, MC. The regiment's next task was to relieve 1/22nd Battalion of the Italian Cremona Division, along the Old Lamone river in the northern sector of Eighth Army's front. In doing so 44 Recce came under command of 12th Royal Lancers, which, coincidentally, was Colonel Spencer's parent regiment. The two regiments formed Recforce, commanded by Lieutenant Colonel K.E.Savill, 12th Lancers.

The new front was long with a line of forward defended localities on the Old Lamone riverbed; there were also forward defensive positions facing the Scolo Pignatta where the Germans had outposts forward of their main line along the Senio and Reno rivers. Although there were seven casualties in the early days in the new positions these were caused by Allied mines laid by a variety of units over several weeks and whose original markings were difficult to distinguish. The defensive positions were good "consisting of well-constructed section-posts connected by crawl trenches [and] all posts were surrounded by wire and mines."[15] There was but slight enemy activity that was almost restricted to moderate small arms fire at night. Virtually no shelling or mortaring took place and, in general, it was the "quietest front the Regiment had had for some time."

The Germans were not entirely inactive for they subjected 44 Recce and 12th Lancers to some propaganda attacks early in April. On the night of 2/3 April a German radio broadcast was aimed at the two regiments:

> You landlubbers of 12th Lancers and 44th Recce, you'll get no Easter eggs and Hot Cross buns this year. There's none for you. Perhaps this time next year you won't be able to eat them. Now get down in your foxholes and weapon pits and listen to this record. Keep away from the River Po. Prisoners taken this month say it is colossal. They say they are bloody glad they haven't got to cross it. Some of them crossing in German transports have been very sick. Can you imagine the terrain between here and the River Po. Canals and rivers they are many. Now you can see why we fought so hard for the Apennine passes. We wanted time and we got time. We Germans fight for what we get. The line of the River Po is impregnable. There are two sides to every question. Why not hear both sides. You can hear them on the German radio with the 47 metre band.[16]

That was followed by another broadcast aimed at Recforce on the 4th. After a record, described as an old favourite, the presenter came in:

> Hullo 12th Lancers, Recce. Headlines make news; news makes money; do you remember the casualties at Arnhem; the 1st Airborne Div... Remember the 1st Canadian Div at the River Lamone and River Reno [figures quoted]. Die quicker pals... [music] Dividends of munitions on Wall Street are soaring because of more casualties so hurry up and die now. How nice to be at home in a nice soft bed... [music] ...Someone out of uniform at home is taking your job; they are not longing for your return so die quicker pal.[17]

A number of British shells finished that second broadcast. At least one other was noted; all three were described as "a little rather puzzling propaganda."

Recforce became Checkforce on 5 April when 6th Cheshires relieved 12th Lancers and Lieutenant Colonel Birch assumed command of the sector. That same day 167 Brigade attacked across the Reno to the right of Checkforce and 44 Recce mounted a Chinese attack on their front. In the space of an hour 500 rounds of 75mm ammunition, 300 mortar rounds and 16 belts per Vickers machine gun were loosed off and drew a considerable proportion of German defensive fire away from 167 Brigade. In subsequent days 44 Recce carried out extensive patrolling. By 12 April the Germans had withdrawn from Checkforce's front and the force was accordingly disbanded that day.

Operation BUCKLAND was now in full swing with the Germans pushed back from the Senio. The battle became more fluid with 56th Division moving quickly north-westwards along Lake Comacchio to outflank Argenta as 78th Division forced the bottleneck of the Argenta Gap. After the breakthrough from the Argenta Gap it had been intended that 44 Recce would protect 56th Division's right flank up to the Po but the task went instead to 27th Lancers. Because of the speed of operations 44 Recce was assigned to support duties, bringing up ammunition, bridging and supplies, as well as providing armoured cars to carry out traffic control duties.

On 15 April the regiment concentrated near Longestina from where, for several days, men were supplied for prisoner-of-war duties while, on the 17th, a party of eighty under Captain Oldland went to assist 1st London Scottish as a boat-carrying party in a river crossing. As the Germans had retreated the operation proved unnecessary. Then, on the 20th, 44 Recce moved east of Portomaggiore and, that afternoon, A and B Squadrons re-organised on an infantry basis to relieve 1st Buffs along the Scolo Bolognese. Both squadrons patrolled forward from their new positions, with B Squadron patrols advancing, unopposed, about five or six miles along the Convogliatone canal; six deserters from 29th PanzerGrenadier Division were captured. A Squadron patrols suffered one casualty when Trooper Robinson lost a foot to an S-mine, several of which also caused civilian casualties.

The regiment moved forward again on 22 April to concentrate north-east of Portomaggiore; once again men and vehicles deployed to assist in supplying the division while a carrying party for boats for the Po crossing was also provided. Three days later came another move, to the Copparo area from where, on the 26th, RHQ and C Squadron moved to Ferrara but had to wait until evening before a bridge was available to cross the Po. After a long, rainy night march, RHQ and C Squadron finally harboured at about midnight.

On 27 April C Squadron advanced to protect 169 Brigade's right flank between the Po and Adige rivers. There was slight German opposition at one point and 62 prisoners were taken. After a "very pleasant day in brilliant sunshine" C Squadron made contact with the Cremona Group to the right and the regiment came together south of Rovigo.

Less C Squadron, 44 Recce crossed the Adige at 7.00pm on 29 April to recce towards Venice. That task was carried out at speed as the regiment wanted to be first in Venice but it was not to be, as 169 Brigade beat them to the city. As the war diary notes "had the bridge over the Adige been completed at 1400 as planned the Regiment would have been first in Venice."[18] The disappointment of missing that distinction was therefore added to the frustration of not seeing as much action as the regiment would have liked in the final operations in Italy:

> For us the break-through was disappointing, as the great number of blown bridges slowed us down so much that infantry often did the job faster, and consequently we were not employed as much as we should have liked.[19]

The war had ended for 44 Recce, which concentrated at Mestre near Venice on 30 April where it remained until called forward to the Isonso river area on 4 May for internal security duties.

***

The Greek episode that involved 4 and 46 Recce was short-lived and the worst of the civil war was over by the time the two regiments arrived. The first in Greece was 4 Recce which landed in late December. Its division had defended Kalamika and liberated Psychiko and on 6 January when resistance ended in Athens, 4 Recce:

> ...patrolled South to Sunium with little opposition and much ovation.

> The Revolution was now coming to an end and the ELAS were being chased to their mountain fastnesses. 'The Chase' was the Regiment's especial type of war, and it went into it with all the dash and efficiency that its long training had produced. C Squadron went to Thebes and thence to Khalkis where an attempt at a parley with ELAS leaders was unfortunately unsuccessful. B Squadron ran North to Levadhia and Amfiklia, but opposition at the Lamia pass prevented further progress. On 18th January C Squadron and RHQ joined B Squadron at Amfiklia, and C Squadron passed through B in another attempt to force the pass, while B attempted the coast road with only limited success. Before further attempts could be made, a truce was effected with the enemy and the Regiment concentrated at Amfiklia, on which village it centred for the rest of the bitterly cold winter.[20]

Into the dying gasps of the ELAS efforts to take over Greece 46 Recce also landed, landing in Athens after a hectic dash to Taranto to board LSTs:

> The first task was a quick swan to ensure that the ELAS forces in the Pellopenese [sic] had withdrawn to the agreed line. The initiation into

Greek hospitality left everyone in a daze which continued throughout our stay among those fierce, friendly folk who could be so warmhearted and so bitter in the same breath. The sudden change that followed when the Regiment became a combination of Carter Paterson, Harrods, a Citizens Advice Bureau and a Court of Solomon in one fell swoop was rather staggering but full of interest. Few of us will ever forget our days in Argos, Nauplion, Corinth, Sikia, Xilokastron, or those long treks over magnificent country to get Red Cross Supplies where they were really needed. The occupation of the remainder of the Pellopenese [sic] and the disarming of ELAS was successfully tackled, 12,750 ex-ELAS troops passing through the Regiment's hands.[21]

So ended the Reconnaissance Corps' involvement in Greece; 46 Recce returned to Italy, too late to see action in the final days of war while 4 Recce faded away in Greece. One of its members penned a poetic tribute to the regiment.

> Now strike the flag, the panther green and gold,
> That for four years has fluttered to the sky
> In seven countries; fold the colours now,
> They are not needed, fold them, lay them by.[22]

21
N-W Europe - the left flank

Despite the Ardennes offensive Adolf Hitler's Third Reich was in its death throes. With the Red Army pushing in from the east the Western Allies turned the German offensive and prepared for the thrust into the heart of Germany. Among the troops who awaited that thrust were men from seven recce regiments: 3 (RNF); 6 Airborne Armoured; 15 (Scottish); 43 (Wessex); 49 (West Riding); 52 (Lowland) and 53 (Welsh).

Although 53rd (Welsh) Division and 6th Airborne Division took part in XXX Corps' attack as part of First (US) Army in early January neither recce regiment was given a significant offensive rôle. The airborne men were deployed south-east of Namur guarding the bridges over the Maas. Patrols were carried out but movement was difficult in the snow; by the end of the month the regiment had moved to the Voorste Steeg area but continued on defensive duties. A thaw in early February brought a temporary ban on tracked vehicles but patrolling continued until 6th Airborne Division returned to Britain at the end of the month.

The battle of the Ardennes was over by 23 January by which time Montgomery had informed Field Marshal Brooke of his intention to take 21 Army Group through the Reichswald forest and up to the Rhine in two operations, the first being GRENADE involving 9th (US) Army, under Montgomery's command at that time, attacking north-eastwards from the Roer towards the Rhine while the second was allocated to First (Canadian) Army: this was Operation VERITABLE, scheduled to begin on 8 February 1945. Before either began, XII Corps carried out Operation BLACKCOCK to clear the Roer triangle: this was assigned to 7th Armoured Division and 52nd (Lowland) Division with assistance from 43rd Division and 8 Armoured Brigade. As Desert Rats and Lowlanders attacked, the Wessexmen provided support; to free infantry 43 Recce held part of the line. A Squadron was assisting 130 Brigade but poor road conditions restricted the squadron's rôle to passing back information and some general liaison work.

For 52 Recce it was a different story as they advanced from Hillensburgh in a blinding snowstorm on ice-bound roads that made movement almost impossible for the anti-tank troop's carriers:

> ...they and the guns they were towing stopped all traffic while their crews toiled away to get them up. All the time it was a struggle against the elements as well as against the Germans. Our part of the battle was on the left flank where we were in contact with the 11th Hussars of 7th Armoured. The enemy retreated gradually and never without a struggle

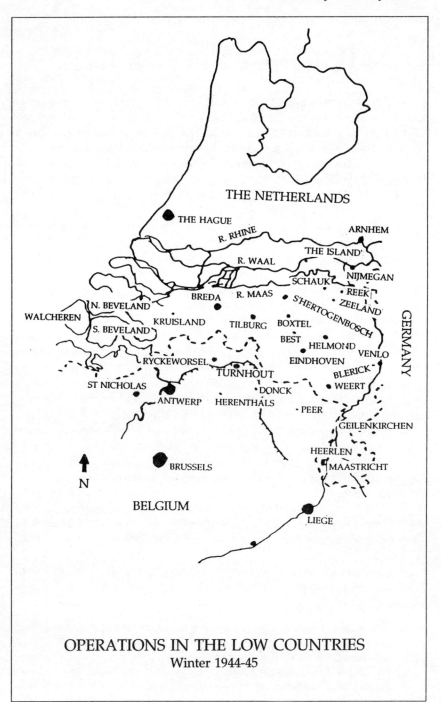

OPERATIONS IN THE LOW COUNTRIES
Winter 1944-45

and often put in a counter-attack. We moved up through Hongen to
Havert and then to Aan Popelaar. We stayed in slit-trenches at Aan
Popelaar for forty-eight of the coldest hours of the whole campaign; at
least B and RHQ did. A Squadron were in reserve and C were out at
Pepinus bridge where they had to cope with refugees as much as with
the Bosch. Jack Horner said that everything had happened in his
command post except that nobody had had twins as yet.[1]

A B Squadron fighting patrol took 21 prisoners plus the surrenders of the
villages of Grosswehrage and Kleinwehragen. When the division took
Heinsberg, 52 Recce occupied Haaren and Driesch. With the Roer triangle
clear the priority became guarding the river line against counter-attack; this
task gave the forward reconnoitrers an unenviable job, keeping 24 hour
watch in freezing conditions under spasmodic enemy shell and mortar fire.
On 5 February, as the thaw set in, the recce squadron of 35th (US) Division
arrived to relieve 52 Recce who moved back to Schinveld. In turn 3 Recce
was awaiting relief by 52 Recce which they had been told would happen
on or about 8 February. Since the beginning of the year 3 Recce had been
on the Maas, based on the villages of Groeningen, Vortum and Sambeek
with two Dutch resistance companies, Nos 2 and 3 Stootropen, under
command. The regiment's arrival in the area coincided with the beginning
of a period of intense cold, with heavy snow, that lasted until a few days
before the relief; on one night 22 degrees of frost were recorded.
    During this spell 3 Recce and their Dutch comrades carried out
interdiction against German patrols in the area with some success: both No
2 Dutch Company at Vortum and C Squadron at Groeningen shot up
patrols after carefully planned ambushes. The regiment also took part in
harassing enemy troops on the far bank of the Maas:

> ...using all the weapons at their disposal from .5in Brownings and
> Vickers MG to the 25 pdrs supporting them. Sometimes RHQ laid on a
> rather bigger strop up, using some of the LAA Regt's Bofors and the
> Middlesex 4.2in mortars. This aggressive use of firepower helped to
> keep the enemy on the other bank very quiet and must have made his
> locations, especially Afferden, extremely unhealthy.[2]

The regiment took the battle to the enemy with Wilforce, a group of two
carrier troops from A Squadron under Major Wilson who patrolled the
enemy side of the Maas from about 10 January. Quickly becoming expert in
the handling of assault boats the force also achieved proficiency in fighting
in buildings and night patrolling, even taking advantage of bright
moonlight on the snow:

> On 28 January a recce patrol with supporting it a fighting patrol were
> put across opposite Sambeek and had a very successful evening. The
> recce patrol under Lt Hodgetts killed two Germans between the river
> and the Afferden-Heijen road: and the fighting patrol captured a
> prisoner and inflicted a number of casualties on the enemy who

approached them near the Lock Gates. The patrol then withdrew and crossing the river under cover of smoke arrived safely back without casualties. It was a first-class night's work and must have caused great consternation to the enemy who had for so long sat secure from patrols on the other side of the river.[3]

Following relief by 52 Recce the regiment moved to Lubbeck near Louvain for maintenance, recreation and rest.

Also engaged on river watching were 49 Recce who spent the first three months of 1945 along the Waal. There was little patrol activity across the river although 49 Recce did take the fight to the enemy on a number of occasions, losing several personnel in the process. Once again Dutch resistance were under command. Both sides used artillery and mortars in harassing programmes; on at least two occasions V1 flying bombs landed near 49 Recce positions but caused no casualties.

Much of the regiment's work was in assisting the Allied artillery's harassing programme and while 49 was on the Waal it had an RA HQ of its own, commanded by a gunner major. Most harassing fire was conducted by 25 pounders but 17 pounder anti-tank guns were used as well, while anti-aircraft guns - both Bofors 40mm and 3.7-inch heavies - joined in from time to time, along with 4.2-inch mortars. There was little the Germans could do in reply as few mortars or field guns faced 49 Recce; plenty of Spandau fire was expended in their direction, however.

On 21 February the regiment carried out Operation JOCK, a river crossing:

> ...at 0100 hours a party of approximately 30 men with two officers (including sappers and naval personnel) crossed from Druten to Ochten 5069 in LCAs; the navy made a perfect land-fall, two patrols landed and after two hours ashore had inflicted considerable damage on the enemy; they returned at 0400 hrs with one dead enemy (from 34 Dutch SS Division), having suffered no casualties themselves.[4]

Remaining in this area until 5 April, 49 Recce had a relatively quiet routine although, towards the end of their spell on the Waal, the Dutch SS who opposed them became more active. A squadron based on the Island found life more varied: contact with the enemy was possible without crossing a river. Many clashes took place,

> ...the most memorable... between a strong patrol of the Assault Company and an enemy party of eleven on 8th March, when, without loss to themselves, our men killed five and took prisoner four of the enemy. This was the first offensive operation in which the comparatively newly formed Assault Company had taken part, and its success was most gratifying.[5]

However, several months in static positions was not gratifying and there

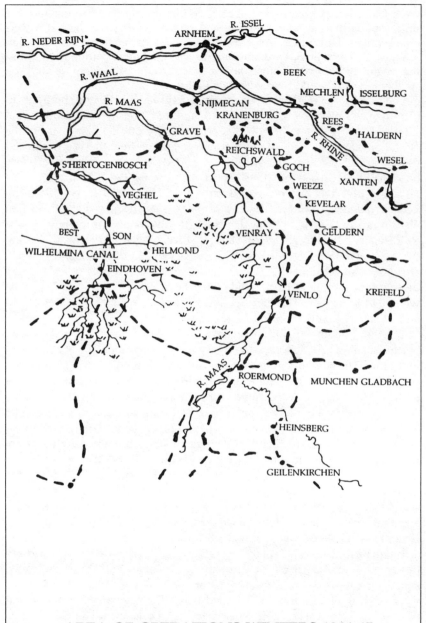

AREA OF OPERATIONS WINTERS 1944-45
Between Rivers Maas (Meuse) & Rhine

were fears that the regiment might have lost its edge as a reconnaissance unit, especially as so many officers and men had left since the last mobile operation in November. As a result, when a Belgian fusilier battalion relieved 49 Recce on 5 April, an exercise was immediately organised to test the regiment's mettle before taking part in the divisional assault on Arnhem, which would finally liberate that town.

Operation VERITABLE opened on 8 February 1945 and brought 15 (Scottish), 43 (Wessex), 52 (Lowland) and 53 (Welsh) into action. First Canadian Army was to have XXX Corps to carry out the first phase of the operation, the breaching of the German defensive line, the Westwall, and the clearing of the Reichswald. Preceded by the greatest artillery bombardment carried out thus far in the war by the British Army, the attacking divisions began their advance at 10.30am on a seven-mile front; against defenders stunned by the artillery, the attackers took their first objectives quickly with 51st Division in the southern corner of the Reichswald by midnight, 53rd Division breaching the "Westwall" during the night and 15th Division taking the villages of Kranenburg and Frasselt. Horrocks had committed 15th, 51st and 53rd Divisions plus two Canadian divisions to the initial battle while Guards Armoured and 43rd Divisions were held in reserve. That put two reconnaissance regiments - 15 (Scottish) and 53 (Welsh) - into the early part of the battle.

For the Scots the operation began with "a nightmare drive in darkness" on the evening of 7 February to Nijmegen. Next morning the attack began with 15th Division's objective being Cleve and, as 46 and 227 Brigades penetrated the Siegfried Line, C Squadron deployed on traffic control parties. A and B Squadrons moved forward to exploit the gap and recce the advance of two mobile columns towards Calcar and Udem respectively. The regiment was also to recce a route from Cleve to the Reichswald to allow 2nd Household Cavalry Regiment to pass through towards Goch. Both regiments were to "flood the country with armoured cars."

But natural flooding caused congestion on the centre-line road and the leading troops were stalled at Nutterden. To allow the attack to continue, searchlights were brought up to provide artificial moonlight as infantry and tanks moved on the town. Two days of tough fighting saw Nutterden cleared and 15 Recce was told to go ahead with the original plan.

B Squadron was still heavily engaged near Cleve in what the war diary described as the usual fog of war; during the night of 9/10 February the squadron captured two German officers and 50 men who thought they were arriving to reinforce the Siegfried Line. (The German commander had moved his sole reserve, 7th Fallschirmjäger Division, to the Cleve area where an Allied breakthrough was most likely.) A Squadron was sent down the road to Calcar meeting heavy opposition at Qualburg. C Squadron relieved A and, by 13 February, had reached Hassalt. Further flooding followed that night as the Germans breached the Alter Rhine

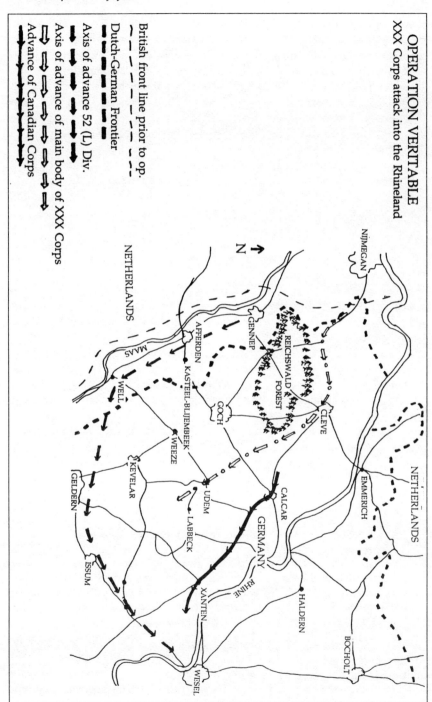

OPERATION VERITABLE
XXX Corps attack into the Rhineland

British front line prior to op.

Dutch-German Frontier

Axis of advance 52 (L) Div.

Axis of advance of main body of XXX Corps

Advance of Canadian Corps

N →

NIJMEGAN

NETHERLANDS

MAAS

AFFERDEN

GENNEP

REICHSWALD FOREST

WELL

KASTEEL-BLIJEMBEEK

GOCH

CLEVE

NETHERLANDS

WEEZE

KEVELAR

UDEM

EMMERICH

GELDERN

LABBECK

CALCAR

GERMANY

HALDERN

BOCHOLT

ISSUM

RHINE

XANTEN

WESEL

dams and the divisional thrust was diverted towards Goch. The RASC drivers received high, and deserved, praise as they brought supplies through the floods ensuring that front-line troops did not go short.

A Squadron reported heavy fighting around Goch on the 19th and 20th which expanded to include all three squadrons along the line Goch-Bucholt by the 23rd. By then, divisional objectives had been achieved and 15th (Scottish) Division was withdrawn to Tilburg to prepare for the Rhine crossing. Many casualties had been suffered throughout the division and 15 Recce had taken its share.

Their fellow Celts of 53 Recce had also concentrated at Nijmegen on 8 February from where traffic control parties, commanded by the squadron leaders of A and B Squadrons, were provided for XXX Corps generally. Carriers were also provided to transport RE stores in the Reichswald.

Traffic control was a far from easy task due to road conditions, heavy rain, frost and traffic volume but it was carried out efficiently and effectively with posts manned at all times and wireless vehicles ensuring the best possible system of control.

The carriers returned to the regiment on 12 February when C Squadron was assigned to 158 Brigade for operations in the Reichswald; the squadron held defensive positions until the 17th. A week later the regiment moved to Goch, concentrating on the edge of the Reichswald with A Squadron protecting 160 Brigade's right flank. As the enemy dominated the nearby country there were no mobile patrols but fighting patrols brought in three prisoners and the squadron was subjected to much enemy fire from a variety of weapons. On the evening of 25 February a German counter-attack was repelled.

B Squadron came under command of 12th KRRC on the 27th taking over a company position as infantry. On St David's Day, with leeks tied to their helmets, the Welshmen were in action again as C Squadron, with a squadron of Sherwood Rangers Yeomanry as Robinforce, advanced to protect 158 Brigade's left flank as that formation moved on Weeze. Having crossed the Muhlen Fleuth the previous night, C Squadron:

> ...dismounted and a series of extremely successful raids were carried out with the fire support of the Sherwood Rangers. Two farm buildings and three small woods were cleared by assault in spite of stiff resistance and it resulted in the capture of 86 prisoners besides a considerable number of enemy killed and wounded for which Lieut D. Addison and Sgt G. Gardner were chiefly responsible. The squadron penetrated to the depth of one and a half miles... and eased the position.[6]

By now the Germans were pulling back and, on the 2nd, A Squadron moved south-west from Weeze covering 8 Armoured Brigade's right flank as it made for Kevelaer. Moving in red, troops cleared neighbouring woods with foot and mobile patrols and flushed out scattered groups of enemy soldiers, most of whom were keen to surrender. Kevelaer fell and, on 3 March, Lieutenant Gardiner's reconnaissance troop pushed forward to Geldern where they met the forward elements of 35th (US) Infantry Division; A Squadron patrols had some skirmishes while C Squadron contacted 3rd Division to the left. The advance continued towards the Rhine with A and B Squadrons carrying out offensive patrols towards Alpen; about 40 Germans were killed by A Squadron patrols in actions under 2nd Monmouths on 6 March.

Next day Wales handed over to Scotland as 52 Recce relieved 53 which moved back to Belgium to prepare for further operations.

VERITABLE had not been long underway when 43rd Division was committed to the battle: after a difficult move from Nijmegen, with shellfire on the road to Cleve, 7 Troop, B Squadron were first to enter the Reichswald where they encountered opposition near Materborn village which was later captured by 7th Somersets, allowing 43 Recce to assume its rôle of reconnoitring in front of the division. As 6 Troop moved forward, supported by tanks from 13th/18th Hussars, they were engaged by machine-gun and Panzerfaust fire which knocked out two heavy armoured cars and an LRC; several men were captured, the tanks also suffered and B Squadron was withdrawn.

Two days later the CO, now Colonel C.H.Kinnersley, took a war correspondent along the Cleve-Calcar road in his LRC. Passing through the forward infantry positions they were caught in a heavy concentration of artillery fire which gave the war correspondent plenty of material for a subsequent article.

It was 15 February before the regiment was operating in its true rôle with C Squadron recce'ing through the village of Niederdam, where B Squadron had been stopped, and turning towards the north-eastern corner of the Cleve forest. There was good news from 53rd Division who had liberated some of the B Squadron captives; 9 Troop made contact with the Monmouths of that division on the edge of the Reichswald.

Further opposition resulted in a number of casualties, mortars, shells, panzerfausten and mines damaging cars and killing Sergeant Darvell, MM and Corporal Horsfall. However, B Squadron's leader, Major Bindon Blood, continued to probe Cleve forest. In one action, to extricate an assault troop, a medical orderly, Lance-Corporal Lane, earned the MM when he dismounted from a carrier, in full view of the enemy, to pick up a wounded man.

As 43 Recce pushed along the road to Goch, 130 Brigade with elements of 15th Division had cleared the town of Cleve allowing an advance towards the escarpment overlooking Goch. This was seized after heavy fighting by units of 43rd Division, an action General Horrocks described as the turning point of the battle. Goch was cleared between 18 and 21 February.

Cleve forest had been cleared before the attack into Goch with the regiment harrying the enemy to protect the advancing infantry. With the forest clear, B Squadron recce'd the main road to Udem and another parallel road. Once again stiff resistance was encountered and the whole regiment was eventually withdrawn. But in the fighting another decoration had been earned when Sergeant Jones of B Squadron directed artillery fire onto an 88 position and then deliberately drew fire from three enemy machine-guns which he subsequently knocked out allowing infantry who had been pinned down to evacuate wounded.

The regiment withdrew to the Bedburg area to re-organise although B Squadron was deployed on traffic control until 22 February. C Squadron then relieved 8 Canadian Recce on the Kalfach river line: by carrying out foot patrols across the river, the squadron provided valuable reports on roads and enemy dispositions in the area. On 26 February 204 Field Company, RE, built a bridge over the Kalfach which was named Recce Bridge and over which A Squadron passed to occupy Wissel that evening. The squadron then moved towards Grieth, meeting further opposition and demolitions en route; during one engagement Sergeant Walklate earned a MM. Near Grieth a German sergeant-major was captured when he cycled up to a group of recce men believing them to be German troops from their RAC-style helmets.

The next objectives were Honnepel and Calcar both of which A Squadron penetrated. But there was opposition at Honnepel where B Squadron's assault troop engaged a German patrol, killing two and capturing the rest. The enemy were cratering all roads with holes some 25 feet wide and up to 12 deep. Progress was difficult as carriers bogged on the soft ground and Colonel Kinnersley decided on a scheme of foot patrolling using assault troops and carrier sections with cars in support:

> Our subsequent operations showed that the cars moving behind a foot patrol in this way formed a continually advancing firm base with considerable fire power from which the patrol could operate; they provided adequate wireless communication and great moral support. In this way a patrol of about eight or ten men were able to advance at night to a considerable depth - much further than an unsupported infantry patrol.[7]

So successful were these operations that the Germans could not withdraw unnoticed. The regiment's endeavours were recognised when Colonel Kinnersley was awarded the DSO.

By the evening of 28 February, 43 Recce was in Appeldoorn which had been taken after a tough fight. The regiment was actively engaged until 12 March, playing its part in the advance towards the Rhine with many of the small actions which typified the experience of recce regiments. One such was on the morning of 3 March when 5 Troop, B Squadron was ordered to establish a firm base on the road to Marienbaum from which to patrol south east towards Xanten. As the troop approached a crossroads south east of Appeldoorn before recce'ing towards Marienbaum:

> [they] encountered sharp opposition and a determined little battle ensued in which Tpr Baker and Sgt Gardiner particularly distinguished themselves, and each won the MM for their courage. Eventually the patrol was ordered to disengage and the RA brought down fire on the enemy positions.[8]

Xanten was captured on 8 March at which time 43 Recce was maintaining OPs along the Rhine. The capture of Xanten meant the end of the German bridgehead - the Schlieffen position - west of the Rhine. Withdrawing to Weeze on 12 March, 43 Recce began to prepare for operations across that river.

As XXX Corps had advanced on Goch, 52nd Division had been pushing down the eastern bank of the Maas on its right with 52 Recce heavily engaged. After its relief by US troops, the regiment had re-organised "as a normal reconnaissance regiment". Because of the earlier loss of its tank squadron, 52 Recce had been under strength by one troop in each squadron, nor did the regiment possess any heavy armoured cars, relying on Dingo scout cars because of its mountain rôle. These shortcomings were now rectified: heavy armoured cars were received and 156 officers and men - three complete scout troops - came as reinforcements from the disbanded 61 Recce. On 8 February a very strong little force came under 52 Recce command at Boxmeer where the regiment relieved 3 Recce: included were 8 Canadian Recce, a medium machine-gun platoon and a 4.2-inch mortar platoon of 7th Manchesters and two Dutch companies; 1 Mountain Regiment, RA was in support.

B Squadron carried out some patrolling across the Maas using assault boats before the regiment moved to Gennep on the night of 15/16 February from where, on the 16th, C Squadron moved out on to the road to Afferden.

The squadron advance was held up by a crater and a road block which were impassable as both sides of the road were flooded. An enemy position opened up and one man was killed in the ensuing action. Next day the crater was filled in and the squadron moved off for Afferden:

> Finally we reached Afferden and were confronted by a great anti-tank ditch... at right angles to the Maas and our line of advance. The flooding of the river had turned this into a formidable water obstacle. The main Nijmegen-Venlo road which hugged the right bank of the Maas stood out like a great causeway through the water and the bit of it from Afferden to the other side of the obstacle was in fact known as "the causeway"; it was very badly cratered and under constant observation from enemy positions about two hundred yards south of the town.[9]

As the advance to the left was stalled before Goch, 52 Recce deployed along the obstacle with RHQ and one squadron in Afferden and another squadron in Rempeld village to the east. For the rest of the month the regiment suffered heavy shelling and mortaring, losing several casualties, of whom two were killed; a counter-mortar officer working in the area said that German mortar positions on that front outnumbered the total mortars believed to be held by the entire German army. On the last day of February a small German recce patrol approached the south end of Afferden and a skirmish followed in which two Germans were killed. On the same day recce parties of 45 Commando arrived to relieve 52 Recce.

That takeover was delayed as the regiment took part in a renewed attack on 1 March. By now the flooding had subsided and enemy positions had been pinpointed and so an assault was planned: B Squadron crossed the anti-tank ditch at first light and captured two enemy positions. With 6th Highland Light Infantry as back-up the regiment advanced on the high ground opposite their start line:

> On the extreme right the combined assault troops of A and C, supported by the fire of a troop of Churchills from the 34th Army Tank Brigade, a battery of mountain gunners and a section of medium machine-guns, put in a subsidiary attack and fought their way across the causeway into the enemy positions. During the night both bodies joined up and established a firm bridgehead from which the advance could be resumed.[10]

Casualties were remarkably light, thanks mainly to the well-directed fire of the supporting artillery. For his part in the planning and execution of the attack, Major James Stormonth-Darling, B Squadron Leader, received the regiment's first MC.

From this firm bridgehead the advance began anew. On 2 March, the commandos took over at Afferden allowing 52 Recce to move forward to Geldern to relieve 53 Recce:

> B Squadron were put under 156 Brigade for their attack on Alpen; their task was to keep the line continuous from 156 Brigade to the Americans on their right. After a very fierce battle, Alpen was captured and at very short notice C Squadron were moved up from Geldern, through the infantry line in front of Alpen, to exploit to the Rhine. The enemy were getting out pretty fast now, and C Squadron, with Peter Vesey's Troop leading on the right and Peter Evans's on the left, had an almost copybook advance to the river at Ginderich.[11]

Many prisoners were taken and rearguards mopped up. From the river bank the regiment could observe German work on the defences of the far bank and frequent mortar and artillery bombardments were called down to interrupt the enemy's endeavours. After over a week in the area 52 Recce moved back to prepare for the Rhine crossing.

Operation VERITABLE had destroyed the Germans west of the Rhine in some of the hardest fighting seen in the European campaign with over 15,000 British and Canadian casualties. In front of 21 Army Group lay the North German Plain where it would deliver the coup de grace to Hitler's armies, now lacking the cohesion needed to present a strategic defence. To deliver the death blow Montgomery's armies had first to cross the Rhine.

22
The Rhine Crossing

Montgomery's plan was for the Rhine crossing to be undertaken by Second (British) Army with both British and Canadian divisions being used, as in VERITABLE. The assault was to take place over a twelve-mile front between Rees and Wesel with XII Corps, under Ritchie, on the right and XXX Corps, under Horrocks, on the left. Ritchie's command included 7th Armoured, 15th, 52nd and 53rd Divisions as well as four independent brigades with the assault crossing at Wesel being undertaken by 1 Commando Brigade. Horrocks commanded 3rd, 3rd Canadian, 43rd and 51st Divisions, the last-named being assigned the assault crossing at Rees; he also had one independent brigade. Both Ritchie and Horrocks had the support of strong artillery and engineer groups and of specialised armoured vehicles, including amphibious Buffaloes and DD or 'swimming' tanks.

The ground troops were not the only element of the operation, code-named PLUNDER: XVIII (US) Airborne Corps was to carry out a massive airborne operation, including 6th (British) Airborne Division. Two airborne divisions would be dropped five miles behind the Rhine, north of Wesel, to seize bridges and ground for 21 Army Group's advance across the river Issel into Westphalia.

Operation PLUNDER would involve six recce regiments with 15, 52 and 53 in XII Corps, 3 and 43 in XXX Corps and 6 Airborne in XVIII (US) Airborne Corps. XXX Corps also included 2nd Derbyshire Yeomanry, 51st (Highland) Division's recce regiment. Of the Reconnaissance Corps' regiments in North-West Europe, only 49 Recce was not committed to the operation.

Under cover of darkness on the night of 23 March assault troops crossed the Rhine in Buffaloes. There were no serious setbacks to the operation: although, tactically, German units still fought with spirit and determination there was no overall cohesion to the defence and most of the attackers' objectives had been taken by dawn. Follow-up units also came across in assault boats and at 10.00am on the 24th the air armada arrived. By dusk the first link-up with 6th Airborne Division had taken place when leading elements of 15th (Scottish) Division contacted the airborne.

C Squadron was the first element of 15 Recce to cross the Rhine, making the journey in Buffaloes without a single enemy shell to disrupt their passage. As they moved through the bridgehead they found why they had been unmolested by the German artillery. So accurate had been the airborne operation that "some of the landings had been in the middle of the

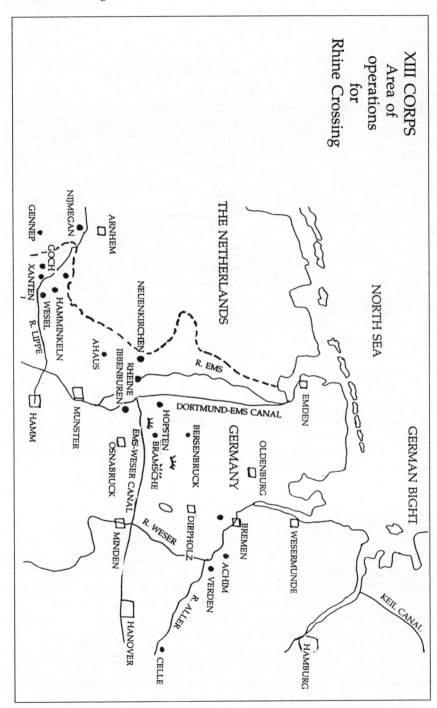

XIII CORPS
Area of
operations
for
Rhine Crossing

enemy gun lines, and the guns now stood, intact but silent, beside their dead crews."[1]

Re-organising at Tilburg the regiment had been told to convert from Humber armoured cars to Daimlers. With little time to carry out the change, and no proper arrangements made by 'higher authority' for conversion training, Colonel Grant Peterkin managed to obtain the release of some old Daimlers from a vehicle reserve depot for training purposes and to enlist the help of instructors from the Derbyshire Yeomanry, Inns of Court and 11th Hussars. The anti-tank battery had also handed in its unloved Carden Lloyd carriers for new vehicles.

In its new Daimlers C Squadron probed to Hamminkeln by dusk that first day, passing the HQ of 3 Parachute Brigade on the way. The Lowland Brigade had asked for a patrol to recce through the woods to the autobahn north of Hamminkeln and this was provided by 4 Troop:

> ...we arrived to find our forward troops under fire from self-propelled guns, and several Shermans burning. Breaking from the woods, we saw two white lorries about four hundred yards away. We thought they were ambulances, and [Trooper] Wilkinson was disappointed at not being able to fire the Browning which the carrier sported in addition to a Besa, three clocks, Staghound seats and the cleanest engine forward of the mobile bath unit. We would have been wise if we had fired, because about forty infantry piled out of these lorries when the range had increased and we could not be sure of bagging any. However, they ran pretty fast.[2]

The rest of 15 Recce crossed the Rhine by pontoon bridge on the morning of the 26th by which stage C Squadron was engaged in observation duties, patrolling the Lowland Brigade front and filling gaps in the line. B Squadron was covering 227 Brigade's left flank while A filled the widening gap between 46 and the Lowland Brigades. The latter had forced a crossing of the Issel against fierce opposition allowing the brigade to strike north-east for Bocholt at which stage 53rd Division passed through.

Heavy fighting was reported on all sections of the bridgehead on the 27th and next day 15 Recce became responsible for the divisional left flank to relieve 227 Brigade for an attack on Haldern on the 29th. But, early that morning, B Squadron patrols, probing north of Mehr, spotted British troops approaching Haldern from the west. When that information was relayed to divisional HQ the attack was cancelled: patrols from 3rd Division had found Haldern unoccupied and a battalion was on its way to occupy the town. As reports of similar enemy withdrawals were being received from all units, it became obvious that the Germans had withdrawn during the night: the chase was now on.

The Scottish Division was, however, withdrawn from operations for a rest along the Rhine and so 15 Recce did not immediately join in that chase.

Those other Scots of 52 Recce had had a lesser rôle in Operation PLUNDER. Only A Squadron - with a commando brigade - took part in the initial assault; the rest of the regiment carried out traffic control duties for XII Corps:

> The rest of the Regiment was given the administrative job of getting the leading battalions and regiments from their concentration area up to the river bank. This job was organised from a tented camp in the woods at Sonsbeck by 12 Corps HQ. The weather was delightful and the birds were singing in the woods and could be heard in the intervals of the barrage. We crossed over about three in the morning on March 29th by the light of a full moon and took up a position near Mehr.[3]

In the initial crossing 53 Recce had no part. After a welcome spell in Belgium, and replacement of the Carden Lloyd carriers, the regiment moved to the area of the river Maas and the village of Maashees where they learnt of the divisional rôle in Operation PLUNDER; this was a follow-up crossing between Rees and Wesel before attacking north-east through Bocholt, Stadtlohn, Ahaus and Gronau whence the attack would swing right to cross the river Ems. So 53 Recce crossed the Rhine over a bridge between Xanten and Rees at 9.00pm on 26 March. First light next morning saw the regiment at Hamminkeln with squadrons already moving out on reconnaissance tasks. At this stage the Welsh Division passed through 15th Scottish:

> It was a usual sort of day... one of those on which nothing startling occurred and no headline news was made but one on which one's life was at stake and all the time one expected the 'ping' of a sniper's bullet or the 'whoop' of an A/Tk gun shell. That day too, and on the next, the Regiment was operating to the east of the main axis to Bocholt. B and C Squadrons patrolled further eastwards still through the sandy tracks and difficult country near Rhede, encountering small parties of enemy and taking prisoners. Here a Troop of B Squadron had a spectacular success rushing a bridge. One section reached the other side of the bridge in the face of heavy opposition but lost its vehicles and had to withdraw to a position of observation. Later A Squadron's Assault Troop arrived and their concerted efforts were too much for the enemy.[4]

On the 28th the regiment deployed on the Ringenburg-Bocholt road to protect the right flank of the divisional advance; during the day they had several actions with casualties and further vehicle losses. Next day RHQ was established in Dingden but B Squadron was unable to advance due to fighting in Bocholt. The town had been cleared by the 30th allowing B to continue its advance in spite of being engaged by the enemy along the way; the squadron led 71 Brigade's advance north to Winterwijk. In mid-afternoon B Squadron encountered German self-propelled guns which knocked out two armoured cars and an LRC but, although some men were wounded, nobody was killed. A Squadron advanced about six or seven miles to Bredevoort, over the Dutch border, where they ambushed a German unit and took 17 prisoners; later they engaged and put to flight over a hundred German troops. C Squadron had lost itself, due to faulty map-reading, to the right of the main axis but, after the capture of Winterwijk, the squadron took the lead on 31 March as 71 Brigade made for Vreden.

A Squadron was working to C's left and both were aware of the importance of seizing intact the bridge over the river Berkel on the outskirts of Vreden. During the afternoon C's leading troop wirelessed back the news that the main bridge was blown but another to the west was still standing. Two troops dashed to the bridge which was being prepared for demolition, and defended by German infantry. C Squadron hit the bridge so fast and hard that the infantry were wiped out and the demolition party denied the chance to destroy the bridge. A second bridge was then taken intact. As a result Sergeant Boxshall was awarded the MM and Sergeant Swift a Mention in Despatches. It was calculated that the seizure of the two bridges saved 53rd Division eleven hours and a difficult bridging operation.

The Welsh recce men were now in hot pursuit of the enemy although there was time to remove the contents of a warehouse in Vreden. The 'booty' was eggs and C Squadron stocked up for Easter, passing on some of their spoils to other parts of the regiment but still managing a crate of eggs per man. Next day was Easter Sunday and the advance continued towards Gronau and Enschede.

The airborne element of the Rhine crossing had the separate codename VARSITY and was meticulously planned to ensure that the mistakes of Arnhem were not repeated. The commander of XVIII Airborne Corps, General Matt Ridgeway, made certain that all his troops would go in on one lift; that they would be within the range of 21 Army Group's artillery; that all essential units would be on the ground before the Germans could assess the intention of the operation; and that there would be no need to rely on resupply aircraft. In every respect Ridgeway was successful.

Major General Eric Bols, commanding 6th Airborne Division, decided that his gliders would make tactical, rather than mass, landings. The aim of the airborne troops was to seize the high ground of the western edge of the Diersfordter Wald to neutralise German forces, including artillery, stationed there who threatened the ground assault forces. In addition the airborne were to capture two road, and one rail, bridges over the Issel for the main breakthrough into Germany. Gliders carrying 6th Airlanding Brigade were to land at Hamminkeln; that brigade included a half-troop of tanks and a 4.2-inch mortar troop of 6th Airborne Armoured Reconnaissance Regiment. The remainder of 6 Armoured Recce was to cross by sea.

The complete VARSITY force was landed in little over an hour and the tanks were soon in action as were the mortars which deployed under the divisional CRA. The entire regiment was operational by the 27th taking part in the crossing of the Issel in which three tanks were knocked out. Next day recce patrols went out to contact 17th (US) Airborne Division and there were many engagements with the enemy: prisoners were taken, some tanks were damaged and there was one hold-up from strong opposition which was eliminated when the regiment called down an air strike.

On 29 March the regiment continued its move forward with the armoured cars of the Inns of Court Regiment. On that day's move many bridges were found intact. Progress was not so smooth on the 30th and recce patrols had to resort to footwork due to craters and heavy artillery fire. Infantry support was called for and orders were received to work around the enemy obstructions. When A Squadron found a loop around the problems the advance was resumed. Contact was made with 3 Recce on the right and the advance continued on 1 April with Greven as the objective.

On XXX Corps' front, 3rd and 43rd Reconnaissance Regiments had been active. Of the two regiments the Geordies of 3 Recce had been first to cross the Rhine, doing so on the 26th after an order to move "immediately." En route they had the, by now unusual, experience of being strafed by enemy aircraft which caused two casualties. The regiment arrived in its concentration area east of the Rhine near Peddenburg at 3.30am on the 27th and shortly afterwards established liaison with 17th (US) Airborne Division which was pushing along the Peddenburg-Schermbeck road.

A Squadron was called on to recce a route for 6 Guards Armoured Brigade and cleared mines to allow tanks of the Scots Guards, carrying men of 513 US Parachute Regiment, to pass through on the road to Munster. By 6.00pm on the 28th the Scots Guards had entered Dorsten by cutting across country south of the main road. A Squadron had passed through Schermbeck before first light to secure a crossroads but had run into vigorous opposition as the crossroads was defended by SP guns, infantry and a road block. A loop was tried but the German infantry were deployed in depth and the effort came to naught. At the end of the day the squadron was withdrawn as was B Squadron which had been protecting the Coldstream Guards' flanks and had also been engaged with the enemy. A patrol from B Squadron reached Wulfen to make contact with 6th Airborne Division:

> Later in the day, C Sqn was brought through to cover the North flank. During the night, the Coldstream Guards reached Haltern. Moving through the dark with them was most impressive as they shot at anything which might be concealing a German. Farms were ablaze, prisoners coming in, and it was raining hard, but somehow the village was cleared, and B Sqn passed through to protect the right flank before

first light, where they had the luck to meet some 'soft' vehicles just as it got light.[5]

As the division moved forward, the right flank, previously protected by the Dortmund-Ems canal across which all bridges had been blown, was exposed as 6th Airborne Division was behind 3rd Division to the north while Ninth (US) Army was also behind to the south: that also exposed the divisional left flank. B and C Squadrons therefore assumed flank protection rôles for the Coldstream Guards throughout the 29th, taking many prisoners and shooting up four enemy vehicles at one crossroads. Towards the end of the day B Squadron handed over to 506 (US) Parachute Battalion. A Squadron patrolled to Lavesum early next morning and during that morning a German withdrawal started.

That afternoon the Coldstream Guards reached Dulmen where they took some time to clear the town due to debris; the US airborne troops had pushed the defenders out. On the 30th B Squadron passed through Dulmen to recce a route for the Scots Guards but were held up near Rorup by SP guns and infantry. C Squadron came up on their right to help but were also stopped by similar opposition and so A Squadron was sent north to Darup where they were firm in the village by nightfall by which time all squadrons were linked by patrols. The Coldstream Guards took Buldern in the afternoon and, the following morning, A Squadron set out from Nottuln to recce the left flank route through Schapdetten where they had a sharp battle. The squadron pulled back that evening to loop and cut the road at Roxel. B Squadron, having contacted 6th Airborne in Billerbeek to the north, had worked round the high ground which was holding up A Squadron; no organised opposition was met on the squadron's route:

> As soon as this was known the whole Regiment was switched round on to this route through Havixbeek, leaving the Guards to the main axis which was still being defended by SPs.

> It was now the night of 31 March, but the Regiment was determined to try to capture the bridge over the Dortmund-Ems canal just East of Munster. So B Sqn pushed on again to Nienberg, which they occupied before first light, while A Sqn struck south to Roxel in an effort to cut off stragglers. We were then only 5 kilos N W of Munster and C Squadron was to pass through B Squadron into the town. But this was not to be, as there were some stout-hearted 88s, which, although shelled throughout the day, made any progress impossible.[6]

An attempt was made by C Squadron on the night of 1/2 April to come down the Greven road but, after a good run across country, they ran into anti-aircraft guns in a ground rôle supported by infantry and were engaged in a sharp skirmish. But, by now, the Scots Guards had arrived at Nienberg and they, with American paratroopers, put in a two-pronged attack from north and west which took Munster and allowed 3 Recce "our first night's sleep for days." On 3 April the regiment went into reserve near Greven for a short rest before resuming their part in the final destruction of the German armies.

Prior to taking part in PLUNDER, 43 Recce had given up some of its Humber armoured cars for Daimlers: two Daimlers were assigned to each troop, alongside two Humbers and a Humber LRC; as the Humber heavies were damaged or lost in action they would be replaced by further Daimlers. Thus equipped, the regiment crossed the Rhine on 27 March to harbour near Speldrop. The bridgehead in XXX Corps' area had not developed quite as fast as anticipated due to tough opposition from Fallschirmjäger and it was the 28th before the regiment began operations.

A Squadron moved off that morning to recce the road from Landfort to Mechelen and capture a bridge along the route if it was intact. But the squadron was held up when 43rd Division infantry had to fight their way into Mechelen. B Squadron, recce'ing the road to Anholt, ran into opposition in woods between Millingen and Anholt:

> Some enemy in a house by the road engaged the cars and hit the leading Daimler, commanded by Sgt Barraclough, on the corner of the turret. The car was ditched and the crew, although suffering from shock and the force of the explosion, were not injured. This was the second occasion on which Sgt Barraclough's car had been knocked out by the enemy.[7]

The following day the regiment continued with similar tasks: squadrons met pockets of stiff opposition but took about sixty prisoners. That night the Germans began pulling out and on 30 March patrols moved out to regain contact with the retreating enemy. The division was to break out to the north that day with 8 Armoured Brigade leading through Anholt before establishing itself in the Varsseveld-Sinderen area; 129 Brigade was to be ready to follow up and consolidate. Once again 43 Recce was assigned a flank protection task although C Squadron was to operate in the wake of the tanks. Despite traffic congestion the tanks reached Sinderen that night where SP guns held up their advance.

The war diary for 31 March notes "much recce in preparation for 'swanning'. Organised resistance has almost ceased."[8] On the following day, Easter Day, the regiment was to be ready to push forward at first light to protect the division's left flank and recce routes forward. One objective was "to flood the country with armour."

There was a delay to the 5.30am start but once on the move:

> ...good progress was made during the day and movement was fast. A small number of isolated enemy pockets were encountered, but these were not sufficiently strong to delay our advance. The morale of the enemy was low and they were in most cases only too anxious to surrender. Total number of prisoners captured during the day was 92.[9]

A captured document suggested that a German counter-attack through 43 Recce's area was being prepared but, although squadrons deployed to meet such a threat, it never materialised; that it did not happen was another indicator of the lack of cohesion among the German forces.

On 2 April C Squadron was placed under 214 Brigade for its advance through Aalten and Groenlo to Borculo. However, the squadron's rôle was compromised by the inclusion of a squadron of The Royals who were to lead the advance in their armoured cars:

> It had always been clear to members of the Regiment that it was wrong for an armoured car regiment to operate in front of a reconnaissance regiment; that either one or the other should be used but not both. As it turned out C Squadron had a very trying day. The conditions which were met were such that, by themselves, C Squadron might have got on quite fast. The opposition met, however, meant that the armoured car regiment, having no dismounted troops, was held up.[10]

By 11.00am the Royals had entered Borculo where they were held up by mines which were cleared by 12 Troop, C Squadron:

> The advance was continued via Geesteren and thence on to the original axis. At 1430 hrs, a vehicle of the Royals was knocked out by Bazooka fire in Dipenheim. 12 Troop were again committed, and their patrol made contact with a firmly established enemy. It was necessary to use the vanguard to deal with this opposition. The vanguard attacked through a firm base established by 12 Troop, and the village was cleared in 60 minutes. The advance was then continued. At 1830 hours C Squadron was ordered to protect the left flank of the Bde Group. Scout troops were deployed to cover the road approaches through Geesteren and Gelselaar. The remainder of the Regiment continued to protect the left flank of the remainder of the Division.[11]

On the afternoon of the 3rd the need to protect the left flank became redundant as the Canadians moved up and the regiment relieved the King's Royal Rifles along the Twente canal south of Hengelo. In this mundane task they suffered the loss of the gallant Lieutenant Lindsay Baker, MC, who fell to a sniper's bullet while taking over a position. His loss was felt the more as he had just returned to duty from hospital. On 4 April the regiment withdrew south-east of Hengelo before resuming operational duties on the 7th, by which time it had changed its khaki recce berets for the black of the Royal Armoured Corps, a change which it was one of the last recce regiments to make.

And so the final phase of operations had begun. In his message to his armies on 23 March, Field Marshal Montgomery had declared that, once across the Rhine, 21 Army Group would chase "the enemy from pillar to post." Already the chasing was underway and another reconnaissance regiment was to join in the job of finishing off the German war.

23
Race to Victory

The final weeks of war in Germany saw 5 Recce join the regiments in North-West Europe. Leaving Palestine in February, the regiment had a short time in Italy before sailing from Naples to Marseilles from where, after a spell in a mistral-stricken, desolate staging camp, it entrained for Belgium, arriving on 14 March. In Belgium 5 Recce re-equipped with Daimler armoured cars before moving off for Germany on 13 April.

Two days later 5th Division joined VIII Corps' advance towards the Elbe on the right of the British sector. After Uelzen fell 5 Recce passed through a brigade of 6th Airborne Division, which was holding a line north-east of the town, to secure the division's start line:

> At 0700 hours on April 19, 1 Sqn, which was to operate on the left, moved off, followed by 3 Sqn and RHQ with 2 Sqn remaining in reserve. The first day was spent in close patrols and a thorough search of the area in front of the FDLs. No spectacular advance was intended as the Division was not ready to follow up. 1 Sqn made contact with 15 (S) Division on its left and reported a number of villages clear and had no contact with the enemy until the leading patrol of 8 Tp had a Daimler brewed up by a bazooka [sic] on the outskirts of Himbergen. Sjt Punter very coolly extricated this patrol without casualties and the village was heavily engaged by armoured cars and 3 in mortars. Sjt Punter was later awarded the MM for his gallantry on this occasion.[1]

Sergeant Bloom, 3 Squadron, also won the MM that day for leading his section in an action near Schwemlitz after he had been wounded when the squadron came under artillery and mortar fire.

Although much information had been gained, the regiment had not contacted the Royals to their right nor the Americans to the south. German resistance had lost cohesion; some units were fighting with determination but with no support while others were prepared to surrender.

On the morning of the 20th a fighting patrol from 1 Squadron entered Himbergen to find the village abandoned. That same morning the squadron suffered the regiment's one and only attack by the Luftwaffe in Germany when a single fighter strafed it at Ronstedt, wounding four men who had taken cover under a Daimler.

Next morning 5th Division began its advance supported by Churchill tanks of 6 Guards Armoured Brigade; 3 Squadron were held up at Hohenzethen and 17 Brigade moved in to clear the village. When it was finally captured Hohenzethen was found to be playing host to a battery of 88s. Meanwhile, 1 Squadron was racing ahead of 2nd Cameronians who were hitching a lift on Churchills. The infantry were called up to clear Bleckede on the Elbe and then Barskamp, to the south-west, was taken by 5th Essex. Barskamp had been attacked by 9 Troop after a pounding by artillery but it was vigorously defended in strength and the troop had to withdraw; two men were killed and the troop leader and three others wounded. Sergeant Turnbull, who rallied the troop, brought down smoke to evacuate the wounded and then withdrew the remainder; he received the MM.

There was some localised fierce resistance again on the 22nd when a 13 Troop patrol captured an 88 but a link up with the Americans persuaded the Germans to pull back across the Elbe. For a week the regiment provided patrols to search for stragglers and destroy enemy arms and equipment.

A bridgehead across the Elbe was established by 15th (Scottish) Division into which 5 Recce crossed on the morning of 2 May. The regiment was soon on its way with 1 Squadron acting as right flank protection to 13 Brigade and 3 Squadron probing ahead of 17 Brigade. Although 3 Squadron contacted Germans at several points there was no organised resistance and the town of Molln, with many military hospitals, was not even defended:

> During this day... it became obvious that enemy resistance had virtually ceased. Prisoners began streaming in thousands towards our lines, and complete units and formations were giving themselves up. During this day the Regiment had its first experience of liberated Displaced Persons, an occurrence with which it was frequently to be bothered later on. 3 Squadron was sent to recce the factories at Schlutup and the seaplane base at Dassow, and were the first troops of the Division and probably the first British troops to reach the Baltic.[2]

That afternoon RHQ, 1 and 2 Squadrons moved via Lubeck to Neustadt where chaos greeted them. Some 2-3,000 German prisoners were in the town square, while an unruly crowd of refugees of assorted nationalities, many very drunk, milled about searching for loot. Some German marines and SS in a barracks near the docks still showed some fight. In the bay two ships burned fiercely after attacks by RAF aircraft: they were said to be filled with refugees, many of whom had drowned while trying to swim ashore.

A troop of 1 Squadron was ordered to escort the prisoners out of town while another troop dealt with German tanks and rounded up escaped prisoners. Other elements of the regiment were to search the docks and barracks area. Captain Attenborough, the Medical Officer, gave assistance to survivors from the ships who were brought ashore after dark. Over the next few days the regiment tried to maintain order and to ensure that the sick, prisoners and refugees were fed. One especially harrowing discovery was a hut full of Jewish prisoners:

> By the light of a torch a mass of humanity crowded together on filthy straw covered with rags and bits of blankets could be seen. The stench was so foul that it was difficult to avoid being sick. On closer inspection the inmates were seen to be living skeletons, with legs and arms little thicker than hockey-sticks. It was quite impossible to do anything for them in the dark, and they were told to stay where they were until daylight.[3]

The surrender of the local garrison was taken and further evidence of atrocities came to light with the opening of a mass grave containing the bodies of 164 people, including women and children, who had been brutally murdered. Later that day the area was handed over to 6th Airborne Division and 5 Recce moved to Travemunde where, on the evening of 4 May, it marked the surrender of German forces to Field Marshal Montgomery.

As 21 Army Group was 'cracking about' on the North German Plain there was unfinished business elsewhere: much of Holland had still to be liberated, including Arnhem. The task which had proved a bridge too far for First Allied Airborne Army in September 1944 now fell to 49th Division. Operating as part of I (Canadian) Corps, the West Yorkshire Division took part in the Canadian sweep into the Netherlands.

C Squadron, 49 Recce crossed the Rhine at Emmerich on 3 April to reconnoitre the east bank of the Neder Rijn and Issel but found little to do as II (Canadian) Corps had moved rapidly through the area; the squadron returned to the regimental concentration area next day.

On 13 April 49 Recce moved to Zevenaar for the assault on Arnhem. A day later the regiment crossed the Issel into the city, putting out a series of recce patrols. The intention was that the regiment would pass through 146 Brigade and exploit northwards once Arnhem was clear. On 16 April that operation began and the squadrons "moved out and had a field day comparable with our best in France, taking 143 prisoners, killing many others and clearing the whole of the right flank of the Division - so much for our fears for their skill in a mobile role."[4] Only B Squadron was excluded from this operation.

The divisional advance continued next day with 49 Recce again on the right flank. The regiment reached Lunteren quickly and C Squadron pushed out westwards, advancing rapidly against light opposition, to take intact the bridge at Renswoude after a short skirmish. But the squadron was recalled by divisional HQ and the Germans again took control of the bridge:

> The reason appeared later - partly in order to allow food convoys for the Dutch [who had starved throughout the winter] to cross the line and partly because negotiations for a German surrender were in progress, a

Standstill Order had come into force on the Grebbe line; on 24th April the infantry (with one squadron under command of 147 Infantry Brigade) moved forward into contact with the line and there remained inactive; no offensive operations were conducted by either ourselves or the enemy and the situation remained unchanged until the final German surrender ... and our subsequent move forward into West Holland on the 7th [May] to implement that surrender.[5]

In the meantime another mobile task had been carried out by the regiment. On 18 April 49 Recce, less C Squadron, concentrated near Otterlo where a regimental group was created which included a tank squadron of 11th Canadian Armoured Regiment, a 25-pounder battery of 69 Field Regiment, 220 Anti-Tank Battery with self-propelled 17-pounders, B Company of 1st/4th King's Own Yorkshire LI and a sapper platoon of 756 Field Company. At 4.30pm that day I (Canadian) Corps ordered the regimental group to Appeldoorn from there it would sweep the area bounded by the Issel river to the east and the Zuider Zee to the west. The group was under Corps command with 49th Division providing a No 12 set as a rear link to Corps HQ:

> This it is agreed is the ideal grouping against a retreating enemy and well within the scope of Regimental command and Signals. It is strongly felt that if a similar Regimental Group had been formed during the pursuit through France more casualties would have been inflicted upon the enemy and considerable time would have been saved.[6]

The group began its task at 8.15am on the 19th and in little over two hours A Squadron had reached Kampen and B Squadron Nunspeet. It had been virtually a triumphal march with wild enthusiasm from local people everywhere. Over a hundred prisoners were taken although most of the Germans had escaped by boat to Amsterdam two days earlier. The group remained in the area another two days, collecting more prisoners from the Dutch resistance. On 21 April the regimental group was broken up and 49 Recce returned to Otterlo with one squadron still detached as the remainder waited for further orders.

Those orders came on 7 May when 49 Recce led the advance into West Holland. A Squadron headed for Utrecht, B for Hilversum and Amsterdam and C for Boarn and Amersfoort. Over the next ten days the regiment accepted German surrenders, escorted prisoners to concentration areas, and guarded those areas until relieved by 7 Canadian Recce on 17 May. By 23 May the West Riding Division had joined I British Corps for occupation duties in Germany and 49 Recce was stationed in Neuenkirchen.

Those regiments which had crossed the Rhine in Operation PLUNDER had, as Montgomery had forecast, cracked about chasing Germans from pillar to post. In the closing weeks of war the German military machine was but a shadow of its former self, unable to sustain an effective defensive posture against 21 Army Group but, like a wounded animal, still capable of inflicting serious wounds on its adversaries. Even in the midst of defeat German soldiers, including Volksturm or home guard, had to be regarded with respect.

When 3 Recce came out of reserve on 6 April it was soon to experience the sharpness of localised German resistance. The following day A Squadron was sent to seize and hold the site of a bridge south of Lingen to allow sappers to build a bridge for 51st (Highland) Division:

> Br. was reached at 1155 and a battle developed with enemy in woods which lasted all day, the enemy gradually pulling back. Posn was handed over to KOSB before last light and sqn moved to Lingen where a position vacated by 1 Norfolks was taken up.[7]

That matter-of-fact entry in the War Diary conceals a tough action in which Sergeant T Cottrell won the Distinguished Conduct Medal.

B and C Squadrons took over from 9 and 185 Brigades on the 8th to hold positions until relieved by 51st Division. Both squadrons had a busy time with C capturing several members of 7th Fallschirmjäger Division which was withdrawing eastwards, cratering roads and blowing bridges as it did so. By the 9th the regiment had been relieved and, with 3rd Division, was on its way to XII Corps to relieve 7th Armoured Division which had almost reached Bremen.

A Squadron was left behind to watch a stretch of the Ems-Weser which they did "for some days until the Commander of 30 Corps crossed over from the enemy side and then they thought it was time to leave."[8] After some problems along the route 3 Recce was established at Heiligenloh by 11 April with RHQ in a gin distillery. B Squadron deployed patrols north-westwards to try to link up with 51st Division but the extent of demolitions made all but local movement almost impossible so that it was not until the 16th that contact was made with the Derbyshire Yeomanry, 51st Division's recce regiment. C Squadron, under 185 Brigade, was filling a gap on the brigade right flank near Verden; 3 Recce was stretched over some fifty miles of country as 3rd Division closed on Bremen. With A Squadron back in the fold all three squadrons were busy patrolling, recce'ing routes or providing flank protection.

A and B Squadrons recce'd around Ippener discovering plenty of enemy activity but handed this task over to 2nd Derbyshire Yeomanry who later occupied the village.

By the time 3rd Division was ready for the assault on Bremen, on 24 April, the regiment's task was complete except for the anti-tank battery which deployed that day in a holding rôle on the left of the line at Stuhr. The regiment's main contribution otherwise to the operation was to provide traffic control.

On the 25th five Russians arrived at the anti-tank battery with information on enemy infantry and gun positions on a nearby airfield. The battery put out recce patrols that day and the next on the basis of that information and several prisoners were taken. Holding a portion of the Delmenhorst-Bremen railway line under 9 Brigade was the next task assigned the regiment; that began on 27 April:

> A Sqn right, B Sqn left carried out vigorous patrolling during daylight within the [regimental] boundaries and reached 98 grid line and Hasbergen which was found clear of enemy. Patrols also went to 8 [Brigade] area in Bremen. Numerous blown bridges and craters reported.[9]

On the evening of 28 April the regiment reverted to divisional command to fill in on the left of the division, with 5 (Canadian) Infantry Brigade to 3 Recce's left:

> The Div. at this time virtually had no operational rôle, only to watch the Canadian right flank on their push up to Oldenburg.

> As the country was very flat and wet, cross-country movement was out of the question, and as the roads had been cratered and heavily mined (here we saw the result of a farmer and his cart going over a magnetic mine) there was little we could do but send out foot patrols. This A and B Squadrons did, keeping what enemy there were under observation, and harassing them whenever within range of the mortars or artillery. On 30 April we took our last two prisoners, but felt that the War was nearly over. It was taking rather a long time to finish, and when the Field Marshal had the 'Cease Fire' sounded at 0800 hrs on 5 May, it came without the thrill and excitement most of us had expected.[10]

The lack of cohesion in the German defences was seen in many ways: when defensive positions were broken and taken, the counter-attacks at which the Germans excelled became much rarer events; and fall-back positions hardly existed - the Germans really were chased across the North German Plain and the advancing Allies often had long runs with little opposition. That is not to say that it was a triumphal procession for many men died in those closing days and there was an added poignancy about such deaths so close to the end of the war.

Swift movement was certainly the experience of 15 (Scottish) Recce in the last month of war in Europe. On 2 April the regiment received the first of a series of orders which were to come so quickly as to mirror the pace of events. That first order:

> ...proved to be the start of what was to be probably the most memorable achievement by the Regiment - continually in action for over a fortnight, leading first the 6th Airborne Division, riding on tanks of the 6th Guards Armoured Division and then our own Division for more than a hundred miles.[11]

The reconnoitrers caught up with 6th Airborne Division after two days "hard driving" at Oldendorf, about fifteen miles west of the Weser river. Once linked with 6th Airborne, the War Diary describes the speed of the division's advance as "illuminating". An average speed of 15mph was sustained "including stops to brush aside light resistance". The regiment was working with two squadrons in front to cover the division's leading elements; A Squadron cleared two villages on the 7th, the day on which 15 Recce crossed the Weser. Next day there was a fierce battle at Ricklingen Bridge that involved 3 Parachute Brigade, C Squadron and elements of B Squadron under Lieutenant Arthur Buck. The bridge was needed by the Americans but was still in German hands.

With his little group Buck was ordered to recce and seize the bridge if possible. This he did, removing demolition charges and capturing the few Germans in evidence. Defensive positions were taken up only to see a Tiger tank appear in the early afternoon:

> My PIAT firer got two or three shots off, but was over keen and missed the vulnerable parts. The tank blazed away, and we did not see the poor lad again.
>
> I ran along to the next wireless carrier, out of the line of fire, and made a desperate request for tanks to be sent up to support us. I felt sure we would stand a good chance of bagging this Tiger if a couple of Churchills could be sent up. "No tanks are available" came the reply. We were on our own; the PIAT was out of action, and the six-pounder was covering a different road.[12]

The Tiger shot up the vehicles one by one. Then a pair of self-propelled guns arrived with several armoured half-tracks. Reaching the bridge the Tiger tried to demolish it by firing 88mm rounds into the parapet but this proved useless and the tank withdrew into the village; Buck's men were firing at it with everything they had. Eventually the 6-pounder was manhandled around but, before it could be brought into action, the German tank drove over it. Buck was forced to order a withdrawal:

> The tenacity and strength of the enemy suggested that this might be the leading patrol of a counter attack on our main column, and I felt that I must get the information to squadron headquarters. I had no vehicles or wireless left, so we had to form up in sections and return on foot.[13]

Eventually Buck's party got back to squadron headquarters at Bordenau and B Squadron stood to and waited for an attack. Some of Buck's men, left on the far side of the bridge, sat tight until 3 Parachute Brigade and C Squadron reached the bridge and drove the Germans off. The Americans then began to cross. In defending Ricklingen bridge Arthur Buck's small force had lost one man dead, another missing and all its vehicles destroyed or damaged.

The Airborne Division was stopped when it crossed the Leine and 15th (Scottish) Division took over with 15 Recce spearheading the advance to

Celle. That town was taken by the Scottish infantry, 15 Recce suffering several casualties in skirmishes en route, including two dead when a German soldier leapt out of a ditch with a Panzerfaust and fired at a scout car. On 15 April C Squadron had a fierce encounter with remnants of the Clausewitz Division at Nettelkamp; this was a Panzer division created to thrust into the Allied lines of communications. Its efforts were thwarted by Glasgow Highlanders at Stadensen,

> and by the resistance at Nettelkamp of the clerks, cooks, mechanics and "odd bodies" of C Squadron headquarters, who fought on under the leadership of Capt. Liddell and Sgt-Major Ward for hours after the troop positions had been over-run.[14]

Five men were killed in the battle, fourteen wounded and thirty-nine missing, most of whom were captured by the enemy, some of whom were French SS. Captivity only lasted a few days of course before liberation came. Eight carriers, four armoured cars and a half-track were also lost; several decorations were won.

On 17 April the regiment met 2nd Special Air Service Regiment, under Lieutenant Colonel B.M.Franks, DSO, MC, and, as Frankforce, the two co-operated with SAS patrols in open jeeps "sharing the hazards of the regiment's armoured car and carrier troops and winning their unstinted admiration."[15] As it advanced towards the Elbe 15 Recce also had support from a 4.2-inch mortar platoon of the Middlesex, which added considerably to the force's punch.

B Squadron led 46 Brigade's advance to Bleckede - meeting and dealing with considerable resistance on the way, including Hitler Jugend - on the Elbe on 20 April; a day later 15th Division occupied an area on the west bank of the river:

> Here the Regiment was allowed a breather after sixteen days of almost continual action, with little sleep and leading the advance of two Divisions for more than 140 miles: a tremendous achievement. Due to casualties the Regiment took the opportunity to reform from three to two full Squadrons, while plans for Operation ENTERPRISE were being made to cross the Elbe.[16]

The operation was intended to take VIII Corps across the Elbe and north into Schleswig-Holstein with the American XVIII Corps crossing east of VIII Corps to protect its right flank while XII Corps would cross and swing left for Hamburg. The assault crossing to create the bridgehead was assigned to 15th (Scottish) Division and 1 Commando Brigade; the Scots thus became the only division of Second Army to assault the Seine, Rhine and Elbe, for which distinction they gained the soubriquet "the crossing sweepers" from war correspondents.

As preparations were finalised, elements of 15 Recce relieved 46 and 227 Brigades along the river. On 29 April, after a massive artillery bombardment, the assault began with crossings at Artlenburg and Lauenburg. That afternoon C Squadron crossed into the bridgehead, suffering some casualties from shelling as they waited to be ferried, and, still with 2 SAS, put out patrols as far as Kollow, a distance of six miles, where an SAS jeep crew took on a battery of 37mm guns with a 2-inch mortar, hitting one gun and forcing the withdrawal or surrender of the other crews. By dusk the patrols had pulled back into a bridgehead that was seven miles wide and up to five miles deep; some objectives had been achieved two days ahead of schedule:

> On 30 April patrols from A and C Squadrons probed west and north.

> C Squadron went north to Kollow again and to Schwartzenbek... Leaving the rest of their patrol on the edge of the woods near this small town, Lieut McFall and Cpl Lavery walked into it and found it looking so unwarlike that they had the impression that people were shopping. Then a German staff car came from the west, so they shot it up. The two occupants took to their heels. The troop took up positions round the road junction; captured an SS officer who arrived by motor cycle combination; and had bacon and eggs at a very good public house, not greatly troubled by the Germans holding the railway station.[17]

To the east, Lieutenant Gillings had taken a patrol from C Squadron south-east of Schwartzenbek meeting SS troops close to the town. He persuaded some to surrender and brought up the SAS intelligence officer, who spoke fluent German, to negotiate the surrender of some 1,800 SS personnel. Although not all of these surrendered, a large number, including officers, did so, providing evidence that the German will to fight was evaporating.

The following day there were further encounters and "minor truces and negotiations, and the munitions factory spread over many acres above the Elbe at Geesthacht, where Nobel invented dynamite, was surrendered."[18] The news of Hitler's death was heard that afternoon. On 2 May 11th Armoured Division smashed through to Lubeck while 15th Division cleared the Sachsenwald and A Squadron patrolled towards Bergedorf and Hamburg where Sergeant Tiny Kirman became "the first link in the chain of negotiations which resulted in the surrender of Hamburg and, ultimately, of the German armies in North-West Europe."[19]

After coming under heavy fire, Kirman's patrol pulled back to allow infantry and tanks to attack. In the midst of battle Kirman saw two German officers approach with a white flag; they asked to be taken to an officer:

> I told them we would have to blindfold them to take them through our lines. The major fussed about this, but in the end they were blindfolded and taken back. They returned, and later two staff cars full of Germans were brought through. By now the rumour of peace negotiations had got round, but the battle continued, although people were coming and

going all the time. After the infantry and tanks had cleared the way we made a small advance. Then we received orders not to go farther.[20]

Kirman also showed considerable tactical enterprise that day as he outflanked enemy positions, eliminated machine-gun posts and gave valued support to the attacking infantry. His day's work earned him the MM.

That the end was near became obvious next day as both squadrons advanced quickly northwards to the Hamburg-Lubeck autobahn. The enemy appeared confused and offered virtually no resistance; A Squadron captured a train and occupied Bargteheide at the end of its day's run while C Squadron captured the castle at Ahrensburg after being diverted from their run towards Hamburg by German officers who told them that, as the city was being surrendered, they could go no further before 2.00pm. Ahrensburg castle was to be 15th (Scottish) Division's headquarters for some time after the war.

At 6.20pm on the 4th, Field Marshal Montgomery accepted the German surrender on Luneburg Heath and the ceasefire took effect the following morning:

> It was the news for which everyone had been waiting for nearly six years, the goal towards which the regiment had fought in four countries. There was no wild excitement, but a great satisfaction and overwhelming relief, mixed oddly with a feeling of emptiness, because the breaking of camp in the chill darkness before dawn, the long drives, the patrols, the hasty meals, and the poring over maps - all the things which were to end - had become so completely the pattern of life. That night the tracer from the Bofors rose lazily to make V signs in the sky.[21]

But there was to be one last action for 15 Recce: a group of SS at Heiderfeld had refused to surrender and had ambushed an SAS jeep. A group from 15 Recce, under Major MacDiarmuid, joined two SAS squadrons in a sweep of nearby countryside and woods to search for the SS men but most seemed to have disappeared and only ten were captured by MacDiarmuid's armoured cars.

In the immediate wake of the German surrender 15 Recce deployed on tasks that included the occupation of Kiel, checking the German troops on the Hamburg road and keeping watch on Segeberg forest. On 8 May, in the absence of Colonel Smith, Major MacDiarmuid issued a Special Order of the Day in which he congratulated all ranks on a "job well and gallantly done." It was a job that had taken 15 Recce some 1500 miles from Arromanches in 316 days and had cost the lives of eighty-three members of the regiment.

The experiences of other reconnaissance regiments in those closing weeks of war followed much the same pattern, differing only in detail. The Wessexmen of 43 Recce had added to their decorations for gallantry almost as soon as they returned to operations on 8 April when Major Bindon Blood earned the Military Cross in a sharp action near Bawinkel. Sergeant George Drake was awarded the Distinguished Conduct Medal for the same action in which he had shown great courage and initiative; an uncle of George Drake had won a DCM in the Great War while serving with the Glosters. C Squadron's 9 Troop found a crossing point for the division over the river Hase at Buckelte. The regiment advanced over several days, meeting light opposition, usually from small groups of soldiers with Panzerfausten and machine-guns; although this was normally dealt with quickly and effectively, there were some casualties as when Lieutenant Patton of A Squadron was killed when his Daimler was hit by a Panzerfaust round.

Cloppenburg proved a nest of strong resistance on 14 April but it was cleared by infantry allowing the advance to continue towards Ahlhorn, near which 43 Recce was to contact 51st Division; the Guards Armoured Division was moving parallel to 43rd and 51st was to cross the paths of both. After some delays this manoeuvre was carried out successfully, but 43rd Division's advance had been brought to a stop as they were squeezed out by the Canadians from the north and 51st Division from the south. Operations towards Ahlhorn had been difficult for 43 Recce as the ground was soft and the countryside provided plenty of cover for ambushes by small parties.

After a few days' rest at Barglay the regiment was in action again for the crossing of the Weser and the attack on Bremen. In this operation scope for movement was restricted and 43 Recce's squadrons fought a plethora of small actions and became very "bazooka-conscious." This phase lasted until 26 April when the city of Bremen was cleared by 3rd, 43rd and 52nd Divisions.

As the advance continued towards Bremerhaven the regiment went into action again in a typical recce task, out in front probing, reporting and finding pockets of enemy resistance. In those final days of war 43 Recce suffered several casualties: an officer was killed by a shell splinter and the crews of two cars were blown up and killed by a buried aerial mine on the 30th while a despatch rider from RHQ was killed by shellfire.

The regiment rested for two days before resuming the advance to Bremerhaven on the 4th, on which evening they heard the news that the war had ended. In the aftermath of war, duties included searching for ammunition dumps, rounding up German servicemen and moving displaced persons into camps. At the end of May the regiment moved to Celle where it was to end its days as a reconnaissance regiment.

Before leaving the Dutch border 53 Recce had fought an action near Gronau on 3 April in which B Squadron distinguished itself by overcoming a strong pocket of enemy resistance including an 88, Spandaus and

Fallschirmjäger. Two assault troop sections attacked the village school which seemed to be the centre of resistance, 3-inch mortars were brought into play and the anti-tank battery fired HE shells. Some thirty prisoners were taken but, after three hours, German resistance was stiffening and the squadron pulled back to the next village. Next morning the enemy had gone, having suffered at least twenty dead.

The regiment crossed the Weser on 12 April and immediately began putting out patrols. That night C Squadron's positions were attacked by German marines on four occasions but each assault was beaten off:

> In the morning we were warmly congratulated by the CO and the Divisional Commander, for during the night chaos had reigned in the bridgehead which had not yet been reinforced with armour owing to the need for bridging, and the Division had been attacked by six battalions of marines with the object of blowing the bridge, and they had very nearly succeeded.

> I was in the only position that was not attacked and did not fire a shot so I can personally take no credit for the Squadron's success; but I can always say I was there.[22]

An attack had also been made on A Squadron, cutting the road between the squadron and RHQ, but the situation was restored next morning by Lieutenant Ferguson's troop as Ferguson prepared to depart for UK leave.

With events stabilised, forward movement resumed and 53 Recce set off on 15 April into a different type of country,

> ...mostly heath land with woods of pine and birch and small undulating hills, the sort of country which could easily harbour persistent parties of enemy. The villages were small, often surrounded by thick woods and... connected... by poor roads. Fighting for the next week was a series of Troop engagements often handicapped by snipers and poor going, while the Division wound its way onwards behind our moving patrols.[23]

Fighting its way to the main road from Rotenburg to the Elbe, 53 Recce was then deployed ahead of the brigades in preparation for the division's part in the assault on Bremen. This was "tough slogging and there was even some stonking reminiscent of Normandy as well, once the Division was in position to wheel west towards Bremen."[24] But the city had fallen to other divisions and 53 Recce moved off on other tasks. In the closing days of war they received the surrenders of large numbers of enemy troops, some of whom informed their captors that they had been ordered to make their way westwards to surrender to British or American forces with whom they could then ally to fight the Russians!

For 53 Recce the war ended in Hamburg where occupational duties soon filled their time. The regiment remained in Germany until disbandment in early 1946.

Bremen had also been an objective for 52 (Lowland) Recce who had left Mehr "in hot pursuit through Oding, Heek and Neuenkirchen to Rheine."[25] There resistance stiffened and the blowing of all bridges across two canals brought a temporary halt to the advance. The regiment recce'd all along the front as a counter-attack was expected but, although there were many clashes, the Germans failed to launch an attack. B Squadron took several prisoners in this phase of operations including one high-ranking Nazi official.

On 6 April the advance resumed with 52 Recce pushing up to Hopsten where the Germans made a stand:

> The prisoners that day were a record bag for us; they kept pouring back from early morning until late at night. When the infantry were in possession of Hopsten we pushed on over to the right and arrived at the appropriately named town of Recke. From here B Squadron were switched away over to the left of the Division and, under command of "Bobforce", they cleared a large area east of the Dortmund-Ems canal just opposite where they had been operating two days earlier.[26]

B Squadron lost its leader, Major James Stormonth-Darling, who was wounded at Recke and succeeded by Ian Inches who commanded until the Weser in spite of having his Dingo knocked out. Demolitions were slowing progress on the division's main advance route and so 52 Recce were sent off to find alternative routes. Progress was fast thereafter with many prisoners being taken and villages cleared. By 12 April, two weeks after crossing the Rhine, the regiment arrived at Neubruchausen on the Weser and began patrolling the river's southern banks.

As the division moved to attack Bremen from the east 52 Recce deployed to protect the right flank which was open to attack from the north:

> We moved up parallel to the leading infantry on their right. As they fought their way forward we punched out to the right using all three squadrons with supporting arms in this rather extended undertaking. We moved from the bridge at Hoya to Verden then on to Achim (where the General held his O groups in our Ops. room) and Langwadel. Finally A Squadron arrived on the autobahn that connects Bremen to Hamburg and cut it effectually.[27]

The Bremen garrison surrendered and 52 Recce moved into the city as a divisional reserve. They were there when all German forces on 21 Army Group's front surrendered. Shortly afterwards they were assigned as part of the force for Operation APOSTLE, the occupation of Norway but that task was cancelled on 19 May and the regiment deployed instead on occupation duties in Germany.

In early April 6 Airborne Recce advanced from Greven with A Squadron recce'ing forward of 6 Airlanding Brigade as it exploited the bridgehead over the Dortmund-Ems canal while the remainder of the regiment provided flank protection on the division's right. On 4 April, C Squadron's assault troop, with a platoon of 22 Independent Parachute Brigade, captured a flak battery which had destroyed a White scout-car; a medium machine-gun section and four mortar jeeps were also missing and had probably fallen victim to the German gunners.

After 15th (Scottish) Division had secured the Elbe bridgehead, 6th Airborne Division moved out to extend the right flank but without 6 Airborne Recce which passed into reserve. The regiment finally crossed the Elbe in early May and had a fast run to the line Lubow-Hohen-Viechlen on the 2nd where it was to contact the Russians. Although no Russians were to be found the regiment took prisoners "too numerous to count."

Contact with the Russians was made next day by a troop of B Squadron and thus the regiment's European war had come to an end. After three weeks of "post hostilities duties" 6 Airborne Recce returned to the UK on 26 May to mobilise for service against the Japanese in south-east Asia. But the dropping of atomic bombs on Hiroshima and Nagasaki ended that plan. Later, however, the regiment was to move to Palestine to undertake internal security duties, where 1 Recce was also involved.

24
The Corps Disbands

Before the echoes of the final shots of the war had died away, a decision was taken to disband The Reconnaissance Corps. The Executive Committee of the Army Council (ECAC) in approving the amalgamation of The Reconnaissance Corps with the Royal Armoured Corps had done so "without prejudice to the future of either corps in the post-war period." But in 1945, as planning took place for what was described as Stage II of the war, i.e. occupation duties, it was realised that "it will be necessary to reduce very considerably the number of Royal Armoured Corps units."[1]

This reduction was to be made, as was the case across the Army, by disbanding war-formed and duplicate Territorial Army units before touching Regular Army and original Territorial units. Using this formula created a real problem for the reconnaissance regiments as there was "only one original Territorial Army unit still in the Reconnaissance Corps, viz 5 Glosters" and the "Corps would in practice disappear as it would be possible to fit in only 5 Glosters. On the other hand, if the existing Reconnaissance Corps units, including War Formed ones, were retained for functional reasons, it would mean placing original Yeomanry and Royal Tank Regiment units in suspended animation."[2]

As it was already clear that the post-war Army would not be able to absorb all the pre-war cavalry and Royal Tank Regiment units if the Reconnaissance Corps was retained to provide the "eyes" for infantry divisions, the recommendation was made to ECAC that:

(a) the role of reconnaissance should remain the responsibility of the Royal Armoured Corps;

(b) reconnaissance units should be found as far as possible by Cavalry or Yeomanry regiments;

(c) the Reconnaissance Corps as such should be disbanded at an appropriate date as circumstances dictate;

(d) the future of each unit of the Reconnaissance Corps should be judged on its merits.[3]

At a meeting on 17 August 1945 the Army Council considered these proposals as a result of which, on 21 September, the War Office issued a letter on the future of the Reconnaissance Corps:

Discussions on the organisation of the post war Army have been taking place and it has been decided that the reconnaissance role should be taken over by Cavalry and Yeomanry Regiments.

The policy will be to allow reconnaissance regiments to waste and as the role is transferred to these Cavalry and Yeomanry Regiments so the recce personnel should, as far as possible, be posted en bloc to such units.

Orders to disband the Reconnaissance Corps will not be issued until some time after the last of the Recce Regiments have been placed in suspended animation or disbanded.[4]

And so, as recce regiments performed occupation duties in Germany and Austria - where some had to deal with the repatriation of Cossacks and Croats - as well as internal security in Palestine and the Far East, the Corps was being run down. In Austria the North Irish Horse replaced 56 Recce as the divisional reconnaissance unit of 78th Division in October 1945, absorbing many of Chavasse's Light Horse as it did so; the Irish yeomanry regiment later (March 1946) replaced 53 Recce as divisional reconnaissance unit of 53rd (Welsh) Division. Across the Army, other cavalry and yeomanry regiments absorbed men from reconnaissance regiments as they replaced those regiments in the infantry divisions.

Reconnaissance Corps regiments faded away in the winter of 1945/46 and in the first half of 1946. By the summer of that year the Corps existed in name only with all regiments disbanded or in suspended animation and the Reconnaissance Training Centre became part of the RAC Training Centre at Catterick. On 1 August 1946 the Reconnaissance Corps was finally laid to rest.

Formed in the heat of war's furnace the Corps had performed its rôle with distinction. Its regiments had not always been used for their primary function of reconnaissance but, when diverted to other tasks, they had never been found wanting. In the aftermath of war an analysis of duties performed by reconnaissance units "in the field emerged as follows:- in reconnaissance, 12%; in protection, 9%; acting as infantry, 34%; miscellaneous and concentrated, 45%."[5]

The experience of the Corps was reflected in the constitution of the new divisional RAC regiments charged with the task of close reconnaissance for infantry divisions which, with their tanks, were not to "be confined to reconnaissance, but will include such other tasks as are compatible with its organisation and equipment."[6]

And so the torch had been passed on to a new generation of soldiers. The achievements of the Reconnaissance Corps reflect the wartime record of the British Army after 1940 and every campaign fought after that date included units of the Corps. In some cases those units suffered a grim fate, as did 18 Recce at Singapore, 50 Recce at Knightsbridge and 1st Airborne Squadron at Arnhem; in others they shared in the successes of victorious armies, as did 44th and 51st at El Alamein and many others, led by 56th in

Tunisia, from the Mediterranean to the heart of Germany itself. As they probed forward to seek out information, or held the line as temporary infantrymen, they had always been true to that unofficial motto of the Corps which provides the title of this history: Only the Enemy in Front; Every other Beggar Behind.

> The lone light flickers, all the World's at rest;
> And those who strove the hardest, sleep the best.[7]

THE END

Notes

Chapter One
1: Bartholomew Committee: PRO WO106/1741
2: Jeremy Taylor, *This Band of Brothers* (Bristol: 1947), pp13-14
3: Bartholomew Committee: PRO WO106/1741
4: Ibid
5: Bartholomew Committee: PRO WO106/1775

Chapter Two
1: *The Reconnaissance Journal*, Memorial Number, Summer 1950, p3
2: Ibid
3: Bob Pite, letter to author
4: War Diary, 4 Recce, 1941, PRO WO166/409
5: This Band of Brothers, p41
6: War Diary, 4 Recce, 1941, op cit
7: Bob Pite, letter to author
8: P.M.Cowburn, *Welsh Spearhead* (Solingen-Ohligs, 1946) p37
9: War Office file, Reconnaissance Corps Badge, PRO WO32/4720
10. John Keegan, *Six Armies in Normandy* (London, 1982) p215
11: War Office file, Reconnaissance Corps Badge, PRO WO32/4720
12: Ibid
13: Ibid
14: D.Smith, MM, letter to author
15: War Diary, 4 Recce, 1941, op cit

Chapter Three
1: *The Reconnaissance Journal*, Vol 2, No 3, p131
2: Ibid, pp131/132
3: Ibid, p131
4: War Diary, 44 Recce, 1942, PRO WO169/4138
5: Operational Order 7, 51 (Highland) Recce, App IV to War Diary, August 1942, PRO WO169/4171
6: War Diary, 51 (H) Recce, 1942, op cit
7: Ibid
8: Leslie Meek, *A Brief History of the 51st (H) Reconnaissance Regiment (1941-1943)* (London, 1991) p30

Chapter Four
1: War Diary, 56 Recce, 1942: PRO WO166/6411
2: K.G.F.Chavasse, interview with author
3: K.G.F.Chavasse, *Some Memories of 56 Reconnaissance Regiment*
4: Major General John Frost, CB, DSO, MC, *A Drop Too Many* (London, 1980) p78
5: *The Reconnaissance Journal*, Vol 1, No 3, pp145/146
6: War Diary, 56 Recce, 1943: PRO WO175/178

Chapter Five
1: G.Glatley, letter to author
2: War Diary, 46 Recce, 1943: PRO WO175/165
3: G.Glatley, letter to author
4: Ibid
5: K.G.F.Chavasse, *Some Memories of 56 Reconnaissance Regiment*

Chapter Six
1: War Diary, 1 Recce, 1942: PRO WO166/6167
2: War Diary, 53 (Welsh) Recce, 1941: PRO WO166/661
3: War Diary, 1 Recce, 1943: PRO WO175/130
4: R.Pite, letter to author
5: War Diary, 4 Recce, 1943: PRO WO175/141
6: Ibid

7: D.Smith, letter to author

Chapter Seven
1: A.R.Prince: *Wheeled Odyssey, The Story of the Fifth Reconnaissance Regiment, Royal Armoured Corps*, p23
2: *This Band of Brothers*, pp111/112

Chapter Eight
1: *Wheeled Odyssey*, pp39/40
2: Ibid, p41
3: *The Reconnaissance Journal*, Vol 4, No 1, p39
4: K.G.F.Chavasse, *Some Memories of 56 Reconnaissance Regiment*
5: *This Band of Brothers*, p125
6: Ibid, p129

Chapter Nine
1: R.Farnworth, 56 Recce OCA Newsletter, Spring 1987
2: *The Reconnaissance Journal*, Vol 4, No 3, pp98/99
3: C.G.T.Dean: *The Loyal Regiment (North Lancashire) 1919-1953* (Preston) p154
4: *The Reconnaissance Journal*, Vol 4, No 3, pp103/104
5: Ibid, p105
6: Ibid, p105
7: Ibid, p105
8: R.Farnworth, op cit

Chapter Ten
1: *This Band of Brothers*, pp145/146
2: Ibid, p147
3: Ibid, p150
4: Ibid, p151
5: Ibid, p152
6: *The Reconnaissance Journal*, Vol 1, No 2, pp72/73
7: J.M.K.Bradford, notes to author
8: War Diary, 2 Recce, 1945: PRO WO172/6953
9: Ibid
10: J.M.K.Bradford, notes to author
11: War Diary, 2 Recce, 1945, op cit
12: Ibid

Chapter Eleven
1: War Diary, 45 Recce, 1943: PRO WO172/2251
2: R.Hand, letter to author
3: War Diary, 45 Recce, 1944: PRO WO172/4592
4: R.Hand, letter to author
5: *This Band of Brothers*, p157
6: War Diary, 45 Recce, 1944: PRO WO172/4592
7: Viscount Slim, *Defeat into Victory* (London, 1956) pp232/233
8: C.E.Lucas-Phillips, *The Raiders of Arakan* (London, 1971) pp83-89
9: *The Reconnaissance Journal*, Vol 2, No 4, p168
10: Ibid, p169
11: Ibid, p169
12: War Diary, 81 (WA) Recce, 1945: PRO WO172/9549-9550
13: Ibid
14: *The Reconnaissance Journal*, Vol 2, No 4, p160

Chapter Twelve
1: War Office paper, The Future of The Reconnaissance Corps: PRO WO32/11520
2: War Office paper, The Amalgamation of The Reconnaissance Corps with The Royal Armoured Corps: PRO WO32/10425

Chapter Thirteen

1: K.G.F.Chavasse, *Some Memories of 56 Reconnaissance Regiment*
2: Ibid
3: Ibid
4: War Diary, 44 Recce, 1943: PRO WO169/8765
5: War Diary, 46 Recce, 1944: PRO WO170/474-475
6: Ibid
7: *Wheeled Odyssey*, p44
8: Ibid, pp44/45
9: *The Reconnaissance Journal*, Vol 1, No 2, pp94/95
10: War Diary, 5 Recce, 1944: PRO WO170/433
11: *The Reconnaissance Journal*, Vol 1, No 2, p95
12: Ibid
13: *Wheeled Odyssey*, p48
14: *The Reconnaissance Journal*, Vol 1, No 4, p95
15: Ibid, Vol 4, No 4, pp162/163
16: Ibid, Vol 4, No 4, p159
17: E.C.West, notes to author
18: E.C.West, notes to author

Chapter Fourteen
1: *This Band of Brothers*, pp160/161
2: P.H.A.Brownrigg, notes to author
3: Ibid
4: *History of 3rd Reconnaissance Regt (NF) in the Invasion and subsequent campaign in North-West Europe, 1944-1945*, p7
5: Ibid, p48
6: Ibid, p50
7: Ibid, p12
8: Ibid, p19
9: Ibid, p22
10: *This Band of Brothers*, p168
11: P.H.A.Brownrigg, notes to author
12: Ibid
13: Ibid
14: Ibid
15: Ibid
16: War Diary, 6 Airborne Armd Recce, 1944: PRO WO171/435

Chapter Fifteen
1: K.Baker, notes to author (from *Newcastle Evening Chronicle*, 11 July 1944)
2: Ibid
3: 49 Recce: Summary of Operations, June 1944 to May 1945, p9
4: Kemsley, W. and Riesco, M.R.: *The Scottish Lion on Patrol* (Bristol: 1950), p53
5: Ibid, p57
6: Ibid, p58
7: Ibid, p65
8: P.M.Cowburn, *Welsh Spearhead: A History of the 53rd Reconnaissance Regiment 1941 to 1946*, p49
9: Ibid, p53
10: R.W.Robinson, notes to author
11: *Welsh Spearhead*, p55
12: R.W.Robinson, notes to author
13: Jeremy Taylor (Ed), *Record of a Reconnaissance Regiment: A History of the 43rd Reconnaissance Regiment (The Gloucestershire Regiment) 1939-1945* (Bristol: 1950) p61
14: Ibid, p70
15: Ibid, 74
16: Ibid, p83

Chapter Sixteen
1: War Diary, 59 Recce, 1943: PRO WO166/6425
2: War Diary, 59 Recce, 1944: PRO WO171/577
3: Ibid
4: Ibid
5: *Record of a Reconnaissance Regiment*, p96

6: Ibid, p97
7: Ibid, p100
8: *The Scottish Lion on Patrol*, p73
9: Ibid: p77
10: War Diary, 15 Recce, 1944: PRP WO171/474
11: David Henderson, Personal Journal
12: J.W.Abbot, Personal Journal
13: *Welsh Spearhead*, p64
14: Ibid, p65
15: Ibid, pp67-68
16: Ibid, p70
17: R.W.Robinson, notes to author
18: War Diary, 53 Recce, 1944: PRO WO171/565
19: *Welsh Spearhead*, p80
20: P.H.A.Brownrigg, letter to author & account of 61 Recce
21: Ibid
22: Ibid
23: Ibid
24: Ibid
25: Ibid
26: Ibid
27: Ibid
28: *History of 3 Recce*, p23
29: Ibid: p29

Chapter Seventeen
1: John Fairley, *Remember Arnhem* (Glasgow, 1978), p25
2: Ibid, p27
3: Arthur Barlow, *Arnhem Aftermath* (privately published), p2
4: R.Minns, letter to author
5: Ibid
6: Ibid
7: *The Reconnaissance Journal*, Vol 4, No 1, pp29-30
8: Ibid, pp30-32
9: Ibid, p32
10: Ibid, pp32-33
11: Ibid, p33
12: Ibid, pp33-34
13: Ibid, Intelligence Officer's report, p34
14: Ibid, p34
15: T.D.W.Whitfield, *Time Spent* (Hamilton, 1946), p59
16: Ibid, 59
17: *Record of a Reconnaissance Regiment*, pp124-125
18: Ibid, pp125-126
19: Ibid, p126
20: Ibid, p126
21: Ibid, p128
22: Ibid, p132

Chapter Eighteen
1: *Time Spent*, p62
2: Ibid, p64
3: Ibid, pp64-65
4: Ibid, p69
5: 49 Recce: Summary of Operations, p13
6: Ibid, pp14-15
7: Ibid, p16
8: P.H.A.Brownrigg, notes to author
9: Ibid
10: P.H.A.Brownrigg, letter to author
11: P.H.A.Brownrigg, notes to author
12: Ibid
13: Ibid
14: Ibid
15: *History of 3 Recce*, p31
16: Ibid, p32
17: *The Scottish Lion on Patrol*, p106
18: Sir John Boynton (Ed), *A Short History of 15*

Recce, p13
19: Ibid, p17
20: Ibid, p18
21: Ibid, p19
22: Ibid, p20
23: Ibid, p20
24: *Record of a Reconnaissance Regiment*, p146
25: *Welsh Spearhead*, p92
26: Ibid, pp93-94
27: Ibid, p98

Chapter Nineteen
1: War Diary, 56 Recce, 1944: PRO WO506-507
2: W.Croucher & E.T.Newton, *The Regimental History of The 56th Reconnaissance Regiment* (London: 1989), p20
3: War Diary, 56 Recce, 1944, op cit
4: War Diary, 4 Recce, 1944: PRO WO170/419
5: Ibid
6: R.Pite, letter to author
7: Ibid
8: War Diary, 4 Recce, 1944, op cit
9: Ibid
10: Ibid
11: Ibid
12: War Diary, 46 Recce, 1944: PRO WO170/474-475
13: Ibid
14: Ibid
15: Ibid
16: Ibid
17: War Diary, 1 Recce, 1944: PRO WO170/394-395
18: Ibid
19: Ibid
20: Ibid
21: Ibid
22: Ibid

Chapter Twenty
1: *The History of the 56th Reconnaissance Regiment*, p26
2: Ibid, p27
3: K.G.F.Chavasse, Some Memories of 56th Reconnaissance Regiment
4: *The History of the 56th Reconnaissance Regiment*, p28
5: C.Ray, *Algiers to Austria: The History of 78 Division, 1942-1946* (London: 1952), p198
6: *The History of the 56th Reconnaissance Regiment*, p30
7: Ibid, p32
8: Ibid, p33
9: Ibid, p33
10: *The Reconnaissance Journal*, Vol 1, No 3, pp173-174
11: Ibid, Vol 3, No 4, p168
12: War Diary, 44 Recce, 1945: PRO WO170/4372
13: *The Reconnaissance Journal*, Vol 3, No 4, p169
14: Ibid, p169
15: Ibid, p170
16: War Diary, 44 Recce, 1945, op cit
17: Ibid
18: Ibid
19: Ibid
20: *The Quadrant*, 4 Nov 1945
21: *The Oak*, 17 Nov 1945, p6
22: *The Quadrant*, op cit

Chapter Twenty-One
1: *Time Spent*, p70
2: *History of 3 Recce*, p34
3: Ibid, pp34-35
4: 49 Recce: Summary of Operations, pp17-18
5: Ibid, pp19-20
6: War Diary, 53 (Welsh) Recce, 1945: PRO WO171/4281
7: *Record of a Reconnaissance Regiment*, p173

8: Ibid, p181
9: *Time Spent*, p73
10: Ibid, p74
11: Ibid, p74

Chapter Twenty-Two
1: *The Scottish Lion on Patrol*, p175
2: Ibid, p176
3: *Time Spent*, p75
4: *Welsh Spearhead*, p113
5: *History of 3 Recce*, p39
6: Ibid, 40
7: *Record of a Reconnaissance Regiment*, p189
8: War Diary, 43 Recce, 1945: PRO WO171/4215-4216
9: Ibid
10: *Record of a Reconnaissance Regiment*, p193
11: War Diary, 43 Recce, 1945, op cit

Chapter Twenty-Three
1: *Wheeled Odyssey*, p53
2: Ibid, p55-56
3: Ibid, p57
4: 49 Recce: Summary of Operations, p21
5: Ibid, pp21-22
6: Ibid, p22
7: War Diary, 3 Recce, 1945: PRO WO171/4133
8: *History of 3 Recce*, p42
9: War Diary, 3 Recce, 1945, op cit
10: *History of 3 Recce*, p43
11: *A Short History of 3 Recce*, p30
12: *The Scottish Lion on Patrol*, p193
13: Ibid, p195
14: Ibid, p204
15: Ibid, p209
16: *A Short History of 3 Recce*, p36
17: *The Scottish Lion on Patrol*, p214
18: Ibid, p215
19: Ibid
20: Ibid, pp215-216
21: Ibid, pp217-218
22: David Henderson, Personal Account
23: *Welsh Spearhead*, p129
24: Ibid, p130
25: *Time Spent*, p76
26: Ibid
27: Ibid, p77

Chapter Twenty-Four
1: Future of The Reconnaissance Corps, PRO WO32/11520
2: Ibid
3: Ibid
4: Ibid
5: *This Band of Brothers*, p227
6: PRO WO32/11520
7: *The Quadrant*, 4 Nov 1945

Index